# PSYCHOBIOLOGY
## BEHAVIOR FROM
## A BIOLOGICAL
## PERSPECTIVE

## Contributors

J. A. DEUTSCH

E. ROY JOHN

MARCEL KINSBOURNE

AUBREY MANNING

W. R. A. MUNTZ

NORMAN M. WEINBERGER

RICHARD E. WHALEN

# PSYCHOBIOLOGY

## BEHAVIOR FROM A BIOLOGICAL PERSPECTIVE

Edited by **James L. McGaugh**

Department of Psychobiology
University of California
Irvine, California

 ACADEMIC PRESS 1971 New York and London

*152*
*P974m*
*148632*

ACADEMIC PRESS, INC.
111 Fifth Avenue, New York, New York 10003

*United Kingdom Edition published by*
ACADEMIC PRESS, INC. (LONDON) LTD.
Berkeley Square House, London W1X 6BA

LIBRARY OF CONGRESS CATALOG CARD NUMBER: 76-170122

PRINTED IN THE UNITED STATES OF AMERICA

# Contents

## Chapter 4.   Appetite Motivation

J. A. DEUTSCH

## Chapter 5.   Attentive Processes

NORMAN M. WEINBERGER

## Chapter 6.   Brain Mechanisms of Memory

E. ROY JOHN

## Chapter 7.    Cognitive Deficit: Experimental Analysis

MARCEL KINSBOURNE

# List of Contributors

Numbers in parentheses indicate the pages on which the authors' contributions begin.

**J. A. Deutsch** (99), Department of Psychology, University of California at San Diego, La Jolla, California

**E. Roy John** (199), Brain Research Laboratories, Department of Psychiatry, New York Medical College, New York, New York

**Marcel Kinsbourne** (285), Division of Pediatric Neurology, Duke University, Durham, North Carolina

**Aubrey Manning** (1), Department of Zoology, University of Edinburgh, Edinburgh, Scotland

**W. R. A. Muntz** (73), Laboratory of Experimental Psychology, University of Sussex, Brighton, England

**Norman M. Weinberger** (129), Department of Psychobiology, University of California Irvine, California

**Richard E. Whalen** (53), Department of Psychobiology, University of California Irvine, California

# Preface

Behavior can be viewed from many perspectives. The behavior of man and the other animals is caused by a myriad of complex and intertwined processes. Because animals are biological beings it is clear that a complete understanding of the nature and causes of behavior will require that behavior be viewed from a biological perspective. This point is so obvious that it is often ignored. Prior to the turn of the century a biological perspective was commonplace among scholars interested in behavior. Behavior was investigated by physiologists and other biologists before psychology emerged as a discipline. For the great pioneers, such as William James, it was clear that the answers to problems of psychology were to be provided by an understanding of physiology. Darwin knew that the principles of evolution applied to behavior as well as to morphology. In fact, Darwin gave special emphasis to the problem of evolution of behavior. The evolutionary view required evidence of similarity between man and the other animals in behavior as well as structure. Although some essential evidence was available before 1900, the comparative-evolutionary view of human behavior has not enjoyed great support during this century. The biological perspective of behavior was not maintained.

Unfortunately, the biological and *a*biological approaches to behavior developed somewhat independently during this century. Almost as if by common agreement the various disciplines concerned with behavior, such as psychology, physiology, ethology, and psychiatry, developed and maintained essentially *intra*disciplinary perspectives.

In recent years, however, there has been a dramatic surge of interest in interdisciplinary approaches to the study of behavior. Psychologists discovered ethology, and vice versa. Despite the territorial problems the discovery has had a highly synergistic effect. Psychologists rediscovered physiology only to find that the discipline had become specialized into numerous important subdivisions, such as neurophysiology, neuroendocrinology, and neurochemistry. Neuroanatomy was complemented by modern neurosurgery. Other disciplines including pharmacology, genetics, biophysics, and engineering have also come to contribute heavily to our understanding of behavior. It is now completely obvious that the study of behavior is not the private franchise of any single discipline. An interdisciplinary approach is not only to be tolerated, it is essential.

The recent renaissance of interdisciplinary research has provided a few "breakthroughs" in our understanding of behavior together with an almost overwhelming collection of undigested "facts." It is no longer possible to write a book containing all existing facts and theories concerning the biology of behavior. And no attempt was made to do so in this book. Rather, this book attempts to approach each problem under consideration from a biological perspective and to present a contemporary analysis of the essential features of the problems. Many of the "facts" in any contemporary book are out of date at the time the book is printed. The current rate of scientific discoveries guarantees short half-lives for facts. Conceptions or perspectives concerning the problems have somewhat longer half-lives than the facts they attempt to encompass. Thus, many of the ideas developed in the book are "undated." To the extent that they are so, they will continue to provide perspectives for facts yet to be discovered.

The book begins and ends with chapters dealing with issues that cut across many specific problems of behavior. Chapter 1 deals with the problem of the evolution of behavior. An understanding of the behavior of any species or of the differences among species requires that the behavior be approached from an evolutionary perspective. The chapter provides extensive evidence concerning the evolution of specific aspects of behavior and in addition illustrates the genetic processes underlying the evolution of behavior. The facts and theories presented clearly indicate the contributions of many disciplines to contemporary views of the evolution of behavior. The last chapter views behavior from a neurobiological perspective. Traditionally, pathology has played an important role in biology. Understanding how a system works is often clarified by knowing what happens when something goes wrong with it. Studies of cognitive deficits in human patients produced by brain lesions have aided our understanding of both behavior and brain function.

Chapters 2–6 deal with specific problem areas. Chapter 2 presents a contemporary analysis of the problem of instinctive behavior. Although the word "instinct" remains with us, the meaning of the word has continuously evolved over the past several decades. The problem of instinct is as important as it is complex. The remaining chapters (3–7) are concerned with processes underlying behavior: sensory processes, motivation, attention, and memory. In each chapter the author has attempted to present the essential issues together with contemporary facts and theories.

These chapters clearly indicate that the problems of behavior are yielding to interdisciplinary neurobiological research. They also indicate that our ignorance still vastly exceeds our understanding. Again, the chapters are selective and critical. They are not intended to be encyclopedic.

There are, of course, many problems of psychobiology that are not dealt with in this book. The choice of problems reflects the interests and biases of the editor and the authors. Certainly, a biological perspective is no less important for other problems of behavior including intelligence, language, emotion, social behavior, and personality.

Although man has been the subject of scholarly inquiry for centuries, as yet we know little about the nature of human nature. We have as pressing need to know more about man—as we do about all endangered species. An understanding of the biological bases of behavior is essential for future planning of man's destiny. If we are to have an adequate environment for man we must know more about man's psychobiological characteristics and requirements. We hope that this book will help to promote the development of a general biological perspective of behavior.

# PSYCHOBIOLOGY
## BEHAVIOR FROM
## A BIOLOGICAL
## PERSPECTIVE

CHAPTER 1 **Evolution of Behavior**

AUBREY MANNING
Department of Zoology
University of Edinburgh
Edinburgh, Scotland

## I. INTRODUCTION

The concept of evolution by natural selection has become the great unifying principle of biology, and before Darwin's "Origin of Species," biology was little more than the accumulation of facts. For the past century the study of evolution has illuminated the past history and present state of every group of animals and plants. Darwin's theory required that selected adaptations be transmitted from one generation to the next, but he himself had little idea of how this was achieved. Following the rediscovery of Mendel's work early in this century, the basic mechanisms of heredity were rapidly revealed. These discoveries in their turn focused attention upon the nature of the genetic material itself, and now the remarkable developments in "molecular biology" over the past few years have almost completed the picture of the chemical basis of heredity.

Evolution has entered into our way of thinking, and it is always

1

implicit in biological studies, but the simple chronicling of what happened in evolution no longer satisfies us. The mainstream of biological research is concerned with mechanisms, and the elucidation of evolutionary mechanisms—some of which will be discussed in this chapter—is one branch of such research.

The development of psychology has proceeded rather separately from that of biology. It has always concentrated upon man, and usually the comparative approach has not been used to study the phylogeny of behavior, but in the hope that animals will act as simplified types of human being. Clearly there are some respects in which mechanisms basic to the organization of all behavior can be best studied in animals. However we lose a whole dimension of animal behavior if we ignore its diverse origins and the selective forces which shaped it to fulfil its present function.

It is not possible to argue that a study of behavioral evolution will necessarily tell us anything about underlying organizations—as we shall discuss later, much the same end result, adaptively speaking, may be produced in a number of different ways. Nevertheless, the manner in which behavior has changed in response to selection in different types of animals reveals much that is of fundamental importance about behavior and may suggest problems of mechanism not obvious in other types of study. For example, what are the origins of the remarkable symbolic communication system which has evolved in honeybees? How is it that selection has produced the extraordinary facility for rapid associative learning in the Hymenoptera (ants, bees, wasps), whereas it is so difficult to demonstrate learning in the other advanced order of the insects—the Diptera (two-winged flies)?

Problems of this type command the attention of both biologists and psychologists, and one of the aims of "psychobiology" is to bring psychology back into the biological sciences where its roots lie.

This chapter will try to introduce both the study of evolutionary mechanisms as applied to behavior, i.e., to discuss behavior genetics as it relates to evolution, and also to examine some of the ways in which selection may operate to change behavior. Any study of evolution is apt to reveal a highly complex series of interacting factors. While one of our aims must be to demonstrate how behavior fits into the whole scheme of adaptation, it is often necessary to concentrate on parts to the exclusion of the whole. This is inevitably an artificial procedure, and it cannot be claimed that the order, headings, or contents of the various sections of this chapter relate to any natural scheme. They are a selection of topics whose close interrelationships will mean there is overlap between them and a good degree of interchangeability.

## II. BEHAVIOR AS ADAPTATION TO THE ENVIRONMENT

Behavior represents the most highly integrated response to its environment which an organism can make. Nowhere else is the dichotomy between plants and animals more clearly shown. The behavior of plants is severely restricted by their immobility and lack of a nervous system. Flowers, for example, can make some simple behavioral responses. They may close when the temperature drops and twist to face the sun, but the plant as a whole can do little. In an environment which is getting colder or drying up, it relies on its physiological flexibility to enable it to survive. Animals also have such flexibility, of course, but they have a second line of defense against change. They can get up and move elsewhere, and further they can do this within a few seconds of the change occurring, if need be. All animals have sense organs to detect changes in the environment and responses which lead them to avoid extremes of heat or cold, moisture or dryness, so that they tend to settle in areas whose characteristics match their physiology.

Some animals can go much further and manipulate their environment to match their needs. A colony of honeybees maintains the temperature of the brood at 34–35°C, and the workers have elaborate behavior patterns which serve to correct any deviation. Some termites are extremely susceptible to dessication, but they cross dry open areas by constructing covered corridors through which they move.

The north temperate zones of North America and Eurasia offer a rich food supply and long hours of daylight during summer, but their winters are severe. Insectivorous birds can exploit these zones for breeding because they have evolved migratory behavior which enables them to spend the winters nearer the equator.

These few examples give some idea of the range and power of behavioral adaptations in fitting an animal for its environment. Because of its behavior, an animal ceases to be a passive agent upon which natural selection acts; it can take a hand in its own evolution and influence the selection which operates upon it. Genetic changes which affect behavior will often have high selective value, and behavioral changes will often affect the subsequent course of evolution.

If behavior is to evolve it must vary, and these variations must be transmitted from one generation to the next. Much of the behavior of human societies is derived from that of past generations through cultural transmission. This will involve direct imitation of parents by offspring, but also responsiveness to written or spoken "instructions" from previous generations. Certainly imitation plays an important part in the normal behavioral *development* of many animals, such as the carnivores and primates among the mammals, which have well-developed parental care. It is much rarer to find good examples of behavioral variants being passed on in this fashion. Hinde and Fisher (1952) discuss the propagation of the habit of opening milk bottles developed by some populations of titmice and Petersson (1959) has been able to plot the spread of a novel feeding pattern among greenfinches (*Chloris chloris*). Among the primates one suspects that cultural transmission is not uncommon, but only Miyadi (1964) has recorded the process in detail in the course of his remarkable field studies on macaques in Japan.

Cultural transmission requires a rather high level of intelligence and imitative ability, certainly far beyond that shown by the majority of animals. In consequence, most behavior must evolve by the operation of natural selection upon inherited variations. It is best to give some consideration to the basic mechanisms of behavioral evolution—its genetics and how it relates to evolutionary changes—before going on to discuss what kinds of environmental factors influence evolution over long periods.

## A. The Development of Behavior

All behavior presents us with a problem in development. When we speak of the inheritance of behavior, we refer to the inheritance of a potential. Tested with a certain range of stimuli and given a certain range of environments prior to the test, an animal will tend to respond within a certain range of possibilities. The performance of some behavior is greatly affected by the animal's experience prior to the test. Obviously the ability to learn has an inherited basis, but the actual behavior we can observe and measure as a result of such ability is of great diversity. The evolution of learning through the vertebrates, for example, might be measured as an increasing potential to solve complex ambiguity problems or as an increase in their potential for acquiring learning sets (Harlow, 1958; Warren, 1965), but it is extremely difficult to detect small changes along this scale.

If we wish to study the genetics and evolution of behavior patterns themselves, it is much simpler to use behavior whose expression is little affected by previous experience. An increasing amount of research is revealing the great influence which an animal's early sensory experience has upon the thresholds of responses and the stimuli which come to evoke them in later life (see reviews in Hinde, 1970; Marler & Hamilton,

1966). By contrast, the form of the motor patterns comprising these responses is extremely resistant to change. Thus its early rearing conditions, social experience, and the amount of handling it receives may all affect the age at which a male rat's sexual behavior is first elicitable. They will also affect the frequency with which the sexual patterns are performed, but the actual motor patterns remain unchanged. In an analogous way the early environment of the larva will affect the type of host caterpillar sought by females of the parasitic wasp, *Nemeritis*, for egg laying, but their oviposition technique is not changed (Thorpe & Jones, 1937).

For this reason the stereotyped patterns so characteristic of arthropods and the courtship and threat displays of fish, lizards, and birds, for example, are particularly suitable for genetical and evolutionary studies. it is possible to study variation in the form and frequency of such behavior patterns from a "baseline" which is relatively environment-independant. To a large extent, if the environment is adequate for the animal to survive in health, such behavior develops unchanged.

In Chapter 2 of this book, Whalen discusses the history of the concept of instinct, so there is no need to dwell on the instinct versus learning controversy here. Nevertheless, the reader may feel that the previous paragraphs tend to set up too strong a dichotomy between instinctive and learned behavior. From the standpoint of its adaptive value and evolution, all behavior, no matter how it develops, begins on an equal footing. Natural selection has no respect for methods; it judges only their end results. In any case, the instinct/learning dichotomy is inadequate because many environmental factors which affect behavior hardly seem to come within the confines of learning, and genes will affect the way animals respond to such factors during their behavioral development.

One strength of the biological approach to behavior is that it enables us to see the roles of instinct and learning in perspective. All animals, at least above the Annelid level, show both ends of this behavioral continuum, but developed to widely different extents. This is inevitable because, while all animals must respond to their environment with well-adapted behavior if they are to survive, various factors may dictate how they meet the specification.

The insects are all small animals, often with very short life spans, and there is rarely any contact between parents and offspring. For example, the elaborate nest-building behavior of many solitary Hymenoptera is performed in a brief period shortly after the female emerges from hibernation. Such an insect has experience of the nest from the inside as a larva but no possibility of imitating its construction, since her parents are dead. In this type of situation selection has favoured the evolution of inherited behavior patterns which are accurately adapted to the normal environment.

At the other extreme is the situation in some mammals, which live much longer and have a long period of infancy with much contact between parents and offspring and also between siblings. Here there are abundant opportunities to learn and to modify behavior during the course of a lifetime; the advantages of preset, inherited responses are far less, and selection has favoured a different type of behavioral development from that of the insects.

Even within an individual, the development of related behavior patterns may vary according to the role they must play. Thus in a number of birds the development of the species-specific song provides a classic example of the interaction between inherited tendencies and learning (Thorpe, 1961; Marler & Hamilton, 1966). The process of acquiring the adult song occupies some weeks or months in the early life of a male. It begins during the first weeks of life when the bird is influenced by the song of its father and other birds nearby, and it is completed after the young male first sings itself and hears other males in the following spring. This prolonged development, with its sensitivity to environmental influences at several stages, may be contrasted with the development of alarm calls in the same species. In all cases so far studied, the species specific, these calls and the various fear responses they evoke occur normally in birds reared in complete auditory isolation, and they appear very early in life. Various selective factors must have combined to produce this contrast in development, and it seems probable that one of them was in danger from predation. Where it may make a difference between life and death to respond perfectly at the first exposure, selection has favored development with a large genetic component.

The study of sexual isolation in various animal groups reveals a similar picture. Sexual isolation may be defined as the behavioral barriers to hybridization between species. It is almost universal among animals and its evolutionary consequences will be discussed later. Here we may note that it requires that animals can identify individuals of their own species and discriminate against foreign ones. The development of this ability is sometimes independent of the early environment, and most insects, for example, are quite unaffected by rearing in the presence of foreign species—they still discriminate their own kind perfectly. On the other hand, in some vertebrates the same end result is achieved in a totally different way. The young animal learns the species characteristics during infancy and is greatly affected if reared by a foster parent of another species. This process of sexual imprinting is best known in pigeons (Whitman, 1919) and ducks (Schutz, 1965), but it is certainly much more widespread. The sexual responses of hand-reared mammals are often directed as much or more towards human beings as to their own kind, a factor which contributes towards the failure to breed rare zoo animals such as giant pandas.

We have just discussed how different vocalizations within the same individual may have quite different developmental histories. The same is true for discrimination of one's own species. Schutz (1965) has found that in most duck species it is only the male which shows sexual imprinting and is affected by early experience; females, no matter how reared, still choose their own males. He suggests that this is because the problem of distinguishing between different females, all of which are more or less cryptically colored in shades of brown, is more difficult than that of distinguishing between different males, each with a highly distinctive nuptial plumage. Selection favors a learning process for the males because it is "difficult" to evolve an accurate genetically determined recognition of the subtle qualities of the duck's plumage. It is "easy" to evolve an inherited responsiveness to the bold features of the drake's plumage. Although an attractive idea, this is probably not the whole answer, but Schutz's work does reinforce the conclusion that selection can evoke different types of adaptive response from the same organism.

## B. The Genetics of Behavior

The study of genetics is basically the study of how differences between animals are inherited. Two individuals which differ in some character are mated and the occurrence of the character is sought for in the $F_1$, $F_2$, and backcross generations. Behavior geneticists have, as far as possible, used the methods of classical genetics, but behavior as a "character" has certain difficulties. The most obvious of these concerns the choice of "units" of behavior for genetic analysis. Mendel succeeded when so many of his contemporaries failed because of his brilliant choice of units. He picked characters in his pea plants which inherited in a clearcut fashion and could be counted.

Behavior, by contrast, seems so diffuse and complex. Further, it can be affected in such a variety of ways. Thus changes to sense organs or muscles or metabolic rate may all depress certain kinds of behavioral response, but the mechanism is totally different in each case.

It is difficult to lay down hard and fast rules about the choice of behavior units for genetic studies. A comparison of parental types and the hybrids between them will often suggest what to use, and we must be ready to subdivide and reclassify as analysis proceeds. Certainly the stereotyped patterns of behavior so characteristic of arthropods and the sexual displays of vertebrates are hopeful choices. These so-called "fixed-action patterns" are easily identified, and each can be distinguished from other related patterns. They are species specific, but a group of close relatives usually shares a common "repertoire" just as they share morphological characteristics. For this reason a close study of behavior can often be of use in systematics—it extends the range of characters which can be compared in deducing phyletic relationships (see Mayr, 1958; Cullen, 1959). Morphological similarities between the sandgrouse (Pteroclidae) and the pigeons (Columbidae) suggest that, although these two families are dissimilar in their general appearance and ecology, they are nevertheless related. This suspicion is supported by the observation that, unique amongst the birds, only these families drink as do mammals, by sucking up directly. Their gait when walking is also strikingly similar and further suggests their common descent.

The units chosen by Mendel for his genetic analysis—stature of plant, colour of seed coat, texture of seed coat etc.—all proved to be under the control of a single gene. We can rarely expect to find such a simple mode of inheritance for a behavior pattern. Nevertheless the way in which genetic changes affect behavior units will give us information both on their genetic control and how they may have evolved.

The elegant work of Rothenbuhler (1964a, b) on honeybees illustrates some of these points. Certain strains of bees are called "hygienic," because if a larva dies, worker bees will uncap its cell and remove the corpse, depositing it outside the hive. The worker from colonies of "unhygienic" strains do not respond in this way. The acts of uncapping cells and removing larvae are quite stereotyped in form, and the difference between hygienic and unhygienic bees is clearcut. This situation provides an excellent opportunity for genetic analysis.

Rothenbuhler found that the colonies of $F_1$ hybrids between hygienic and unhygienic bees were all unhygienic. He then backcrossed hybrids to the "recessive," i.e., hygienic, strain and produced 29 colonies. These showed a most remarkable segregation of behavior into four classes as follows:

*Class 1.* 8 colonies which neither uncapped cells containing dead larvae nor removed larvae; i.e., they were unhygienic.

*Class 2.* 6 colonies which uncapped cells and removed larvae; i.e., they were hygienic.

*Class 3.* 9 colonies which uncapped cells but went no further and left the dead larvae untouched.

*Class 4.* 6 colonies which did not uncap cells, but which would remove the corpses from cells artificially uncapped by the experimenter.

This result immediately suggests that one's intuitive separation of hygienic behavior into two "units"—uncapping cells and removing larvae—has genetic as well as behavioral validity. Further, the segregation ratio of the four behavioral classes listed above (which does not differ significantly from 1:1:1:1) suggests that each "unit" is controlled by a single gene. Thus we may denote the gene for uncapping cells as *u*, and that for removing corpses as *r*. Both are recessive, and while the hygienic parental strains have the constitution *uurr*, that of the dominant unhygienic strain is *UURR*. The crosses described above can then be represented as follows:

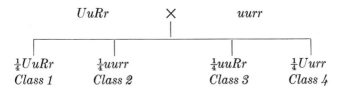

$$UuRr \qquad \times \qquad uurr$$

| $\frac{1}{4}UuRr$ | $\frac{1}{4}uurr$ | $\frac{1}{4}uuRr$ | $\frac{1}{4}Uurr$ |
| Class 1 | Class 2 | Class 3 | Class 4 |

Although we describe the genes *u* and *r* as "controlling" uncapping and removal, this does not imply that only they are responsible for the development of the complex mechanisms behind each behavior pattern. In fact, Rothenbuhler's work shows that this cannot be so, because there were always a few cells and dead larvae treated by bees of the unhygienic colonies. In other words, the behavior patterns were not absent, but performed only at a tiny fraction of their frequency in hygienic colonies.

The genes in Rothenbuhler's honeybee strains act as "switches" determining whether the fixed action patterns appear or not in virtually an all-or-nothing fashion. "Switch-genes" are familiar from other types of genetic study, particularly those concerned with the inheritance of complex wing patterns in butterflies (see Sheppard, 1961). Here single-genes are sometimes found affecting the action of a group of genes which in combination control the formation of a particular wing pattern. Analysis has often shown that the latter group of genes is closely linked upon a chromosome and thus tends to inherit as a single unit. Clearly selection will be in favor of linkage between genes which all contribute towards the optimum development of a character. In this way, there will be reduced risk of individuals inheriting a gene combination which is less than optimum.

Although critical evidence is lacking as yet, it is very reasonable to suggest that groups of closely linked genes may control the development of many fixed action patterns of the type we have been considering. There is, for example, Lorenz's work on the courtship behavior of hybrid ducks. A number of closely related duck species share a common repertoire of fixed action patterns performed by the drakes when they court females. These patterns were originally described by Lorenz (1941) and his pupils (see also Johnsgard, 1965). In some cases the drake $F_1$ hybrid between two species shows a courtship pattern not performed by either parent, but which is familiar from other members of the species group. This must mean that the block of genes responsible for the development of the pattern has remained "intact" in the parent species, although its expression as behavior never occurs. In the hybrids, the action of other genes which "switch off" this expression is reduced, and the pattern appears again. Certainly the simplest explanation of how the block of genes remain intact is that they are closely linked. We should need to look at the behavior of $F_2$ hybrids and backcross to test this explanation, but unfortunately most $F_1$ hybrids between species are subfertile or sterile.

There are other examples of behavior patterns which inherit completely or not at all. They lend some support to the hypothesis about linkage outlined above, but we must remember that there are many difficulties of interpretation. If we observe the effects of a mutant which causes a gross wing deformity in the fruit fly, *Drosophila*, it is easy to identify the incomplete or abortive wing. It may be much more difficult to identify abortive attempts to perform a behavior pattern. Perhaps we do not see the incomplete inheritance of fixed action patterns in hybrids because we simply fail to identify them as such.

In general it must be admitted that we can learn relatively little about the inheritance of behavior from the study of species hybrids. Usually hybridization is possible only between closely related species whose repertoire of fixed action patterns is very similar. This means that they have most of their genes in common, and the behavior of hybrids is little affected, at least qualitatively.

Fixed action patterns represent complex sequences of muscle contractions (see Fig. 5, for example) strictly dependent on structural and functional characters of parts of the nervous system, and it seems certain that very many genes must control their development. One suggests that they have evolved gradually by the accumulation of genes each of small effect, and later in this chapter we shall examine some of the ways in which selection may act. Here it is worth noting that perhaps the most direct way of relating the genetics of behavior to evolution is to examine the behavioral effects of relatively slight genetic changes and to compare them with the differences between closely related species.

The type of genetic change we can study depends to some extent on the nature of the material. In animals which are much used in genetical research, such as mice or *Drosophila*, it is relatively easy to obtain two stocks which differ by only a single gene. In these and other animals it is also possible to compare stocks which have been intensively inbred or selectively bred for some morphological or physiological character, such as body size or egg production. Finally, it may be feasible to take a population of animals and to select individuals for breeding according to their behavioral characteristics. In this way we can discover how much of the variability in the original population had a genetic basis. There are good reviews of all these different types of study in Fuller and Thompson (1960) and Hirsch (1967).

The types of behavioral change which have been studied are, of course, very diverse, but they may be loosely grouped under two categories.

First, there are what may be called "general effects" in which genetic changes affect the sensory threshold or motivational state of animals. Tryon's famous experiment, in which he selectively bred rats for speed of learning an elevated maze, produced changes of this type. Subsequent analysis of these lines by a number of workers revealed how pervasive were the behavioral results of selection. For example, the "bright" rats tended to concentrate on spatial or kinesthetic cues in running through a maze; "dull" animals relied more on visual cues. Hence in problems of a different type from that used in selection, the "dull" animals sometimes scored better than the bright. (All these experiments are well summarized by Fuller & Thompson, 1960, p. 208.)

Another genetical experiment with rats provides a further example of this "general" type. Broadhurst (1967) selectively bred from animals which had high and low "emotional" responses to being placed in a mildly stressful, open field situation. The resulting "reactive" and "nonreactive" lines differed in a number of respects, but it is clear that the reactive rats are more easily aroused by external stimuli of various types, and thus the genes responsible may have repercussions on their behavior in a variety of situations.

The second category of effect by genes is one which can be more directly related to the type of work with bees and ducks which was discussed earlier. Numerous observations have demonstrated that genetic changes can affect the frequency with which specific behavior patterns are performed.

For instance, among mammals, inbred strains of mice (McGill, 1962) and guinea pigs (Goy & Jakway, 1959; Jakway, 1959) differ in various components of their sexual behavior. A number of measures were used in these studies. Some of them involved latencies or duration of performance—how long males took to mount females, how long females sustained the lordosis posture—others were more direct frequency measures involving the number of times particular patterns were performed. In all of them, the quantitative differences between strains were striking. With the guinea pigs, genetic analysis showed that the number of genes involved and their dominance varied between the different measures. In particular, genes affecting components of male and female behavior were quite distinct, although the nature of their effects was very similar.

Similar quantitative changes can often be produced quite rapidly by selective breeding from a population which is screened for some behavioral component. Thus by selection for only three generations, Wood-Gush (1960) was able to change quite dramatically the frequency of various sexual behavior patterns in domestic cocks. Turning to insects, selective breeding for mating speed in the fruit fly, *Drosophila,* was successful in producing lines which differed more than tenfold in their average time to mate (Manning, 1961). Part of this difference was due to changes in the frequency with which males of the two types performed the characteristic courtship movements.

During selection experiments, we are producing relatively large changes involving many genes, but there is evidence that single genes also can affect behavior in a similar quantitative fashion. In some insects it is relatively easy to produce two strains which differ by only a single pair of genes (although we must accept that sometimes there may be a few other genes very closely linked to them). Cotter (1967) used two strains of the flour moth *Ephestia* differing only at the *a* locus. Male moths bearing the *a* gene showed a shorter latency of response to the females' sex pheromone, and they also showed other behavioral changes. Cotter could show that the heterozygote was intermediate in some respects so that the behavioral change was inherited as a partial dominant.

Similar studies have been made with *Drosophila* where mutants such as *yellow, ebony, vestigial,* and *white* are all known to affect the sexual behavior of male *Drosophila* carrying them (see Manning, 1965, for references). Superficially all appear to do so in the same way; they reduce the frequency with which the flies perform various elements of the courtship display. However we have no means of knowing where the genes act in the long chain of mechanisms between a male fly perceiving a female and the actual performance of the courtship display; it seems unlikely to be at the same link in each case, particularly as the morphological effects of these mutants are so diverse.

In fact, from the evolutionary point of view the way in which the gene acts to change behavior may be of much less importance than the end result, and it is now possible to link this brief discussion of behavior genetics with the processes of evolution itself. We have laid emphasis on the *quantitative* nature of genetic effects, whether it has been the "switch gene" determining the performance of a behavior pattern in an all-or-none fashion or the much smaller effects of, say, the *yellow* gene in *Drosophila*.

Almost all attempts to change behavior by selective breeding from natural populations have been successful. This means that much of the behavioral variability we observe has a genetic component, and natural populations may be highly variable for genes which affect behavior in a quantitative fashion. Such genes are, of course, the raw material of behavioral evolution, and we may examine the early stages of evolutionary divergence between populations to see whether we can find evidence of their being put into use.

## C. The Microevolution of Behavior

The best material for such an examination comes from the comparative study of a group of closely related species. Here we find a common repertoire of fixed action patterns, and the divergence from a common ancestral type will have involved a series of specializations and other adaptive changes which represent some of the earliest stages of evolution, usually called "microevolution." We can be fairly confident that the behavioral divergence within a species group will not involve large genetic changes.

Casual observations on a group can tell us little of value because it is essential to have a very complete knowledge of the whole repertoire of a species' behavior before we can make a valid comparison between it and a close relative. Fortunately there are a number of excellent comparative ethological studies, inspired by the pioneering work of Whitman, Lorenz, and Tinbergen. We may list the following as a representative sample dealing with a variety of groups: Crane (1949, 1952, 1957) on jumping spiders (Salticidae), mantids, and fiddler crabs, respectively; Blest (1957) on moths; Spieth (1952) on *Drosophila;* Baerends and Baerends-van-Roon (1950) on Cichlid fish; Crook (1963) on weaver birds; Dilger (1960, 1962) on lovebirds; Lorenz (1941) and Johnsgard (1965) on ducks; Whitman (1919) on pigeons; and Tinbergen (1959) on gulls.

Several types of quantitative difference between relatives have been repeatedly described from such comparative studies. We can summarize the most important under two headings; Blest (1961) and Manning (1965) go into more detail.

## 1. Differences in Threshold for the Elicitation of Homologous Behavior Patterns

The lesser black-backed gull (*Larus argentatus*) and the herring gull (*L. fuscus*) have almost identical alarm calls, but those of the lesser black-back are much harder to elicit. A human observer skirting a nesting area including both species will commonly arouse only the herring gull (Goethe, 1954).

Blest (1957) and Crane (1952) have described how different species of saturnioid moth and mantid, respectively, vary greatly in the level of stimulus required to evoke defensive displays. Some mantids will display to visual stimuli alone—a large object moving close to the head—while others require powerful tactile stimuli. Most moths require some kind of tactile stimulus, but while in distasteful species with the most vivid warning colors, the lightest touch suffices, the more cryptic species require a hard prod.

Here we are dealing with threshold differences in a response to simple stimuli, but threshold changes can also be observed in more complex responses which can be evoked by a combination of different stimuli. The courtship display of *Drosophila*, for example, involves a complex interplay of visual, olfactory, auditory, and tactile stimuli between male and female (Spieth, 1952; Manning, 1965). In no case do we know in detail the way in which stimuli from different modalities summate to evoke sexual responses, but certain gross differences between species are conspicuous. The sexual behavior of some species (e.g., *D. subobscura, D. suzukii*) is dependent on the presence of light, while other species (e.g., *D. melanogaster*) are quite unaffected (see Spieth & Hsu, 1950; Grossfield, 1966). This certainly suggests that the former are more dependent upon visual stimuli, and it can be no coincidence that it is these species which have elaborate displays in which the insects face one another, and in *D. suzukii* the males' wings, adorned by black tips, are moved slowly in front of the females' eyes (Manning, 1965). It may not be simply sexual behavior which is affected by the absence of light; indeed there is evidence that in some light-dependent species of *Drosophila* (e. g., *auraria*), light is required to raise the level of locomotor activity to a level where males and females will encounter one another; in the dark, *D. auraria* scarcely ever moves. The essential distinction remains; such species obviously have lowered thresholds of responsiveness to light, compared to the light-independent ones. Crane (1949) has described similar differences between groups of salticid spiders, some of which rely almost entirely on their eyes for orientation and exploration of their environment, while others are primarily "tactile and olfactory" animals.

An analagous example of changes in sensory thresholds comes from studies on the reproductive cycles of wild and feral pigeons in Britain. Three pigeons of the genus *Columba* are common residents: the wood pigeon (*C. palumbus*), stock dove (*C. oenas*), and the rockdove (most familiar as the "domestic pigeon," *C. livia*). In all three species the onset of sexual behavior at the beginning of the breeding season is related to increasing day-length as spring approaches. Light leads to stimulation of the hypothalamus which, in turn, initiates the secretion of gonadotropins by the pituitary gland. Lofts, Murton, and Westwood (1966, 1967) have shown that the amount of light required to initiate hormone secretion and hence sexual behavior is considerably higher for the wood pigeon than for the stock dove, while domestic pigeons are often in breeding condition all the year round.

## 2. Differences in the Frequency with Which Homologous Behavior Patterns Are Performed

This is perhaps the commonest difference which we observe between related species, and examples are provided by almost every comparative study. It is obviously only marginally distinct from the threshold changes we have just considered, because differential threshold changes will lead to one pattern increasing or decreasing in frequency with respect to others. For example, Tinbergen (1959) provides an excellent review of the work of his group on the reproductive behavior of gulls. Here there is a clearly recognizable common repertoire of displays, but each species has a characteristic range of frequencies with which they appear during social interactions. Lorenz (1941) and Johnsgard (1965) have described analogous differences between duck species. Among insects, the comparative study of the courtship displays of *Drosophila* species reveals numerous examples of this type. The closely related *D. melanogaster* and *D. simulans* each show two conspicuous wing-displays: "scissoring," in which both wings are slowly opened together, and "vibration," in which one wing is extended and rapidly vibrated in the vertical plane. Scissoring is the dominant wing display in *D. simulans* and is only rarely observed during the courtship of *D. melanogaster* males. Conversely vibration is much more frequent in the latter species (Manning, 1959).

Scissoring is so rare in *D. melanogaster* that only prolonged observations reveal that this motor pattern still forms part of the courtship repertoire. Sometimes, as in the duck example we considered earlier (p. 10), a frequency change is so extreme that one species never performs a pattern. Thus for all intents and purposes, there has been a qualitative change in the species' repertoire, although as the hybridization results show, the necessary neural organization to perform the pattern may still be there.

This type of example draws attention to the essential artificiality of trying to separate "quantitative" and "qualitative" changes to behavior. So far we have considered microevolutionary changes which are most reasonably considered quantitative, but much that is so characteristic of a particular species' behavior involves subtle feature of form and emphasis in a movement or posture which are not easily described in qualitative terms. Figures 1 and 2 illustrate two examples of interspecific variations in the form of a pattern from birds. Figure 3 shows an analagous example from *Drosophila*. In each case the common origin of the movement or posture is clear, but each species has a completely distinctive "look" about it.

For the purposes of description, it has been useful to try to classify microevolutionary changes under separate headings, but obviously the actual process of microevolution will involve simultaneous changes in a number of features. Figure 4 shows, in diagrammatic form, the evolu-

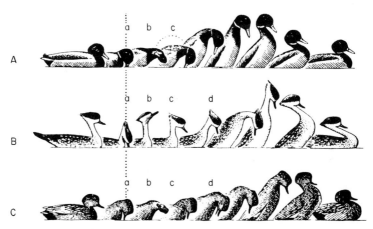

Fig. 1.    An homologous fixed action pattern—the "grunt-whistle"—as performed on the water by drakes of three closely-related duck species: A, the mallard (*Anas platyrhynchos*); B, the crested duck (*A. specularoides*); and C, the gadwall (*A. strepera*). The timing and emphasis of the movement vary between the species. Thus the mallard and the gadwall show much greater emphasis of the sideways "flip" of the head after the bill is dipped into the water. The mallard begins rearing up the body slightly earlier than crested duck or gadwall. (Drawn from a film sequence after van der Wall, 1963.)

Herring gull                              Lesser black-back

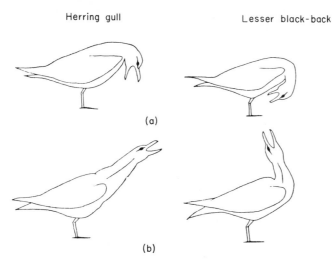

(a)

(b)

FIG. 2.    Variations in the form of the homologous "long-call" movement in:
(a) the closely-related Herring gull (*Larus argentatus*); and (b) lesser black-backed
gull (*L. fuscus*). Each species begins with the head thrown down and then raises
it into the thrown-back position. The two species differ in the development of
these positions. (After Brown, 1967.)

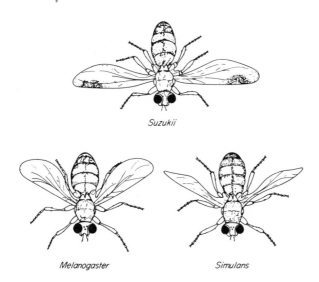

*Suzukii*

*Melanogaster*                          *Simulans*

FIG. 3.    The maximum extent of the "scissoring" display by males of *Drosophila
suzukii, melanogaster,* and *simulans.* In *melanogaster* and *suzukii,* the wings are
held fairly flat, though extended much further in the latter species where they
have black patches near the tips. In *simulans,* the wings are raised briefly and
their trailing edges dropped. (After Manning, 1965.)

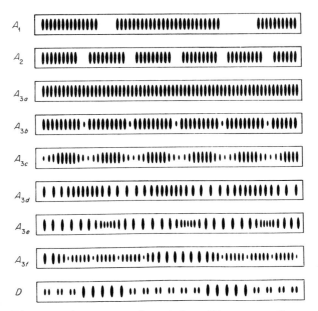

Fig. 4. Diagrammatic representation of the trilling song patterns of crickets, arranged in approximate order of increasing complexity. Height of marks represents amplitude of sound. Changes in amplitude, repetition rate, and pattern are all shown. (After Alexander, 1962.)

tionary changes which have occurred in the calling songs of some crickets. The pulses of sound, produced by rubbing the hardened forewings together, have changed in frequency, amplitude, and patterning to produce a whole range of distinctive "songs" (Alexander, 1962).

## D. Summarizing Microevolutionary Changes: The Link with Genetics

In our discussion of genetic effects we noted that quantitative changes were common, and it often seemed reasonable to interpret them as being due to threshold changes somewhere in the control system. It is very easy to relate this type of genetic effect to the quantitative differences observed between closely related species—they are exactly analogous and indicate that relatively small genetic changes can produce the specific differences we observe in many groups.

It is very easy to speak in general terms of threshold changes as responsible for interspecific differences, but we must remember that in no case do we know the actual mechanism behind the changes we observe. We noted earlier that several different single gene mutations in *Dro-*

*sophila* all reduce the frequency of courtship patterns in males, but we could not at present choose between the various ways in which they might produce this effect. The same is true of interspecific differences. For instance, Hinde (1959), in a comparative study of the courtship displays of four species of finch, found both quantitative and qualitative differences of the types we have been discussing. In particular, the frequency of patterns believed on other grounds to be aggressive was higher in the goldfinch (*Carduelis carduelis*) and the canary (*Serinus canarius*) than in the chaffinch (*Fringilla coelebs*) and the bullfinch (*Pyrrhula pyrrhula*). This difference could be caused by threshold changes in the control mechanisms of the patterns themselves, i.e., very much on the motor output side. Alternatively, the goldfinch and the canary might have a generally lowered aggressive threshold and thus respond more aggressively in any situation. Thirdly, it may be relevant that females of these two species have similar plumage to males, whereas female chaffinches and bullfinches are distinctly colored. This might mean that the latter species evoke less aggression from their mates because they offer fewer stimuli in common with rival males.

However, returning to the more straightforward qualitative differences illustrated in Figs. 1–3, there seems no reason to doubt that here too we are observing the end results of threshold changes. Recent physiological work on the control of fixed-action patterns shows how genes could affect such changes. In an excellent review, Hoyle (1964) discusses the ways in which stereotyped motor patterns may be controlled. There must be a central coordinating center—a small group of interconnected neurons perhaps—which in response to the appropriate signal produces a patterned output to a series of "lower" centers with more direct control over groups of related muscles. These in turn will control centers for single muscles, and so on. The output is such that each muscle group is brought into action at the right point in the sequence, contracted to the necessary extent and for the necessary time, and so on. The result is the smoothly coordinated, stereotyped sequence of muscle contractions that go to make up the behavior pattern we observe. Only in a few of the simplest cases have we anything like a full picture of the muscle sequences involved. Figure 5 shows an analysis of the swallowing reflex in the dog, and even here there are about twenty muscles to be considered.

Sometimes there is good evidence that the output of the top coordinating center is complete in itself and that it requires no information to be fed back from muscles as they contract in order to bring in the next muscles in the sequence. The swallowing reflex of the dog appears to be quite independent of any feedback during its course. In other

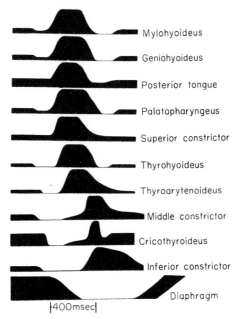

Mylohyoideus

Geniohyoideus

Posterior tongue

Palatopharyngeus

Superior constrictor

Thyrohyoideus

Thyroarytenoideus

Middle constrictor

Cricothyroideus

Inferior constrictor

Diaphragm

|400msec|

FIG. 5.    Simplified summary of the sequence of muscular activity involved in the swallowing of the dog. The height of shading represents the intensity of action in each muscle. (After Doty & Bosma, 1956.)

cases, while the coordinating center can operate without feedback, the exact form of the movement is susceptible to outside modification as it proceeds. The flight control center of locusts is a case of this type (Wilson, 1964). Finally, the sequential changeover from one muscle group to another may be entirely dependent on feedback from the muscles in action—locomotion in some vertebrates is controlled in this way (see Hoyle, 1964; Hinde, 1970, Chap. 3).

Whatever the exact system of control it is clear that the correct sequence depends upon a very precise arrangement of thresholds for firing both between and within the coordinating centers and the subordinate ones. Genetic changes affecting thresholds at any site within such a system will cause a distortion in the form of the movement. A muscle group may come into action sooner than before, or contract more strongly, or be held contracted for longer, and so on. The accumulation of small changes of this type would result in modifications like those seen in Figs. 1–3. Figure 6 shows a particularly beautiful example of microevolutionary variations on a simple pattern which must have been produced by threshold changes. Hunsaker (1962) had described the head-bobbing movements characteristic of male lizards of the genus

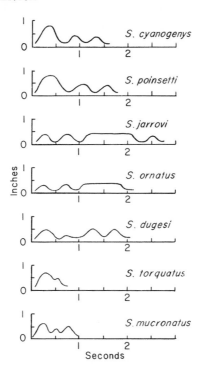

Fig. 6.    The specific head-bobbing movements of some *Sceloporus* lizards. The movements of the head are represented as a line with height on the vertical axis and time on the horizontal axis. Variations in amplitude, speed and pattern of movement are all clearly shown. (After Hunsaker, 1962.)

*Sceloporus.* They bob their heads in a number of situations—after feeding or when they encounter other individuals, for example—and the movement is actually performed by a series of "press-ups" with the front legs extending and relaxing to move the head and shoulders up and down. Hunsaker showed that females are helped to identify their own males by the characteristic form of the bobbing in each species. The variations in speed, amplitude and pattern must all be produced by subtle differences in the output from some center which controls the sequence of alternate contractions in the extensor and flexor muscles of the front legs.

In conclusion, it seems possible to account for most microevolutionary changes in terms of the accumulation of small threshold variations. These correspond very well to the known effects of genetic changes as discussed earlier. In many cases the circumstantial evidence is strong that genes are operating to affect the central nervous system directly. It is, for example, very difficult to conceive how else the difference between the lizard bobbing patterns could be produced. Clearly there is an important and almost untouched field of research into the physiological nature of genetic effects upon behavior. It is a difficult field, not least because the most convenient animals for physiology are not necessarily those best suited for the kind of comparative approach just described. Ginsburg (1967) discusses work with different inbred strains of mice which shows some of the potentialities of linking physiology, genetics, and behavior.

So far we have deliberately ignored the adaptive value of the behavioral changes under consideration. This has been done in order to focus attention on the raw material and "basic mechanics" of behavioral evolution. Now we can bring adaptiveness into the foreground and consider the selective forces which have caused behavior to evolve. We must also range beyond microevolution to discuss some of the larger-scale changes which result from selection operating over long periods of time.

## III. HOW SELECTION OPERATES

The dynamics of evolution by natural selection have been thoroughly explored, and the classic work of Fisher, Haldane, and Sewall Wright was the foundation for the synthesis between Darwin's original theory and modern genetics. Good accounts of the modern viewpoint, which is as relevant to the evolution of behavior as of any other character with a genetic basis, are provided by Grant (1963) and Mayr (1963).

Selection operates upon individuals, but we can best consider its action upon the characters of a population which is interbreeding and therefore shares a common pool of genes. Most behavioral characters will be affected by many genes, and, if we assume that the genetic variation is distributed normally, then we can represent the two main ways in which selection operates as in Fig. 7. "Stabilizing" selection eliminates those genotypes which depart too far from the mean in either direction. It will tend to sharpen the peak around the mean but there will soon come an equilibrium point beyond which no further perfection is possible. Stabilizing selection can only occur if the environment itself is stable, at least in so far as it affects the character in question. If the environment is changing, selection may impose a progressive bias towards change, shifting the population mean as shown in Fig. 7, because it eliminates only one tail of the distribution.

The diagram plots genetic variation and, if there is a simple direct relationship between genes and the character they control, then the same normal curves could serve to represent the character. Stature or body

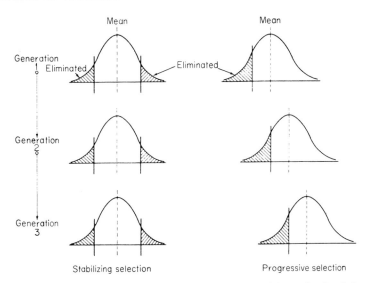

Fig. 7. Two modes of selection: on the left, "stabilizing selection," in which organisms that deviate too far from the population mean in either direction are at a disadvantage; and on the right, "progressive selection," which tends to shift the population mean because only deviants in one direction are at a disadvantage. (After Grant, 1963.)

weight in man are characters whose genetic control is of this type. However, a normal distribution of genetic variability need not result in a parallel distribution of phenotypes. Particularly with behavioral characters, it may be almost impossible to score a continuous range of expressions, and one is forced to lump them into a few classes. The members of each class will not all be the same genetically, but their behavior is effectively indistinguishable. This type of situation may pose difficulties for genetic analysis and harks back to the question of choice of behavior units we considered earlier (p. 7). Fuller and Thompson (1960, p. 88) discuss the problem in more detail.

One of the commonest objections raised against Darwin's theory of evolution by natural selection was that small changes, conferring only a slight advantage upon the organisms that carried them, could not possibly spread through a population quickly enough. Part of this objection was answered when the enormous extent of geological time became known, but part of it arose from ignorance of the powers of sustained selection generation by generation. In fact, even if a gene has a selective value as low as 0.001 (i.e., for every 1000 individuals lacking the gene that survive each generation, 1001 survive that carry it) and even if it is totally recessive so that individuals must carry it in double dose to benefit, it will still spread through a population. Calculations show that it would take about 120,000 generations of selection to change such a gene's frequency in a population from about 1% to 100%. This is slow, though not too slow for the evolution of many groups of animals. However, this is not a typical situation. First, many genes will have far higher selective values than one in a thousand, and rate of spread increases dramatically with increasing advantage. Secondly, genes do not act individually; selection operates on the whole organism and its whole genotype. If a gene confers an advantage, other genes which enhance its effect will also be selected for, and so the net selective advantage will increase. Indeed in some cases it appears likely that selection can make favorable recessive genes into dominant ones, while unfavorable genes can be rendered recessive in their action.

Natural selection then may change the genetic structure of populations quite rapidly. However, there are many other factors apart from the intensity of selection which will determine the rate at which evolution can take place. The rate at which new mutations crop up in the population is one of these factors, but it is unlikely to be a limiting one. Factors connected with the size of a population are probably much more important. The majority of evolutionary geneticists agree that the most rapid evolution will occur when a large population is split up into smaller groups which are isolated from one another for considerable periods but crossbreed occasionally.

In a large, continuous population new mutations and recombinations of genes tend to be swamped before selection can "get hold" of them. Conversely in very small populations, there is a smaller gene pool to choose from and the number of new recombinations is much reduced. Further, if the population is too small, gene combinations may be lost purely by chance. The small, temporarily isolated "pockets" from a large population gain the best of both worlds. They are in contact with a large gene pool from time to time, but within each "pocket," favorable recombinations have a chance to become established during a period of isolation.

There is considerable evidence to show that these arguments are not purely theoretical. It is well known that populations on offshore islands of large land masses tend to be much more divergent from each other and the mainland population than do variants within the latter population. This holds even when the islands are really very close to the mainland; in other words it is not isolation alone which has produced the divergence but isolation coupled with occasional contacts with the large, mainland population. Mayr (1963) gives examples of this phenomenon which is particularly well shown by bird populations in Australasia.

In very small, permanently isolated populations the rate of evolution, and even its direction, may be affected through particular combinations of genes becoming fixed or lost by chance alone. This phenomenon, called "genetic drift" by Sewall Wright has certainly played a part in the evolution of some groups. It is a concept which must be used with caution and not evoked simply in order to explain characters to which one can ascribe no adaptive value at the time. Drift may turn evolution along one path rather than another, but only if both paths are advantageous; selection will eliminate chance combinations of genes if they have any deleterious effects.

## A. Group Selection and Individual Selection

Selection appears to be a narrowly selfish process. It is concerned only with individuals, and phrases like "the preservation of the species" arise from a basic misunderstanding of how selection operates. The species is preserved only if the individuals which constitute it are well adapted and leave an adequate number of progeny. However, as we have seen, the success of individuals may be affected by the size and degree of isolation of the population they come from. It is quite appropriate to speak of "a well-adapted population," and individuals carrying a selection of genes from its gene pool will be at an advantage if they compete with other individuals from another, less well-adapted population.

The biology of many animals involves varying degrees of social life such that they live in cohesive groups at least for part of the year. Consequently there has been much speculation on the possibility that "group selection" occurs. Suppose the members of a group all share a character which increases the fitness of the group making it more likely to prosper and split into two. Clearly there is no problem about such a character's evolution if it improves the fitness of individuals also; it will spread by selection in the usual way. However it could happen that a character which improves the fitness of the group as a whole is disadvantageous to individuals. A group comprised of such individuals will survive better in competition with other groups, it is more likely to split into two, and thus the total proportion of individuals bearing this character will increase. In such a case, selection will have operated upon the group and not upon the individuals.

Once such a situation has arisen and all individuals have the character, it is easy to maintain, but the problem comes when we consider how it could evolve in the first place. It is a problem particularly relevant to the evolution of behavior and the most influential recent protagonist of group selection (Wynne-Edwards, 1962) has argued that much of the social behavior of animals has evolved in this way. He is particularly concerned with the relationship between animals and their food supply, claiming that most species have ways of limiting their own reproductive rate so as to avoid overpopulation. Wynne-Edwards considers that much social behavior with its communal gatherings, displays, territorial fighting, etc., has evolved in order that the breeding groups may in some way assess their own density and regulate their reproduction accordingly. Of course, he does not envisage any conscious understanding of the situation, but suggests, for example, that if the density within a group is abnormally high, this is detected during some kind of communal display and the members of the group have an inherited response which affects their reproductive behavior accordingly. For instance, birds might lay fewer eggs or even fail to breed at all in a year when their population was unusually high.

Other authorities, notably Lack (1954, 1966) consider that animal populations always live close to the limits of their food supply and that individuals reproduce at the maximum feasible rate. For example, the gannet (*Sula bassana*), a long-lived seabird, does not breed until it is several years old and then lays only one egg each year. Wynne-Edwards would suggest that although individuals might be able to breed earlier and rear two or more young per year, colonies in which they raise only one have prospered better because they live well within their food supply. Lack, on the other hand, would suggest that gannets laying one egg per year will, taken over their whole breeding life, leave more descendants than those laying two or more eggs.

Wynne-Edwards amasses a vast amount of data to support his hypothesis but, although everyone admits that there are awkward facts which are, at present, hard to explain on the basis of individual selection, it cannot be said that Wynne-Edwards' arguments on the power of group selection are convincing.

It is very difficult to envisage how breeding restraint can evolve unless it is of advantage to individuals. It might perhaps enable them to conserve their strength in a period of scarcity so that they can breed again as soon as conditions improve. Even if we assume that group selection has operated and all individuals have so reduced their reproductive rate that groups live within their food supply, this situation would be widely unstable. Suppose some variant individuals crop up which reproduce at double the group selected rate; what can prevent the genes responsible from spreading through the population, since they confer such large short-term gains? Herein lies the universal drawback to the group selection concept.

From the behavioral point of view there seems no problem over the evolution of most social behavior and the responsiveness to other individuals which is needed to maintain the cohesion of a group or society. The pioneering work of Allee (1938) and his students has shown how much the individual gains from social life even if this amounts to little more than passive aggregation. Group selection, even if it were possible, is quite unnecessary to account for the evolution of social behavior.

The controversy outlined above is currently enlivening much research on the borderlines between behavior, genetics, and ecology. The reader is recommended to the books by Wynne-Edwards and Lack, and also to excellent critical commentaries by Smith (1964) and Wiens (1966).

## B. The Evolution of Altruism

There is a particular type of behavioral character which can spread through a population even though disadvantageous in the immediate sense to individuals possessing it. Most small birds utter alarm calls when they see a predator approaching. By doing so they must increase, even if only slightly, their own chances of detection. A clue to the evolutionary history of such behavior is provided by the observation that birds are most persistent in calling—or in feigning injury, another potentially dangerous behavior pattern—when they are close to their own young. Clearly it is often "worthwhile" genetically to sacrifice one's own interests for the sake of one's offspring. Just how worthwhile it is will depend on many circumstances—whether one breeds once or many times, how many offspring there are in a brood, and so on. Following Smith (1964) we may call the process whereby such altruistic behaviour evolves "kin selection." It evolves not because it favors the individual directly, but because other individuals carrying similar genes benefit. Many of the diverse patterns of behavior we lump under the term "parental behavior" must have evolved in this way. Often animals with well-marked maternal care learn the characteristics of their own young and discriminate against others. This is just as adaptive in the converse direction—one does not waste effort to assist unrelated animals.

Kin selection may be effective outside the familiar parent/offspring relationship. An individual inherits half of its genes from its mother and half from its father. Hence its genetic affinity to either parent is 50%, and this is the same as the average genetic affinity between full siblings. If for the moment, we regard the purpose of life as the perpetuation of one's genes, then it is just as profitable to sacrifice oneself for brothers and sisters as for sons and daughters; in each case, it would be necessary to ensure that one saved two lives, on average, in order to make the sacrifice worthwhile. On the same argument one would need to save four grandchildren or eight first cousins!

Hamilton (1964) has examined the evolutionary consequences of kin selection in detail, and in doing so has made one brilliant suggestion bearing on a problem that has long puzzled biologists—the evolution of sociality among insects. True social life has evolved in only two orders of insects, the Isoptera (termites) and the Hymenoptera (ants, bees, and wasps), but there is good evidence that in the latter order it has evolved *independently* no less than ten times on a minimum estimate (Wilson, 1966). Why should the Hymenoptera show such an extraordinary "facility" for social life which evades other insects even if they show subsocial aggregations of various types which might seem hopeful starting points for true sociality? Hamilton points out that the characteristic features of Hymenopteran social life are that it involves cooperation between sisters, the majority of which are sterile. New colonies of the honeybee are founded by the old queen emigrating with some of her daughters, leaving behind a young queen with a large number of her sisters. The latter then cooperate to rear the daughters of their single fertile sister.

Now the Hymenoptera have an unusual system of sex determination: males are produced from unfertilized eggs and are haploid, while females result from fertilized eggs and are diploid. Because the male Hymenopteran has only one set of chromosomes his gametes are all identical, and this means that all his daughters (which develop from fertilized eggs) have 50% of their genes in common from him. In addition, these daughters share with each other, on the average, 25% of their mother's genes, so their total genetic affinity is 75%. Since their affinity with their mother is the normal 50%, this means that Hymenopteran sisters are more similar to each other than each is to their mother. Reverting to the kin selection argument, in the Hymenoptera it is more advantageous to assist in the rearing of a sister than to produce a daughter of one's own. Once this conclusion, so simple and elegant, has been attained, then it is easy to appreciate how their manner of sex determination may have played an important part in predisposing the Hymenoptera to evolve social life. To quote from Hamilton (1964),

> Consider a species where the female consecutively provisions and oviposits in cell after cell so that she is still at work when the first of her female offspring ecloses, leaves the nest and mates. Our principle tells us that even if this new

adult had a nest already constructed and vacant for her use she would prefer, other things being equal, returning to her mother's and provisioning a cell for the rearing of an extra sister to provisioning a cell for a daughter of her own.

Obviously kin selection was not the entire basis for the evolution of social life in the Hymenoptera (see Kennedy, 1966). Many other factors were involved—one of the most important emerges from the quotation above, length of life must be prolonged so that the generations overlap—but one can hardly doubt that we have here a unique example of how the course of behavioral evolution was profoundly affected by purely genetic factors.

## C. The Correlation between Behavior and Morphology

We have discussed earlier the way in which inherited behavior forms part of the animals' whole adaptive response to its environment. In the course of evolution, morphology and behavior have become closely associated and interdependent so that the overall correlation between them is commonplace. We are not surprised that predatory animals behave differently from herbivorous prey animals. A carnivorous mammal inherits particular types of alimentary canal, teeth, and jaws; it also inherits certain predatory tendencies which become perfected into hunting behavior.

Nevertheless there is often a much more detailed coadaptation of behavior and structure which is worth examining briefly, particularly as there are one or two cases which pose problems concerning their evolution.

Lorenz (1937) first suggested the term "Auslöser" (which Tinbergen, 1951, translated as "social releasers") for these features of a fellow member of the same species to which an animal reacts particularly strongly. These may be vivid patches of color as on a bird plumage, the enlarged fins of a Siamese fighting fish, or the Nasanoff scent gland on the abdomen of a worker honeybee. Lorenz pointed out that in every case the releaser is especially evolved for communication and that usually it is perfectly adapted to emphasize some display posture or movement. Bird displays invariably "show off" their plumage to the maximum effect—vivid tail feathers are spread, wings drooped to reveal wing bars, and so on. The fighting fish display laterally with their exaggerated fins spread out. The worker bee opens the Nasanoff gland and disperses its scent by fanning its wings. Here then we have the most beautiful detailed correspondence between structure and behavior.

Lorenz argued that in most cases the movement must have arisen before the releaser which now serves to enhance its effect. Many birds when strongly aroused erect the feathers on the top of the head, but only in a few groups have these feathers become elaborated to form a crest and in still fewer do the crest feathers have a contrasting color. This is good circumstantial evidence that feather erection is phylogenetically older than crests themselves. The eyespots on the hind wings of some moths and butterflies (see Fig. 9) are hidden in the normal rest position but are flashed into view during the defensive display when the insect is disturbed. The eyespots themselves could have no selective advantage if the movement which displays them did not already exist. On the other hand, a sudden spreading of the wings would have some startling effect even if there were no eyespot pattern to be revealed. The presence of the movement could then give selective advantage to the development of a contrasting pattern on the hind wing and set the stage for the evolution of eyespots.

Sometimes quite close relatives differ markedly in form and behavior. In Sect. II, D, when discussing threshold changes in microevolution, we mentioned that different species of moth required different levels of tactile stimulation to elicit the defensive display. The group contains species which have adopted opposite stratagems for defense. Some are cryptically colored so as to resemble closely the leaves or bark of the trees on which they rest during the daytime—these species are all palatable to common predators such as lizards and monkeys. Other species have developed vivid red, orange, and black aposematic or warning coloration and appear to be violently distasteful to predators which refuse to touch them.

The threshold for the defensive display, which all the moths show in some form, is correlated with their coloration. The cryptic species require strong stimulation—their best defense is to remain still, relying on their camouflage until all else fails. The aposematic species react quite differently—the more obviously they flaunt their conspicuousness, the better, and they display at the least touch or to a visual stimulus alone (Blest, 1957).

This contrast between the behavior of cryptic and aposematic species is found throughout the animal kingdom. The behavior of cryptic animals has always evolved so as to support their camouflage, while aposematic species never made any attempt to conceal themselves. Cott (1957) gives abundant examples of the remarkable range of adaptive coloration and associated behavior to be found in every group of animals.

To conclude this section, we may consider one example where the fit between behavior and morphology is almost too good. This concerns the remarkable phenomenon of egg mimicry by parasitic cuckoos. Several groups of birds—the cuckoos, cow-birds, and honey-guides, for example—include members which do not build nests but lay their eggs in the nest of other species where they are incubated. Hamilton and Orians (1965) provide a good discussion of factors which may have influenced the evolution of this habit; Southern (1954) considers the egg mimicry of cuckoos in more detail.

The European cuckoo (*Cuculus canorus*) lays its eggs in the nests of small passerine birds and in accordance with this habit, its eggs are very small for a bird of its size and they hatch after a short incubation period. These adaptations fit the cuckoo for parasitism in general, but it goes much further than this. Figure 8 shows how the cuckoo's eggs have quite different color patterns matching the host species in which they are laid. There is evidence that matching is necessary because passerine species which are often parasitized by cuckoos discriminate against (i.e., remove) odd eggs in their nests more than do unparasitized species (Rensch, 1924). Host and parasite are engaged in an evolutionary contest, the outcome of which is bound to drive the cuckoo into better and better matching of its eggs.

Egg pattern must be genetically determined, and therefore we are faced with the problem of how the female cuckoo matches her selection of host to her egg pattern. There is the further problem of how the gene complex controlling egg pattern is kept intact—each female would need to insure that she mates with a male cuckoo carrying the right genes.

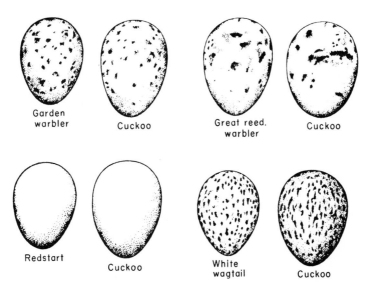

FIG. 8.    Egg mimicry by cuckoos which parasitize different host species. (After Welty, 1962.)

We do not yet have full answers to these problems, but field studies have helped greatly. They confirm that female cuckoos specialize in one host species, and in most areas of Europe the local cuckoos have one main host. Thus the cuckoo population is effectively split up into races, or "gentes" as they are usually called, with a fair degree of geographical isolation between them. The fact that one area may be inhabited by cuckoos parasitizing species A while species B, which is the main host of cuckoos in another area, is not parasitized is good circumstantial evidence that coexistence of two gentes is disadvantageous. Presumably it is impossible to avoid hybridization, and for the same reason there seems little chance of a second gens evolving in an area where one is already well established.

A degree of geographical isolation will make it less likely that a female cuckoo will mate with the wrong sort of male, but she still has to select the "correct" host, and in most areas several potential host species will be common. After spending the winter in Africa, cuckoos like many other migrant birds return to almost the exact spot where they were reared. This habit would aid host selection but would not be sufficient on its own. There must be in addition some kind of learning process, akin to imprinting, by which a nestling female cuckoo becomes attached to its host species. (Note that cuckoos *cannot* be susceptible to sexual imprinting upon their foster parents.)

There are several awkward facts which still have to be explained. In Scandinavia, cuckoos parasitizing meadow pipits have a rather diffuse distribution which does overlap with other gentes; how do they maintain their independence? Again, if gentes are reproductively isolated from one another, why do they not show any divergences in plumage or other characters which might be expected to accumulate? In fact the main geographical races of the cuckoo, based on size and plumage characteristics, cut across the distribution of gentes; i.e., Scandinavian cuckoos, of all gentes, are more similar in appearance to each other than they are to cuckoos in eastern Europe which may be parasitizing the same sorts of host species.

More research is needed, although the material is admittedly rather intractable, but enough is known to demonstrate the intricate interdependence of structure and behavior which fits the cuckoos for their remarkable mode of life.

### D. "Perfectionism" and Compromise in the Evolution of Behavior

Selection operates upon whole organisms not upon isolated characteristics. Consequently if we consider any feature in isolation, it is rarely found to be developed to the maximum level which it might exhibit if selection also operated in isolation.

Compare the two visual releasers shown in Figs. 9 and 10. The effectiveness of the eye spots on the wings of *Caligo* depends on the almost universal fear for large eyes shown by insectivorous birds; it is by this character that the latter recognize their own predators, hawks and owls. Once *Caligo* had, evolutionarily speaking, begun to assemble an eye pattern, selection continued in one direction and with few limitations. The pattern involves only the organization of the pigmented scales on

Fig. 9.    Eye spots on the hindwings of butterflies of the genus *Caligo*. Every detail of the pattern serves to entrance the resemblance to a large vertebrate eye lit from above. (Material by courtesy of E. C. Pelham-Clinton, Royal Scottish Museum.)

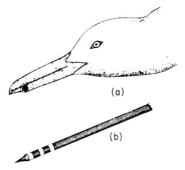

FIG. 10.    An accurate, 3-dimensional model of a herring-gull's head (a) compared
with a "supernormal" bill (b). The latter received 26% more pecks from young
chicks. (After Tinbergen & Perdeck, 1950.)

the wing, it does not affect the wing as a propulsive organ, nor is there
any competing tendency towards camouflage. As a result the eye spot
has become a near-perfect representation of a large vertebrate eye.

More commonly, long before such perfection is attained, competing
factors will take effect. The herring-gull's bill (Fig. 10) is bright yellow
with a red spot on the lower mandible. The latter serves as a releaser,
attracting the pecks of the newly hatched chick when it seeks food from
its parents. Tinbergen and Perdeck (1950) have shown that the artificial
bill also shown in Fig. 10 is more efficient at eliciting pecks from naive
chicks than a normal bill, but in view of its feeding habits it is easy
to understand why the herring gull has not evolved a bill of this shape.

Of course we are rarely in a position to make such judgments about
the perfection of behavioral adaptations. The feeding responses of birds
or the nest-building behavior of digger wasps, for example, seem perfectly
adaptive, but it would be almost impossible to discover whether they
could be improved. It is in the study of display patterns that more
meaningful comparisons are sometimes possible.

For instance, Marler (1959) discusses the alarm calls made by passerine birds to a hawk flying overhead (see Fig. 11). They all share
certain characteristics which make them difficult to locate—the sound
is a pure tone which fades in and fades out gradually. These qualities
are in striking contrast to the calls of similar species made when they
mob an owl; here there is a premium on easy location in order that
other birds can join in the mobbing (Fig. 12). The similarity between
the alarm calls of unrelated birds could simply be an example of "conver-
gent evolution"—the same environment evoking a similar response. However since passerines of different species respond to one another's alarm
calls it is possible that selection has deliberately favored the calls becom-

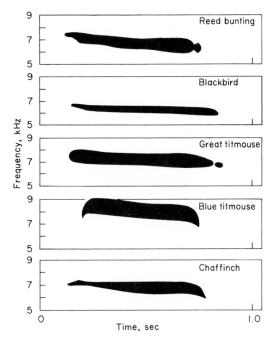

FIG. 11.    Sound spectograms of calls of five species of British bird used when a hawk flies over. They share the characteristic of being difficult to locate. (After Marler, 1959.)

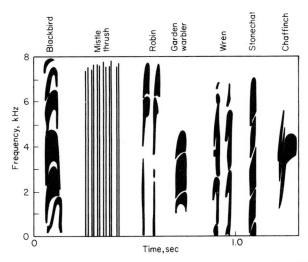

FIG. 12.    Sound spectograms of calls of seven species used while mobbing an owl. They are more diverse than the alarm calls but share the characteristic of being easy to locate. (After Marler, 1959.)

ing similar so as to increase interspecific effectiveness. By this means the group of species concerned has evolved towards the best possible alarm call.

The situation is quite different for the territorial songs of birds. The function of song is to advertise the presence of the male, and it serves both to attract females and warn off other males. Apart from very general characteristics such as loudness and ease of location, there is no further detailed "specification" to be met, i.e., there is no "ideal" song. Indeed there is selective advantage in songs being highly variable, both between species, to avoid hybridization (a factor to be discussed in Sect. V) and to a lesser degree within a species, so that females can identify their own mates easily. Marler (1952) has shown that no two male chaffinches have identical songs, and even in a species such as the white-crowned sparrow which has well-marked local dialects, individual differences remain (Marler & Tamura, 1964).

Such song variations are not, of course, based upon genetic variation alone. They arise from the male bird's sensitivity to features of its early environment—the song of its father and neighboring birds, for example. Clearly where distinctive individual variation is advantageous, it is much more likely to arise in this way. Variability in response is closely related to behavioral flexibility within the individual, and obviously the ability to vary one's response to changing environmental demands is one of the great selective advantages of the evolution of learning potential in long-lived animals.

Learning may enable an animal to make its own individual optimum "compromise" between the various demands of its environment. Barnett (1963) discusses how wild rats establish a compromise between two conflicting tendencies, that to approach and investigate new objects in their environment ("neophilia") and that to avoid new objects ("neophobia"). A rat's response to a new object is influenced by its past experience, the responses of other individuals in its society, and its state of hunger. A rat's behavior will change and a compromise be set at different levels according to changing circumstances during its lifetime.

We can often observe an evolutionary compromise between conflicting tendencies whose levels are largely determined genetically. Very many birds are territorial and the establishment and holding of a territory depends on the bird showing an adequate compromise between attack and escape tendencies. There must be a balance struck, because overdevelopment of either tendency is certain to be disadvantageous. A hyperaggressive individual is likely to carve out a large territory, but he is also likely to be too aggressive towards females who come near. The size of territory varies greatly between birds; it may be an acre or more in Passerines but only a few square feet in a gull. However, in each case the area is hotly defended against intruders early in the breeding season. The evolution of attack and escape tendencies has repercussions on the sexual behavior of vertebrates. The work of ethologists has revealed how most courtship displays have their origin in the conflict between sexual, attack, and escape tendencies (see Tinbergen, 1953; Bastock, 1967). Within the family of gulls (Laridae) there is good evidence that selection has favored different levels of compromise between attack and escape tendencies (see Tinbergen, 1959). This is particularly well shown by a rather aberrant gull the kittiwake (*Rissa tridactyla*). Most gulls nest on level ground and there is rarely any shortage of nest sites, but the kittiwake nests on narrow cliff ledges and competition for suitable sites is severe. By this habit the kittiwake escapes a good deal of the predation of eggs and young which is quite severe in the ground-nesting gulls. The competition for nest sites has driven the kittiwake to become more aggressive; and fierce battles are common when the birds return to the breeding cliffs. This extra aggressiveness has repercussions on many other aspects of the kittiwake's behavior. Aggression between mates persists much longer than in the other gulls, and to counteract it, there is a well-developed appeasement display. In order to accommodate this change to cliff-nesting, the kittiwake has had to "accept" a high level of aggression, and selection has produced a compromise which is struck at a different level from the other gulls. Cullen (1957) describes numerous other changes to the behavior of both adults and chicks which all clearly stem from this one starting point.

The evolution of colonial nesting itself often involves compromise. On the one hand dispersion of nests will tend to help concealment, but concentration of nests will improve mutual protection. Tinbergen (1957) and Cullen (1960) discuss these tendencies in gulls and terns, and in the latter group, Cullen provides evidence that close relatives have evolved distinctly different stratagems to meet the problem of predation during the nesting period.

The performance of any conspicuous display is likely to endanger the performer to some extent. Hence it is common to find among male animals that whereas during the breeding season, the necessity to obtain a mate swings the selective balance in favor of conspicuousness, more retiring habits return as soon as reproduction is finished. Most male birds stop singing once their mate has begun incubation, and not uncommonly they lose their nuptial plumage as well. Once again we see evidence that selection has struck the balance at different levels depending on other factors. In monogamous species there is rarely a great exaggeration of male secondary sexual characters. This is particularly true in those cases as in many passerine birds, where the male plays an active part in feeding and protecting the young. In polygamous species on the other hand, a high proportion of males are excluded from reproducing each year but the few males that do breed mate with many females. There is intense competition for females and this has led to the extreme exaggeration of secondary sexual characters. The fantastic plumage of male birds of paradise, the tail of a peacock, the antlers of deer and the gigantic bulk of male elephant seals, have all resulted from selection between males—true sexual selection in the sense originally discussed by Darwin (see Smith, 1958, Bastock, 1967). Although in some colonial animals, such as baboons, the large males may help in colony defense, polygamous males play no direct part in caring for the young. They function largely as reproducing mechanisms and consequently there is less selective advantage in their maintaining themselves outside the narrow reproductive context. A highly conspicuous male who mates with a large number of females in his first season and then is killed by a predator, will often leave more descendants than a male who survives many years but is less efficient at attracting females.

## IV. THE ORIGINS OF BEHAVIOR

A high proportion of any animal's fixed action patterns are clearly and directly related to the function they serve. This is particularly true of patterns connected with the most basic homeostatic behavior—breathing, feeding, and drinking. Thus the elaborate feeding behavior of a bee is a complex amalgam of inherited and learned patterns whose form and function obviously evolved alongside the elongated lapping mouth parts, hairy body surface, and pollen storage "baskets" on the hind legs.

However there are other types of behavior, and particularly some displays, in which the connection between form and function is much less obvious. *Drosophila* males court females using various types of wing display; jumping spiders wave their legs; pigeons bow in front of their females; while pheasants strut round the female trailing their wings. We have no *a priori* ground for assuming that the females concerned were initially more likely to respond to these particular displays. Why then have these movements been chosen by selection and not others which might seem equally effective?

Over the past two decades the work of the ethologists has succeeded in making evolutionary sense out of many display patterns, although many functional problems remain (see particularly, Tinbergen 1952, 1953; Bastock, 1967). They have convincingly shown that displays take their origin from behavior functionally associated with such patterns as feeding, drinking, care of the body surface, parental behavior, attack, or escape. The territorial system of many vertebrates has introduced an element of conflict into the courtship situation, because when a female enters a male's territory she is certain to arouse attack and escape tendencies as well as sexual ones. Thus, not only these tendencies may find expression in the male's behavior towards her, but so-called "displacement activities"—the behavioral result of a conflict—may also occur.

This is not the place to discuss the nature and causation of displacement activities, a topic well covered by McFarland (1966), Hinde (1970), and Bastock (1967); here we are concerned only with their role in the evolution of display patterns. It appears that selection has been remarkably "opportunistic" to the extent that almost any pattern which was likely to occur in a sexual conflict situation might be pressed into service and form the basis for a display.

For example, many birds commonly show "displacement" preening movements of various types when in conflict. Courtship displays clearly based upon preening are found in many species, notably grebes, ducks, and some finches. Feather or hair erection is also a common "by-product" of conflict and physiological arousal; it also forms a common element in the threat and courtship displays of birds and mammals. In an analogous way patterns derived from feeding, drinking, and breathing movements also appear in displays.

Presumably the displays we now see were originally selected out of a wider range because their performance increased reproductive efficiency in some way. They may have stimulated the female or arrested her attention so that she did not move away. Once one movement began to get the edge over others, selection would favor males performing this movement more frequently, and, once a pattern of courtship was established, females who responded most favorably would also be at an advantage.

The evolution of releaser structures which emphasize the effect of a display has already been discussed (p. 29), and many of the best examples come from courtship. The incorporation of displacement preening into the courtship of ducks has led to the evolution of the "speculum," a patch of bright feathers on the wing, which is displayed during the preening movement. Morris (1956), Andrew (1956), and Daanje (1950) all review in more detail the origins of vertebrate displays and their associated releasers.

Although we have concentrated upon vertebrates, many of the display patterns of invertebrates have a similar history. There is little or no evidence that conflict, in the vertebrate sense, is involved in the courtship of arthropods, and consequently displacement activities are not "available" as suitable material upon which selection can be elaborate. In crickets, Huber (1962) suggests that the wing movements used to produce the song patterns are derived from the flight movements of ancestors which still had functional wings. The wing displays of *Drosophila* probably have the same origin (Ewing & Manning, 1967). The courtship movements of male longhorned beetles are made after the male has mounted the female's back. At first she tries to dislodge him, and the male's licking of her head and thorax may serve to calm her. This licking movement is little modified in form from normal feeding and the more primitive long-horned beetles use this movement alone. Michelson (1964, 1966) has traced all the more complex rhythmic movements used by other species back to this one simple feeding pattern.

It is not just in sexual displays that we can trace the history of behavior patterns from origins that are functionally quite unrelated. Andrew (1963) suggests that facial expressions in primates and perhaps their vocalizations also, which are now so important in communication, arose from movements designed to protect the face when approached by danger. Many tropical fresh water fish build nests of air bubbles glued together at the water surface. Braddock and Braddock (1959) suggest that this habit depended upon the evolution of air breathing in such fish, which requires them to visit the surface periodically to take in air, some of which is guffed out as bubbles when they do so.

Finally, the classic work of von Frisch (1968) has revealed the remarkable dance communication system of the honeybee. By means of a dance performed on the vertical combs, a returning forager can indicate to her fellow workers the approximate distance and direction of the food source upon which she has been feeding. Among other things, this dance requires that the performer transpose the angle between the sun and the food source into an angle between the straight run of her dance and gravity (see Fig. 13). The "spectators" follow the movement of the dancer closely, tracing her steps as they keep their antennae in contact with her abdomen. Subsequently, they make the reverse transposition when they leave the hive—heading off at an angle to the sun which equals the angle the dance made to gravity. This ability in an arthropod might seem almost unbelievable, but recent work with ants, beetles, flies, and moths, among others, has shown that all the elements of the bee dance are paralleled in other insects. The essential difference is that, in the honeybee, selection has elaborated certain basic aspects

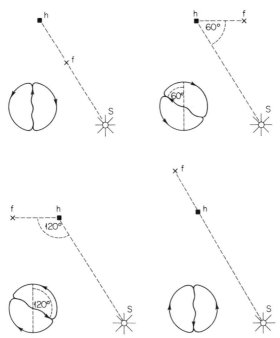

Fig. 13.    The manner in which the straight path of a honeybee's dance on the vertical comb is related to the direction of the food source with respect to the sun. In each case the angle between the dance path and the vertical equals that between the food source and the sun when viewed from the hive. Directly upwards means that the food source is in the same direction as the sun. (After von Frisch, 1968).

of the way insects orientate themselves with respect to gravity and light and formed them into a means of communication. In solitary insects, so far as we know, these elements have no signal function. Bastock (1964) ably discusses the evolution of the bee dance from its humble origins.

In all these examples of the evolution of displays, there are two outstanding features. Firstly, the opportunism of selection, which we mentioned at the outset; the remarkable way in which behavior of diverse origins has been pressed into service because it happened to appear in the right context for a display. Secondly, the "shaping" process which has occurred after the movement becomes the "target" for selection has basic similarities throughout. Changes in its frequency of performance and its qualitative form—whose mechanisms were discussed in the section on microevolution—have combined together with the evolution of releaser structures to enhance the signal value of the movement. In ethological terminology it has become "ritualized" into a clear-cut, conspicuous, and unambiguous display. Tinbergen (1952), Morris (1957), and Blest (1961) discuss the ritualization process in more detail; see also the symposium edited by Huxley (1966).


## V. SEXUAL ISOLATION

It is appropriate to end this chapter with a topic illustrating that behavior not only evolves under the pressure of selection but can also influence the course and speed at which evolution occurs. Any factor which affects an animal's choice of a mate will also affect the exchange of genes within a population. If, for example, females tended to prefer males of a particular color or mated only with males of high status in a hierarchy of dominance, then particular genotypes would increase or decrease irrespective of any other selective forces operating on them. There is abundant evidence that assortative mating of this type does occur within populations and thereby influences their evolution (see King, 1967; Lill, 1968a, b), but here we have space to consider only the assortative mating that occurs between populations.

Sexual isolation may be defined as "any behavioral barrier to mating between members of different populations." It forms one category of a whole series of potential isolating mechanisms, whose nature and action are well reviewed by Mayr (1963). A species is sometimes described as a group of populations which can potentially interbreed among themselves but are isolated from other comparable groups, and much work on isolating mechanisms is concerned with how species are kept distinct from one another. Once again the phrase "preservation of the species" is liable to crop up in the literature, but it can be ignored. There is nothing sacrosanct about a species; it will stay distinct only if there is a good selective reason for doing so.

Among plants it is quite common to find that where two closely-related species overlap, there is a zone of hybridization, and sometimes this zone is quite extensive. Hybridization is much rarer between animal species, and hybrid zones are usually narrow. For example, in the British Isles the carrion crow (*Corvus corone*) occupies the south, while the hooded crow (*C. cornix*) occupies the north and west, especially around the coasts. There is a narrow zone where hybrids occur, but there is no sign of the hybrids spreading into the two parent populations which remain completely distinct. Observations of this type strongly suggest that hybrids are at a disadvantage and cannot compete with either parent species, and the reason for this is not difficult to understand. The group of populations that comprises the species "carrion crow" shares a common gene pool. This pool has evolved as the result of selection operating on individuals so as best to adapt them to their particular environment. The gene pool of the "hooded crow" species has evolved in a more northern environment, which has consequently imposed different selection pressures. When these two species interbreed, the hybrids inherit a mixture of their genes, and this mixture is unlikely to be an adequate compromise. It is less well suited to either environment, and though hybrids survive they are no match for either parent species.

This situation will still hold even if two closely-related species have an overlapping distribution. The willow warbler (*Phylloscopus trochilus*) and the chiff-chaff (*P. collybita*) live together in the same woodlands through much of Europe. However close observation shows that they do not occupy exactly the same habitat. The willow warbler gets most of its food from bushes and the lower branches of large trees whilst the chiff-chaff feeds in the higher branches. It seems likely that they are driven by mutual competition to specialize in that part of their common habitat where they are most successful. This hypothesis is supported by the fact that on the Canary Islands, where the willow warbler is absent, the chiff-chaff feeds at all levels.

Because species which overlap are driven into specialization, the gene pool of each must be specialized too, and hybrids will suffer in just the same way as described for the hybrid crows. This is, in fact, one of the mildest outcomes of hybridization between species. Many hybrids, even between quite close relatives, are completely sterile because the two parental genotypes are too different to combine successfully when gametes are being formed. (See Mayr, 1963, for a full discussion of these topics.)

Herein lies the selective force keeping species distinct; individuals who mate with members of other species will leave fewer or less successful descendants and hence be at a considerable disadvantage. Obviously selection will favor any mechanisms which help in the correct identification of a mate. The selective value of many of the microevolutionary changes to displays, discussed in Sect. II, D, probably lies in the specific distinctiveness they confer. Changes to form, speed, and frequency of performance will all tend to impart a characteristic "flavor" to a display, making it a useful identification signal.

A number of animals have evolved "assembly signals" emitted by one or both sexes which serve to attract mates from a distance. The calls of frogs and toads, the songs of cicadas, the flashing of fireflies, and the odors emitted by female moths are examples. In almost all cases, these signals are extremely species specific, and the responsiveness of one sex is precisely matched to the signal emitted by the other. Marler and Hamilton (1966) give numerous examples with full references. Often the species concerned appear to rely entirely on this assembling system for sexual isolation. Thus Blair (1955) observed that toads of the genus *Microhyla* would hybridize freely if females were lured to the wrong species of male. Perdeck (1958) describes the same phenomenon in grass-hoppers. The majority of animals have some kind of "close-range" identification system which prevents interspecific mating. This may be based on visual, chemical, or auditory displays, usually depending on the dominant sensory modality of the groups concerned. Contact chemical stimuli are important in a number of insects, visual signals are important in lizards, birds, and butterflies, and so on. Again, Marler and Hamilton (1966) provide a rich source of specific examples.

It is very common to find that females are much more discriminating than males. In *Drosophila,* for example, males will usually approach almost any moving object of about the right size and, although females of very dissimilar species are rejected on contact, most males will court females of species closely related to their own—it is the female who discriminates more precisely (see Manning, 1965). Liley (1966) describes a similar situation in four closely-related Poeciliid fishes. Inexperienced males court indiscriminately at first, but after some experience they learn to confine their attention to their own females, because only the latter respond to them. Females discriminate correctly from the outset.

This situation bears some resemblance to that found in ducks (Sect. II,A), where males become sexually imprinted upon their mothers, but females show inherited responsiveness to the characteristic male plumage and courtship pattern. However it is difficult to generalize about inherited and acquired species recognition, because there is considerable variation among quite closely-related animals. Godfrey (1958) found that males of different geographically isolated populations of the bank vole (*Clethrionomys glareolus*) could identify females of their own strain by scent and chose to mate with them. He had circumstantial evidence that they could do this irrespective of their early experience. On the other hand Mainardi, Marsan, and Pasquali (1965) have shown that although female domestic mice learn the characteristic smell of their strain during infancy and discriminate against other males, male mice are little affected by their early experience in this respect and show much less discrimination against foreign females.

Extra selectiveness by females makes good evolutionary sense because they usually have much more to lose by an incorrect choice. Many female insects mate only once in their lifetime and thus an unsuccessful mating effectively sterilizes them. In vertebrates also, females usually contribute much the most material and "effort" to reproduction, and mating may be followed by a long period of gestation or egg formation, during which they cannot mate again. On the other hand, the males of most groups of animals have much less to gain from strict discrimination. Many are, at least potentially, polygamous and can mate several times in quick succession. Selection may well favor lower selectivity, because it is better to risk an occasional infertile mating than to miss any chance of a fertile one.

So far we have been considering sexual isolation between established species, but obviously behavioral discrimination will be most critical at the earliest stages of the divergence between two populations. Suppose a formerly continuous population has become split into two. For example, a sustained dry period might cause a continuous woodland habitat to become broken up with trees surviving only on two isolated areas of higher ground. The environments of the two subpopulations and their gene pools will never remain exactly the same. After many generations in isolation, wetter conditions return, woodland spreads back into the lower ground and the habitat is once more continuous. Will the two subpopulations interbreed when they meet?

It is possible that during their period in isolation genes affecting sexual recognition and sexual isolation will have accumulated purely as a by-product of genetic divergence, in which case the two subpopulations may tend to discriminate against each other as soon as they meet. Alternatively they may show no discrimination and interbreed freely. The final outcome, in either eventuality, is likely to depend on the fitness of the hybrids. If these can compete successfully, then the two populations will merge unless an extremely effective sexual isolation system has arisen, by chance, during the period of separation. If the hybrids are not successful, then selection will promptly favor the accumulation of genes which promote sexual isolation.

Evolutionary geneticists have been interested in determining how early in the divergence between populations sexual isolation can occur and whether it arises as a "byproduct" or by selection. The strongest evidence that selection for sexual isolation has occurred on occasions comes from comparing isolation between species which do not live in the same area ("allopatric species") with isolation between species which do have an overlapping distribution ("sympatric species"). For example, several closely-related species of cricket live in the same areas of the eastern United States, so that several different types of male may be calling at the same time. In every case, their songs are quite distinct, and indeed some species have first been separated by their songs and only later have taxonomists found morphological differences confirming that two species are concerned (Alexander, 1962; Walker, 1964). Conversely, three allopatric species of *Gryllus* (*campestris* from Europe, *bermudiensis* from Bermuda, and *firmus* from North America) have obviously been isolated from each other for many thousands of generations. Although they have diverged to a considerable extent morphologically, their calling songs remain identical.

The only reasonable explanation for such facts is that selection favors divergence of song where species overlap, and that in the absence of such selection, songs remain remarkably stable. This is understandable because once a suitable song has evolved, variants are likely to be "misunderstood" by females, and, in the absence of any conflicting tendency, selection will be strongly "stabilizing" (Fig. 7a).

When selection does favor discrimination of members of one's own population from those of another mixed with it, then intraspecific signals can begin to change. A change to one partner which aids discrimination will impose selection upon the other to respond appropriately. Most species show a beautiful correspondence between signaller and receiver. For instance, Walker (1957) has shown that the calling rate of a male tree cricket (*Oecanthus nigricornis*) declines with the temperature, and the responsiveness of the female adjusts to match it, i.e., at low temperatures females are most attracted by a slower calling rate.

A number of workers have attempted to produce or increase sexual isolation artificially by selective breeding. In *Drosophila* successful experiments have been made by Koopman (1950), Knight, Robertson, and Waddington (1956), Crossley (1963), and Kessler (1966) in all of which two populations were mixed and hybrids removed as they appeared so that only those flies that mated with their own kind left any descendants. These experiments all produced marked results within some 10–20 generations, however in each case the populations concerned differed in some fairly striking fashion to begin with—they were genetically marked by mutant genes. Thus, although they would hybridize at the outset of the experiment, there was already some basis for discrimination once selection was imposed. This might be the equivalent of a natural situation when two populations meet after a long period of isolation during which they have diverged morphologically.

It must be admitted that we lack direct evidence that sexual isolation can evolve unless there is some such divergence to begin with. Robertson (1966) reared a population of *Drosophila melanogaster* for many generations on a special diet—called EDTA. This diet was, at first, extremely unfavorable, but the flies slowly adapted to it, and Robertson could show that this adaptation involved considerable genetic changes. Hybrids between the EDTA flies and a normal population were far less successful than their EDTA parents when reared on EDTA food and equivalently less successful than normal flies when reared on normal food.

Having reached this stage, Robertson allowed the two populations to mingle to a limited extent and provided both sorts of food. These would appear to be the optimum conditions for the evolution of sexual isolation for selection will strongly favor those flies which mate with their own kind. In fact, after 25 generations there was no detectable isolation between the t·o populations although they had definitely inter-bred to a considerable extent. Robertson's experiments remind us that our evidence that selection for sexual isolation has been important in the divergence of species, though persuasive, is still only circumstantial. Manning (1965) provides a further discussion of this problem with especial reference to *Drosophila* (see also Ewing & Manning, 1967).

In conclusion, it must be noted that changes in mate discrimination and sexual behavior are not the only way in which sexual isolation is achieved. A species' detailed choice of habitat is also important, because even though they may live in the same area two species will always specialize (see p. 43) and may meet only rarely. In the laboratory *Drosophila pseudoobscura* and *D. persimilis* will hybridize freely, and in considerable areas of North America their distribution overlaps. Yet, although they have been diligently searched for, hybrids are excessively rare in nature. It is known (Pittendrigh, 1958) that in the area of overlap, *D. pseudoobscura* tends to seek the darker and therefore moister parts of the environment while *D. persimilis* prefers lighter places. This divergence in microhabitat selection must drastically reduce the number of contacts between the species.

Waddington, Woolf, and Perry (1954) have shown that some genetic changes affect the microhabitats chosen by *Drosophila*. Such genes may be important in the evolution of populations because not only can they affect specialization when populations are competing in a common habitat, they may be partially "autoisolating" as in the example given above.

## REFERENCES

Alexander, R. D. Evolutionary change in cricket acoustical communication. *Evolution*, 1962, **16**, 443–467.

Allee, W. C. *The social life of animals.* New York: Norton and Company, 1938.

Andrew, R. J. Intention movements of flight in certain passerines and their use in systematics. *Behaviour*, 1956, **10**, 179–204.

Andrew, R. J. The origin and evolution of the calls and facial expression of the primates. *Behaviour*, 1963, **20**, 1–109.

Baerends, G. P., & Baerends-van Roon, J. M. An introduction to the ethology of cichlid fishes. *Behaviour Supplement*, 1950, **1**, 1–243.

Barnett, S. A. *A study in behaviour*. London: Methuen, 1963.

Bastock, M. Communication in bees. *Penguin science survey*. Harmondsworth: Penguin, 1964, Pp. 181–200.

Bastock, M. *Courtship: an ethological study*. New York: Aldine, 1967.

Blair, W. F. Mating call and stage of speciation in the *Microhyla olivacea-M. carolinensis* complex. *Evolution*, 1955, **9**, 469–480.

Blest, A. D. The evolution of protective displays in the Saturniodea and Sphingidae (Lepidoptera). *Behaviour*, 1957, **11**, 257–309.

Blest, A. D. The concept of ritualization. In W. H. Thorpe & O. L. Zangwill (Eds.), *Current problems in animal behaviour*. London & New York: Cambridge University Press, 1961, Pp. 102–124.

Braddock, J. C., & Braddock, Z. I. Development of nesting behaviour in the Siamese fighting fish *Betta splendens*. *Animal Behaviour*, 1959, **7**, 222–232.

Broadhurst, P. L. The biometrical analysis of behavioural inheritance. *Science Progress, Oxford*, 1967, **55**, 123–139.

Brown, R. G. B. Species isolation between the herring gull *Larus argentatus* and lesser black-backed gull *L. fuscus*. *Ibis*, 1967, **109**, 310–317.

Cott, H. B. *Adaptive colouration in animals*. London: Methuen, 1957.

Cotter, W. B. Mating behavior and fitness as a function of single allele differences in *Ephestia kühniella* Z. *Evolution*, 1967, **21**, 275–284.

Crane, J. Comparative biology of salticid spiders at Rancho Grande, Venezuela. Part IV. An analysis of display. *Zoologica*, 1949, **34**, 159–214.

Crane, J. A comparative study of innate defensive behavior in Trinidad mantids (Orthoptera, Mantoidea). *Zoologica*, 1952, **37**, 259–293.

Crane, J. Basic patterns of display in fiddler crabs (Ocypodidae, Genus *Uca*). *Zoologica*, 1957, **42**, 69–82.

Crossley, S. An experimental study of sexual isolation within a species of *Drosophila*. D. Phil. Thesis. University of Oxford, 1963.

Crook, J. H. Comparative studies on the reproductive behaviour of two closely related weaver bird species (*Ploceus cucullatus* and *Ploceus nigerrimus*) and their races. *Behaviour*, 1963, **21**, 177–232.

Cullen, E. Adaptations in the Kittiwake to cliff-nesting. *Ibis*, 1957, **99**, 275–302.

Cullen, J. M. Behaviour as a help in taxonomy. *Systematics Association Publication*, 1959, **3**, 131–140.

Cullen, J. M. Some adaptations in the nesting behaviour of terns. *Proceedings of the 12th International Ornithological Congress, Helsinki, 1958*, 1960, 153–157.

Daanje, A. On locomotory movements in birds and the intention movements derived from them. *Behaviour*, 1950, **3**, 48–98.

Dilger, W. C. The comparative ethology of the African parrot genus *Agapornis*. *Zeitschrift für Tierpsychologie*, 1960, **17**, 649–685.

Dilger, P. C. The behavior of love birds. *Scientific American*, 1962, **206**, 88–98.

Doty, R. W., & Bosma, J. F. An electromyographic analysis of reflex deglutination. *Journal of Neurophysiology*, 1956, **19**, 44–60.

Ewing, A. W., & Manning, A. The evolution and genetics of insect behaviour. *Annual Review of Entomology*, 1967, **12**, 471–494.

Frisch, K. von. *The dance language and orientation of bees*. Cambridge, Massachusetts: Harvard University Press, 1968.

Fuller, J. L., & Thompson, W. R. *Behavior genetics.* New York and London: Wiley, 1960.

Ginsburg, B. T. Genetic parameters in behavioral research. In J. Hirsch (Ed.), *Behavior-genetic analysis.* New York: McGraw-Hill, 1967. Pp. 135–153.

Goethe, F. Vergleichende Beobachtungen zum Verhalten der Silbermöwe (*Larus argentatus*) und der Heringsmöwe (*Larus fuscus*). *Proceedings of the 11th International Ornithological Congress,* 1954, 577–582.

Godfrey, J. The origin of sexual isolation between bank voles. *Proceedings of the Royal Physical Society of Edinburgh,* 1958, **27,** 47–55.

Goy, R. W., & Jakway, J. S. The inheritance of patterns in sexual behaviour in the male guinea pig. *Animal Behaviour,* 1959, **7,** 142–149.

Grant, V. *The origin of adaptations.* New York and London: Columbia University Press, 1963.

Grossfield, J. The influence of light on the mating behavior of *Drosophila.* In M. R. Wheeler (Ed.), *Studies in genetics.* University of Texas Publications 6615, 1966, 147–176.

Hamilton, W. D. The genetical evolution of social behaviour. I and II. *Journal of Theoretical Biology,* 1964, **7,** 1–16, 17–52.

Hamilton, W. J., & Orians, G. H. Evolution of brood parasitism in altricial birds. *Condor,* 1965, **67,** 361–382.

Harlow, H. F. The evolution of learning. In A. Roe & G. G. Simpson (Eds.), *Behavior and evolution.* New Haven, Connecticut: Yale University Press, 1958. Pp. 269–290.

Hinde, R. A. Behaviour and speciation in birds and lower vertebrates. *Biological Reviews,* 1959, **34,** 85–128.

Hinde, R. A. *Animal Behaviour.* 2nd edition. New York: McGraw-Hill, 1970.

Hinde, R. A., & Fisher, J. Further observations on the opening of milk bottles by birds. *British Birds,* 1952, **44,** 393–396.

Hirsch, J. (Ed.) *Behavior-genetic analysis.* New York: McGraw-Hill, 1967.

Hoyle, G. Exploration of neuronal mechanisms underlying behavior in insects. In R. F. Reiss (Ed.), *Neural theory and modeling.* Stanford: Stanford University Press, 1964. Pp. 346–376.

Huber, F. Central nervous control of sound production in crickets and some speculations on its evolution. *Evolution,* 1962, **16,** 429–442.

Hunsaker, D. Ethological isolating mechanisms in the *Sceloporus torquatus* group of lizards. *Evolution,* 1962, **16,** 62–74.

Huxley, J. (Ed.) A discussion on ritualization of behaviour in animals and man. *Philosophical Transactions of the Royal Society of London,* 1966, **251,** 247–562.

Jakway, J. S. The inheritance of patterns of mating behaviour in the male guinea pig. *Animal Behaviour,* 1959, **7,** 150–162.

Johnsgard, P. A. *Handbook of waterfowl behaviour.* London: Constable, 1965.

Kennedy, J. S. Some outstanding questions in insect behaviour. *Symposium of the Royal Entomological Society of London,* 1966, **3,** 97–112.

Kessler, S. Selection for and against ethological isolation between *Drosophila pseudoobscura* and *Drosophila persimilis. Evolution,* 1966, **20,** 634–645.

King, J. A. Behavioral modification of the gene pool. In J. Hirsch (Ed.), *Behavior-genetic analysis.* New York: McGraw-Hill, 1967. Pp. 22–43.

Knight, G. R., Robertson, A., & Waddington, C. H. Selection for sexual isolation within a species. *Evolution,* 1956, **10,** 14–22.

Koopman, K. F. Natural selection for reproductive isolation between *Drosophila pseudoobscura* and *Drosophila persimilis. Evolution,* 1950, **4,** 135–148.

Lack, D. *The natural regulation of animal numbers.* London and New York: Oxford University Press, 1954.

Lack, D. *Population studies of birds.* London and New York: Oxford University Press, 1966.

Liley, N. R. Ethological isolating mechanisms in four sympatric species of Poecilliid fish. *Behaviour Supplement,* 1966, **13**, 1–197.

Lill, A. An analysis of sexual isolation in the domestic fowl: I. The basis of homogamy in males. *Behaviour,* 1968, **30**, 107–126. (a)

Lill, A. An analysis of sexual isolation in the domestic fowl: II. The basis of homogamy in females. *Behaviour,* 1968, **30**, 127–145. (b)

Lofts, P., Murton, R. K., & Westwood, N. J. Gonadal cycles and the evolution of breeding seasons in British Columbids. *Journal of Zoology London,* 1966, **150**, 249–272.

Lofts, P., Murton, R. K., & Westwood, N. J. Interspecific differences in photosensitivity between three closely related species of pigeons. *Journal of Zoology London,* 1967, **151**, 17–25.

Lorenz, K. Z. The companion in the bird's world. *Auk,* 1937, **54**, 245–273.

Lorenz, K. Z. Vergleichende Bewegungsstudien an Anatinen. *Journal für Ornithologie Leipzig,* 1941, **89,**1 94–293.

Mainardi, D., Marsan, M., & Pasquali, A. Causation of sexual preferences of the house mouse. The behaviour of mice reared by parents whose odour was artificially altered. *Atti Societa Italiana Scienze naturali,* 1965, **104**, 325–338.

Manning, A. The sexual behaviour of two sibling *Drosophila* species. *Behaviour,* 1959, **15**, 123–145.

Manning, A. The effects of artificial selection for mating speed in *Drosophila melanogaster. Animal Behaviour,* 1961, **9**, 82–92.

Manning, A. Drosophila and the evolution of behaviour. *Viewpoints in Biology,* 1965, **4**, 125–169.

Marler, P. R. Variation in the song of the chaffinch, *Fringilla coelebs. Ibis,* 1952, **94**, 458–472.

Marler, P. R. Developments in the study of animal communication. In P. R. Bell (Ed.) *Darwin's biological work.* London and New York: Cambridge University Press, 1959. Pp. 150–206.

Marler, P. R., & Hamilton, W. J. *Mechanisms of animal behavior.* New York: Wiley, 1966.

Marler, P. R., & Tamura, M. Culturally transmitted patterns of vocal behavior in sparrows. *Science,* 1964, **146**, 1483–1486.

Mayr, E. Behavior and systematics. In A. Roe & G. G. Simpson (Eds.), *Behavior and evolution.* New Haven, Connecticut: Yale University Press, 1958. Pp. 341–362.

Mayr, E. *Animal species and evolution.* London and New York: Oxford University Press, 1963.

McFarland, D. J. On the causal and functional significance of displacement activities. *Zeitschrift für Tierpsychologie,* 1966, **23**, 217–235.

McGill, T. E. Sexual behaviour in three inbred strains of mice. *Behaviour,* 1962, **19**, 341–350.

Michelsen, A. Observations on the sexual behaviour of some longicorn beetles, subfamily Lepturinae. *Behaviour,* 1964, **22**, 152–166.

Michelsen, A. On the evolution of tactile stimulatory actions in longhorned beetles

(Cerambycidae, Coleoptera). *Zeitschrift für Tierpsychologie*, 1966, **23**, 257–266.
Miyadi, D. Social life of Japanese monkeys. *Science*, 1964, **143**, 783–786.
Morris, D. The feather postures of birds and the problem of the origin of social signals. *Behaviour*, 1956, **9**, 75–113.
Morris, D. "Typical intensity" and its relation to the problem of ritualization. *Behaviour*, 1957, **11**, 1–12.
Petersson, M. Diffusion of a new habit among greenfinches. *Nature*, 1959, **184**, 649–650.
Perdeck, A. C. The isolating value of specific song in two sibling species of grasshoppers (*Chorthippus brunneus* Thunb. and *C. biguttulus* L.). *Behaviour*, 1958, **12**, 1–75.
Pittendrigh, C. S. Adaptation, natural selection, and behavior. In A. Roe and G. G. Simpson (Eds.), *Behavior and evolution*. New Haven, Connecticut: Yale University Press, 1958. Pp. 390–416.
Rensch, B. Zur Entstehung der Mimikry der Kuckuckseier. *Journal für Ornithologie, Leipzig*, 1924, **72**, 461–472.
Robertson, F. W. A test of sexual isolation in Drosophila. *Genetic Research, Cambridge*, 1966, **8**, 181–187.
Rothenbuhler, W. C. Behaviour genetics of nest cleaning in honey-bees. I. Responses of four inbred lines to disease-killed brood. *Animal Behaviour*, 1964, **12**, 578–583. (a)
Rothenbuhler, W. C. Behavior genetics of nest cleaning in honey-bees. IV. Responses of $F_1$ and backcross generations to disease-killed brood. *American Zoologist*, 1964, **4**, 111–123. (b)
Schutz, F. Sexuelle Prägung bei Anatiden. *Zeitschrift für Tierpsychologie*, 1965, **22**, 50–103.
Sheppard, P. M. Some contributions to population genetics resulting from the study of Lepidoptera. *Advances in Genetics*, 1961, **10**, 165–216.
Smith, J. M. Sexual selection. In S. A. Barnett (Ed.), *A century of Darwin*. London: Heinemann, 1958. Pp. 231–244.
Smith, J. M. Group selection and kin selection. *Nature*, 1964, **201**, 1145–1147.
Southern, H. N. Mimicry in cuckoo's eggs. In J. Huxley (Ed.), *Evolution as a process*. London: Allen & Unwin, 1954. Pp. 219–232.
Spieth, H. T. Mating behavior within the genus *Drosophila* (Diptera). *Bulletin of the American Museum of Natural History, New York*, 1952, **99**, 401–474.
Spieth, H. T., & Hsu, T. C. The influence of light on the mating behavior of seven species of the *Drosophila melanogaster* group. *Evolution*, 1950, **4**, 316–325.
Thorpe, W. H. *Bird song*. London & New York: Cambridge University Press, 1961.
Thorpe, W. H., & Jones, F. G. W. Olfactory conditioning and its relation to the problem of host selection. *Proceedings of the Royal Society B.*, 1937, **124**, 56–81.
Tinbergen, N. *The study of instinct*. London & New York: Oxford University Press, 1951.
Tinbergen, N. "Derived" activities; their causation, biological significance, origin, and emancipation during evolution. *Quarterly Review of Biology*, 1952, **27**, 1–32.
Tinbergen, N. *Social behaviour in animals*. London: Methuen, 1953.
Tinbergen, N. The functions of territory, *Bird Study*, 1957, **4**, 14–27.
Tinbergen, N. Comparative studies of the behaviour of gulls (Laridae): a progress report. *Behaviour*, 1959, **15**, 1–70.

Tinbergen, N., & Perdeck, A. C. On the stimulus situation releasing the begging response in the newly-hatched herring gull chick (*Larus a. argentatus* Pont.). *Behaviour*, 1950, **3**, 1–38.

Waddington, C. H., Woolf, B., & Perry, M. Environment selection by *Drosophila* mutants. *Evolution*, 1954, **8**, 89–96.

Walker, T. J. Specificity in the response of female tree crickets (Orthoptera, Gryllidae, Oecanthinae) to calling songs of the males. *Annals of the Entomological Society of America* 1957, **50**, 626–636.

Walker, T. J. Cryptic species among sound-producing ensiferan Orthoptera (Gryllidae and Tettigonidae). *Quarterly Review of Biology*, 1964, **39**, 345–355.

Wall, W. van de, Bewegungsstudien an Anatinen, *Journal für Ornithologie Leipzig*, 1963, **104**, 1–15.

Warren, J. M. Primate learning in comparative perspective. In A. M. Schrier, H. F. Harlow, & F. Stollnitz (Eds.), *Behavior of nonhuman primates*. Vol. I. New York and London: Academic Press, 1965. Pp. 249–281.

Welty, J. C. *The life of birds*. Philadelphia and London: Saunders, 1962.

Whitman, C. O. The behavior of pigeons. *Carnegie Institute of Washington Publication*, 1919, **257**, 1–161.

Wiens, J. A. On group selection and Wynne-Edwards' hypothesis. *American Scientist*, 1966, **54**, 273–287.

Wilson, D. E. The origin of the flight-motor command in grasshoppers. In R. F. Reiss (Eds.), *Neural theory and modeling*. Stanford: Stanford University Press, 1964. Pp. 331–345.

Wilson, E. O. Behaviour of social insects. *Symposium of the Royal Entomological Society of London*, 1966, **3**, 81–96.

Wood-Gush, D. G. M. A study of sex drive of two strains of cockerel through three generations. *Animal Behaviour*, 1960, **8**, 43–53.

Wynne-Edwards, V. C. *Animal dispersion in relation to social behaviour*. Edinburgh, Scotland: Oliver and Boyd, 1962.

# CHAPTER 2

# The Concept of Instinct

RICHARD E. WHALEN

Department of Psychobiology
University of California
Irvine, California

## I. INTRODUCTION

The concept of instinct has been with us for some time—Beach (1955) has traced it as far back as the Greeks. Scholarly argument has been used to defend this notion (Eibl-Eibesfeldt & Kramer, 1958; Lorenz, 1965; Tinbergen, 1951), and polemic and data have been employed in its attack (Beach, 1955; Lehrman, 1953). Instinct has not had an untroubled life, but despite these viscissitudes the concept has survived the years remarkably unchanged. "Instinct" is viable.

But, what is an instinct? What is meant by the term "innate?" The answers to these questions may seem obvious, but they are not. For example, Sluckin (1965) in his interesting and valuable review of the imprinting phenomenon tells us that the terms "instinctive" and "innate" are interchangeable and that there exist innate patterns of response,

This paper is respectfully dedicated to Frank A. Beach, whose teaching has had a profound influence upon the development of these ideas, on the occasion of his sixtieth birthday innate drives, innate preferences, and innate recognitions.* Thus "instinct" is quite complex and applies not only to gross behavior, but to such subtle things as preferences. "Instinct" is not easily defined.

To this writer, the instinct notion contains two similar, but distinct, kernel hypotheses. The first is that an instinct is an unlearned behavior or behavior characteristic. The second is that instincts are genetically determined. Despite the antiquity of these hypotheses, both are in current use as distinguishing characteristics of the instincts. The first hypothesis is embodied in a statement by Rock, Tauber, and Heller (1965) concerning the perception of movement by newborn guppies and praying mantises:

> The fact that apparent movement is seen only at certain speeds and spatial separations, that it can be seen by a variety of species, as well as by decorticated animals, has suggested to many that the effect is innate. Nevertheless, it is possible that such perception of movement is learned on the basis of experience with real movement.

The second hypothesis was included by Michael (1961) in a discussion of the sexual behavior of female cats: (this behavior) ". . . is genetically coded into the activity of the central nervous system."

Several years before Rock *et al.* and Michael employed these hypotheses as quasiexplanatory concepts in the analysis of behavior, both of the kernel hypotheses had been analyzed and found inadequate. Beach (1955), for example, took issue with the use of a dichotomy, any dichotomy (e.g., learned–unlearned) in the classification of behavior. He stated the case as follows:

> This (dichotomy) forces psychologists to deal with a two class system, and such systems are particularly unmanageable when one class is defined solely in negative terms, that is in terms of the absence of certain characteristics that define the other class. It is logically indefensible to categorize any behavior as unlearned unless the characteristics of learned behavior have been thoroughly explored and are well known.

---

* According to Sluckin (1965): "Such young birds—domestic chicks, ducklings and goslings, to name a few—tend to follow their parents almost as soon as they are out of the egg. This initial tendency in the young to cling to, or to follow, parent-figures may be described as instinctive or innate, by which is meant that the young are not trained and do not have to learn to behave in this manner" (p. 1) . . . "An innately determined pattern of responses normally unites the neonate with its mother, or mother substitute" (p. 16) . . . "Nevertheless the approach and following tendency, or drive is innate and primary" (p. 23) . . . "Since this was so in the case of chicks that had been in the dark prior to the test, there is little doubt that these preferences are innate" (p. 33) . . . "Such instinctive recognition might occur in some species but not in others" (p. 49).

The second kernel hypothesis was analyzed by Lehrman (1953):

> The use of "explanatory" categories such as "innate" and "genetically fixed" obscures the necessity of investigating developmental *process* in order to gain insight into the actual mechanisms of behavior and their interrelations. (Further) It is clear, however, that to say a behavior pattern is "inherited" throws no light on its *development* except for the purely negative implication that *certain types* of learning are not involved.

In spite of these cogent analyses of instinct by Beach and by Lehrman, the instinct concept remains unmodified in contemporary thought about the nature of behaviors which are not obviously learned as such. There is no simple explanation for this fact. Data arguments in disproof of instinct theory have been advanced (Lehrman, 1953), but these arguments have certainly had little effect upon contemporary thought about instincts. Indeed, data arguments appear doomed to fail. It has often been said that a theory is never overthrown by data, but is only replaced by a better theory. If this is so, the stability of traditional instinct concepts would indicate that no superior instinct theory has yet been generated. For these reasons, no attempt will be made in this paper to disprove traditional instinct theory. Rather this paper will present an analysis of instinct theory and will discuss some "noninstinct" hypotheses about the determination and control of behavior.

## II. TRADITIONAL INSTINCT APPROACH

According to traditional instinct theory, behaviors exist which are unlearned and genetically determined. This concept may be characterized by the following equation:

$$R_{\text{instinct}} = f \text{ (genotype)} \qquad (1)$$

This equation states that the instinctive response is solely a function of the genotype of the organism. Evidence in support of this hypothesis is generally drawn from what Lorenz (1965) calls the deprivation experiment: the organism is reared to maturity under conditions which prevent it from having contact with one or more naturally occurring stimuli. For example, a female rat is separated from its mother shortly after birth and is reared without contact with other rats. When mature, the sexual and maternal behaviors of this animal are studied. The existence of "innate information" is assumed if the deprived organism displays the appropriate behavior at the appropriate time. As stated by Lorenz (1965, p. 107),

If the information which is clearly contained in the behavioral adaptation to an environmental given is made inaccessible to the individual's experience and if, under these circumstances, the adaptedness in question remains unimpaired, we can assert that the information is contained in the genome.

Following Lehrman (1953), one can raise several questions about the validity of the deprivation experiment as a technique for proving that behaviorally relevant information is contained in the genome. The most serious argument against the idea that the genome contains behaviorally relevant information is that such a formulation is not consistent with modern genetic theory. No phenotype, morphological or behavioral, is the simple, direct resultant of gene action as this concept implies. Genes cause the development and organization of structure, which in turn, may have ultimate effects upon behavior potential. For example, it now seems clear that the differentiation of the potential of male and female rats to exhibit their characteristic mating patterns is due to the action of gonadal hormones secreted at a critical period of maturation. Rats of both sexes stimulated by gonadal hormones shortly after birth will exhibit male, but not female, mating responses in adulthood (Grady, Phoenix & Young, 1965; Harris & Levine, 1965; Whalen & Nadler, 1965; Whalen & Edwards, 1967). Male and female rats not stimulated by gonadal hormones during the critical period develop the potential to display both male and female responses in adulthood (Grady et al., 1965; Whalen & Edwards, 1966, 1967; Feder & Whalen, 1965). These studies imply that the genes do not directly encode information about whether or not a rat will be able to display male and/or female behavior in adulthood. Rather, this behavior potential is determined by the presence or absence of gonadal hormone stimulation in infancy. The genes, of course, do have an *indirect* influence on the sexual differentiation process.

A similar argument could be made with respect to other so-called instincts. In no case do we know the exact role played by the genes in the ultimate expression of behavior. What is clear, however, is the fact that the proximal determinants of behavior are some "distance" from gene action. That is to say, the behavior of an organism is determined by its neural organization, and neural organization is several metabolic and physiologic steps from primary gene action.

It is clear also that genes do not work alone to determine behavior. This point was made particularly well in a recent paper by De Fries, Hagmann, and Weir (1966) on the control, by the genome, of open-field behavior in mice. De Fries et al. interbred two inbred strains of mice (BALB/cJ and C57BL/6J) which differ greatly in activity and defecation scores when placed in a novel open field. The F5 generation which was obtained by random matings contained both albino and pigmented mice. The albinos exhibited significantly less activity and significantly more defecation than the pigmented animals when the mice were tested under the "usual" conditions. The usual condition in such studies includes testing under relatively bright light. When these same animals were tested under dim red light, activity and defecation scores were almost the same in albino and pigmented animals. The expression of the genome was crucially dependent upon the environment! Behavior thus emerges from genes *acting in environments*. Primary gene actions on enzyme and metabolic activity are themselves not independent of the environment. In fact, genes without environments would not yield organisms, much less behaving organisms. *We are thus led to reject the concept of instinct expressed in Eq. 1.*

## III. THE ONTOGENETIC APPROACH

Since, as Lehrman asserted (1953), behavior must be considered the result of gene and environment action, it is appropriate to conceptualize the determinants of behavior as follows:

$$R = f \text{ (genes + environment)} \tag{2}$$

This formulation says that behavior is the result of genetic and environmental influences, regardless of whether the behavior in question is what is traditionally called "instinctive" or "learned." Lehrman clarified the application of this concept (1953) in a discussion of rat nestbuilding:

> . . . rat nest building probably does not mature autonomously—and it is *not* learned. It is not "nest-building" which is learned. Nest-building develops in certain situations through a developmental process in which at each stage there is an identifiable interaction between the environment and organic processes . . .

This hypothesis of the determination of behavior may be called the ontogenetic or epigenetic (Moltz, 1965) theory. According to this theory, which stresses the emergence of behavior from organism–environment interactions, the genetic and environmental determinants of behavior are inextricably confounded. As a result, the ontogenetic theory does not provide for the independent estimation of the genetic and environmental influences upon behavior. Research based on the ontogenetic theory focuses upon the behavior of individuals, and, of course, *in individuals,* environmental and genetic influences are confounded.

Although the ontogenetic approach has provided significant information about the bases of behavior as exemplified by the research of Beach (1942), Lehrman (1955), and Schneirla, Rosenblatt, and Tobach (1963), this theory does not allow for the independent estimation of the contribution of genes and environment to behavior. Ideally, a theory of instinct would provide for this analysis.

## IV. THE VARIANCE APPROACH

Since we must accept the conclusion that "instinctive" behaviors are not directly and entirely determined by gene action, it is important to find a way to estimate the relative "instinctiveness" of a behavior. The variance model provides such an approach to behavior analysis. According to this model, not only is behavior determined by genetic and environmental factors, but, in addition, these factors are separable. Unlike the ontogenetic approach, the focus is not upon individuals, but rather upon individual differences in the behavior of members of a population. According to the variance model, the behavior of an individual can be characterized by a single score or measurement, the value of which is determined by both the genotype and the environment of the individual. Moreover, the behavior of a population of individuals may be characterized by group averages and by measures of the differences between individuals. The measure most often used to describe individual differences in behavior is the variance $(\sigma^2)$. For a population, therefore, one can measure the variance of a behavioral phenotype $(\sigma_p^2)$. This statistic is determined by variability caused by genetic differences between individuals $(\sigma_g^2)$ and by (micro-) environmental differences between individuals $(\sigma_e^2)$. These relationships may be stated as follows:

$$\sigma_p^2 = \sigma_g^2 + \sigma_e^2 \tag{3}$$

where $\sigma_p^2$ is total phenotypic variance, $\sigma_g^2$ is genetic variance, and $\sigma_e^2$ is environmental variance.

This model states that the phenotypic variance, a measure of the magnitude of individual differences in behavior, is the result of individual differences in genetic characteristics plus individual differences in environments. It is important to note, however, that this equation rests on the assumptions that the separate variances due to genetic and environmental influences are independent and additive and that the different gene influences which contribute to $\sigma_g^2$ are themselves additive. Deviations from additivity may be produced by genetic interactions (Fuller & Thompson, 1960). While we must be constantly aware of the possibility of nonadditive interactions, such interactions may often be disregarded in initial studies of the polygenically-based behaviors which are the focus of instinct theory. In spite of these problems, this model, in combination with standard variance statistics, does allow for the independent estimation of gene and environment contributions to behavior, as will be shown later. Within the framework of the variance model, one can derive the heritability ($h^2$) of a phenotype. Heritability is a measure of the proportion of individual differences in phenotype which is due to individual differences in genotype. In variance notation:

$$h^2 = \sigma_g^2/\sigma_p^2$$

$$= \sigma_g^2/(\sigma_g^2 + \sigma_e^2) \tag{4}$$

It is important to reiterate here that the variance analysis is an analysis of populations and not of individuals; heritability is a population characteristic and not an individual characteristic, just as "instinct" must be a population characteristic and not an individual characteristic.

## V. INSTINCT AND HERITABILITY

Traditional instinct theory implies that the behavior of the parents may be inherited by the offspring. In fact, the transmission and evolution of behavior is the reason for instinct theory. The inheritance of behavior is a fundamental implication of the kernel hypothesis that instincts are genetically determined. The analysis of heritability ($h^2$) outlined above is no more than a technique for evaluating this implication. As noted above, heritability provides a measure of the degree of genetic transmission of a behavioral phenotype from parents to offspring.

The simplest form of instinct theory (Eq. 1) states that instinctive behavior is entirely a function of the organism's genotype. Were this true, in Eq. 4, $\sigma_e^2$ would be reduced to zero, $\sigma_p^2$ would equal $\sigma_g^2$, and $h^2$ would equal 1.00. Analysis has shown that this "ideal" can never be realized, since gene action cannot occur in the absence of the environment. Thus, in the real world of organisms, $h^2$ can only approach 1.00, and in most cases, $h^2$ will be appreciably less than 1.00, even for the "instincts." Behaviors traditionally considered instinctive would, of course, be expected to have relatively high heritability when compared to behaviors traditionally considered learned.

The heritability model of instinct based on the analysis of individual differences in behavior is valuable in several respects. First, it captures the true essence of all instinct concepts, namely that behavior may be inherited. Moreover, the heritability analysis provides a way of measuring the potential inheritance of a behavior. There is an important point here which may be missed. The heritability model relies on the analysis of individual differences to separate genetic from nongenetic determinants of behavior. The model does not state that it is differences rather than similarities in behavior which are heritable as Lorenz seemed to imply when he said "our assertion that this similarity is innate, that is, based on genetical information, has at the very least the same likelihood of being correct as the opposite one, that dissimilarities in identically reared organisms are innate" (1965, p. 42). In fact, the heritability analysis relies on selective breeding experiments which aim at making the individuals in the populations under study as similar as possible genetically.

Second, the model stresses the fact that a behavior is neither an instinct nor a noninstinct. Using the model, it is possible to determine the relative degree of genetic control over a behavioral phenotype in a population, thus eliminating the need to dichotomize behaviors into learned and unlearned categories. It might be suggested that some arbitrary heritability score, for example, $h^2 = 0.80$, be used to dichotomize instincts from noninstincts. This would be neither desirable nor possible in any meaningful way. Heritability is never a measure of a total behavior such as nest-building but of only one parameter of the total behavior pattern, such as frequency, intensity, or duration of nest-building. The full characterization of a behavior would require many different heritability estimates for the different components and parameters of the behavior.

Third, the model states that *all* behaviors are under joint genetic and environmental control. "Learned" behaviors are not considered to be different in *kind* from the instincts. In this way, the similarities of all behaviors are emphasized. The potential importance of this consideration was discussed by Verplanck (1955) and will be expanded upon later in this paper.

Finally, the model allows for the definition of "instinctiveness" without relying upon the deprivation experiment. The model does not require that a behavior appear at the appropriate time of life after the organism has been reared in isolation from particular stimuli for that behavior to be defined as an instinct (cf. Lorenz, 1965). Such demonstrations are interesting and do contribute to our understanding of the stimulus determinants of behavior, but they are not relevant to the heritability of behavior, since heritability is a population characteristic which cannot be established using the deprivation experiment.

## VI. DIFFICULTIES WITH THE MODEL

The greatest problem which the heritability model of instinct faces is the difficulty which investigators may have in thinking of instinct as a characteristic of a population rather than as a characteristic of an individual. It is important, nonetheless, to begin thinking of "instincts" as characteristics of a population. As Lorenz (1965) has so ably pointed out, the behavior of organisms is adapted to the environment, and this adaptation is the result of the genetically determined evolution of behavior. This adaptation, however, is not the adaptation of any given animal to its environment; it is the adaptation of the species to the environment of the species. The different individuals which comprise a species are usually quite variable genetically, and it is this variability which permits the evolution of behavior. Species evolve, individuals do not; behavior patterns within a species evolve, the behavior of individuals does not.

Lorenz (1965) feels that the heritability model suffers in other ways. He has said, "The formulation that it is not characters but differences between characters which may be described as innate is, in my opinion, an unsuccessful attempt to arrive at an operational definition" (p. 41). In way of reply to this form of criticism, it should be noted that the heritability model is no more or less "operational" than is the deprivation experiment model which Lorenz defends. Whether the model is "successful" is an empirical question not really subject to debate.

Finally, the heritability model requires that "genetic" (i.e., selective breeding) experiments be performed if the instinctiveness of a behavioral phenotype is to be evaluated, and such experiments are expensive in time and money. Most investigators would be unwilling to undertake breeding experiments to determine heritability and thus establish the degree of genetic control over a behavior.

## VII. MEASUREMENT OF HERITABILITY

Several techniques may be used for the estimation of heritability, each resting on a slightly different logic. Two of these techniques will be described here briefly. The reader is referred to Falconer (1960), to Fuller and Thompson (1960), and to Hirsch (1967) for more detailed descriptions.

## A. Variance Analysis

According to Eq. 4, heritability is defined as $h^2 = \sigma_g^2/\sigma_e^2 + \sigma_g^2$. The derivation of $h^2$ using this model requires separate estimates to be made of $\sigma_g^2$ and $\sigma_e^2$. These estimates, however, cannot be derived from a single heterozygous population such as is typically used in behavioral experiments. The phenotypic variance of such populations is always the result of genetic and environmental variances. To estimate separately the genetic and environmental variances it is necessary to use selective breeding procedures. By inbreeding one can obtain homozygous strains which are isogenic for some characteristic. The rate at which inbreeding will yield homozygous strains is a function of the degree of inbreeding. It has been estimated that a strain will approach homozygosity in 30 generations with brother–sister matings, and in about 45 generations with double first cousin matings (Hall, 1951).

In the inbred, isogenic strain, all individuals of each sex possess the same genotype. Measures of variance in such isogenic strains thus must be measurements of environmental variability, $\sigma_e^2$. That is to say, behavioral variability among individuals of the same genotype must represent environmental variability. It follows from this analysis that a comparison of the phenotypic variability of an inbred isogenic population with the phenotypic variability of a randomly-bred heterozygous population, will permit an estimation of $h^2$. The logic is as follows:

1. Phenotypic variance of a heterozygous population $\sigma_p^2 = \sigma_g^2 + \sigma_e^2$;
2. Phenotypic variance of a homozygous population $= \sigma_e^2$;
3. Genetic variance $= (1) - (2)$, or $\sigma_p^2 - \sigma_e^2 = \sigma_g^2$;
4. $h^2 = \sigma_g^2/\sigma_p^2 = (3)/(1)$.

In this description the $\sigma^2$s on which $h^2$ is based represent "true" variances of the phenotypes and genotypes in the total population. Since the total population is rarely available for study, it is necessary to obtain unbiased estimates of the variances using standard statistical techniques (e.g., Snedecor, 1956).

The experimental strategy for obtaining the appropriate variance estimates is as follows: Individuals in a parent population are randomly divided into three groups. Group 1 $S$s are selectively bred for high phenotypic scores (for example, by intermating the top 10% of the group);

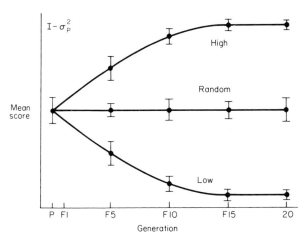

FIG. 1.    Idealized effect of selective breeding on phenotypic scores. Selection pressure increases or decreases mean population scores over successive generations. Over generations, subpopulation variances decrease.

Group 2 $S$s are selectively bred for low phenotypic scores; Group 3 $S$s are randomly bred each succeeding generation. The likely effects of such selective breeding are illustrated in Fig. 1.

From Fig. 1 it may be noted that: (1) Randomly bred animals maintain relatively constant scores on the phenotypic measure. If this is not the case, it is likely that testing techniques are changing with each generation or that there is genetic drift. (2) Selectively bred animals deviate from the randomly-bred population in the direction of the applied selection pressure. The rate and amount of deviation will be determined by the heritability of the phenotype and by the severity of the selection pressure. (3) After several generations the applied selection pressure no longer produces additional divergence from the randomly bred population. As the lines become isogenic, selection pressure will have a reduced effect. (4) The variance of the phenotypic scores becomes progressively smaller as the selectively bred lines become isogenic, i.e., as genetic variability is reduced.

At generation "$x$," when selection pressure no longer leads to a measurable change in phenotypic score, one can assume that the phenotypic variability is due solely to environmental variability. Variances derived from the scores of the high and low lines at this point will provide unbiased estimates of $\sigma_e^2$. A conservative estimate would be obtained by taking the mean variance of the high and low lines. The variance derived from the randomly-bred line may be used as an unbiased estimate of $\sigma_g^2 + \sigma_e^2$, since members of this population are heterozygous for the phenotype in question and are influenced by both genetic and environmental events. The variances obtained from the inbred and randomly bred strains at generation "$x$" are applied to Eq. 4 to obtain an estimate of heritability. This score would be used as a measure of the relative "innateness" of the behavioral phenotype.

This variance technique has been used to good advantage by Hirsch and Boudreau (1958) in their study of phototaxis in *Drosophila melanogaster*. In this study, the tendency of a heterozygous population of flies to approach a light was measured. High-scoring flies were interbred as were low-scoring flies. Their offspring were then tested for phototaxis, and again the extreme scoring animals were mated among themselves, highs with highs and lows with lows. This selection pressure was applied for 29 generations. It was found that the two subgroups progressively diverged from each other, and that the within-group variances became smaller over successive generations.

Hirsch and Boudreau selected the variances for each group at generations 28 and 29 for analysis. These variances were averaged and the mean taken as an estimate of $\sigma_e^2$. The variance of the initial parent population was used to estimate $\sigma_g^2 + \sigma_e^2$. The mean variance at generations 28 and 29 of the selected groups was found to be 2.77. The variance of the parental population was 6.38. Substituting in Eq. 4:

$$\sigma_g^2 + \sigma_e^2 = 6.38$$

$$\sigma_e^2 = 2.77$$

$$\sigma_g^2 = 6.38 - 2.77 = 3.61$$

$$h^2 = 3.61/6.38 = 0.57$$

It was concluded that 57% of the phenotypic variance was due to genetic variance. The "instinctiveness" of this behavior characteristic for this population was thus established.

## B. Regression Analysis

A second technique for the estimation of heritability involves the use of regression analysis. As with the variance technique, groups are selectively bred for high or low scores in a behavioral phenotype. Over successive generations, these groups progressively diverge from each other and from a randomly-bred line. The rate of divergence reflects the degree of heritability. A highly heritable trait will exhibit rapid divergence as noted above. The regression analysis uses the rate of divergence as an estimate of $h^2$.

The regression analysis differs from the variance analysis in that the regression analysis utilizes data from all generations, not only from those generations which are isogenic. For this reason, estimates of heritability using the regression analysis are not based simply on the divergence between high and low lines, but on the relationship between group divergence and the selection pressure which is applied. The effective selection pressure, called the "selection differential," is measured by the difference between mean phenotype score of the individuals selected as parents for the next generation, and the mean of the entire population from which these parents are selected. For example, a population of 50 organisms is tested and yields a mean phenotype score of 10. From this population 10 individuals with a mean score of 15 are selected as parents for the "high" line and 10 individuals with a mean score of 5 are selected as parents for the "low" line. The selection differential in each case is 5, as is the mean selection differential for the two lines. This process would be repeated at each generation, each generation providing a mean phenotype score of to-be-parents and a mean selection differential.

To obtain an estimate of heritability from these data one correlates the difference between the mean phenotype scores of the high and low lines at each generation with the cumulative selection differential. The slope of the line obtained is used to estimate $h^2$. Heritability in this case is defined as follows:

$$h^2 = b$$

where $b$ is the slope of the regression line.

An excellent use of the regression technique is contained in Manning's (1961) analysis of mating in *Drosophila melanogaster*. Manning was interested in the heritability of mating speed, the time from combination of males and females until mating occurred. The parental population consisted of two genetically heterozygous groups of 50 flies. These were mated, and the first and last 10 pairs to mate in each group were selected as the parents for the F1 generation. Fifty of the offspring from each of these groups were mated, and again the first and last 10 to mate in each group were selected as parents for the subsequent generation. This selection pressure was applied for 25 generations.

The sublines selected for fast mating showed a progressive reduction in mating latency, while the lines selected for slow mating showed a progressive increase in mating latency.

At the end of the experiment, Manning correlated the divergence of the high and low lines with the cumulative selection differential. The slope of the regression line was found to be 0.30, indicating that 30% of the phenotypic variance was due to genetic variance.

For the cases cited above, we must be quick to point out that the heritability scores obtained (a) are only estimates of heritability, (b) reflect only the additive genetic components, (c) truly apply only to the population studied, and (d) provide only very incomplete information on the relationships which exist between genome and behavior. In each case, heritability estimates were obtained using limited populations tested under a single set of experimental conditions. Nonetheless, even with these limitations the Hirsch and Boudreau (1958) and Manning (1961) experiments do provide models for behavior–genetic analysis. It is only through such analysis that we can learn about gene-behavior relations, and it is only through such genetic analysis that we can ultimately learn about the mechanisms of behavior evolution and about the "instinctiveness" of instincts.

## VIII. THE CONTROL OF BEHAVIOR

The heritability analysis described above deals with only one aspect of the kernel hypotheses of instinct theory, namely the hypothesis that instincts are genetically determined. The instinct notion also contains the hypothesis that instincts are unlearned behaviors. This latter hypothesis is extremely difficult to deal with, since it implies, as Beach (1955) pointed out, that we understand the nature of learning. This assumption more than another has obfuscated our understanding of the determinants of animal behavior. The confusion here is between "learned" and "trained." Nest-building behavior may be learned in the sense that the expression of this behavior may be crucially dependent upon prior experiences, yet such behavior is not trained or conditioned as such. One must keep these two facets of learning distinct. Possibly a good model to keep in mind is that provided by the "latent-learning" studies. In these studies, an animal is exposed to some environment, e.g., a maze, yet is given no goal as defined by the presence of an incentive such as food. In this situation the animal shows no reduction in "errors" or cul-de-sac entries. When an incentive is added to the situation the animal shows a more rapid reduction in cul-de-sac entries than he would have, had the incentive been present on the first exposure to the environment. Obviously the animal had learned something about its environment, even though it did not indicate such learning before the introduction of the incentive. What was learned during the "unrewarded" trials was not trained or conditioned as such, yet learning certainly occurred. We must in this case (and an argument can be made for all cases) distinguish between learning and training.

If one restricts "learning" to training, one might well conclude that instincts are unlearned, or more properly nonlearned, behaviors. In his recent discussion of instinct, Lorenz (1965) does not distinguish between "learned" and "trained" and as a result is led to the conclusion that some behaviors are nonlearned. For example, Lorenz defines learning in the following way: "The core of the concept (i.e., learning) will be represented by classical conditioning and other "higher" forms of learning and marginally it will merge imperceptively into more lowly forms of adaptive modification of behavior" (p. 11). (By "other higher forms of learning" Lorenz seems to mean trial-and-error or selective learning.) He then goes on to say "The assumption that learning 'enters into' every phylogenetically adapted behavior mechanism is neither a logical necessity nor in any way supported by observational and experimental fact" (p. 18). This latter conclusion is certainly justified, but only if by learning one means classical or instrumental conditioning. This conclusion is not justified if one means by learning "experience-dependent changes in behavior." The study of the development of bird song provides some interesting examples of experiential determinants of behavior which cannot be readily classified as examples of classical or instrumental conditioning. Konishi (1965) studied the ontogeny of song in male American robins which were deafened or raised in isolation from other birds. The isolated birds developed calls which resembled normal song but with some distortion. The deafened birds developed calls which showed even less similarity to normal song than that of the isolated birds. Apparently the opportunity to hear the song of adult birds is necessary for the development of normal song in this species. Further, the development of normal song is facilitated but cannot be brought to completion if the bird only has an opportunity to hear himself sing. In this species, and in several other species studied by Konishi (cf. Marler & Hamilton, 1966), auditory stimulation from other birds and auditory feedback are necessary for the development of the mature song which characterizes the species. One would not say, however, that bird song in the robin was "conditioned" in the usual sense, that is, in the sense that the total song pattern developed because components of the pattern were elicited or emitted and were "reinforced" by some external reinforcer such as food, water, or pain. The learning involved in the ontogeny of bird song does not fit the classical conditioning or selective learning paradigms of the experimental psychologist. This, of course, does not mean that learning is not involved.

The point that the classical conditioning and selective learning paradigms do not deal with all learning should be obvious. This point has been made before and forms one of the basic tenants of epigenetic theory. Moltz (1965), for example, discussed the problem in this way:

> This last example reveals the narrow conception of learning held by most instinct theorists. They reason that, if no source of reinforcement can be identified in connection with a particular response, then the response is perforce not learned. . . . They have not, however, thereby demonstrated the reality of behavior elements that are uninfluenced during ontogeny by extrinsic stimulus conditions, or by what may be more simply labeled experience.

## IX. EXPERIENCE AND THE DEVELOPMENT OF BEHAVIOR

The now classical example of experientially determined behavior which does not have the characteristics of Pavlovian conditioning or trial-and-error learning is "imprinting." Lorenz (1965) defined imprinting as the "learning of objects toward which to direct one's responses."

This concept is based on the observation that precocial birds will direct their social and sexual responses toward the object or organism to which they were exposed during some limited period following hatching. In the laboratory, the customary and appropriate experimental paradigm consists of allowing the newly hatched bird to follow some stimulus, a model of the parent, for example. At some time after this exposure, the chick is returned to the experimental situation which now contains two stimuli, the stimulus the chick had followed on the initial exposure and some other relatively similar stimulus, for example, a model of a parent of some other species. If the chick spends most of its time in the vicinity of the stimulus to which it had been exposed initially, the chick is said to be imprinted. The stimulus determinants, response determinants, and critical period characteristics of this phenomenon have been extensively studied. Since Sluckin (1965) has so lucidly reviewed this literature it will not be discussed here. What is clear from this research is that the exposure of the bird to striking stimuli during a limited period of development influences its later behavior. Responses, in the sense of particular motor movements do not seem to be learned. Unfortunately, exactly what is learned by the animal in this situation is not yet clear. Regardless of this problem, we must conclude that experience other than conditioning does determine the organism's adaptation to its environment. Similar processes may be the basis for bird song and for control of migratory behavior in some fish (Hasler & Larsen, 1955).

Experience also alters the behavior of adult animals in ways which do not fit the usual conditioning paradigm. For example, with fighting experience, male rats exhibit a progressive reduction in their latency to initiate aggression (Karli, 1956). With experience, the probability that a rat will kill a mouse increases (Heimstra & Newton, 1961; Whalen & Fehr, 1964). With experience the dominance hierachy of chickens is established (Ratner, 1961). With mating experience, the latency with which intromission will occur in the initially naive female cat is reduced (Whalen, 1963). With mating experience, the effects of castration on mating in male cats and dogs is ameliorated (Beach, 1950, Rosenblatt & Aronson, 1958). With suckling experience, the kitten comes to choose a particular nipple (Ewer, 1959). With feeding experience, the parental feeding behavior of the ring dove changes from tactile to visual control (Lehrman, 1953). This list could be extended almost indefinitely. All of these studies show that the sensory interaction of the organism with its environment has a profound effect upon the probability, frequency, intensity, and direction of its response patterns, patterns which themselves are not learned as such (i.e., trained) in the situations examined. For example, in the initial feeding experience, ring doves are not trained to display the regurgitation response, yet experience in performing this response determines the stimuli which in the future will elicit regurgitation (Lehrman, 1955).

The simple but critical point is that, in Moltz's (1965) words, "the environment is not benignly supportive, but actively implicated in determining the very structure and organization of each response system." We cannot accept today the classical instinct theorist's hypothesis that because a response system develops in animals which are separated from their conspecifics during maturation that that response system develops independent of the environment. As in the epigenetic view (Moltz, 1965; Lehrman, 1953) we must assume that behavior patterns develop, because at all stages of development organisms of particular genetic characteristics interact with environments of particular stimulus characteristics.

We must never assume that the so-called isolation experiment can provide information about what is experience independent, since we can never isolate the organism from experience. Even such a subtle thing as exposure to patterned light influences the development of those neuronal systems which seem to underly perception (Hubel, 1967) and the development of the visual control of behavior (Riesen, 1961). Even such a subtle thing as the brief exposure of the developing organism to his own testicular secretions controls sexual and social development (Young, Goy, & Phoenix, 1964; Whalen, 1968). When one broadens the concept of learning to include all of the experiences of the maturing organism the notion that behaviors develop in the absence of experience fades and disappears.


## X. CONCLUSION

Despite periodic harassment, the concept of instinct remains with us. Despite the fact that no behavior develops in the absence of environmental stimulation, there are still those who believe that there are unlearned behaviors which are simply genetically determined. Despite our recent gigantic strides toward an understanding of genetic mechanisms, there are still those who prefer to believe that genes contain information about the environment of the total organism. Despite the fact that classical instinct notions are outmoded, they remain with us. These ideas will doubtless remain with us until a younger generation adopts the following ideas: (1) all behavior is influenced by the genome of the organism; (2) all behavior is influenced by the experience of the organism; and (3) all "instincts" are characteristics of populations which are *entirely* dependent upon the genome *and entirely* dependent upon the experience of the population.


## REFERENCES

Beach, F. A. Comparison of copulatory behavior of male rats raised in isolation, cohabitation and segregation. *Journal of Genetic Psychology*, 1942, **60**, 121–136.

Beach, F. A. Sexual behavior in animals and man. *Harvey Lectures* 1950, **XLVIII**, 254–279.

Beach, F. A. The descent of instinct. *Psychological Review*, 1955, **62**, 401–410.

De Fries, J. C., Hagmann, J. P., & Weir, M. W. Open-field behavior in mice: evidence of a major gene effect mediated by the visual system. *Science,* 1966, **154**, 1577–1579.

Eibl-Eibesfeldt, I., & Kramer, S. Ethology, the comparative study of animal behavior. *Quarterly Review of Biology*, 1958, **33**, 181–211.

Ewer, R. F. Suckling behavior in kittens. *Behaviour*, 1959, **15**, 146–162.

Falconer, D. S. *Introduction to quantitative genetics.* Edinburgh: Oliver & Boyd, 1960.

Feder, H. H., & Whalen, R. E. Feminine behavior in neonatally castrated and estrogen-treated male rats. *Science,* 1965, **147**, 306–307.

Fuller, J. L., & Thompson, W. R. *Behavior Genetics*. New York: Wiley, 1960.

Grady, K. L., Phoenix, C. H., & Young, W. C. Role of the developing rat testis in differentiation of the neural tissues mediating mating behavior. *Journal of Comparative and Physiological Psychology,* 1965, **59**, 176–182.

Hall, C. S. The genetics of behavior. *In* S. S. Stevens (Ed.), *Handbook of experimental psychology.* New York: Wiley, 1951.

Harris, G. W., & Levine, S. Sexual differentiation of the brain and its experimental control. *Journal of Physiology (London),* 1965, **181,** 379–400.

Hasler, A. D., & Larsen, J. A. The homing salmon. *Scientific American,* 1955.

Heimstra, N. W., & Newton, G. Effects of prior food competition on the rat's killing response to the white mouse. *Behaviour,* 1961, **17,** 95–102.

Hirsch, J. (Ed.). *Behavior-genetic analysis.* New York: McGraw-Hill, 1967.

Hirsch, J., & Boudreau, J. C. Studies in experimental behavior genetics. I. The heritability of phototoxis in a population of *Drosophila melanogaster. Journal of Comparative and Physiological Psychology,* 1958, **51,** 647–651.

Hubel, D. H. Effects of distortion of sensory input on the visual system of kittens. *The Physiologist,* 1967, **10,** 17–45.

Karli, P. The Norway rat's killing response to the white mouse. *Behaviour,* 1956, **10,** 81–103.

Konishi, M. Effects of deafening on song development in American robins and black-headed grosbeaks. *Zeitschrift für Tierpshychologie,* 1965, **22,** 584–599.

Lehrman, D. S. A critique of Konrad Lorenz's theory of instinctive behavior. *Quarterly Review of Biology,* 1953, **28,** 337–363.

Lehrman, D. S. The physiological basis of parental feeding behavior in the ring dove (*Streptopelia risoria*). *Behaviour,* 1955, **7,** 241–275.

Lorenz, K. *Evolution and the modification of behavior.* Chicago: University of Chicago Press, 1965.

Manning, A. The effects of artificial selection for mating speed in *Drosophila melanogaster, Animal Behaviour,* 1961, **9,** 82–92.

Marler, P. R., & Hamilton, W. J. III. *Mechanisms of animal behavior.* New York: Wiley, 1966.

Michael, R. P. An investigation of the sensitivity of circumscribed neurological areas to hormone stimulation by means of the application of estrogens directly to the brain of the cat. *In* S. S. Kety and J. Elkes (Eds.), *Regional neurochemistry: international neurological symposium.* Oxford: Pergamon Press, 1961.

Moltz, H. Contemporary instinct theory and the fixed action pattern. *Psychological Review,* 1965, **72,** 27–47.

Ratner, S. C. Effect of learning to be submissive on status in the peck order of domestic fowl. *Animal Behaviour,* 1961, **9,** 34–37.

Riesen, A. H. Stimulation as requirement for growth and function in behavioral development. In D. W. Fiske & S. R. Maddi (Ed.), *Function of varied experience.* Homewood: Dorsey Press, 1961.

Rock, I., Tauber, E. S., & Heller, D. P. Perception of stereoscopic movement: evidence for its innate basis. *Science,* 1965, **147,** 1050–1052.

Rosenblatt, J. S., & Aronson, L. R. The decline of sexual behavior in male cats after castration with special reference to the role of prior sexual experience. *Behaviour,* 1958, **12,** 285–338.

Schneirla, T. C., Rosenblatt, J. S., & Tobach, E. Maternal behavior in the cat. In H. L. Rheingold (Ed.), *Maternal behavior in mammals.* New York: Wiley, 1963.

Sluckin, W. *Imprinting and early learning.* Chicago: Aldine, 1965.

Snedecor, G. W. *Statistical methods.* Ames: Iowa State College Press, 1956.

Tinbergen, N. *The study of instinct.* London & New York: Oxford University Press, 1951.

Verplanck, W. S. Since learned behavior is innate, and vice versa, what now? *Psychological Review*, 1955, **62**, 139–144.

Whalen, R. E. The initiation of mating in naive female cats. *Animal Behaviour*, 1963, **11**, 461–463.

Whalen, R. E. Differentiation of the neural mechanisms which control gonadotropin secretion and sexual behavior. In M. Diamond (Ed.), *Perspectives in reproduction and sexual behavior*. Bloomington: Indiana University Press, 1968. Pp. 303–340.

Whalen, R. E., & Edwards, D. A. Sexual reversability in neonatally castrated male rats. *Journal of Comparative & Physiological Psychology*, 1966, **62**, 307–310.

Whalen, R. E., & Edwards, D. A. Hormonal determinants of the development of masculine and feminine behavior in male and female rats. *Anatomical Record*, 1967, **157**, 173–180.

Whalen, R. E., & Fehr, H. The development of the mouse-killing response in rats. *Psychonomic Science*, 1964, **1**, 77–78.

Whalen, R. E., & Nadler, R. D. Modification of spontaneous and hormone-induced sexual behavior by estrogen administered to neonatal female rats. *Journal of Comparative and Physiological Psychology*, 1965, **60**, 150–152.

Young, W. C., Goy, R. W., & Phoenix, C. H. Hormones and sexual behavior. *Science*, 1964, **143**, 212–218.

# CHAPTER 3

# Sensory Processes and Behavior

W. R. A. MUNTZ

Laboratory of Experimental Psychology
University of Sussex
Brighton, England

## I. INTRODUCTION

Much of behavior is stimulus controlled: that is, the animal's response depends on a specific stimulus reaching the receptors and, through them, affecting the central nervous system (CNS). In order to understand such behavior, it is clearly necessary to know the characteristics of the animal's sensory mechanisms, since these will determine which stimuli are confused, perceived only with difficulty, or fail to have any effect on the CNS at all.

There is a very large literature on the physiology of the senses in various animals. Comparatively few attempts, however, have been made to use these physiological findings to explain behavior. The first part of the present chapter considers the problems involved in correlating sensory physiology and behavior, and the second part describes some of the findings that have been made in this field.

## II. THE BEHAVIORAL RELEVANCE
## OF PHYSIOLOGICAL FINDINGS

A. Factors Influencing the Behavioral Relevance
of Physiological Findings

A lot of information is available on the physiology of the sense organs. Often, however, this is of little help in predicting how an animal will respond in a given stimulus situation. There are several reasons for this. In the first place, physiological studies are usually done on animals which are anesthetised, or under curare, or immobilized in some other way. Such procedures are necessary for technical reasons to allow the experiments to be carried out, but their effects on the sensory mechanisms being studied are usually unknown. Where evidence is available, it is clear that physiological techniques may have a marked effect on the characteristics of sensory processes. The use of nembutal anesthesia, for example, has been shown to affect the characteristics of the retinal ganglion cells of the rabbit, causing the size of their receptive fields to increase enormously (Thompson, 1953, quoted in Granit, 1962), and barbiturate anesthesia has been shown to cause a characteristic repetitive bursting pattern of firing in the retinal ganglion cells of the rat (Brown & Rojas, 1965). Similarly, anesthesia has been shown to alter the characteristics of neurones in the cat's auditory and visual cortex (Katsuki, 1961; Robertson, 1965) and to abolish inhibitory components in the response of neurones in the somatic cortex of monkeys (Mountcastle, 1957). Other physiological experiments are done on isolated parts of the animal, such as the isolated retina, or on animals with parts of the CNS removed, as in decerebrate preparations. These procedures may also affect the properties of the system being studied by, for example, isolating the sense organ from the effects of efferent fibers passing from the brain to the receptors. A good example of the effects of efferent activity is given by Wall (1967), who showed that marked changes occurred in the receptive field properties of cells in the spinal cord, depending upon whether efferent activity was allowed or not. In some cases, the cells even responded to different modalities in the presence or absence of efferent impulses originating in the brain stem, being dominated by proprioceptive stimuli in the former case, and by cutaneous stimuli in the latter case.

Efforts have been made to overcome these difficulties by recording or stimulating through chronically implanted electrodes in the CNS of intact, unanesthetized, animals. Wurtz (1969), for example, trained monkeys to fixate a small visual stimulus and then recorded from neurones in the visual cortex. He was able to show that the receptive fields of the neurones under these conditions were similar to those obtained when anesthesia was used. A more dramatic example is provided by the work of Brindley and Lewin (1968). In this case, an array of 80 radio-driven stimulators was implanted into a human patient who had been almost completely blind for four years. These stimulators were in contact with the surface of the occipital cortex, and when one of them was activated the patient saw a small spot of light. The apparent position of this spot depended on which stimulator was activated and usually agreed well with previous data on the central mapping of the visual fields in man. While techniques such as these obviously hold great promise for the future, however, their contribution so far has not been great, and almost all physiological work on sensory processes is still of necessity done under conditions where the relevance to normal life is uncertain.

The usefulness of physiological data has also often been reduced by the fact that, until recently, physiological experiments have usually been dominated by physical concepts. For example, analogies have been drawn between the eye and the camera, and between the retinal mosaic and the grain of a photographic film. The skin is visualized as covered with pressure receptors and small thermometers. Physiological study has consequently concentrated on the analysis of perception using stimuli which are adapted to such ideas. Afferent fibers from the skin are analyzed by stimulating with different temperatures and plotting the rate of firing of the fiber against the temperature. In this way, fibers tuned to different temperatures may be found and specified as warm receptors or cold receptors (for example, Zotterman, 1953). However, it is well known that, in fact, temperature is judged relative to the ambient temperature to which the receptors are adapted. Thus it can be shown that, if one hand is placed in hot water and one in cold water, and then both hands are placed in warm water, this will feel hot to the hand adapted to cold, and cold to the hand adapted to heat. Similarly, in vision, stimuli of a simple physical character, such as spots of light, or monochromatic light, are usually used. These stimuli are, however, almost never found in normal life, and most of the afferent fibers from the eye respond best to more natural stimuli, such as edges and movements (e g., Lettvin, Maturana, McCulloch, & Pitts, 1959).

The reason why the use of physically orientated stimuli has been disappointing is that the function of the sense organs is not the faithful reproduction of the physical world. Rather, it is the selection and accentuation of those aspects of the physical world that are important to the behavior and survival of the animal. The absolute intensity of light is unimportant in this respect, but changes in the intensity of light, which indicate that some event has occurred, are important. It is such things—edges, intensity changes, temperature gradients—which are biologically significant, and we may expect that the sensory mechanisms of animals will usually be specialized to respond to them. A realization of this has altered the whole emphasis of research in this area.

One striking exception should be noted, however, namely the application of Fourier analysis to sensory processes. This stems from the fact that any periodic waveform can be analyzed into, or synthesized from, a series of sinusoidal waveforms. If, therefore, it is known how a sensory system responds to sine waves of different amplitudes and frequencies, it should be possible to calculate how it will respond to any other waveform with which it is presented (provided that the system is linear). Since the response to a sine wave is relatively easy to study, this approach appears promising. The most obvious application is in the study of hearing (e.g., Licklider, 1951), but it has also been applied to various mechanoreceptors (Janson & Rack, 1966) as well as to vision (Sperling, 1964; Campbell & Robson, 1968).

Finally, comparisons between physiological and behavioral data have frequently been done across species. In behavioral experiments on sensory systems, for example, humans are often most used, because they are very good experimental subjects whose behavior can be controlled by verbal instructions. However, they are not good experimental subjects for physiology and anatomy, and only a limited number of experimental techniques, such as the electroretinogram or evoked potentials, can be applied. Most electrophysiological data has therefore been obtained with lower vertebrates and invertebrates. Physiological findings on the compound eye of *Limulus*, for example, have been used to explain the phenomenon of Mach bands in human vision (Ratliff, 1965). Although this particular comparison is very interesting, it is dangerous to generalize from man to other animals, since their sensory capacities are usually very different.

It will probably never be possible to obtain detailed electrophysiological data from man. It therefore seems vital to obtain accurate behavioral data from other animals. Obtaining such data is tedious, but recent developments in animal psychophysics have shown that it is possible to obtain data from lower animals comparable in accuracy to those obtained with man. One important development in this area has been the application of tracking techniques for determining thresholds. The basis of this technique, first used in comparative work by Blough (1957), is that the stimulus strength on any trial depends on the animal's per-

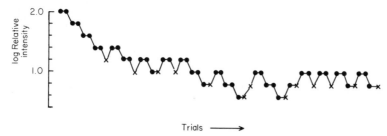

FIG. 1.    Tracking record during a visual threshold determination with a fish. The figure shows the first 56 trials of an experimental session in which there were 400 trials in all. Correct responses shown by filled circles, incorrect responses by crosses.

formance on the previous trials. If, for example, the animal performs correctly on a given trial, the stimulus strength will be reduced on the next trial. If, however, the animal performs incorrectly, the stimulus strength will be increased, making the discrimination easier. In this way, the stimulus strength is made to vary from trial to trial around the animal's threshold, and trials are not wasted by presenting stimuli well above or below threshold.

An example of such a tracking record is shown in Fig. 1. In this case the subject, a fish, was trained to respond to a circle of light in a two-choice situation. In this situation, the fish will respond at the 50% correct level by chance even if the stimulus is well below threshold. The tracking procedure reduced the intensity of the stimulus by a fixed amount (0.2 log units) after every two consecutive correct responses and raised it by the same amount following every incorrect response. This should result in the stimulus oscillating around the intensity level at which 70% correct responses are made. Figure 2 shows the percentage of correct responses that occurred at different intensity levels in this experiment, and the frequency with which the different intensities were in fact presented. It can be seen that the procedure successfully concentrated the intensity around the 70% level.

Tracking procedures of one sort or another have now been used with a wide variety of species for determining thresholds in several modalities. Visual thresholds have been determined in this way in fish (Muntz & Northmore, 1970), turtles (Muntz & Sokol, 1967; Muntz & Northmore, 1968), pigeons (Blough, 1957), starlings (Adler & Dalland, 1959), squirrels (Silver, 1966), monkeys (Symmes, 1962; Schrier & Blough, 1966), and man (Oldfield, 1955). Auditory thresholds have been obtained similarly in fish (Jacobs & Tavolga, 1967), cats (Elliott, Frazier, & Riarch, 1962), and monkeys (Behar, Cronholm, & Loeb, 1965), and taste thresh-

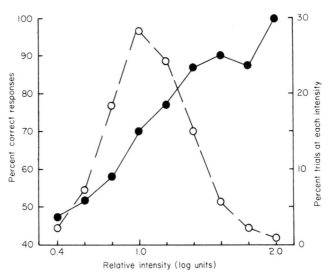

Fig. 2.    Psychometric function resulting from the record shown in Fig. 1. The filled circles and the left-hand axis show the percentage of correct responses at the different stimulus intensities used. The plain circles and right-hand axis show the percentage of trials given at each intensity level.

olds have been obtained in the rat (Koh & Teitelbaum, 1961). While accurate thresholds can, of course, also be obtained in other ways, the economy of effort resulting from the use of tracking procedures makes them very important.

## B. Comparisons of Physiological and Behavioral Data

Attempts to explain behavior using physiological data involve comparisons between physical and behavioral measurements, and some hypothesis about the relationship between the two must be made. The most convincing of such hypotheses is that when two stimuli cause physically indistinguishable signals to be sent from the sense organs to the brain, the sensations produced by the stimuli, as reported by the subjects through words or other actions, will also be indistinguishable (Brindley, 1960). This hypothesis, which few people would deny, means that the animal must be used as a null-detector. In threshold experiments, for example, the intensity of the stimulus is reduced until the animal responds identically whether the stimulus is present or not. No further assumptions (such as that when the animal responds more strongly, the stimulus is in some sense more effective in stimulating the sense organs) are involved.

Experiments in this class cover the great majority of psychophysical experiments, as well as a large number of physiological experiments, especially those where thresholds are measured, and it is no coincidence that it is in the field of thresholds that the strongest correlations between physiology and behavior are found. One of the earliest such correlations to be made was between the spectral absorptive characteristics of the pigment (visual purple or rhodopsin) that can be extracted from the human retina and human scotopic spectral sensitivity (Konig, 1894; Dartnall, 1962). The results of this comparison are shown in Fig. 3. It can be seen that the threshold at any wavelength is exactly proportional to the number of light quanta that the pigment absorbs at that wavelength. This means that lights of different wavelengths that have the same effect on the pigment also have the same effect on behavior.

The above example involves stimuli that have identical effects on receptors. A rather more complex example may be taken from the work of Erickson (1963), who recorded the electrical activity of gustatory neurones in the chorda tympani of the rat. Erickson's records were taken from third-order neurones, but the same principle applies: stimuli which

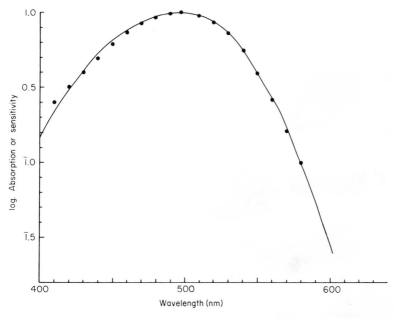

Fig. 3.    Comparison between the spectral absorbance of visual purple (continuous line) and human scotopic sensitivity (filled circles). Data for visual purple from Dartnall (1962), and for human scotopic sensitivity from Wyszecki and Stiles (1967).

have an identical effect on all the neurones are sending identical messages to the brain, and so should be indistinguishable. The stimulus specificity of these neurones is not very marked. Nevertheless, they respond more strongly to some chemicals than to others. The results were presented in the form of *cross-unit curves,* in which a number of neurones are arranged along the abscissa and the rate of firing of each nerve to different chemical stimuli is given by the ordinate. When this is done, it is found that the cross-unit curves of some chemicals are very similar, showing that a fiber that responds strongly to one chemical will also respond strongly to the other, and that a fiber that responds weakly to one chemical will respond weakly to the other as well. The cross-unit curves of potassium and ammonium chloride, for example, are very similar, and differ markedly from the cross-unit curve of sodium chloride. This leads to the prediction that rats will find it difficult to discriminate between the first two salts, but will discriminate them readily from sodium chloride. Training experiments confirmed that this was so.

Using the animal as a null detector, however, is unfortunately in many ways one of the less interesting types of experiment, because in most cases it is the differential responsiveness to different suprathreshold stimuli that is important in predicting behavior: animals in their natural life are seldom confronted with threshold stimuli. In such cases, other assumptions must be made, such as that an increase in the number of nerve impulses in the afferent pathways leads to an increase in the probability of the animal responding correctly. If by making such assumptions a sufficient number of correlations can be found between the physical, physiological, and behavioral events, it is plausible to assume that they are causally connected. Two examples where such correlations have been made may be taken from work on hearing and vision in the frog. Thus Frishkopf and Goldstein (1963) showed that the afferent fibers from the ear of the bullfrog consisted of two types: simple units with peak sensitivity at around 1500 Hz, and complex units with peak sensitivities at around 400 Hz. Energy at intermediate levels was found to inhibit the complex units. A large proportion of the energy of the bullfrog's call falls within these two areas, with little in the intermediate frequencies, so that the bullfrog's call is a very good stimulator of both the simple and the complex units. Capranica (1965) carried out behavioral studies which showed that the frog's behavior agreed well with these details. The frogs responded to the calls of another frog by calling themselves, and he found that they also responded well to a combination of two tones, one in the range of the complex units, and one in the range of the simple units. Here again, intermediate tones abolished the response.

A similar relationship between afferent activity and behavior can be shown in the escape behavior of frogs. Under suitable conditions, frogs escape towards the light, and some wavelengths are more effective than others in controlling this behavior. The experimental situation used consists of a small box, with two windows from which the animals can escape. These windows are illuminated with different wavelengths of light, and the number of times the frogs escape through differently illuminated windows counted (Muntz, 1962; Chapman, 1966). The resulting spectral response curve is very similar to the response curve of the afferent fibers passing from the retina to the diencephalon (Fig. 4). The behavior of the intact animal and the retinal projection to the diencephalon is also similar in that inhibition can be demonstrated in each case, for it can be shown that adding green light to blue light reduces its effectiveness.

The taste mechanisms of the fly provide another good example of a direct correlation between afferent activity from the sense organs and behavior (Hodgson, 1961). In these experiments a fluid-filled microelectrode was placed over one of the hairs on the fly's proboscis, and this was used both to stimulate the hair (by passing various chemical substances into it) and to record the activity of the nerve fibers in the hair. Each hair has only two sensory nerve fibers, which may be distinguished by the size of their nerve spikes, since one of them (the L

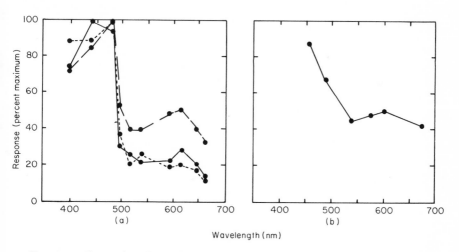

FIG. 4.    Comparison between the spectral properties of the retinal projection to the diencephalon and phototactic behavior in the frog. (a) Number of impulses (as a percentage of the maximum) given by three individual optic nerve fibers in response to different monochromatic stimuli. (b) Percent choices of differently illuminated windows in the phototactic situation.

fiber) always gives a larger spike than the other (the S fiber). It was found that the L fiber responded to most chemicals, but not to sugars, while the S fiber responded preferentially to sugars. In one experiment four polyhydric alcohols were used, which all have the same atoms in the molecule, differing only in the arrangement of these atoms. Three of these (sorbitol, dulcitol, and mannitol) gave L responses but no S responses, while the fourth (inositol) stimulated the S fibers. These responses for the S fibers agree very well with the behavior of the whole fly, which had been previously studied by Dethier (1956), those chemicals which cause responses in the S fibers also causing proboscis extension and feeding in the fly.

With higher animals, this degree of correlation between physiology and behavior has not often been observed. This may mean that behavior is less dependent on peripheral coding mechanisms, but it is also possible that the correlations have simply not been attempted. Good correlations have been found between physiological work in one species and behavior in another (generally man). For example, the firing pattern of the afferent fibers from the ear of the cat may be compared to results obtained in human psychophysical experiments (Katsuki, 1961). Similarly, attempts have been made to correlate the output of cat retinal ganglion cells with human data on the psychometric function (Fitzhugh, 1957). Such correlations are often all that can be attempted, since behavioral and physiological data are seldom available for the same species. The inherent dangers, however, are obvious.

The best examples of behavioral–physiological correlations that have been reported with higher animals are probably those that have been obtained with monkeys. These animals have several advantages: in particular, it is likely that their sensory processes are very similar to man's, so that the great body of human psychophysical data can be compared directly to monkey physiology with some chance of success. They are also amenable to behavioral experiments, so that any point in question can be checked. As an example, detailed psychophysical work on monkeys has been done in the field of color vision (DeValois, 1965a, b). The results indicate that the color vision of the macaque is almost identical to that of man, while the color vision of the squirrel monkey resembles that of the protanomalous human (Jacobs, 1963; DeValois, 1965a, b). DeValois and his collaborators have carried out a series of experiments, in which recordings were made from the lateral geniculate nucleus of the monkey. They found two classes of cell: spectrally opponent cells, and spectrally nonopponent cells. The former class give opposed responses to different parts of the spectrum, showing, for example, an increased rate of firing for short wavelengths and a decreased rate of firing for long wavelengths. The nonopponent cells on the other hand, show a firing pattern that is unaffected by wavelength. DeValois attempts to deduce how the three parameters of color vision (hue, saturation, and brightness) are coded by comparing the outputs of these cells with human psychophysical data. For example, the spectral sensitivity of the nonopponent cells is very similar to the human photopic luminosity function, suggesting that these cells carry brightness information. The spectral sensitivity of the opponent cells, on the other hand, bears no resemblance to the human photopic function. DeValois suggests that these carry information on hue, not brightness. If this were so, we might expect that the difference between the sensitivity of the opponent and nonopponent cells at any point of the spectrum would reflect how saturated that part of the spectrum appeared, for it would show the ratio of hue information to brightness information at that wavelength. When the difference between the two classes of cell is compared to the human saturation discrimination function, the agreement is good. DeValois makes several other comparisons as well, which are given in DeValois (1965a, b).

Correlations such as those described in the previous five paragraphs are often convincing. The underlying assumptions must, however, be kept in mind. It is not by any means certain that increased activity in the afferent nerves is always correlated with an increase in subjective magnitude. It is even less certain that, as is sometimes assumed (e.g., Stevens, 1961), the change in neural activity with stimulus intensity has the same mathematical form as a sensory scale of subjective magnitude judgements, although this may be true in some cases. As Rosner and Goff (1967) point out, early physiological experiments were greatly influenced by Fechner's law. As a result many experiments were carried out in which the impulse rates of peripheral receptors were measured and found to follow a logarithmic relation (e.g., Granit, 1955). More recently Fechner's law has given way to the power law (Stevens, 1961). Rosner and Goff (1967) have shown that much of the early data fits a power function at least as well as a logarithmic function, and recent physiological studies nowadays usually use power functions rather than logarithmic functions to explain their results (e.g., Easter, 1968).

## III. SENSORY SYSTEMS AND BEHAVIOR

### A. The Interdependence of Sensory Functions and Behavior

It is often assumed that animals are potentially able to respond to any of the stimuli that are capable of affecting their sense organs. However, it is now well known that animals only respond to selected stimuli out of the total potential stimulation reaching them. The problem of exactly which stimuli are effective in controlling the various types of behavior has been studied in detail by the ethologists, and many of the findings in this field have been summarized by Tinbergen (1951). In a classic example, von Uexküll (1934) describes the behavior of the tick as being limited to three components, each component being controlled by a different stimulus. The tick remains attached to a branch until it is stimulated by one of the chemicals secreted by a mammal's skin, namely butyric acid. This stimulus, and this stimulus alone, causes the animal to release its hold on the branch and drop, with luck, onto the animal passing beneath. As von Uexküll puts it, "Like a gourmet who picks the raisins out of a cake, the tick has selected butyric acid alone from among the things of her environment." Other components of the tick's behavior require different releasing stimuli: mechanical stimuli involved in landing on the hairs of the animal's back release the response of running about, and the stimulus of heat releases the response of boring in towards the skin. An important point is that different aspects of the potential stimulation control different segments of the behavior. The tick drops off the branch in response to butyric acid, and bores into the skin in response to heat. It does not drop off the branch in response to heat, nor does it bore into the skin in response to butyric acid, though clearly the sense organs are affected by both. The behavior of the cabbage white butterfly (*Pieris brassicae*) provides another example of the specificity of releasing stimuli (Ilse, 1937). This animal shows quite different color preferences when feeding and when laying eggs. In the former case, blues and reds are preferred; in the latter case, greens. These preferences appear to be related to the fact that the butterflies feed on flowers but lay their eggs on leaves. The point is that neither spectral function is in any sense more "real" than the other: each describes the animal's behavior in different circumstances, and they both reflect the animal's sensory capabilities.

From the above examples, it is clear that the sensory cues to which the animals respond depend on the behavior that is being studied. The interdependence of the behavior studied and the way in which the stimuli are analyzed obviously has important consequences for the study of sensory systems, since it means that an animal's sensory capacities can only be discussed in the context of the experimental situation.

Much ethological work is concerned with rather complex stimuli, controlling specific behavior patterns. Often our interest in sensory problems may concern the capabilities of the sense organs to resolve much simpler stimuli. We may, for example, wish to know the minimum quantity

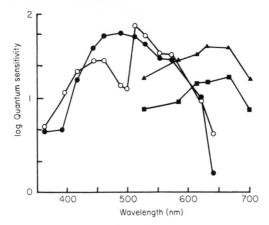

FIG. 5.    Spectral sensitivity curves for *Xenopus laevis* (the clawed toad). Filled and plain circles, melanophore response to black and white backgrounds, respectively (data from Silver, 1963). Triangles and squares, optomotor response at two levels of background intensity (data from Cronly-Dillon & Muntz, 1965).

of light at different wavelengths that the animal can respond to, with the intention of correlating the results with the properties of the visual pigments. Figure 5 shows several such curves that have been obtained with *Xenopus*, the clawed toad. Two of these were obtained by measuring the smallest quantity of light necessary for the animals to change the color of their skin to match a black and a white background, respectively (Silver, 1963). The third and fourth curves show the threshold for the optomotor response (Cronly-Dillon & Muntz, 1965). The spectral sensitivity of *Xenopus* has also been measured using the animal's phototactic behavior (Denton & Pirenne, 1954): the results in this case are essentially the same as the results obtained using the response to a black background. Using different behavioral responses, therefore, leads to three quite distinct relationships between wavelength and sensitivity. Furthermore, none of the spectral sensitivity curves obtained bears any obvious relationship to the visual pigments which can be extracted from the eyes of these animals. The situation is very complex, and it is clearly unreasonable to talk about *the* spectral sensitivity of *Xenopus;* we can only talk about the spectral sensitivity of *Xenopus* in a given experimental situation.

So far, all the examples quoted have involved unlearned behavior patterns in lower animals. The same considerations hold true, however, for higher animals and learned behavior patterns: here also the animal's apparent sensory capacities depend on the behavioral situation that is used. One of the best known examples concerns the form discriminating capabilities of the rat. For a long time it was believed that these animals were essentially incapable of discriminating forms, although they were able to discriminate brightness differences readily (Munn, 1930). However, when a new apparatus was used, the Lashley jumping stand, it was found that they could discriminate forms without difficulty (Lashley, 1938). The jumping stand, unlike the previous apparatuses that had been used, apparently forced the animals to pay attention to visual information. The history of rat vision shows how our information on sensory processes depends on the apparatus used: it also shows the danger of making a negative statement. A more recent example is due to Dobrzecka, Szwejkowska, & Konorski (1966). These experiments showed that dogs depend on different kinds of information in two training situations. The first training situation involved an instrumental task: the animals had to raise the right or left leg depending upon the stimulus presented. In the second situation, only one response was involved, which the animals had to perform in the presence of one of the stimuli and withhold in the presence of the other. The stimuli to be discriminated were also of two types, differing either qualitatively (a buzzer versus a metronome) or in their position (a buzzer in front or behind the animal). The results showed that in the instrumental situation, where two responses were involved, the animals were only able to learn using the directional cues, performance being very poor when the qualitatively different stimuli were used. The reverse was true in the other training situation, where the animals could learn on the basis of the qualitative cues, but were usually unable to learn when the directional cues were used. Similar results were also obtained with monkeys.

The sensory capabilities of an animal, measured behaviorally, thus depend on the experimental situation, and we cannot assign any sensory capacity to an animal except when it is considered in relation to some specified situation. The same is true when the sensory capacities are measured physiologically, for here also the results obtained depend on the techniques used to obtain them. For example, in freshwater turtles, the spectral sensitivity curve obtained using the electroretinogram is quite different from that obtained using evoked potentials recorded from the optic tectum (Granda & Stirling, 1965). A similar situation has been shown for humans, cats, rabbits, and hens (Armington, 1966; Ingvar, 1959; Vatter, Koller, & Monnier, 1964; Armington & Crampton, 1958); in all cases spectral sensitivity curves obtained through measuring evoked potentials at the occipital cortex or optic tectum differ from those obtained using the electroretinogram.

## B. Peripheral and Central Coding

The coding of sensory information starts peripherally, at the level of the receptor cells themselves, for these respond more strongly to certain forms of energy than others and so select, out of the total environment, those events that can affect the central nervous system. Thus, due to the optics of the eye, a given receptor cell in the retina responds only to light from a certain part of the visual field. Similarly, retinal receptors respond preferentially to certain wavelengths of light: we have seen, for example that the human rod responds most strongly to light of 500 nm, and is insensitive to deep reds. The same is true of other receptors: the hair cells of the inner ear respond to certain frequencies more strongly than to others, the taste buds of the tongue respond selectively to certain chemicals, and so on.

The stimulus specificity of the receptors constitutes the first step in discrimination, since any two stimuli that have the same effect on all the receptors must necessarily send identical messages to the brain and so will be indistinguishable. Stimulus specificity, however, can only result in very simple forms of coding. More complex forms of coding require interactions between the outputs of the different receptors. These may occur at the level of the sense organs, which in many cases contain a considerable amount of nervous tissue, giving ample opportunity for effects such as lateral interaction. As we have seen, in some cases, such as in vision and hearing in frogs, the output of the sense organs may be directly correlated with the animal's behavior, suggesting that almost all the relevant sensory coding has taken place at the peripheral level. In other animals, the degree of coding occurring at the level of the sense organs is less, but there can be little question that it occurs to some degree in all species.

The output of the sense organs is passed on to the brain by the afferent nerves. In general, for those sense organs that have large surface areas, the different parts of the sense organ project to different parts of the brain in an orderly way, so that one or more maps of the receptor surface may be plotted out on the surface of the brain. The details of such maps have been reviewed many times (e.g., Ruch, 1951). Since a map of the surface of the sense organ appears on the surface of the brain, this means that a map of the outside world will also appear there. This has led in the past to the idea that the function of the sense organ is to transmit a picture of the outside world as faithfully as possible to the brain, where it becomes available for analysis. If this were true, we should know nothing more about sensory coding than before, except that it is done centrally and not peripherally. Also, as Adrian (1947) put it,

> For those who think precisely, this conjures up a disquieting figure of a little hobgoblin sitting up aloft in the cerebral hemispheres with a series of maps to look at. Both physiologists and philosophers have drawn attention to the fact that there is no such person.

The examples given in the previous sections have shown, however, that the sense organs do not simply transmit a picture of the outside world to the brain. As a result of peripheral coding, activity in a given afferent fiber means that a certain *event* has occurred at the point in question, and the central nervous maps represent the distribution of these events in the outside world, not the distribution of physical energy.

In all probability, sensory coding cannot be localized to a single nervous structure for any animal, but occurs throughout the afferent pathways, the responses being progressively elaborated as we move centrally. This can be seen very clearly in the microelectrode results obtained by Hubel and Wiesel (1959, 1962, 1965) on the visual system of the cat. In this animal, recordings have now been obtained from the retinal ganglion cells (Barlow, Fitzhugh, & Kuffler, 1957) the lateral geniculate neurones, the striate (Area 18), and the peristriate (Area 19) cortex. The responses show a progressive elaboration as we move centrally. Some of the findings and possible mechanisms are summarized in Fig. 6. At the level of the retinal ganglion cells, the receptive fields are circular, with on centers and off surrounds or vice versa. The same is true at the level of the lateral geniculate nucleus, but at the level of the cortex quite different relationships are found. In Area 17 the neurones fall into one of two classes, simple and complex. The simple cells have elongated receptive fields and the general form shown in Fig. 6. This results in their response being greater to a contour or bar of light falling in a given direction, for only in certain directions will the amount of excitation caused by the stimulus exceed the amount of inhibition. The diagram shows a possible set of connections between the geniculate and the cortex which could underlie such a simple cortical neurone. It is assumed that a large number of lateral geniculate neurones (of which three are shown) have receptive fields with on centers arranged along a straight line on the retina. All of these project on to a single cortical cell, which they excite.

The complex units differ from the simple units in that they have vary large receptive fields, of the order of 40. They also have a preferred orientation, but the position of the stimulus is not important, and the

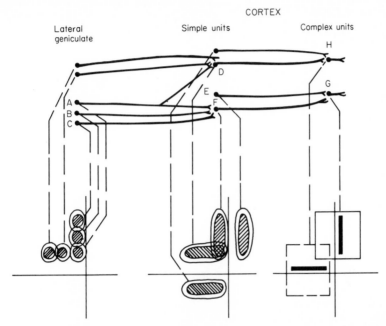

Fig. 6.    A possible scheme to account for the simple and complex units of the cat's visual cortex. In the top half of the figures, neurones of the lateral geniculate nucleus are shown projecting to the simple units of the cortex, which in turn project to the complex units. Each neurone is connected by a dashed line to a representation of its receptive field. The lateral geniculate neurones have circular receptive fields, with on centers (hatched) and off surrounds (plain), or vice versa. The simple units have elongated receptive fields, and the complex units respond to a suitably orientated edge anywhere in their receptive fields. The figure only shows a few of the many types of unit that are found in the cat's visual system.

cells respond to the stimulus irrespective of where this lies (provided it is within the 40° receptive field). It is easy to see that such complex units could arise by convergence from simple units, as illustrated in the figure.

Similar converging projections could account for the hypercomplex Class I and Class II units described by Hubel and Wiesel for Area 19. Hypercomplex Class I units respond to contours in a given direction provided that these are not too long and can be accounted for by assuming appropriate excitatory and inhibitory connections from simple cortical units. Hypercomplex Class II respond to the same stimuli as Class I, but, like the complex units, they have large visual fields and respond to the appropriate stimulus irrespective of its exact localization.

These results show how stimulus coding can be elaborated by successive projections between different parts of the CNS. The projections involve both divergence and convergence at all levels, as illustrated in Fig. 6. Thus geniculate cells A, B, and C converge onto the simple cortical unit F, and the simple units E and F converge onto the complex unit G. Divergence is also involved: the geniculate cell A, for example, projects to the simple units F and D. Such an arrangement requires a large number of transmission pathways but would be economical in that a given neurone can contribute to an activity of several different types of neurones at the next level of analysis. Thus a neurone such as A represents a certain fairly simple stage in sensory analysis. This element of the analysis can then be combined in many ways to yield more complex responses: combined with different neurones, for example, it can contribute to a large number of simple cortical neurones representing many directions.

Such a system of successive recombinations has been proposed for other sensory systems as well. In color vision it has been proposed that three receptor types, responding preferentially to different parts of the spectrum, contribute to the perception of both luminosity and hue, in the former case by combining additively, and in the latter by some differential response involving inhibition (e.g., Guth et al., 1969). It seems probable that systems of this type, involving different combinations of receptor outputs, are common in the nervous system. The CNS has many more transmission pathways than cells, which fits in with this view.

A striking fact about stimulus coding in the CNS is that different types of information are sent to physically different areas of the brain. This has been shown to happen, in different cases, in three distinct ways. In the first case, the output of the different coding mechanisms may be sent to completely different areas of the brain. For example, in both frogs and pigeons most of the visual information projects to the optic tectum, but information on color is sent to the thalamus (Muntz, 1962; Maturana, 1962). The second type of separation occurs when the sensory outputs representing different events are organized in layers. This is seen very clearly, for example, in the work of Lettvin et al. (1959) on the visual system of the frog. Here four classes of retinal ganglion cell have been described, projecting to the optic tectum, which respond to four quite distinct types of stimulation. When a microelectrode penetrates at right angles to the surface of the tectum, it picks up impulses from these four types of cell in turn, but the position of the effective stimulus in the visual field remains the same. This means that there are four superimposed maps of the visual world in the tectum, each map giving information on whether a certain event has occurred, and also of the locus of this event.

Separation into layers has been shown in other cases as well. It occurs, for example, in the optic tectum of the fish (Jacobsen & Gaze, 1964), although in this case the separation is not so marked. It has also been shown to occur in the lateral geniculate nucleus of mammals, where different layers receive information from only one eye, as well as receiving information from different ganglion cell types (DeValois, Smith, Kanoly & Kitai, 1958; Daniel, Kerr, Seneviratne & Whitteridge, 1961; Bishop, Kozak, Levick & Vakkur, 1962). As Walls (1953) put it, the geniculate may be likened to a pile of maps: ". . . laminae No. 1, No. 4, and No. 6 are related to each other as are three maps of the country, one of which is geodetic, a second climatological, and the third agricultural." Any neurone passing at right angles through such a pile of maps will be able to sample, for one locus in the visual field, whether any one of several events has occurred. Neurones that do pass at right angles to the maps in this way are known to occur both in the frog tectum (Ramon, 1955), and the mammalian lateral geniculate body (Bishop *et al.*, 1962). Separation into superimposed laminae is also not restricted to the visual system, for Wall (1967) has shown that the cells in the dorsal horn of the cat are separated into laminae with different receptive properties.

A third method whereby physical separation has been achieved has been demonstrated for both touch and vision in the mammalian cortex (Mountcastle, 1957; Hubel & Wiesel, 1962). Here neurones representing different perceptual events are organized into columns which lie at right angles to the brain surface. Within each column, all the neurones respond to the same type of stimulus, so that the cortical surface is a mosaic representation of the external world, and any small area only contains one type of information.

Recent work thus supports the idea that the outputs of different classes of sensory fiber are segregated in the CNS. It has been known for a long time that different sensory modalities, such as touch, olfaction, and vision, are dealt with initially by distinct areas of the brain. It now appears that the same general rule holds even within one sensory modality. Stimuli that are coded differently by the nervous system, even though they may be received through the same sense organ, may be considered to constitute different "submodalities," and to influence different parts of the brain.

Where an animal's behavior is under fairly direct control by a sense organ, such an organization may have advantages in that the "submodalities" can then project directly on to the appropriate motor systems. We have seen in Sect. II that an animal's apparent sensory capabilities depend on the behavioral situation that is used. In some cases this may be related to the separation of different types of sensory information in the CNS. For example, as already described, the retinal projection to the diencephalon of the frog has characteristics that agree well with the animal's escape behavior, whereas the projection to the tectum has other characteristics and is presumably involved in other types of behavior. This is supported by some recent experiments of Ewert (1968) on the toad. These have shown that lesions to the diencephalon disrupt escape behavior and facilitate feeding behavior, whereas lesions to the tectum have the opposite effect. Electrical stimulation of the diencephalon and tectum were also shown to cause escape and feeding behavior, respectively.

## C. Relative Advantages of Peripheral and Central Coding

It is clear that sensory coding takes place peripherally at the level of the sense organs, as well as centrally, in the brain. One clear advantage of peripheral coding is that irrelevant information is discarded at an early stage, and less nervous activity has to be wasted on it. Selecting the important aspects of the stimulus at the peripheral level economizes on the number of nerve fibers that must be devoted to transmitting sensory information to the brain and on the number of nerve cells within the brain which must be devoted to analyzing this information. Especially in lower animals, where the number of nerve cells may be relatively small, this economy may be extremely important. There are, however, also clear disadvantages in coding stimuli at a peripheral level. The number of nerve cells available in the sense organ is much less than the number available in the brain. This means that the types of coding possible at the peripheral level will be less sophisticated than the coding that would be possible if all the information were passed on to the brain, and the richness of the stimulus controlled behavior that is open to the animal will be correspondingly reduced.

Peripheral coding would thus appear to be an advantage if the animal is living in a restricted environment, in which case the potential stimuli available to it are limited, and within the capacity of the nervous structures associated with the sense organ. It would also be an advantage if the animal has a small number of nerve cells in the brain, in which case the economy gained is an overriding advantage. Central coding, on the other hand, is an advantage in rich environments, where the number of potential stimuli are very large, but requires that the animal have a well-developed brain.

The advantages and disadvantages of peripheral and central coding are reminiscent of the advantages that have been discussed in relation to learned and instinctive behavior (e.g., Manning, 1965). As Manning puts it, with instinctive behavior the animal contains within the nervous system a coded "picture" of the normal environment and of the appropriate responses to make to it. In a purely instinctive animal, no neural structures need to be wasted, but the system is inflexible and unable to deal with unexpected events. It has been suggested that instinctive behavior patterns are particularly well developed in animals such as the arthropods, where the number of nerve cells in the brain is small. It is interesting, therefore, to consider the extent to which peripheral coding dominates in animals which are rich in instinctive behavior, while central coding dominates in animals which rely more on learning. At first sight, much of the evidence that is available appears to be compatible with this view. Thus one vertebrate in which peripheral coding is very highly developed is the frog. Here, in both the visual and the auditory systems, we have seen that the afferent fibers running from the sense organs to the brain respond to very special and highly organized features of the stimulus and in many cases appear to be adequate to control behavior with little or no further processing. It is also true that frogs have a minimal capacity for learning (Yerkes, 1903) and are dominated by fixed behavior patterns. At the other extreme, mammals such as the cat and the monkey show comparatively little peripheral coding. In vision, for example, concentric fields are the most complex type commonly found, and units of the same level of complexity as those found in the frog retina only occur in the cortex (Hubel & Wiesel, 1962, 1968).

Other vertebrates occupy intermediate positions. The pigeon shows a great deal of peripheral coding (Maturana, 1962), and birds in general have a large instinctive repertoire, combined with considerable learning ability as well. Fish also show a considerable degree of peripheral coding (Jacobsen & Gaze, 1964), although it does not appear as marked as in the frog.

The invertebrates, with some exceptions such as the octopus, apparently show much more dependence on inherited behavior patterns than the vertebrates, and in insects and arthropods such behavior reaches its highest development. In some cases, such as the bee, learning occurs as well, but in other cases little or no learning has been demonstrated, and behavior is limited to a series of rigid responses to the environment. The instinctive behavior patterns may be very complex, as is the case in the communication system of bees (von Frisch, 1955). Peripheral coding is also very well developed in the arthropods. It has been shown, for example, that sound is analyzed at the level of the tympanic membrane in moths (Roeder & Treat, 1961). In vision, the compound eye is not separated from the brain by a relatively long optic nerve as it is in vertebrates. Nevertheless, it has been shown that the seven or eight component retinular cells or a single ommatidium are differentiated according to spectral sensitivity (Langer & Thorell, 1966) and their response to polarized light (Waterman & Horch, 1966), and Horridge *et al.* (1965) have described twenty different types of unit in the optic lobe of the locust. These units are presumably between two and four synapses removed from the receptors and, in this respect, comparable with the ganglion cells of the vertebrate retina.

Unfortunately, there are a large number of complications and exceptions to the general statements made in the preceding paragraphs. In the first place, we do not know enough about the relationship between innate and learned behavior in different animals. Even the distinction between the two behavior types is open to question, and anything approaching a complete study of behavior has been undertaken on only a very few species. In the second place, there are numerous exceptions to the general picture presented. Not all mammals show only simple forms of peripheral coding, correlated with a highly developed learning ability. This may be true, for example, in the rat (Brown & Rojas, 1965), but highly complex forms of sensory coding have been shown to take place at the level of the retinal ganglion cells in the rabbit (Levick, 1967), an animal that certainly learns with ease (van Hof, 1967), even though it may have a rich instinctive repertoire as well.

Further, within one animal, coding may take place peripherally in some modalities and centrally in others. If we take lateral inhibition in the cat as a simple example of sensory coding, this has been shown to take place at the retinal level for vision (Barlow *et al.*, 1957). For the modality of touch, however, there is no evidence for lateral inhibition at the peripheral level, though it has been shown to occur centrally (Mountcastle, 1957). In hearing, we again find that lateral inhibition may be demonstrated at the peripheral level (Katsuki, 1961). It seems unreasonable to propose that the cat depends more on instinctive behavior when using some modalities than others.

## REFERENCES

Adler, H. E., & Dalland, J. I. Spectral thresholds in the starling. *Journal of Comparative & Physiological Psychology,* 1959, **52,** 438–445.

Adrian, E. D. *The physical background of perception.* London & New York: Oxford University Press, 1947.

Armington, J. C. Spectral sensitivity of simultaneous electroretinograms and occipital responses. In H. M. Burian and J. H. Jacobsen (Eds.), *Clinical electroretinography.* Oxford: Pergamon Press, 1966.

Armington, J. C., & Crampton, G. H. Comparison of spectral sensitivity at the eye and optic tectum of the chicken. *American Journal of Ophthalmology,* 1958, **46,** 72.

Barlow, H. B., Fitzhugh, R., & Kuffler, S. W. Change of organisation in the receptive fields of the cat's retina during dark adaptation. *Journal of Physiology,* 1957, **137,** 338–354.

Behar, I., Cronholm, J. N., & Loeb, M. Auditory sensitivity of the Rhesus monkey. *Journal of Comparative & Physiological Psychology,* 1965, **59,** 426–428.

Bishop, P. W., Kozak, W., Levick, W. R., & Vakkur, G. J. The determination of the projection of the visual field on to the lateral geniculate nucleus of the cat. *Journal of Physiology,* 1962, **163,** 503–539.

Blough, D. S. Spectral sensitivity in the pigeon. *Journal of the Optical Society of America,* 1957, **47,** 827–833.

Brindley, G. S. *Physiology of the retina and the visual pathway.* London: Arnold, 1960.

Brindley, G. S., & Lewin, W. S. The sensations produced by electrical stimulation of the visual cortex. *Journal of Physiology,* 1968, **196,** 479–494.

Brown, J. E., & Rojas, J. A. Rat retinal ganglion cells: receptive field organisation and maintained activity. *Journal of Neurophysiology,* 1965, **28,** 1073–1090.

Campbell, F. W., & Robson, J. G. Application of Fourier analysis to the visibility of gratings. *Journal of Physiology,* 1968, **197,** 551–566.

Capranica, R. R. *The evoked vocal response of the bullfrog.* Cambridge, Massachusetts: M.I.T. Press, 1965.

Chapman, R. M. Light wavelength and energy preferences of the bullfrog: evidence for color vision. *Journal of Comparative & Physiological Psychology,* 1966, **61,** 429–435.

Cronly-Dillon, J. R., & Muntz, W. R. A. The spectral sensitivity of the goldfish and the clawed toad tadpole under photopic conditions. *Journal of Experimental Biology,* 1965, **42,** 481–493.

Daniel, P. M., Kerr, D. I. B., Seneviratne, K. N., & Whitteridge, D. The topographical representation of the visual field on the lateral geniculate nucleus of the cat and monkey. *Journal of Physiology,* 1961, **159,** 87P–88P.

Dartnall, H. J. A. The photobiology of visual processes. In *The Eye,* H. Davson (Ed.), New York: Academic Press, 1962.

Denton, E. J., & Pirenne, M. H. The visual sensitivity of the toad, *Xenopus laevis. Journal of Physiology,* 1954, **125,** 181–207.

Dethier, V. G. Chemoreceptor mechanisms. In R. G. Grenell and L. J. Mullins (Eds.), *Molecular structure and functional activity of nerve cells.* American Institute of Biological Sciences, 1956.

DeValois, R. L. Behavioural and electrophysiological studies of primate vision. In W. D. Neff (Ed.), *Contributions to sensory physiology.* Vol. I. New York: Academic Press, 1965. (a)

DeValois, R. L. Analysis and coding of color vision in the primate visual system. *Cold Spring Harbor Symposium Quantum Biology,* 1965, **30,** 567–579. (b)

DeValois, R. L., Smith, C. J., Karoly, A. J., & Kitai, S. T. Electrical responses of primate visual system. I. Different layers of macaque lateral geniculate nucleus. *Journal of Comparative & Physiological Psychology,* 1958, **51,** 662–668.

Dobrzecka, C., Szwejkowska, G., & Konorski, J. Qualitative versus directional cues in two forms of differentiation. *Science,* 1966, **153,** 87–89.

Easter, S. S. Excitation in the goldfish retina: evidence for a non-linear intensity code. *Journal of Physiology,* 1968, **195,** 253–272.

Elliott, D. N., Frazier, L., & Riarch, W. A tracking procedure for determining the cat's frequency discrimination. *Journal of Experimental Analysis of Behavior,* 1962, **5,** 323–328.

Erickson, R. P. Sensory neural patterns and gustation. In *International Symposium of Olfaction & Taste, Proceedings I.* Oxford: Pergamon Press, 1963.

Ewert, J.-P. Der Einfluss von Zwischenhirndefekten auf die Visnomotorik im Beute—und Fluchtverhalten der Erdkrote (*Bufo bufo* L.). *Zeitschrift für Vergleichende Physiologie,* 1968, **61,** 41–70.

Fitzhugh, R. The statistical detection of threshold signals in the retina. *Journal of General Physiology,* 1957, **40,** 925–948.

Frishkopf, L. S., & Goldstein, M. H. Responses to acoustic stimuli from single units in the eighth nerve of the bullfrog. *Journal of Acoustical Society of America,* 1963, **35,** 1219–1228.

von Frisch, K. *The dancing bees.* New York: Harcourt, 1955.

Granda A. M., and Stirling, C. E. Differential spectral sensitivity in the optic tectum and eye of the turtle. *Journal of general Physiology,* 1965, **48,** 901–917.

Granit, R. *Receptors and sensory perception.* New Haven: Yale University Press, 1955.

Granit, R. The visual pathway. In *The Eye,* vol. 2, H. Davson (Ed.), New York: Academic Press, 1962.

Guth, S. L., Donley, N. J., and Marrocco, R. T. On luminance additivity and related topics. *Vision Research,* 1969, **9,** 537–576.

Hodgson, E. S. Taste receptors. *Scientific American,* 1961, **204,** May, pp. 137–144.

Horridge, G. A., Scholes, J. H., Shaw, S. R., and Tunstall, J. Extracelluar recordings from single neurones in optic lobes. In *The physiology of the insect central nervous system,* Ed. J. E. Treherne and J. W. L. Beament (Eds.). New York: Academic Press, 1965.

Hubel, D. H., and Wiesel, T. N. Receptive fields of single neurones in the cat's striate cortex. *Journal of Physiology,* 1959, **148,** 574–591.

Hubel, D. H., and Wiesel, T. N. Receptive fields, binocular interaction and functional architecture in the cat's visual cortex. *Journal of Physiology,* 1962, **160,** 106–154.

Hubel, D. H., and Wiesel, T. N. Receptive fields and functional architecture in two nonstriate visual areas (18 and 19) of the cat. *Journal of Neurophysiology,* 1965, **28,** 229–289.

Hubel, D. H., and Wiesel, T. N., Receptive fields and functional architecture of monkey cortex. *Journal of Physiology,* 1968, **195,** 215–243.

Ilse, D. New observations on responses to colours in egg-laying butterflies. *Nature,* 1937, **140,** 544–545.

Ingvar, D. H. Spectral sensitivity as measured in cerebral visual centres. *Acta Physiologie Scandanavica Supplement,* 1959, **46,** 159.

Jacobs, D. W., & Tavolga, W. N. Acoustic intensity limens in the goldfish. *Animal Behavior,* 1967, **15,** 324–335.

Jacobs, G. H. Spectral sensitivity and color vision of the squirrel monkey. *Journal of Comparative & Physiological Psychology,* 1963, **56,** 616–621.

Jacobsen, M., & Gaze, R. M. Types of visual response from single units in the optic tectum and optic nerve of the goldfish. *Quarterly Journal of Experimental Physiology,* 1964, **49,** 199–209.

Janson, J. K. S., & Rack, P. M. H. The reflex response to sinusoidal stretching of soleus in the decerebrate cat. *Journal of Physiology,* 1966, **183,** 15–36.

Katsuki, Y. Neural mechanism of auditory sensation in cats. In W. A. Rosenblith (Ed.), *Sensory communication*. Cambridge, Massachusetts: M.I.T. Press, New York: Wiley, 1961.

Koh, S. D., & Teitelbaum, P. Absolute behavioural taste thresholds in the rat. *Journal of Comparative & Physiological Psychology*, 1961, **54**, 223–229.

Konig, A. Uber den menschlichen Sehpurpur und seine Bedentung fur das Sehen. *S.B. Akademie der Wissenschaften Berlin*, 1894, 577–598.

Langer, H., & Thorell, B. Microspectrophotometry of single rhabdomeres in the insect eye. *Experimental Cell Research*, 1966, **41**, 673–677.

Lashley, K. S. The mechanism of vision: XV. Preliminary studies of the rat's capacity for detail vision. *Journal of General Psychology*, 1938, **18**, 123–193.

Lettvin, J. Y., Maturana, H. R., McCulloch, W. S., & Pitts, W. H. What the frog's eye tells the frog's brain. *Proceedings of the Institute of Radio Engineers*, 1959, **47**, 1940–1951.

Levick, W. R. Receptive fields and trigger features of ganglion cells in the visual streak of the rabbit's retina. *Journal of Physiology*, 1967, **188**, 285–308.

Licklider, J. C. R. Basic correlates of the auditory stimulus. In S. S. Stevens (Ed.), *Handbook of experimental psychology*. New York: Wiley, 1951.

Manning, A. *Drosophila* and the evolution of behaviour. *Viewpoints in Biology*, 1965, **4**, 125–169.

Maturana, H. R. Functional organisation of the pigeon retina. *Proceedings of the International Union Physiological Science* (*XXII International Congress, Leiden*), 1962, **3**, 170–180.

Mountcastle, V. B. Modality and topographic properties of single neurons of cat's somatic sensory cortex. *Journal of Neurophysiology*, 1957, **20**, 408–434.

Munn, N. L. Visual pattern discrimination in the white rat. *Journal of Comparative Psychology*, 1930, **10**, 145–166.

Muntz, W. R. A. Effectiveness of different colours of light in releasing the positive phototactic behaviour of frogs, and a possible function of the retinal projection to the diencephalon. *Journal of Neurophysiology*, 1962, **25**, 712–720.

Muntz, W. R. A., & Northmore, D. P. M. Background light, temperature, and visual noise in the turtle. *Vision Research*, 1968, **8**, 787–800.

Muntz, W. R. A., & Northmore, D. P. M. Vision and visual pigments in a fish, *Scardinius erythrophthalmus* (the rudd). *Vision Research*, 1970, **10**, 281–298.

Muntz, W. R. A., & Sokol, S. Psychophysical thresholds to different wavelengths in light adapted turtles. *Vision Research*, 1967, **7**, 729–741.

Oldfield, R. C. Apparent fluctuations of a sensory threshold. *Quarterly Journal of Experimental Psychology*, 1955, **7**, 101–115.

Ramon, P. Quoted in *Histologie du systeme nerveux de l'homme et des vertebres*, by S. Ramon y Cajal, Madrid, Instituto Ramon y Cajal, 1955.

Ratliff, F. *Mach bands*. San Francisco: Holden–Day, 1965.

Robertson, A. D. J. Anaesthesia and receptive fields. *Nature*, 1965, **205**, 80.

Roeder, K. D., & Treat, A. E. The reception of bat cries by the tympanic organ of noctuid moths. In W. A. Rosenblith, (Ed.), *Sensory communication*. Cambridge, Massachusetts: M.I.T. Press, New York: Wiley, 1961.

Rosner, B. S., & Goff, W. R. Electrical responses of the nervous system and subjective scales of intensity. In W. D. Neff (Ed.), *Contributions to sensory physiology*, Vol. 2. New York: Academic Press, 1967.

Ruch, T. C. Sensory mechanisms. In S. S. Stevens (Ed.), *Handbook of experimental psychology*. New York: Wiley, 1951.

Schrier, A. M., & Blough, D. S. Photopic spectral sensitivity of macaque monkeys. *Journal of Comparative & Physiological Psychology,* 1966, **62**, 457–458.

Silver, P. H. Two spectral sensitivity curves of *Xenopus laevis* obtained by using the melanophore response to light on white and black backgrounds. *Journal of Physiology,* 1963, **169**, 1–9.

Silver, P. H. A Purkinje shift in the spectral sensitivity of grey squirrels. *Journal of Physiology,* 1966, **186**, 439–450.

Sperling, G. Linear theory and the psychophysics of flicker. *Documenta Ophthalmological* 1964, **18**, 3–15.

Stevens, S. S. The psychophysics of sensory function. In W. A. Rosenblith (Ed.), *Sensory Communication.* Cambridge, Massachusetts: M.I.T. Press, New York: Wiley, 1961.

Symmes, D. Self-determination of critical flicker frequencies in monkeys. *Science* 1962, **136**, 714–715.

Tinbergen, N. *The study of instinct.* London & New York: Oxford University Press, 1951.

Van Hof, M. W. Visual acuity in the rabbit. *Vision Research,* 1967, **7**, 749–752.

von Uexküll, J. A stroll through the worlds of animals and men. In C. H. Schiller (Ed.), *Instinctive Behaviour,* (1957). New York: International University Press Inc., 1934.

Vatter, O., Koller, Th., & Monnier, M. Die spektral sensitivitat der Retina und des optischen Cortex beim Kaninchen. *Vision Research,* 1964, **4**, 329–343.

Wall, P. D. The laminar organisation of dorsal horn and effects of descending impulses. *Journal of Physiology,* 1967, **188**, 403–424.

Walls, G. L. The lateral geniculate nucleus and visual histophysiology. *University of California Publication Physiology,* 1953, **9**, No. 1.

Waterman, T. H., & Horch, K. W. Mechanism of polarised light perception. *Science,* 1966, **154**, 467–475.

Wurtz, R. H. Visual receptive fields of striate cortex neurones in awake monkeys. *Journal of Neurophysiology,* 1969, **32**, 727–742.

Wyszecki, G., & Stiles, W. S. *Color science.* New York: Wiley, 1967.

Yerkes, R. M. The instinct, habit, and reactions of the frog. I. Associative processes of the green frog. *Psychological Review, Monograph Supplement,* 1903, **4**, 579–597.

Zotterman, Y. Special senses: thermal receptors. *Annual Review of Physiology,* 1953, **15**, 357–372.

CHAPTER 4  # Appetitive Motivation

J. A. DEUTSCH

Department of Psychology
University of California at San Diego
La Jolla, California

## I. INTRODUCTION

*148632*

In this chapter, we shall talk about hunger, thirst, and reward. Though reproductive activity is often dealt with under this title, in this volume it is dealt with in Chapter 2 (R. E. Whalen, "The Concept of Instinct"). It is to be noted that the title of this chapter is based on a classification according to introspective criteria. There are classes of motivation where we feel we have an appetite for something, where we have an urge to seek it out. Other classes of drives are called aversive, because there are things in the environment which we try to escape or to avoid. Such a distinction need not be taken to be a basic distinction; according to some theories, the distinction is only superficial. According to such theories (e.g., Hull), when we see an organism seeking out food, it is trying to escape from the aversive stimuli proceeding from its viscera. The ingestion of food provides an escape from the visceral stimulation. In this way hunger drive is reduced to the same paradigm as escape from electric shock. The only, but theoretically trivial, difference is that in the case of hunger the stimuli are coming from inside the organism, whereas in the case of electric shock they are coming from the outside. The same analysis can, of course, be applied to thirst or sex. We must therefore keep an open mind about the distinction between aversive and appetitive drives. However, it is true that they are introspectively different, and this may be an important clue.

## II. HUNGER AND THIRST

The requirement for various types of nutrient is brought about by growth of the organism, energy losses due to movement, and various metabolic factors, the most prominent of which in warm blooded animals is the maintenance of a certain body temperature. Water losses which must be made up by the animal are chiefly due to evaporation from the body surface and most inevitably from the lungs during breathing. Water losses also occur, because in the case of most animals certain substances must be eliminated dissolved in water (through micturition). Requirements of both food and water must be made up in the case of most animals through some active effort. When dehydration occurs in a land-living organism, this must in some way be translated into appropriate activity. The organism must start looking for water either by utilizing previous learning or by adopting some strategy of search which has been selected by evolution in its species. Having found water, it must then ingest it in quantity appropriate to its water requirement. We might also expect that in the case of most animals it will ingest this requirement as quickly as possible. The water hole is a favorite hunting ground for predators. Slow drinkers suffer a selective disadvantage. Similar considerations apply to hunger. In the case of hunger, however, we are not dealing with a unitary drive. Depending on the species, many different substances must be selected.

To be able to perform the varied behaviors we have briefly outlined, the organism must have the physiological and neural equipment appropriate to the task. We shall begin by asking how water and food deficiency is translated into the neural activity which then initiates water and food seeking behavior.

## III. WHAT PRODUCES THIRST?

Strangely enough, a simple lack of water as such does not seem to produce thirst. Darrow and Yannet (1935) have shown that a simple lack of water does not produce thirst in dogs, provided there is simultaneous loss of salt. Further, it is well known that injection or drinking of a volume of water will cause thirst, provided the water contains more salt per unit volume than the body fluids. From this, it could be deduced that what causes thirst is an increase in the concentration of salts in the body fluids; however, this is only true in a partial way. Gilman (1937) was able to show in an ingenious way that, if the increase in concentration occurred both inside the cells of the body and outside the cells, in the fluid bathing the cells, thirst did not result. So it seems that it is an increase of concentration of extracellular fluid relative to the concentration inside the cells which produces thirst. This indicates that somewhere in the body there is a mechanism which can detect such a disparity. We shall inquire where such a mechanism is situated later (p. 105).

## IV. WHAT PRODUCES HUNGER?

While the state of affairs which initiates thirst is fairly well established, we cannot as yet be sure what it is that initiates hunger. One of the difficulties in finding out is that there are many different kinds of hunger. For instance, animals may be hungry only for salt or for protein. The theorists who have advanced hypotheses about hunger appear mainly to have been concerned with caloric hunger. These hypotheses view hunger mainly as a response to a shortage of food seen as fuel to keep the body warm and to provide energy for movement.

The three chief theories which have been advanced are the thermostatic theory of Brobeck, the glucostatic theory of Mayer, and the lipostatic theory of Kennedy.

### A. The Thermostatic Theory

As its name indicates, Brobeck's (1948) thermostatic theory implies that hunger arises in order to control temperature in the body. Animals eat in order to prevent their temperature from falling, and they stop eating when they are becoming too warm. It is, in fact, the case that temperature rises after a meal. The property of food which produces such a rise in temperature is called its "specific dynamic action." The hypothesis is supported also by the fact that high temperatures depress eating and low temperatures increase eating. Also foods such as proteins, which increase temperature after eating, also produce satiation more quickly.

However, there are objections against this theory: Kennedy (1953) has pointed out that fat should be eaten in excess to produce obesity, because its specific dynamic action is not as high as that of protein, but its caloric value is higher. However, animals do not overeat fat as compared to protein.

Andersson and Larsson (1961) report an experiment which partly supports the thermostatic theory. They implanted a device in the hypothalamus of goats (preoptic area and rostral hypothalamus) which caused cooling or heating of that region of the central nervous system. Cooling of the area increased eating but decreased drinking. On the other hand, warming the area increased drinking and decreased eating. However, the shifts in temperature used to obtain these effects were very large, and they were much larger than the changes in temperature which would probably occur during normal hunger and thirst, or satiation. Furthermore, when the regions of the hypothalamus which were sensitive to the effects of temperature (as measured by alterations of intake) were surgically removed, no gross abnormalities of intake resulted. The goats simply ate at temperatures at which normal goats would not eat; they did not drink more at such temperatures, although normal goats did. According to the thermostatic hypothesis, we would expect such goats to eat excessively because they are not sensitive to an increase in temperature, which in theory causes normal animals to stop eating. The experiment shows that temperature does affect intake through a specific locus in the hypothalamus, but it seems to be only a subsidiary factor. The main regulation of intake is probably performed in some other way.

## B. The Glucostatic Theory

The glucostatic theory, as its name indicates, suggests that hunger is due to an attempt on the part of the organism to keep glucose constant. Mayer (1955) has suggested that it is not the absolute level of glucose that is monitored, but the difference in glucose between the arteries and the veins. A large difference between the arteries and the veins implies that a large amount of glucose is being taken up from the blood by the tissues en route between the arteries and the veins. Stunkard, Van Itallie, and Reis (1955) have shown that there is a correlation between such a measure and hunger. Herberg (1962) has also shown that small injections of glucose into the ventricles of a rat depress hunger.

## C. The Lipostatic Theory

This theory, put forward by Kennedy in 1953, proposes that the organism regulates the overall fat deposited in its body, through some biochemical consequence of the stored fat. Some evidence for this theory comes from the fact that animals can keep within very close limits of body weight and will return to their previous weight when they have been artificially fattened (Teitelbaum, 1962).

## V. WHERE DO CHANGES PRODUCING HUNGER AND THIRST ACT?

A once popular view held that changes acted on peripheral structures to produce hunger or thirst. The notion that all behavior was due to stimulation impinging on receptors and was then translated into responses by pathways leading to effectors made such a view popular. In the same way, hunger and thirst could be looked upon as special reflexes. Not only is there a great deal of evidence against such a view (summarized by Deutsch & Deutsch, 1966), but the real place where the changes due to hunger and thirst occur are now fairly accurately known. It seems that the physiological changes leading to hunger and thirst act directly on structures within the nervous system.

The demonstration of such sites in the central nervous system is especially dramatic in the case of thirst. The general method used is as follows: The animal (such as a cat or rat) is anesthetized, and its head is placed in a stereotaxic instrument. It has been found that brain structures bear a fairly constant spatial relation to places on the animal's skull, such as the entrance to the ear. If we know where the animal's ear canals are and where his top incisors are, we can then specify how many millimeters away in a certain direction, say, the red nucleus is from both of these bony structures. The stereotaxic instrument takes advantage of this constant relation between the skull and the brain. The animal's head is clamped using certain bony landmarks such as the ear canals. Each point in the animal's skull can then be represented by a system of three numbers, which give the distance along the three dimensions of a particular brain structure away from, say, the ear canals when the tilt of the head is held at some arbitrary point by clamping, say, the top incisors. Maps of the brain, called stereotaxic atlases, which give the coordinates in three dimensions of the various brain structures, have been prepared from sections of the animal's head. A part of the stereotaxic instrument is a probe which can be accurately positioned along the three spatial coordinates.

When the anesthetized animal has been clamped in the stereotaxic instrument, an incision is made in the scalp and a small hole drilled in the skull at the place where an electrode or a cannula is to be inserted into the brain. In the case of experiments on thirst, cannulas are generally used, which are narrow tubes, often sawed-off hypodermic needles. These are inserted to the desired depth with the use of the stereotaxic probe. The end of the cannula which protrudes above the skull is then fastened with dental cement to screws which have been inserted in the skull. The cannula is then closed off with a stopper, which should fit along the whole length of the cannula. This prevents dirt from entering the cannula and also prevents the cannula from becoming clogged. The scalp is then sown up around the cannula and the animal left to recover. Upon recovering from the anesthesia, the animal shows little or no distress and seems unaffected by the implant.

When such a cannula has been implanted, it is possible to inject small amounts of substances through the cannula into a brain structure. Such an ability is obviously very useful when we wish to determine the site of action of the factors producing thirst. Andersson and McCann (1955) injected very small amounts of a 2–3% sodium chloride solution into a region of the hypothalamus of a goat. It is true that a large injection of sodium chloride solution at this concentration would produce drinking wherever it was injected into the body. However the amounts used by Anderson and McCann were so very small (0.003–0.01 cc), that if injected anywhere else in the body they have no effect. We can therefore assume that the injections made by Andersson and McCann must have been close to the structures which are normally sensitive to the changes producing thirst. Miller (1961) showed a similar phenomenon in cats. Small injections of 2% sodium chloride produced drinking if injected into the third ventricle in cats. This is a concentration which is roughly two and a half times as high as that normally found in body fluids. On the other hand, an injection of distilled water into the same place, which would of course tend to dilute body fluids, actually reduced drinking. Similar effects have been obtained in rats by Herberg (1962). Injections of minute amounts of hypertonic saline into the lateral ventricles of a rat produced almost immediate drinking. It seems that the neural structures which initiate drinking in response to a physiological change are very close to the surface of the ventricles. Since the ventricles are a set of interconnected cavities within the brain, filled with cerebrospinal fluid, an injection into the ventricles can quickly affect any structure lining these fluid-filled cavities.

It has also been possible to elicit thirst by electrical stimulation of structures within the brain. Andersson and McCann (1955) were able to elicit drinking in goats by stimulating electrically in the area where injection has been shown to produce drinking. Further these same investigators have shown that destruction of such an area leads to a cessation of drinking. Animals in whom such areas have been lesioned show thirst lessened in proportion to the amount of lesioning of the relevant area.

## VI. HAS THIRST REALLY BEEN PRODUCED?

It could be argued that the experiments above only show that an animal might be stimulated to drink, but that the animals were not necessarily thirsty. In answer to this objection, it should first be pointed out that the acts of drinking are directed. The animal does not simply produce drinking movements. It orients itself correctly with respect to water. Furthermore, Andersson's goats would seek out sources of water about which they had previously learned. Miller (1961) taught cats to perform a response to obtain water when they were thirsty. He then injected hypertonic sodium chloride into their third ventricle, and they began to perform the same response to obtain water as they had previously learned.

## VII. CENTRAL NERVOUS SYSTEM
## LOCI LINKED TO HUNGER

As we saw above, the factors which produce hunger, or the various types of hunger, remain unknown. It has therefore been impossible to evoke hunger by minute injections of whatever it is that normally triggers eating. This has been possible in the case of thirst, so that the evidence in the case of thirst is very compelling. However it has been possible to elicit eating by electrical stimulation. Instead of implanting a tube (cannula), electrodes have been placed by means of a stereotaxic instrument with tips in the lateral area of the hypothalamus. These electrodes are essentially short lengths of thin wire, coated with insulating material right up to the tip. Only a small area is left exposed at the end. In that way we can know just where the current passing out of the electrode is having its effect. The electrode is made of material such as stainless steel which is nontoxic to brain tissue. When small currents are passed through such electrodes permanently implanted in the area of the lateral hypothalamus, an animal begins to eat (Delgado & Anand, 1953; Anand & Dua, 1955). If lesions are made of the lateral hypothalamic area on both sides, then an animal does not become hungry and will starve in the midst of food (Anand, Dua, & Shoenberg, 1955). But such lesions may not produce simple loss of hunger: Teitelbaum and Epstein (1962) have shown that a loss of thirst may be the most important ingredient of the animal's symptoms, and that the unwillingness to eat may just be a consequence of dehydration. However, the lesion seems to produce more than a loss of thirst; it seems actually to produce an aversion to drinking. For instance, Williams and Teitelbaum (1959) found that animals with this lesion would take a much stronger shock to avoid drinking then would normal animals. Rats were trained to avoid shock by drinking. Much higher levels of shock were required to make rats with lesions of the lateral hypothalamus drink, although their learning ability is not adversely affected by such lesions. It is not altogether surprising that the results of even such small lesions as were made should turn out to be so complex. There appears to be a great deal of intermingling of pathways in the lateral hypothalamic area. For instance, animals often find stimulation of this area rewarding. In fact, such intermingling of functionally different units is probably the rule in the nervous system. That is one reason why studies employing surgical lesions have proved to be so difficult to interpret.

In any case, it is unlikely that the lateral area of the hypothalamus is where bodily changes are monitored and then translated into neural activity. Rather the lateral hypothalamic area contains a pathway leading away from an area which monitors bodily states. By stimulating at various points in the brain of the cat, Wyrwicka and Doty (1966) were able to elicit feeding from points in the globus pallidus from which fibers pass into the lateral hypothalamic area. The same pathway then passes into the ventral tegmentum and then to the ventrolateral boundary of the central gray. Feeding can be elicited by stimulation all along this pathway. This study is a timely reminder that functions in the brain do not reside at a certain point just because they may be evoked there by stimulation or abolished by a lesion.

The specificity (and perhaps even the fixity) of the loci evoking hunger and thirst has recently been called in question by Valenstein, Cox, and Kakolewski (1968). They have shown that rats in which electrodes would evoke drinking would show eating or gnawing when water was not available. This indicates that the electrode was not stimulating a single system but many systems to varying degrees. It was also shown that once the rat had obtained experience with the activity that was not its first choice, it persevered with such an activity even though the subject of its first choice (such as water) was reintroduced. It looked as if the specificity of the locus had changed due to experience. However when interpreting the experiment, we should note that the loci evoking drive activity can also under some circumstances provide reward for the animal (e.g., Coons & Cruce, 1968). The secondary activity, while getting evoked, might at the same time become rewarded and so become an instrumental act. To support this interpretation, there is the observation of Valenstein *et al.* (1968) that other behavior was observed to be elicited by the stimulation in some animals. For instance one rat "frequently positioned itself in one part of the cage, and with the onset of stimulation a specific path was traversed on the way to the drinking bottle." The author has frequently seen the development of such stereotyped behavior as a result of rewarding electrical stimulation.

## VIII. IS IT REAL HUNGER WHICH IS PRODUCED BY ELECTRICAL STIMULATION?

As in the case of artificially evoked drinking, electrically evoked eating resembles normal hunger in all important respects. Wyrwicka, Dobrzecka, and Tarnecki (1959) trained food-deprived goats to place a foreleg on a tray in order to obtain a reward of oats. The goats were then satiated, and lateral hypothalamic stimulation was then turned on. The goats then began to place their foreleg on the tray again. Nor was this simply a movement elicited by the stimulation, because when the goats were not given their usual reward of oats for performing the movement, they gradually stopped lifting their leg. The habit extinguished in the same way when the goats were normally hungry. It is interesting to note that, when lateral hypothalamic stimulation was discontinued, the goat only made one or two movements to obtain oats and then stopped. It looks as if the induced drive dissipates very rapidly once electrical stimulation is withdrawn. Coons, Levak, and Miller (1965) performed an experiment in which a rat was taught to press one of two bars in a Skinner box for a reward of food when its lateral hypothalamus was electrically stimulated. When the first bar stopped producing a food reward, the rat learned to switch to the other bar. The rat did not press when satiated without lateral hypothalamic stimulation. However when the rat was made normally hungry, for a time it pressed the bar last rewarded during lateral hypothalamic stimulation, even though no food was then given for such a response. Tenen and Miller (1964) stimulated the lateral hypothalamus to see if increases in such stimulation would induce rats to drink milk progressively more adulterated with quinine. It was found that, the hungrier a rat, the more readily it will drink a bitter solution. It was also found that increases in the intensity of electrical stimulation made the rat ready to drink an increasing concentration of quinine in its milk.

The experiments quoted above are necessary to find out if hunger is really being elicited by brain stimulation. This is made clear by studies where brain stimulation produces feeding behavior but differs from normal hunger in other ways. Harwood and Vowles (1966) stimulated the forebrain of the ring dove electrically. Such stimulation prolonged bouts of pecking and eating directed to food but not bouts directed to non-nutritious matter, such as grit or feces. From this, it might be thought that the stimulation produced hunger in the same way as lateral hypothalamic stimulation produced hunger in the rat. However, using this stimulation it was impossible to elicit by such electrical stimulation the performance of a habit learned by the ring doves to obtain food. This shows that the stimulation does not induce motivation for a habit previously learned while the ring doves were hungry. If ring doves are taught to obtain food by repeatedly pecking a key and are given a reward only for a certain proportion of presses, they speed up their pecking if they are made more hungry. However, forebrain stimulation did not increase the rate of responding in such a situation. This is another way of showing that the stimulation did not evoke real hunger but only components of feeding behavior. (However, such a conclusion is not completely necessary. It might be argued that electrical stimulation as employed in this experiment may have introduced other components besides hunger. Such components can produce generalization decrement. If an animal has learned a habit or discrimination, it is frequently unable to perform it when an apparently irrelevant stimulus is introduced into or taken away from the situation. There is no reason why an electrical brain stimulus can not function as an irrelevant stimulus.)

## IX. WHAT OTHER PROPERTIES DO THESE CENTRAL DRIVE MECHANISMS HAVE?

One of the interesting discoveries concerning these central mechanisms of drive is that the transmitter substances used in them are different for hunger and thirst. This information has been obtained by the injection of drugs into the central nervous system. The rationale for the injection of drugs to study the hunger and thirst systems is as follows: Transmission of information in the nervous system depends on the spread of what may be regarded as an electrical disturbance along the various parts of the neuron. However, in the case of the mammalian nervous system, when the information crosses from one neuron to another (the crossing point being called a synapse), another type of carrier is used, namely, the movement of minute particles of substance, across the gap between the two neurons. When the action potential travels to the end region of one neuron, this region, known as the presynaptic ending, ejects a substance called transmitter into the minute cleft between the two neurons. This cleft, called the synaptic cleft, is about 200 Å wide. The transmitter rapidly diffuses across the synaptic cleft to its other side. The other side, the postsynaptic region of the next neuron, is sensitive to the transmitter and responds by initiating an electrical change. In this way, the neural message is carried electrically and chemically alternately.

There are probably many different kinds of transmitter used at various synapses in the nervous system: the two identified so far with any certainty are acetylcholine and norepinephrine. By injecting these transmitters or substances with the same action on their particular postsynapatic endings, we can produce the action of the transmitter ejected by the presynaptic ending. In this way, it is possible to stimulate, at least temporarily, the synapses which use a certain type of transmitter. We say temporarily, because if acetylcholine, for instance, is not rapidly removed before being reapplied, blocking of the synapse results, since no more electrical action potentials are generated by the neuron on the postsynaptic side. However, blocking results only if the amount of transmitter or substance with a similar action is high. If the level is low, the injected transmitter or substance simply adds to the effect produced by the transmitter ejected by the synapse itself, thus facilitating transmission.

It has been found (Grossman, 1960; Miller, 1965) that the injection of small amounts of transmitter, or substances producing the same action as transmitter, can evoke eating or drinking. Drinking is produced by the injection of the acetylcholine-like substance, carbachol. Eating, on the other hand, is evoked by injection of norepinephrine. Quartermain and Miller (1966) have shown that rats will drink for about twenty minutes after a minute injection of carbachol into the preoptic area of the hypothalamus. However, if the rats are not given water after injection, but the presentation of water is delayed for various periods of time, drinking seems to be induced by carbachol for at least sixty minutes. This shows that carbachol-induced thirst can be shut off by drinking in a similar way that normal thirst can be.

Attempts have been made to trace the pathway mediating hunger and thirst by the placement of small amounts of drug in various loci (e.g., Fisher & Coury, 1962). However, Routtenberg (1965) points out that the results obtained by this method may reflect spread of drug through the ventricles. A similar objection is made by Deutsch and Deutsch (1966).

## X. REGULATION OF AMOUNT EATEN OR DRUNK

When an animal eats or drinks, the amount it takes in is closely matched to its physiological deficit. We may ask how the animal knows that it has had enough. One of the answers to this question is based on the notions of stimulus–response psychology. According to this school of thought, a response on the part of the organism is initiated and maintained by a stimulus. When the stimulus is withdrawn, the response ceases. The way this view then accounts for regulation of eating or drinking is to assume that certain stimuli generated by the physiological deficits in hunger (or thirst) trigger the response of eating (or drinking). As soon as eating (or drinking) has reversed the initiating physiological deficit, the stimuli triggering the responses of eating (or drinking) cease and so, of course, do the responses. This type of arrangement is like that in a thermostat. A fall in temperature causes a change in a thermometer. As a result of this change, the thermometer switches on the furnace. The furnace then heats the air around the thermometer, until the change in temperature which caused the thermometer to fall below a certain point is reversed. Then the thermometer no longer keeps the furnace on.

The system employed by this thermostat is like that of any other simple homeostat. Such a system may be employed whenever we wish to keep the level stable around a given point. Although such a system is very simple, it is by no means the only system which can be employed. One of the features of this system is that activity to restore a deficit continues until the deficit is made up. If such a system is used in the organism to regulate eating (or drinking), we expect eating (or drinking) to continue while the physiological deficit persists.

One way to find out if it is the reversal of the initiating deficit which produces cessation of drinking is to measure how long it takes to reverse the initiating deficit. We can do this by taking a thirsty animal and placing water directly into its stomach. Having done this, we wait for various lengths of time before we allow the animal access to water. If the animal drinks after a certain time interval, we can assume that the initiating change in thirst takes at least as long as this to reverse. Bellows (1939) has performed such an experiment. He found that it takes 15 minutes after a preload of about 8% of body/weight directly in the dog's stomach before the dog will not drink when allowed access to water. On the other hand, Bellows found that, when it is thirsty, a dog can drink 10% of its body weight in four minutes. This indicates that the dog stops drinking a long time before the change initiating drinking is reversed. It is clear that if the dog kept drinking until the initiating change was removed, it would overdrink grossly.

However, it should be pointed out that there is a conflict of evidence here. Towbin (1949) reports that the amount a dog drinks is considerably lessened after placing water directly in the stomach even when the dog is allowed to drink immediately afterwards. Tobin also showed that such immediate lessening of drinking can also be brought about by inflating the stomach with a volume of air or inflating a balloon in the stomach. This at least shows that cessation of drinking in the first part of Towbin's experiment was not due to a reversal of the change which brings about drinking in the first place.

Light has been shed on this conflict of evidence by Miller and Kessen (1954). In their experiment, rats were placed in a T-maze and given a choice between the two goal boxes. In one, a balloon was inflated in their stomachs. This apparently satiated the rats. However they learned to avoid the goal box in which their stomachs were distended by means of the balloon. The most likely explanation of the result is that rapid distention of the stomach causes nausea. Nausea, of course, mimics satiation insofar as a nauseated animal will not drink. On the other hand, nausea differs from satiation inasmuch as an animal finds satiation rewarding but not nausea. It is likely that a slow rate of injection of water into the stomach does not cause nausea, whereas a fast rate does.

To test what happens when the rate of injection is kept low in order to avoid nausea, Miller, Sampliner, and Woodrow (1957) took rats and studied the effects of injection of water on their thirst. They found that water injected slowly had considerable effect on thirst immediately after injection. However their injection took about 12 minutes to complete, and it is possible that considerable reversal of the condition which produced thirst had already taken place. Indeed, Novin (1962) was able to show a considerable diminution of body fluid tonicity within 12 minutes of the start of drinking. He used the ingenious technique of measuring the electrical conductance of the body fluids through implanted electrodes while the rat was drinking.

We have seen then that Bellows found no effect on drinking immediately upon loading the stomach with water. On the other hand, Towbin and Miller *et al.*, found considerable effects. In Towbin's experiment, the effect was probably due to nausea. In Miller, Sampliner, and Woodrow's experiment, the possibility of nausea was carefully excluded, and we concluded that their result was due to absorption from the stomach. The question is then why the results of Bellows are different. The critical difference is probably due to the use of different kinds of animals in the two experiments. Bellows used dogs while Miller *et al.*, used rats. The difference in result is likely to be due to a difference in size between the two animals. When water is placed in the stomach, two main effects occur: first, water makes its way out of the stomach into the tissues; and, second, salts make their way out of the tissues into the stomach. In other words, the fluids inside and outside the stomach tend towards an osmotic equilibrium. The rate at which such a trend towards equilibrium can take place is governed, among other things, by the area of contact between the fluids.

Although the rate of exchange will be higher in a dog due to the larger surface area of its stomach, the amount of fluid to be exchanged will be even larger. As the linear dimensions of an animal increase (such as height or length), the measurements of its surface area tend to increase more or less as the square of the linear dimensions. However, measurements such as the volume tend to increase more or less as the cube of the linear dimensions. If the surface of the stomach increased at the same rate as its volume, then it would take the same time (other things being equal) for a rat and a dog to reach osmotic equilibrium with the content of their stomach. However, for geometric reasons, the volume of a dog's stomach is very much larger in proportion to its surface than a rat's. We therefore expect a preload in a dog's stomach to be much slower in reversing the physiological deficit than in the case of the rat. It is therefore likely that the conclusion from Bellow's experiment is correct, namely, that drinking (at least, in the case of larger animals) is over long before the physiological change which produces drinking is over.

There are other ways in which we can try to discover if reversal of the initiating change switches thirst off. For instance, we can see if an animal will keep drinking if no water is allowed to reach its stomach. According to the simple homeostat view, the animal should keep drinking, at least until it is exhausted. Such an experiment can be done using the technique of esophageal fistulation. This consists of cutting the esophagus and sowing both cut ends to the surface of the neck, so that as the animal drinks the water escapes through an opening on the neck.

When this happens, the animal is said to be sham drinking. The general consensus of such experiments is that the animal does not keep on drinking. However some experimenters (such as Adolph, 1941) show that the amount drunk under such circumstances is almost the same as when water is allowed to enter the stomach. Other experimenters (such as Bellows, 1939; and Towbin, 1949) calculate that dogs will overdrink anywhere from 155–250%. However, the difference in result here is probably more apparent than real and very likely stems from different methods of calculating how much the dog would have drunk with the esophagus intact. Adolph (1941) weighed the dog and used the reduction in body weight as an index of the amount of water needed by the dog. On the other hand, Towbin placed differing amounts of water in the dog's stomach and left them there for an hour. This should be sufficient time for a reversal of the physiological deficit. He then gave the dog access to water and assumed that the least amount of water necessary to stop the dog from drinking an hour later was also the amount that the dog had drunk. However, such an assumption is probably false for the following reason: Robinson and Adolph (1943) found that a dog will only begin to drink when it has lost 0.4% of its body weight in water, so that if the real deficit of the dog in Towbin's experiment is, say, 0.6% of body weight, and Towbin inserted 0.3% of its body weight of water in its stomach, the dog will be left with a deficit of 0.3% of body weight. He will consequently not start drinking, as he needs to have a deficit of 0.4% of body weight to start drinking. (However, once he starts drinking, he continues drinking until the whole body weight is regained. This, of course, is another reason to believe that drinking is not stopped by reversal of deficit.) It is therefore apparent that drinking can be held off by a much smaller amount of fluid inserted in the stomach than the dog will actually drink.

Another way of measuring the influence of various factors discussed above was devised by Deutsch and Blumen (1962). Instead of attempting to introduce water into the stomach before the onset of drinking or preventing water from reaching the stomach, the physiological benefit resulting from drinking was cancelled out or counteracted. A small poly- ethylene tube was implanted in the stomach. As the rat drank water, a small volume of hypertonic saline was pumped into the stomach through the tube whenever the rat made a lick. The volume and the concentration of saline was carefully adjusted so that the mix of water and hypertonic saline arriving in the stomach through the esophagus and the implanted tube produced saline at the normal concentration of the rat's body fluid. In such a way, drinking did not produce the normal reversal of the physiological change which initiates drinking. The advantage of this method is that the rat, when it is not in the experiment, can feed and drink quite normally. This is not the case with an animal with an esophageal fistula.

## XI. COUNTERINJECTION

It is also easy to test the same animal when it is drinking and when drinking is allowed to have normal physiological consequences. Instead of indirect calculation of what the animal should drink, we can actually measure what it normally drinks. Using this technique, we showed that a rat behaves in an almost identical way for the first 25 minutes after access to water, whether its physiological deficit is being reversed or not. It drinks rapidly at first, stopping almost completely after 15 min- utes when it is 22 hours thirsty. However after a pause of about 10 minutes, the rat with a deficit begins to drink again. The rat in which the deficit has been reversed does not begin again. This shows that there is something about drinking itself, without regard for its physiologi- cal consequences, which can inhibit thirst. However such an inhibition is only temporary, because without reversal of the physiological change drinking begins again.

So far we have only discussed results obtained in thirst, but similar questions have been asked about hunger. Attempts have been made to establish the effects of preloads of food in the stomach (Kohn, 1951; Berkun, Miller, & Kessen, 1952). Even though nausea can be excluded as an explanation, the insertion of food into the stomach seems to lead to an almost immediate inhibition of hunger. This should be contrasted with the case of drinking, where a preload of water seems to have little immediate effect. However, because of the speed with which the inhibi- tion takes place, it is unlikely that the inhibition of eating can be due to a reversal of the change which initiates eating. The process of digestion is somewhat slow.

Smith and Duffy (1955) attempted to discover in more detail how this inhibitory action of the stomach on hunger works. Does the stomach react simply to distention or can it "discriminate" nutrients from nonnutrients? In order to answer this, they preloaded the stomach with kaolin (white china clay), and so inert, nonnutritious bulk, and nutrient substances (enriched milk, sugar solution). They found that kaolin had no effect on hunger independent of quantity, but that nutrient substances had. They also noted that the larger the amount of the nutrient substance, the larger the inhibitory effect. From this evidence, it seems that there is something about the entry of food into the stomach which functions as a signal to stop eating. This is not the case in thirst, where the factors switching off drinking are related to drinking itself. This is true of the act of eating also, but only to a minor extent. An amount of food ingested by mouth has a slightly larger effect on subsequent eating than that same amount of food placed in the stomach (Berkun et al., 1952).

Hull, Livingstone, Rouse, and Barker (1951) attempted to measure what would happen if a dog were allowed to eat, but if no food reached the stomach. Although the dog weighed 10 kg before his esophagus was transected, he ate 8 kg of food before stopping for 5 minutes. Even then his stopping was probably due more to exhaustion than to satiation. This supports the idea that the stop signal in eating is somehow generated mostly in the stomach.

It can be seen from the above review that the simple homeostatic view of the control of drive does not fit the evidence as it has been collected in the laboratory. Something occurs which switches off drive, even though the initiating factors are still present. We must therefore consider alternative views.

## XII. THE AFFERENT INHIBITION VIEW OF SATIATION

We have seen in the case of the evidence we have reviewed, that thirst, for example, is produced by an increase in the tonicity of the extracellular fluid, and that it can be reversed by a decrease of tonicity of such fluids. This may be done, for example, by placing water in the stomach and waiting. So it appears that thirst can be turned on by the presence of a certain physiological deficit, and that it can be turned off by the removal of this deficit. This fits in well with our knowledge of structures in the hypothalamic region sensitive to such a deficit. On the other hand, we have also seen that, during normal drinking, ingestion of water stops before the physiological deficit has been reversed. It seems that something occurs during drinking which inhibits thirst. It has been suggested that drive states are normally inhibited by specific afferent messages produced during activities such as eating, drinking, or copulation (Deutsch, 1953, Deutsch & Jones, 1960; Stellar, 1954).

As the inhibition by the afferent stimuli wears off, the slower-acting reversal of the initiating deficit will have taken place. Also, given a certain level of afferent message resulting from an activity such as drinking, it will take longer to inhibit a higher level of thirst. Furthermore, the greater the amount of afferent message, the quicker will a given level of thirst be inhibited. In this way, intake will be proportionate to deficit.

Physiologically speaking then, we get a picture of a center which is excited or irritated by a physiological deficit, and which is at the same time sensitive to inhibitory influences from afferent pathways, presumably those leading from the tongue and the upper digestive tract. The first would be true of such drives as drinking, and the second would be true of such drives as hunger. There is a very convenient property of the afferent pathway employed in inhibiting thirst which enables us to manipulate the number of impulses reaching the thirst center over that pathway as the animal is drinking. Water, in the case of the rat, inhibits a steady rate of spontaneous firing in the gustatory pathway. When hypotonic salt is placed on the tongue, activity in this set of nerve fibers increases. However, when water is placed on the tongue, spontaneous rate of firing in these nerves decreases. In this way, the taste of water is signaled by a decrease in the spontaneous rate of firing in the gustatory nerve in the rat. Apparently the same arrangement is also to be found in man. In other animals, such as the monkey, there are two sets of fibers each of which separately convey information regarding either salt or water. In these animals, the rate of firing in the water and salt pathways is reciprocal. When water is placed on the tongue, the activity in the water fibers increases, and activity in the salt fibers decreases. When salt is placed on the tongue, activity in the water fibers decreases, and activity in the salt fibers increases. Even when there are two pathways, the water signaling system is essentially the same. In the rat and man, where there is a single pathway, the arrangement is simply less redundant than in other animals, and therefore easier to speak about. From this neurophysiological evidence concerning taste, it might be predicted on the afferent inhibition view of satiation that it should take animals longer to become satiated when they are drinking mildly salty water than when they are drinking distilled water, because the amount of decrease of spontaneous firing in the case of distilled water is very much higher than the amount of decrease in firing in the case of salty water. Hypotonic saline will act on the receptors as if it were diluted water. It will be less effective in inhibiting thirst than pure water. From this, we can predict that given a choice between pure water and hypotonic salt solution, the rat will drink more of the hypotonic salt solution than of the water. This is not because it prefers such a solution, but simply because it takes a longer time to be satiated by the hypotonic salt solution.

In fact, this theoretical prediction seems to be confirmed, as it has been known for a long time that rats, given a choice between water and saline both freely available in the cage at the same time, will drink more saline than water. This has been shown by (Nelson, 1947; Bare, 1949; Young, 1949). Of course, the fact that animals drink more saline than water might not be due taste factors. It might simply be that they have to drink more saline in order to produce an equivalent reversal of the deficit, which originates first. However, it has been shown by Stellar and McCleary (1952) and Mook (1963), using animals with esophageal fistulae, that saline is overdrunk in relation to water even when the fluid cannot reach the animal's stomach. A similar demonstration concerning hypotonic saline has been given by Deutsch and Blumen (1962), using the technique of counterinjection. Rats will drink much more saline than water, even when the physiological consequences as a result of the ingestion of both liquids are made the same by the addition of different strengths of saline into the stomach while the animal is drinking. However, it might be argued, from the evidence that has just been summarized, that animals do not drink more saline, simply because it takes more saline to switch off thirst. It might be argued that rats drink more saline, because they actually prefer it, in the same way that we prefer the taste of sweet-tasting solutions. The diluted-water theory of saline overdrinking and the preference theory of saline overdrinking can, however, be differentiated by a simple experiment. If rats are given the choice between equal amounts of saline and water, then they should prefer the saline on the preference theory of saline overdrinking. However, the diluted-water theory of saline overdrinking predicts that the rats should actually prefer the water to the saline, because a given amount of water will produce more satiation of thirst than the same amount of saline. Therefore, the animal should learn to go to the side where a greater amount of satiation or reward is actually obtained. Deutsch and Jones (1959, 1960) performed such an experiment: they found the rats would learn to run to the sides of a T maze which contained the water, rather than that side which contained an equal amount of hypotonic saline. A further prediction which differentiates between the two theories is that saline overdrinking is simply a manifestation of thirst according to the diluted water-theory. By the preference theory, if animals prefer saline, they should prefer saline regardless of whether or not they are thirsty. Consequently, Deutsch and Jones placed animals in a situation containing equal amounts of saline and water in the two arms of a T maze when they were not thirsty. It was hardly possible to run the animals. Most of them refused to run, and there was no particular preference for either the saline or the water: the animals only rarely touched either reward substance in the two goal boxes. This shows that the animals did not have an appetite for saline when they were not thirsty, and this is not what would be expected according to the saline preference theory. Other experimeters have tried to repeat Deutsch and Jones' (1959, 1960) experiments. Some have been successful, such as Chiang and Wilson (1963); however. Falk and Teitelbaum found that they could not repeat the experiment, because the animals tended to prefer saline when they were nonthirsty and showed no preference for water when they were thirsty. However, Wiener and Deutsch (1967) were able to show that the discrepant results of Falk and Teitelbaum were probably due to the use of a particular strain of rat which is highly susceptible to salt deficiency, and also to a possible salt deficiency on the part of the particular animals that Falk and Titlebaum used. It has, of course, long been known that rats will drink salt in large quantities when they are actually salt deprived. The phenomenon we have been discussing is apparent in nonsalt-deprived rats. It has been shown by Wolf (1964) that saline drinking due to salt deprivation is, in fact, a completely different phenomenon from saline overdrinking, which is not associated with salt deprivation. He has shown that the two phenomena can be dissociated by the use of lesions in the dorsal part of the lateral area of the hypothalamus. These lesions will abolish an increase of salt intake in response to salt deficiency, which produces an increase in salt intake in normal animals. However, animals with the lesions still show overdrinking of hypotonic saline, as expected in animals not deprived of salt and without lesions. This seems to show that there are, in fact, two different phenomena, and that we must be careful to separate them when we are studying salt overdrinking. Tests of the theory of diluted water are vitiated by the use of animals with salt deficiency. The experiments on diluted water then strengthen the supposition that it is afferent messages which shut off thirst. Similar experiments are lacking in the case of hunger, although, as we saw above, such an idea is made very likely by the observation that the simple insertion of food into the stomach produces a prompt satiation of hunger. It looks as if the stomach passes some type of message to the central nervous system, inhibiting the centers in the central nervous system which are affected by physiological deficits. In the case of hunger, however, the messages which are relayed to the central nervous system are unlikely to be neural messages cutting off the afferent input from the stomach. That is, the neural afferent input from the stomach does not alter food intake significantly, as has been shown by Grossman, Cummins, and Ivy (1947). It seems much more likely that the shut-off message produced by the stomach is humoral in nature. It is well known that the upper gastrointestinal tract produces various types of hormones, which then trigger activity in other parts of the tract, stimulating, for example, the secretion of bile. It is not unlikely that the same or similar humoral messages are also employed in order to shut off hunger. If this is the case, we then expect a certain locus in the central nervous system to pick up such humoral messages and to translate them into neural activity, which then inhibits the loci in the nervous system, which are excited by the physiological changes occurring during hunger. We do not at present know what such hormonal messages are, so we cannot use techniques of chemical stimulation to verify such a hypothesis. However, it is known that there are loci in the central nervous system which, when ablated, produce a state of overeating and result in obesity in the animals on which such lesions are inflicted. These loci are to be found in the ventromedial nucleus of the hypothalamus. This was discovered by Hetherington and Ranson (1942) and thoroughly investigated by Teitelbaum and Campbell (1958). It has been found that, immediately upon the occurrence of such a lesion, animals will eat very large quantities of food and display extreme symptoms of hunger. As a result, they grow very obese. Eventually they do not show such signs of extreme hunger, although they remain obese. In fact, their main symptom seems to be that they keep on eating food, although they will not work as hard for it as normal animals, and they will tend to avoid food which has been slightly adulterated, say, by the addition of the bitter tasting substance quinine. However, Teitelbaum and Epstein (1962) have shown that the initial stage of voracious eating can be reinstated by putting the animal on a deprivation schedule, so that it loses all the weight that it initially gained after the operation. After the animal is given access to food again, it will show the same symptoms of voracious overeating initially displayed after the operation. It seems likely that part of the afferent path from the stomach to result in inhibition of hunger has been eliminated in animals lacking the ventromedial hypothalamus. Teitelbaum (1964) has found that animals with ventromedial lesions will not press a lever to give themselves intra-gastric injections of nutrient substance, a task mastered readily by normal rats. Therefore, it seems that some type of reward is mediated through the ventromedial nucleus of the hypothalamus in the normal animal. Teitelbaum also found that, if a sweet taste is coupled with the intragastric injections in the case of the animal with a ventromedial lesion, the animals learn to pump nutrient solution into their stomachs quite readily. This presumably happens because mouth factors do play some part in satiation, as we saw above, and the provision of taste factors in this case restores an afferent message which can then provide at least a small part of afferent inhibition.

Further evidence that the shut-off mechanism in hunger is carried by some type of factor in the blood stream is provided by an experiment conducted by Hervey (1959). Hervey made artificial Siamese twins of two rats by sewing them together in such a way that there could be a slow diffusion of substances from one rat into the other. In this arrange-ment, if one rat had the ventromedial nuclei of the hypothalamus re-moved, its partner would then become exceedingly thin. The rat with hypothalamic lesions would become very obese. This can be interpretated by assuming that as the very obese rat ate, it produced substances which stimulated the ventromedial nuclei of its partner and so inhibited eating in its partner. However, as it had no ventromedial nuclei itself, it kept eating, and of course as it did so, it kept inhibiting the hunger in its partner, which consequently did not eat at all.

So far, we have discussed only the quantitative regulation of eating and drinking. However, it is obvious, when we consider dietary habits, that such habits also have large qualitative components. That is, we must not only look at how much we eat, but also the physiological reasons for choosing what we eat. There are substances which we like, and those which we reject. Animals tend to eat only very specific sub-stances. Although some preferences and aversions are learned, there is evidence that many are, in fact, unlearned. Tinbergen and Perdeck (1950) showed that the newly hatched herring gull chick pecked at things resembling the beak of its parent. The newly hatched herring gull chick not only pecked at exact copies of the adult herring gull beak, but even more strongly at what might be called caricatures of such a beak. Rheingold and Hess (1957) found that similar results could be obtained with newly hatched domestic chicks. In their experiment, the chicks used had never eaten or drunk. The experimenters attempted to find out what evoked the response of drinking in chicks. The drinking response is a highly stereotyped response and thus very easily measurable. So that learning factors could be excluded, each chick was allowed to respond only once. Six different substances were placed around the chick in a semicircle, and the chick was required to choose between these. Among these substances were tap water, blue colored water, red colored water, a circle of polished aluminum, mercury, and a hard translucent plastic which looked like water. It was shown that most of the chicks tried to drink the mercury. Progressively fewer chose plastic, blue water, tap water, aluminum, and red water in that order. Experience with normal drinking for seven days made very little difference to the relative order of preference of the substances. So it seems that chicks are born with what we might call an idea of what to drink, and that mercury comes closer to this idea than does actual water. Fantz (1957) showed that similar factors occur when we use hunger as a motive in domestic chicks. He used various shapes of small objects to see which the chicks preferred to peck at. The results show that chicks without any experience peck much more frequently at round objects than at jagged objects. This is presumably because seeds in nature have rounded rather than jagged shapes, and chicks born with a preference for picking rounded objects are therefore more likely to ingest nutritious cereal. The bias thus serves to eliminate trial-and-error behavior which might be costly in time to the new-born chick, and insures that the chick is much more likely to obtain the nutrition it needs.

Not only are there stimuli which are attractive to the animal, but also those which the animal will reject or avoid. If a bitter substance like quinine is placed in a child's mouth, the child will unhesitatingly reject it by spitting out the contents of the mouth and puckering up his face. A very bitter taste is similarly aversive to other animals such as rats, monkeys, or chickens. Related to such built-in aversions are the consequences of the lesions of the amygdala. It has been noted that animals with lesions of the amygdaloid complex will eat objects such as feces and drink very bitter solutions. It is possible that these structures are in some way related to the neural circuits necessary for the presence of the two aversions that we have discussed above.

## XIII. SPECIFIC HUNGERS

It should be stressed that hunger is not a unitary drive. When animals become deficient in different substances, they seek out foods containing such substances separately. As physiological requirements alter, an animal will also alter the diet that it selects. This ability to select is seemingly very efficient. Davis (1928) has shown that young children are able to select an adequate diet if allowed a free choice. Richter (1942) has shown similar phenomena with rats. In fact, rats that select their own diet actually grow more rapidly than animals offered the standard laboratory diet. Pregnant rats increase their intake of fat, protein, and minerals but lower their intake of sugar. This is due to the different dietary requirement produced by the growth of the fetuses inside the mother. After the young are weaned, the mother selects the same diet as she did before pregnancy (Richter, 1942). There are two ways in which animals have been shown to adapt to differing dietary requirements. The first way is based on built-in mechanisms. It seems that as soon as a certain physiological deficiency arises, certain tastes become attractive to the animal. Epstein and Stellar (1955) were able to demonstrate that a craving for salt arises without any previous experience of the beneficial effects of salt when the animal is short of sodium. However, such built-in preferences, on the basis of stimuli to which the needed substance gives rise, can of course lead to mistakes, especially in the laboratory, where it is often possible to mimic the stimulus properties of the beneficial substances. For example, lithium chloride has a very similar taste to sodium chloride and will therefore be ingested by a rat lacking salt. However, lithium chloride is poisonous, and it is unlikely that such a confusion would occur in nature, because lithium chloride is rare and would probably not have been encountered in nature in the entire history of the rat species. The second way in which an animal can select needed substances is through learning. Certain deficiencies can be made up very quickly; that is, the relief of symptoms due to the deficiencies can be very rapidly reversed. In circumstances such as these, the animal will learn to seek out tastes which are associated with this rapid relief of symptoms. This has been shown, for example, by Harris, Clay, Hargreaves, and Ward (1933). Vitamin B deficient rats were able to discriminate and eat the diet containing vitamin B. However, this ability only appeared if the number of diets among which the animal had to choose was not too large. Presumably, otherwise the association between the relief of symptoms and particular taste would be incorrectly made. It is interesting to note that rats were unable to learn about diets containing vitamins A and D. This is probably the case because relief of A and D vitamin deficiency is somewhat slow. Scott and Verney (1947a, b) also showed that an appetite for the B-complex of vitamins was acquired. They flavored food containing these vitamins with anise, and animals deficient in the B-complex learned to eat food flavored with anise rather than plain food. In a control experiment, Scott and Verney added the vitamin to the plain food rather than the food flavored with anise. In this case, the rats learned to eat the plain food rather than the flavored food. This showed that the original result was not due to the rat's preference for the anise taste.

The results obtained with the selection of beneficial substances such as vitamin A and D stand in contrast to those found with noxious substances. It seems that animals cannot learn to select certain vitamins, because the beneficial consequences occur too long after the relevant substances have been tasted. It has been shown (Garcia, Ervin, & Koelling, 1966; Kimmeldorf & Hunt, 1965; Smith & Morris, 1964) that, if the ingestion of a substance is followed by some aversive event, such as X-ray irradiation, the rat will show an aversion to the taste which preceded the noxious stimulus. Revusky (1968) has shown that consumption of sucrose followed 7 hours later by X-ray irradiation produced an aversion to sucrose in rats.

## XIV. REWARD

So far we have asked what factors lead to and what factors switch off hunger and thirst. Now we must ask what makes eating and drinking rewarding. Hull (1951) believed that it was the reduction of a physiological need which made an activity rewarding. This means that the reversal of the initiating change which leads to hunger and thirst should produce reward. However, there are many facts which argue against such a notion. First is the fact that it often takes a long time for a physiological need to be reversed after an act such as eating. If we consider such activities as mating, it is difficult to see how any physiological need is actually reversed as a result of copulation. However such activities do seem to be rewarding. Not only can the idea that physiological reduction produces reward be questioned on general grounds, but it can also be doubted on experimental evidence. For example, Sheffield and Roby (1950) found that saccharine, a nonnutritive sweet substance, acts as a reward for rats traversing a runway, and that it continues to do so without losing its effectiveness.

In order to escape some of the implausibilities of the notion that physiological need reduction leads to reward, other theories suggest that the simple reduction in the stimuli, to which the physiological need reduction gives rise, functions as reward. The idea is that physiological need states do not cause drive directly, but do so because they generate some type of neural activity. As we saw above, it was thought that they do this to generate some type of peripheral message, which is then carried to the central nervous system. It was suggested that perhaps reduction in these afferent messages, without the necessary reduction in the physiological need which was producing them, functions as a reward. However, even this idea is unlikely. Sheffield, Wulff, and Backer (1951) and Whalen (1961) found that incomplete copulation in male rats served as a reward in a choice situation. The male rat intromits a large number of times before ejaculation takes place. It is, therefore, possible to allow a male rat to intromit, and then take him away from the female before ejaculation takes place. It is unlikely that intromission per se reduces the sexual drive in the rat. In fact, common sense says that no diminution of drive takes place at all due to such a procedure. In spite of this, male rats appeared to find such an activity rewarding. Sheffield, on the basis of these findings, proposes that the actual performance of the consummatory act provides reward. He considers acts of eating, drinking, or copulating in some way rewarding. However, such a view is unlikely, because Miller and Kessen (1954) report that the rat finds simple insertions of food in its stomach rewarding. It chooses the arm of a T maze where a nutrient solution is directly injected into the stomach. Here, the normal act of eating is absent. Furthermore, Deutsch and Jones (1960) have found that rats prefer to drink an equal volume of water to the same volume of hypotonic saline. Here, the total amount of consummatory activity in both cases is the same. However, what determines preference, and so presumably reward value, is in fact the stimulation which arises from the consummatory activity. Hagstrom and Pfaffmann (1959) have shown that there is a correlation between the amount of activity in the chorda tympani nerve part of the afferent taste pathways generated by various sweet solutions and the reward value of these solutions. Relations have also been found by Hutt (1954) and Guttman (1954). We therefore conclude that it is the arrival of certain specific peripheral messages normally generated by the consummatory activity which produces reinforcement or reward.

## REFERENCES

Adolph, E. F. The internal environment and behavior: III Water content. *American Journal of Psychiatry,* 1941, **97,** 1365–73.

Anand, B. K., & Dua, S. Feeding responses induced by electrical stimulation of hypothalamus in cat. *Indian Journal of Medical Research,* 1955, **43,** 113–22.

Anand, B. K., Dua, S., & Shoenberg, K. Hypothalamic control of food intake in cats and monkeys. *Journal of Physiology,* 1955, **127,** 143–52.

Andersson, B., & Larsson, B. Influence of local temperature changes in the preoptic area and rostral hypothalamus on the regulation of food and water intake. *Acta Physiologica Scandinavica,* 1961, **52,** 75–89.

Andersson, B., & McCann, S. M. Drinking, antidiuresis and milk ejection from electrical stimulation from the hypothalamus of goats. *Acta Physiologica Scandinavica*, 1955, **35**, 191–201.

Bare, J. K. The specific hunger for sodium chloride in normal and adrenalectomized white rats. *Journal of Comparative & Physiological Psychology*, 1949, **42**, 242–53.

Bellows, R. T. Time factors in water drinking dogs. *American Journal of Physiology*, 1939, **125**, 87–97.

Berkun, M. M., Kessen, Marion L., & Miller, N. E. Hunger-reducing effects of food by mouth measured by consummatory response. *Journal of Comparative & Physiological Psychology*, 1952, **45**, 550–54.

Brobeck, J. R. Food intake as a mechanism of temperature regulation in rats. *Federation, Proceedings of the American Physiological Society*, 1948, **7**, 13.

Chiang, H. M., & Wilson, W. A. Some tests of the diluted-water hypothesis of saline consumption in rats. *Journal of Comparative & Physiological Psychology*, 1963, **56**, 660–65.

Coons, E. E., Levak, Milena, and Miller, N. E. Lateral hypothalamus: Learning of food-seeking response motivated by electrical stimulation. *Science*, 1965, **150**, 1320–21.

Coons, E. E., & Cruce, J. A. F. Lateral Hypothalamus: Food current intensity in maintaining self-stimulation of hunger. *Science*, 1968, **159**, 117–19.

Darrow, D. C., & Yannet, H. The changes in the distribution of body water accompanying increase and decrease in extracellular electrolyte. *Journal of Clinical Investigation*, 1935, **14**, 226–75.

Davis, C. M. Self-selection of diet by newly weaned infants. *American Journal of Diseases of Children*, 1928, **36**, 651–79.

Delgado, J. M. R., & Anand, B. K. Increase of food intake induced by electrical stimulations of the lateral hypothalamus. *American Journal of Physiology*, 1953, **172**, 162–68.

Deutsch, J. A. A new type of behavior theory. *British Journal of Psychology*, 1953, **44**, 304–17.

Deutsch, J. A., & Blumen, H. L. Counter-injection: A new technique for the analysis of drinking. *Nature*, 1962, **196**, 196–97.

Deutsch, J. A., & Deutsch, D. *Physiological psychology*. Homewood, Illinois: Dorsey Press, 1966 (1st printing), 1967 (2nd printing).

Deutsch, J. A., & Jones, A. D. The water-salt receptor and preference in the rat. *Nature*, 1959, **183**, 1412.

Deutsch, J. A., & Jones, A. D. Diluted water: an explanation of the rat's preference for saline. *Journal of Comparative & Physiological Psychology*, 1960, **53**, 122–27.

Epstein, A. N., & Stellar, E. The control of salt preference in the adrenalectomized rat. *Journal of Comparative & Physiological Psychology*, 1955, **48**, 167–62.

Fantz, R. L. Form preferences in newly hatched chicks. *Journal of Comparative & Physiological Physiology*, 1957, **50**, 422–30.

Fisher, A. E., & Coury, J. N. Cholinergic tracing of a central neural circuit underlying the thirst drive. *Science*, 1962, **137**, 691–93.

Garcia, J., Ervin, F. R., & Koelling, R. A. Learning with prolonged delay of reinforcement. *Psychonomic Science*, 1965, **5**, 121–22.

Gilman, A. The relation between blood osmatic pressure, fluid distribution and voluntary water intake. *American Journal of Physiology*, 1937, **120**, 323–28.

Grossman, M. I., Cummins, C. M., & Ivy, A. C. The effects of insulin on food intake after vagotomy and sympathectomy. *American Journal of Physiology*, 1947, **149**, 100–102.

Grossman, S. P. Eating or drinking elicited by direct adrenergic or cholinergic stimulation of the hypothalamus. *Science*, 1960, **113**, 301–32.

Guttman, N. Equal-reinforcement values for sucrose and glucose solutions compared with equal sweetness values. *Journal of Comparative & Physiological Psychology*, 1954, **47**, 358–61.

Hagstrom, E. C., & Pfaffmann, C. The relative taste effectiveness of different sugars for the rat. *Journal of Comparative & Physiological Psychology*, 1959, **52**, 259–62.

Harris, L. J., Clay, J., Hargreaves, F., & Ward, A. Appetite and choice of diet. The ability of the vitamin B deficient rat to discriminate between diets containing and lacking the vitamin. *Proceedings of the Royal Society, (London)*, Ser. B, 1933, 113–161–90.

Harwood, D., & Vowles, D. M. Forebrain stimulation and feeding behavior in the ring dove (Streptopelia Risoria), *Journal of Comparative & Physiological Psychology*, 1966, **62**, 388–96.

Herberg, L. J. Physiological drives investigated by means of injections into the cerebral ventricles of the rat. *Quarterly Journal of Experimental Psychology*, 1962, **14**, 8–14.

Hervey, G. R. The effects of lesions in the hypothalamus in parabiotic rats. *Journal of Physiology*, 1959, **45**, 336–52.

Hetherington, A. W., & Ranson, S. W. The spontaneous activity and food intake of rats with hypothalamic lesions. *American Journal of Physiology*, 1942, **136**, 609–17.

Hull, C. L. *Essentials of behavior*. New Haven: Yale University Press, 1951. Pp. 6, 12, 137.

Hull, C. L., Livingston, J. R., Rouse, R. O., & Barker, A. N. Time sham, and esophageal feeding as reinforcements. *Journal of Comparative & Physiological Psychology*, 1951, **44**, 236–45.

Hutt, P. J. Rates of bar pressing as a function of quality and quantity of food reward. *Journal of Comparative & Physiological Psychology*, 1954, **47**, 235–39.

Kennedy, G. C. The role of depot fat in the hypothalamic control of food intake in the rat. *Proceedings of the Royal Society*, Ser. B, 1953, **140**, 578–92.

Kimmeldorf, D. J., and Hunt, E. L. *Ionizing radiation: Neural function and behavior*. New York: Academic Press, 1965.

Kohn, M. Satiation of hunger from food injected directly into the stomach versus food ingested by mouth. *Journal of Comparative & Physiological Psychology*, 1951, **44**, 412–22.

McCann, S. M. Effect of hypothalamic lesions on the adrenal cortical response in the rat. *American Journal of Physiology*, 1953, **172**, 265–75.

Mayer, J. Regulation of energy intake and the body weight. The glucostatic theory and the lipostatic hypothesis, *Annals of the New York Academy of Science*, 1955, **63**, 15.

Miller, N. E. Learning and performance motivated by direct stimulation of the brain. In Sheer, D. E. (Ed.), *Electrical stimulation of the brain*. Austin, Texas: University of Texas Press, 1961. Pp. 387–97.

Miller, N. E. Chemical coding of behavior in the brain. *Science*, 1965, **148**, 328–38.

Miller, N. E., & Kessen, M. L. Is distention of the stomach by a balloon rewarding or punishing? *American Psychologist*, 1954, **9**, 430–31.

Miller, N. E., Sampliner, R. I., & Woodrow, P. Thirst-reducing effects of water by stomach fistula vs. water by mouth measured by both a consummatory and an instrumental response. *Journal of Comparative & Physiological Psychology*, 1957, **50**, 1–6.

Mook, D. G. Oral and postingestional determinants of the intake of various solutikons in rats with esophageal fistulas. *Journal of Comparative & Physiological Psychology*, 1963, **56**, 645–59.

Myers, R. E. Interocular transfer of pattern discrimination in cats following section of crossed optic fibers. *Journal of Comparative & Physiological Psychology*, 1955, **48**, 470–74.

Nelson, D. Do rats select more sodium than they need? *Federation Proceedings*, 1947, **6**, 169.

Novin, D. The relation between electrical conductivity of brain tissue and thirst in the rat. *Journal of Comparative & Physiological Psychology*, 1962, **55**, 145–54.

Quartermain, D., and Miller, N. E. Sensory feedback in time response elicited by carbachol in preoptic area of rat. *Journal of Comparative & Physiological Psychology*, 1966, **62**, 350–53.

Quartermain, D., Paolino, R. M., & Miller, N. E. A brief temporal gradient of retrograde amnesia independent of situational change. *Science*, 1965, **149**, 1116–18.

Revusky, S. H. Aversion to sucrose produced by contingent X-irradiation: temporal and dosage parameters. *Journal of Comparative & Physiological Psychology*, 1968, **65**, 17–22.

Rheingold, H. I., and Hess, E. H. The chicks preference for some visual properties of water. *Journal of Comparative & Physiological Psychology*, 1957, **50**, 417.

Richter, C. P. Total self-regulatory functions in animals and human beings. *The Harvey Lecture Series*, 1942 (a), **38**, 63–103.

Robinson, E. A., and Adolph, E. F. Pattern of normal water drinking in dogs. *American Journal Physiology*, 1943, **139**, 39–44.

Routtenberg, A. The effects of chemical stimulation in dorsal midbrain tegmentum on self-stimulation in hypothalamus and septal area. *Psychonomid Science*, 1965, **3**, 41.

Scott, E. M., & Verney, E. L. Self-selection and diet. VI. Appetite for carbohydrates. *Journal of Nutrition*, 1947, **34**, 401–7. (a)

Scott, E. M., & Verney, E. L. Self-selection and diet. VI. The nature of appetites for B vitamins. *Journal of Nutrition*, 1947, **34**, 471–80. (b)

Sheffield, F. D., and Roby, T. B. Reward value of non-nutritive sweet taste. *Journal of Comparative & Physiological Psychology*, 1950, **43**, 471–81.

Sheffield, F. D., Wulff, J. J., & Backer, R. Reward value of copulation without sex drive reduction. *Journal of Comparative & Physiological Psychology*, 1951, **44**, 3–8.

Smith, J. C., & Morris, D. D. The effects of atropine sulphate and physostigmine on the conditioned aversion to saccharin solution with X-rays as the unconditioned stimulus. In T. J. Haley and R. S. Snider (Eds.), *Response of the nervous system to ionizing radiation: Second international symposium.* Boston, Massachusetts: Little, Brown, 1964. Pp. 662–72.

Smith, Moncrieff, & Duffy, M. The effects of intragastric injection of various substances on subsequent bar-pressing. *Journal of Comparative & Physiological Psychology*, 1955, **48**, 387–91.

Stellar, E. The physiology of motivation. *Psychological Review*, 1954, **61**, 5–22.

Stellar, E., & McCleary, R. A. Food preferences as a function of the method of measurement. *American Psychologist*, 1952, **7**, 256.

Stunkard, A. J., Van Itallie, T. B., & Reis, B. B. The mechanism of satiety: effect of glucagon on gastric hunger contractions in man. *Proceedings of the Society for Experimental Biology and Medicine*, 1955, **7**, 256.

Teitelbaum, P. Appetite. *Proceedings of the American Philosophical Society*, 1964, **108**, 464–72.

Teitelbaum, P., & Campbell, B. A. Ingestion patterns in hyperphagic and normal rats. *Journal of Comparative & Physiological Psychology*, 1958, **51**, 135–41.

Teitelbaum, P., & Epstein, A. N. The lateral hypothalamic syndrome. *Psychological Review,* 1962, **69,** 74–90.

Tenen, S. S., & Miller, N. E. Strength of electrical stimulation of lateral hypothalamus, food deprivation and tolerance for quinine in food. *Journal of Comparative & Physiological Psychology,* 1964, **58,** 55–62.

Tinbergen, N., & Perdeck, A. C. On the stimulus situation releasing the begging response in the newly hatched herring gull chick (*Larus argentatus* Pont.). *Behavior,* 1950, **3,** 1–39.

Towbin, E. J. Gastric distension as a factor in the satiation of thirst in esophagostomized dogs. *American Journal of Physiology,* 1949, **159,** 533–41.

Valenstein, E. S., Cox, V. C., & Kakolewski, J. W. Modification of motivated behavior elicited by electrical stimulation of the hypothalamus. *Science,* 1968, **159,** 1119–21.

Whalen, R. E. Effects of mounting without intromission and intromission without ejaculation on sexual behavior and maze learning. *Journal of Comparative & Physiological Psychology,* 1961, **54,** 409–15.

Wiener, N., & Deutsch, J. A. Effects of salt deprivation and strain differences on tests of the diluted water hypothesis. *Journal of Comparative & Physiological Psychology,* 1967, **64,** 400–03.

Williams, D. R., & Teitelbaum, P. Some observations on the starvation resulting from lateral hypothalamic lesions. *Journal of Comparative & Physiological Psychology,* 1959, **52,** 458–65.

Wolf, G. Effect of dorsolateral hypothalamic lesions on sodium appetite elicited by desoxycorticosterone and by acute hyponatremia. *Journal of Comparative & Physiological Psychology,* 1964, **58,** 396–402.

Wyrwicka, W., Dobrzecka, C., & Tarnecki, R. On the instrumental conditioned reaction evoked by electrical stimulation of the hypothalamus. *Science,* 1959, **130,** 336–37.

Wyrwicka, W., & Doty, R. W. Feeding induced in cats by electrical stimulation of the brain stem. *Experimental Brain Research,* 1966, **1,** 152–60.

Young, P. T. Studies of food preference, appetite and dietary habit. IX. Palatability versus appetite as determinants of the critical concentrations of sucrose and sodium chloride. *Comparative Psychological Monograph,* 1949, **19,** 45–74.

# CHAPTER 5  Attentive Processes

NORMAN M. WEINBERGER

Department of Psychobiology
University of California
Irvine, California

Supported by PHS Research Grant #MH 11250 from the National Institute of Mental Health. My thanks to Carol Rumford for outstanding secretarial assistance in the preparation of this chapter.

Bibliographic assistance was received from the UCLA Brain Information Service, which is part of the Neurological Information Network of NINDS and is supported under contract #DHEW PH-43-66-59.

129

## I. INTRODUCTION

The purposes of this chapter are twofold: (1) to offer a point of view for investigating the neural bases of attention; and (2) to evaluate our current understanding of this problem in light of criteria implicit in this viewpoint. Literature cited and discussed has been chosen for illustrative and discursive purposes only, and no attempt has been made to provide a comprehensive review of the area. Recent reviews are available (Lindsley, 1960; Horn, 1965; Worden, 1966; Thompson & Bettinger, 1970). Additionally, Hernandez-Peon provided a summary of his own work on attention shortly before his untimely death (Hernandez-Peon, 1966). Contemporary treatments of attention from a purely behavioral point of view are also recommended to the interested reader (Trabasso & Bower, 1968; Norman, 1969; Moray, 1969).

> "Explain yourself," said the caterpillar to Alice. "I'm afraid I can't," replied Alice "for I'm not quite myself you see."—LEWIS CARROLL, "Alice's Adventures in Wonderland."

It is customary at the outset for the author to explain himself, to say what he means by the title of his offering. Although we may agree that it is at least as important in science as in Wonderland to explain ourselves and to define our terms, still this does not itself ease the task. "Attention" is not quite "itself" you see. White (1964) discusses dozens of common usages of the term. Even within science today, definitions of "attention" vary from descriptive to explanatory, from hypothetical construct to entelechy, and from purely behavioral to predominantly neurophysiological. Faced with a phenomenon so unsure of itself, it might be well to trace in detail the usages of "attention" through the years. Hopefully, this will prove to be unnecessary for the author finds himself lacking enthusiasm at the prospect of performing such a survey. However, it would be helpful to consider some treatments of "attention" before attempting to arrive at a definition well suited to our purposes.

### A. A Brief Historical Perspective

As with many problems of behavior, the roots of attention are old and can be traced explicitly to philosophical approaches to the problem. One vexed question concerned how it was that sensory impressions became known or conscious. Introspection "revealed" that some sense data or ideas were most conspicuous or clear in consciousness at a given moment, although the contents of consciousness could change from one moment to the next. Leibnitz coined the term "apperception" to refer to the processes whereby clarity of consciousness was achieved by the combination of innumerable "petites perceptions." For example, the sound of a wave was considered to be composed of many individual perceptions of the sounds of the drops of water within the wave (Boring, 1957). Thus reified, "apperception" became a convenient vehicle for considering the determinants of sensory clarity, providing the structuralist school of experimental psychology with a "process" which could act upon mental elements to form conscious compounds. The analogies of mental to physical elements and compounds were not accidental.

Further development of the concept of apperception may be traced from Leibnitz to Kant, Herbart, Wundt, and Titchner (Pillsbury, 1908; Boring, 1957). While the details need not concern us, there were two results pertinent to the present discussion. First, "apperception" became used to refer to various things aside from the original definition. To the Leibnitzian conception of apperception as the process of an idea rising into conscious clarity, Herbart added the assimilation of one idea to those previously in consciousness (i.e., the "apperceptive mass"); Wundt additionally considered apperception to be the resultant state of clarity, so that it referred both to the process producing clarity (explanation) and the result of the action of the process (description). As apperception became indistinguishable from "attention" as used in common parlance, the central issues of attention became related to clarity of sensations in consciousness.

> It seems to be beyond question that the problem of attention centers in the fact of sensible clearness . . . (Titchner, 1908).

The relation of attention to clarity was itself unclear, for it could be the state of clarity, or an explanation for or a process producing clarity. Use of the same term in both an explanatory and descriptive manner presaged some of the present confusion with definitions of attention.

In contrast to this view, the "functionalists," notably William James, stressed the selective aspects of attention. One can do no better than let James speak for himself on this matter: "Millions of items of the outward order are present to my senses which never properly enter my experience. Why? Because they have no *interest* for me. *My experience is what I agree to attend to*" (James, 1890).

Paschal (1941) has pointed out that, while James spoke eloquently in attacking clarity and espousing selectivity, it was the structuralists rather than the functionalists who pursued experimentation and carried the day. But having attached itself to consciousness, attention did not adapt well to the behavioristic revolution which toppled consciousness-centered psychology during the second and third decades of this century. Although we may now lament the neglect of attention in behavior theories, perhaps the theorists themselves are not actually culpable, for attention as mental clarity was a dinosaur which simply could not adapt to the ice age of behaviorism. Within the fields of psychiatry and neurophysiology, largely insulated from experimental psychology, the cloak of consciousness of "mental contents" still clings to attention. Thus, we find that attention ". . . involves the selective passage of relevant sensory information to consciousness . . ." (Hernandez-Peon, 1966).

"Attention" was largely disregarded by the behaviorists; those who could not bring themselves to this position sought behavioristic respectability for it by behavioristic redefinition. Thus, according to Dashiell (1928), attention was a form of posturing: "When a person takes up an attitude that will facilitate his response to some particular stimulus or stimuli, that attitude goes by the name of attending or attention." Additional response components of attention were considered to include adjustment and orientation of receptors, respiratory and circulatory changes, and general muscular tension (Paschal, 1941). However, attention so defined played no major role in either subsequent theory or experiment, for even if these bodily adjustments usually accompanied the selective act, they could not be identified with the process of selection itself, but might simply constitute ". . . the physiological concomitants or consequences of . . ." attention (Paschal, 1941). The behavioristic insistence upon operational definitions permitted the resurrection of attention into contemporary experimental psychology under the guise of response-oriented definitions.

While attention as selection rather than mental clarity survived, it was not as James had envisaged. In his classic discussion, James (1890) had distinguished between two general classes of things to which attention could be directed, that is, which could be selected. "Attention . . . is either to (a) objects of sense (sensorial attention); or to (b) ideal or represented objects (intellectual attention)." This division accords well with both common sense and experience, an agreement which is not necessary for valid science but may prove comforting to some readers. Surely, few would disagree that selection may be for stimuli which currently excite receptors, or for the traces or representations of such stimuli, which have been termed "memories," "covert stimuli," or even "ideas," "concepts," "thoughts."

This whole problem area of cognitive processes has developed somewhat independently of stimulus selection. It will not be discussed further in this essay, not because psychology has ignored cognition, which it certainly has not, but rather because the neural basis of "intellectual attention" or selection for thoughts, etc., has hardly been broached. Research has been characterized by concern for a much easier task, that of "sensorial attention" or stimulus selection related to the normal excitation of sensory receptors. It is to this issue which we now direct our "attention," but not without acknowledging that perhaps we are limiting ourselves to no more than 50% of what will be recognized one day as the total subject matter of attention. Fortunately, our coming understanding of sensorial attention should be useful when we come to study the neurology of intellectual attention.

## B. Contemporary History, Western Developments

It is true that experimental psychology largely discarded the appelation "attention" during the late twenties, but the problem of stimulus selection was not dropped as was the problem of clarity in consciousness. Indeed, one of the central issues in classical learning theory may be considered to be indistinguishable from stimulus selection, the "continuity–noncontinuity" issue which arose in the thirties. Briefly, the issue concerned the necessary and sufficient conditions for learning. The extreme S–R or continuity position held that all receptor excitations (stimuli) which were followed by reinforcement (reward or punishment) became associated with the rewarded behavior. Opposed to this view, the "cognitive" theorists or noncontinuity proponents held that not all stimuli which preceded reinforced behavior would become conditioned, but only those which the organism selected (attended). In other words, receptor excitation itself may be a necessary condition for association, but it is not a sufficient condition. (Thus William James may be considered an early cognitive theorist.)

More recently, theories have dealt with this issue in modified form, mainly in the area of discrimination learning (e.g., Riley, 1968). For example, Lawrence (1963) has proposed that organisms learn two habits: (1) an appropriate covert coding response limited to some part of the total stimulus array present; and (2) an association between the coding response and an overt behavioral response. Overt behavior will change as the animal utilizes or shifts stimulus coding responses (Goodwin & Lawrence, 1955). Broadbent's (1958) formulation of "filter theory" in learning is based upon differential stimulus selection. MacIntosh (1965) and Sutherland (1968) have proposed attentional theories of discrimination learning based upon the belief that the more an animal learns about one stimulus dimension, the less it learns about another simultaneously rewarded dimension. Estes' (e.g., 1959) stimulus sampling theory of learning is clearly founded upon the notion that only a portion of the total constellation of stimuli present at any one moment become effectively capable of being associated with responses. More recently, Trabasso and Bower (1968) have approached the learning of simple classifications from the point of view of attention. These few examples demonstrate that "attention" or stimulus selection continues to occupy a place of interest in experimental psychology long after it had been apparently exorcized.

While learning theorists often have been concerned with attention as it relates to the acquisition of new behaviors, many present-day workers who identify themselves with the area of attention are concerned mainly with performance rather than associative factors (e.g., Buckner & McGrath, 1963; Sanders, 1967). This area seems to have been given new life by the second world war, when practical problems of vigilance, such as watch keeping, radar tracking, and signal detection were of crucial importance. Most of the research in this area involves determination of the stimulus variables and their parameters which affect performance of "vigilance" tasks. Subject variables, such as level of arousal have also been studied, and we will return to this particular topic later in another context. More recently, signal detection theory (Green & Swets, 1966) has developed as a reformulation of classical psychophysics and has emerged as a viable approach in its own right.

All of the foregoing approaches are related, in some way, to the more general problem of the limitations of sensory processing, and *in toto* this literature strongly indicates that some stimuli which impinge upon organisms may fail to have any discernable effect upon ongoing or subsequent behavior, or both.

## C. Eastern European Developments

An entirely independent development, initiated by Pavlov (1927), pursued by his successors, and almost completely unknown to Western investigators for three decades, concerns behavior evoked by novel stimuli in general, and the orienting reflex in particular. The work best known in English-speaking countries is that of Sokolov (1960, 1963a, 1963b). There are at least two major contributions of Eastern European investigators to the area which we refer to here as "attentive processes." One concerns the research in interoceptive conditioning, which greatly enlarged our conceptions of what stimuli may be effective in the control of behavior (Razran, 1961). While western investigators concentrated upon the use of external stimuli, usually those exciting the visual and auditory systems, these scientists demonstrated that interoceptive stimuli (e.g., from stomach or bladder distension) could also serve quite well as conditional stimuli. Additionally, demonstrations of interoceptive—interoceptive conditional reflexes indicated that they could serve as both conditioned and unconditioned stimuli (e.g., duodenal distension followed by a change in intestinal pressure). Finally, the establishment of conditional reflexes by any combination of intero- and exteroceptor stimulation as either CS or US once and for all enlarged the scope of stimulus selection investigations and necessarily with it, the candidate brain mechanisms subserving stimulus selection.*

The second important addition to knowledge concerned the complex physiological and behavioral consequences of (a) simply presenting a stimulus to an organism without subsequent reward or punishment, and (b) repeating such stimulus presentation. Most important for the present discussion, the former elicits an orienting reflex (OR); the latter results in its extinction, or in Western terminology, habituation. An important characteristic of the orienting reflex, which consists of a constellation of behavioral and physiological components, is that it takes the same form regardless of the particular nature of the stimulus which elicits its appearance. The major parameter responsible for evocation of the OR appears to be stimulus novelty per se. Magnitude of the OR seems to be a function of relative novelty, as it is extinguished by repeated presentation of the previously novel stimulus. Thus, appearance of the OR may serve as an index that the organism has selected novelty or stimulus change. If not apparent now, the importance of this will become clear later. An equally important aspect of the OR is that the constellation of responses of the organism seems to serve the function of enhancing the ability of the animal to analyze and deal with environmental stimuli.

The Eastern tradition or approach has had a greater influence upon the Western than the reverse. Extensive investigations of the orienting response have been undertaken in the West, much of this work apparently stimulated by the work of Sokolov and his reports of the research of others which were available in English, beginning in the early 60's (Sokolov, 1960, 1963a, 1963b). The topic of habituation itself, however, has had a long and acceptable tradition of investigation in the West quite apart from the Pavlovian developments (e.g., Humphrey, 1933; Harris, 1943). It is the dissection of the overall behavior of an organism

---

* Somato–somato and viscero–viscero associations seem to be formed more easily than somato–viscero and viscero–somato (Garcia & Ervin, 1968).

into its component responses that is particularly characteristic of the Eastern European endeavors.

## D. Summary

The current problem of attention is concerned with stimulus selection. It contains elements of two very different traditions, both of which have become actively concerned with the processes pertinent to the adequate reception of stimuli, and the selection of only some fraction of the total stimulus environment in order to promote adaptive organismic behavior.

The problem to which this chapter is addressed is that of the neural mechanisms which underly such stimulus selection. Before turning to the topic of brain mechanisms in attention, it is absolutely essential first to consider certain behavioral aspects of attention. We will begin with a discussion of the aspects of a stimulus which may serve as the basis for selection, the so-called "objects of attention."

## II. OBJECTS OF SENSORIAL ATTENTION

In the course of designing experiments, investigators choose certain stimuli, often with careful thought given to the particular nature of the stimulus, sometimes not. Aside from the obvious requirements that an organism must have a receptive apparatus appropriate for the stimulus used, and that some experiments require the use of certain stimuli because of the particular question being posed, the experimenter has quite a bit of latitude.

Let us assume that in an avoidance learning experiment the investigator chooses to present as the conditioned stimulus (CS) an intermittent 3000 Hz tone for five seconds through a speaker mounted on the rear wall of the chamber. The experiment is run, and the animals reach some criterion of excellence in avoiding shock. If the experimenter has employed a sensitization, habituation, or differential (nonpunished) stimulus control, then he may conclude safely that animals which consistently performed the required response during the CS and prior to the US learned to avoid shock. However, he may not conclude that animals "selected," "attended," or were "controlled by" a 3000 Hz tone, or even an auditory stimulus, or merely by the onset of any stimulus. This limitation of interpretation is due to the fact that several stimulus categories are confounded in this "straw" experiment; the experimenter does not know which of these are the objects of the animal's attention.

## A. Those Confounded Categories

Let us consider five basic stimulus categories, each of which may vary in intensity and duration:

(1) *presence–absence* (simply a change in the ambient stimulus situation) ;
(2) *sensory modality* (e.g., visual, auditory) ;
(3) *locus*, in space (e.g., portion of the visual field), time, or both;
(4) *modality-specific attribute* (e.g., wavelength, frequency) ;
(5) *pattern*, in space (e.g., shape) or time (e.g., a tune).

The reader is invited to think of others, but these five will do for present purposes.

To return to the avoidance experiment, it was claimed that the experimenter could not determine, solely on the basis of the experiment described, which aspects of the CS controlled the behavior. That is, a subject could have selected: (1) the change in his environment (ambient stimulus situation) caused simply by stimulus onset; (2) the presence of sound; (3) a sound in back of it; (4) a 3000 Hz tone; (5) an intermittent tone pulsed five times per second (i.e., patterned stimulation). In colloquial and anthropomorphic terms, the animal might say (if it could speak), respectively: (1) "Something happened"; (2) "I heard something"; (3) "I heard something behind me"; (4) "I heard a (3000 Hz) tone"; (5) "I heard tone pips." Further, it is possible that the animal could have been responding to the stimulus by also taking into account its intensity and duration. Thus, "I heard a pulsed 3000 Hz tone behind me, of 40 db above ambient noise level, presented five seconds, each pulse of which is 700 msec in duration, separated by 300 msec of tone absence." Of course, this last possibility seems remote, yet note that such specific selection simply corresponds to the CS as it would be specified in the "Methods" section of the experimenter's journal manuscript.

This extreme "straw" experiment was described not as an example of reality so much as to make the simple point that the experimenter may not know the particular basis upon which his subjects respond. Of course, for many purposes this may not be of interest, but for understanding the neural bases of learning (the association between the CS and US) or attention (the processes underlying selection of the CS from among other stimuli), determination of what was selected is essential. If one animal selects stimulus change occasioned by CS onset, while another is controlled by the presence of a tone, and yet a third attends to a patterned change in ambient stimulus conditions, we might expect reasonably that the neural events sought would not be identical for the three animals. Even if a more simple stimulus were used, let us say a single click, stimulus presence or onset (change in ambient stimulus conditions) would be confounded with sensory modality, and also possibly with locus, and modality-specific attributes (because a click contains certain frequency components). Additionally, the click does possess an intensity and duration. Some solutions to the problem of confounding of stimulus categories will be considered specifically in the following section on the measurement of attention. At this point, however, it becomes necessary to adopt a provisional definition of attention. Later, we will attempt to evaluate its utility in understanding the neural bases of stimulus selection.

## B.  A Behavioral Definition of "Attention"

The most commonly used operational definition of attention originated with Skinner (1953) and may be summarized as follows: *An animal is considered to attend to a stimulus dimension if changing that stimulus dimension also changes its behavior.* If changing the dimension does not change the behavior, we consider that the animal did not attend the dimension.* It is in this sense that one speaks of "stimulus control" of behavior. ("Stimulus control" is considered to be equivalent to "the animal selects" or "attends to" the stimulus.)

As an example, suppose a rat is rewarded for pressing a bar in the presence of a 3000 Hz tone and is trained to a high level of correct performance. We may determine whether the dimension of audio frequency was selected (attended) by changing it to 500 Hz, or on different trials to use a range of different frequencies above and below 3000 Hz. If the performance does not change when the new frequencies are present, then bar-pressing was not controlled by tonal frequency (but perhaps, although not definitely, by the presence of sound). If the behavior does change, preferably systematically so that the highest rates of responding occur during stimulation closest to 3000 Hz, we consider that the rat is attending to frequency. Of course, this definition of attention is not limited to dimensions or parameters within a modality. It can apply equally well to any of the five categories listed above, plus their combinations and permutations involving intensity and duration. In the case above, we might substitute a light for the tone to determine whether

---

* Of course, this definition applies only to situations in which the subject is capable of (1) receiving the stimuli in question and (2) responding.

the rat was attending to mere presence of a stimulus or to the auditory modality.

## C. Breadth of Selection

To return to the five major stimulus categories listed above, it would seem that they are arranged in a hierarchy, from stimulus presence to stimulus pattern. Thus attending to a visual pattern, for example a checkerboard, might also imply knowledge of or attention to the fact that the stimulus is: (1) present, (2) visual, (3) located in a particular part of the visual field, (4) black and red, and perhaps even that it is brightly illuminated (intensity) and remains in view as long as gaze is continued (duration).

However, we cannot assume that all of these categories are attended to, in the sense that they may not control behavior, even though they are "noticed." For example, Trabasso and Bower (1968) presented subjects with cards which contained four letters in a row. The task was to sort the cards into two piles. The relevant category was the second letter on the card (either L or B). Letters in the other positions (1st, 3rd, 4th) were randomly paired with L and B. Following learning, additional trials were given in which the letter in the fourth position was redundant with the relevant letter in the second position (e.g., R with L, W with B); during these overtraining trials, the subjects were required to speak the letters as they sorted the cards (correctly into the L and B piles). Following this, tests were given in which the L and B were replaced by blanks. None of the subjects were able to sort correctly into two piles (R and W), although clearly they had noticed these letters because they had recited the letters previously and, further, had recited R only following L, and B only following W. Thus, seeing, recognizing, and even repeating the letters did not ensure that these letters were selected, that is, acquired stimulus control over sorting, even though they were always paired with the letters (L and B) which did exert such control.

This clever differentiation between noticing and attending points up the risk of assuming that knowledge of a stimulus category (even when paired with reward) guarantees its selection. A reasonable alternative to this assumption is to consider "breadth of selection" to be an empirical question, perhaps one that may have to be answered for each experimental situation employed. This is the position taken by Bruner, Matter, and Papanek (1955) in their consideration of the "continuity–noncontinuity" controversy which was mentioned above.

As a demonstration of the validity of this empiricist position, these authors investigated the effects of deprivation level and amount of original training upon the acquisition of single-alteration behavior during performance of a black–white discrimination problem. Rats deprived of food for either 12 or 36 hours underwent discrimination training in an apparatus consisting of four pairs of doors successively arranged between the start and goal boxes. During initial training, the brightness cues were placed on the doors randomly with regard to their position (left or right), but following either 30 or 100 training trials, the brightness cues were alternated so that errorless behavior on a trial consisted not only of selecting the correct brightness cue (e.g., black) but also of exhibiting single-alternation behavior through the four pairs of doors (e.g., right–left–right–left). Animals were then tested for learning of the single alternation (i.e., attention to position) by using gray cue cards to eliminate the brightness dimension. The results indicated that animals receiving 30 training trials and 12 hours of deprivation learned most about single alternation; those receiving overtraining (100 trials) and running under the high deprivation level (36 hours) learned the least. Overall, overtraining retarded acquisition of single alternation to a greater extent than did high deprivation. The importance of this study, however, is not in comparing the effects of deprivation and amount of training, but rather the demonstration that the degree of selection of the position cue could be manipulated. Breadth of selection can be investigated experimentally and may depend upon the particular parameters and variables employed in a study. The concept of "breadth of attention," often considered "narrowed attention," continues to receive attention in experimental psychology (Wachtel, 1967) and approaches to behavioral pathology (Callaway & Stone, 1960).

In addition to the situational variables discussed above which may modulate the breadth of stimulus selection, animals may exhibit preferences for certain stimulus categories which are relatively insensitive to experimental manipulation. Familiar examples within the ethological literature include so-called "sign stimuli" or "releasers" which typically elicit a particular behavior. A well-known example is the red dot on the herring gull's beak which evokes gaping in the young. Stimulus preferences which are less specific regarding the detailed nature of the stimulus are also found; these seem to be less closely tied to a specific response or behavior pattern also. Thus, pigeons apparently will select color cues, if available, in preference to orientation cues, even though both are always present and rewarded (Newman & Benefield, 1968). Cats seem to have a strong preference for auditory stimuli. Jane, Masterson, and Diamond (1965) found that they selected auditory rather than redundant visual cues and continued to do so even after extensive lesions of the auditory system.

The category or dimension preferred need not be immutable but can change according to the nature of the task which confronts the animal. Dobrzecka, Szwejkowska, and Kornorski (1966) provided dogs with the opportunity to select either the "quality" of an auditory CS (buzzer vs. metronome) or the direction of its source (in front or behind) in a differential conditioning situation. When the task involved responding with the right leg to one stimulus and with the left to another, they chose directional cues and exhibited very poor learning when only quality cues were available. However, when the task involved responding to one stimulus and withholding response to the second stimulus, they generally selected quality cues.

Of course we must exclude from this discussion those stimulus preferences which are based solely upon sensory receptor or system limitations that preclude the possibility of behaving to other stimuli. Thus, while the male gypsy moth can detect an unmated female's scent over long distances, he can smell little or nothing else, for his olfactory receptive apparatus is sensitive only to the molecules which she secretes. He has, in other words, a "virgin gypsy moth detector," but hardly an olfactory system in the common sense of the term. Stimulus selection based upon such specialized mechanisms is interesting in its own right, but we should recall that at the outset we restricted considerations of attention to instances in which only a part of the total *potential stimuli* present are selected.

### D. Evidence for the Selection of Stimulus Categories

Up to this point, we have assumed tacitly that animals may indeed attend to the stimulus categories delineated: (1) presence–absence, (2) modality, (3) locus, (4) modality dimension, (5) pattern. But simply enumerating categories does not demonstrate selection for "the presence of an intermittent increase in ambient stimulus levels on my right" or "a three-second decrease in red light above me coincident with taps on my right great toe." All possible combinations have not, in all probability, been investigated; it would not be surprising if such highly specific selection were demonstrable after suitable training. However, all this is a bit beside the point. It is necessary simply to point out that animals can and may select some stimulus categories which are usually overlooked by an experimenter.

The most widely used categories are probably: (3) locus (e.g., left or right stimulus card), (4) modality dimension (e.g., color), (5) pattern within a modality (e.g., shape) and intensity (e.g., brightness). These have been used so extensively that they need no further support here. A few examples of the "neglected" categories will suffice at least to entice the reader to consider them; whether that consideration be acceptance or challenge to their claim as controllers of behavior is less important.

Pattern, irrespective of modality, may control the avoidance behavior of mice (Oliverio & Bovet, 1969). DBA/2J mice were trained in a shuttlebox with a pulsed tone (3000 Hz at 3 pulses per second) as CS. Following acquisition, the mice were divided into two groups matched for acquisition rate, and a light was substituted for the pulsed tone. For one group, the light was steady, while for the other, it was pulsed at 3 per second. The mice receiving steady illumination failed to avoid, while those receiving illumination pulsed at the rate of the original tone CS continued to avoid at a high level, suggesting that pattern (of 3 per second stimulation) independent of modality controlled the avoidance behavior.[*]

Selection for modality was shown in this same study, with other groups of mice. Animals trained with a steady tone as the CS failed to show any transfer when tested with a steady light. That is, the animals selected or attended to the auditory modality, not simply to an increase in ambient stimulus conditions due to tone or light onset. It is intriguing to compare this with the previous finding of attention to a pattern without regard for modality.

Of the five major categories, the "simplest" remains attention to a change in ambient stimulation. We have noted previously that the presentation of any stimulus confounds modality with stimulus onset. These can be disentangled by holding modality constant and manipulating stimulus onset and offset. Weinberger and Lindsley (1965) tested behavioral and EEG arousal in sleeping cats and found arousal to both stimulus onset (clicks or white noise) on a background of quiet, and to stimulus offset (3 sec interruption of stimulation) on a background of 16 hours of stimulus presentation (clicks or white noise) (See also Rowland, 1957). Habituation of EEG arousal with aperiodically presented trials followed the same rate for both the onset and offset condi-

---

[*] However, these data may be interpreted differently. Although the mice were supposedly trained in darkness, the effects of stimulus change (light onset) were confounded with pattern. It is possible that a pulsed novel stimulus caused the animals to run. This issue would be clarified by use of a complete factoral design which analyzes the effects of training sequence, modality, pattern, and novelty.

tions. Thus behavioral and EEG arousal were controlled by change (presence or absence) in the ambient stimulus situation.

Thompson (1959a) found that the amount of transfer of an avoidance response from a light to a tone depended upon the amount of training with the light as the CS. Cats trained to the level of 55% correct showed greater selection of the tone than those trained to the 90% level, which exhibited none. Such cross-modality transfer may be interpreted as selection of stimulus onset or change in ambient conditions. These results also indicate that selection strategy may change as a function of amount of experience or level of performance; selection for change was replaced by selection for modality by the time the 90% criterion was achieved. (See also Bruner, Matter, & Papanek, 1955.)

Change in ambient conditions, rather than audio frequency, may be controlling so-called frequency discrimination in cats under some circumstances. Thompson (1959b) compared three methods of frequency discrimination training: (1) "Absolute," in which shock avoidance was contingent upon responding to a 1500 Hz tone on a background of silence. Discrimination was examined by also presenting a nonpunished 1000 Hz stimulus ("negative stimulus") on some trials. (2) "Alternation," in which the CS consisted of alternating 1500 and 1000 Hz tone pips, and the negative stimulus was 1000 Hz tone pips alone. (3) "Repetitive," in which the background consisted of continuous 1000 Hz pips, and the CS was a period of change to alternating 1000 and 1500 Hz pips. The cats were required to reach a criterion of correct responses to the CS, and for the first two methods also to refrain from responding to the negative stimulus. Attainment of the criterion was most rapid for the repetitive condition, intermediate for the alternation condition, and very slow for the absolute condition in which differential behavior to the two stimuli required twice the number for the alternation and ten times as many trials as the repetitive condition.

L. M. Kitzes (personal communication) has pointed out that the repetitive condition requires only that the animals detect a change in ambient conditions and does not in itself demonstrate identification of specific frequencies. The absolute condition does demand such identification or recognition and was characterized by prolonged responding to both the negative and positive stimuli, a result consonant with attention to change. The alternation procedure requires differentiating a change also, but not simply a change from the background, because the negative stimulus also represented the same patterned change from ambient levels; rather it required a detection of the fact that the CS consisted of some change in frequency. These results suggest that learning to attend to change ("detection") may be easier than attending to a modality dimension ("recognition"), and that the category of change in ambient conditions might warrant further experimental and theoretical consideration.

Stimulus duration has received some consideration as a category for selection. Sokolov (1963b) found that a tone presented repeatedly for a fixed duration will lose its ability to elicit an orienting reflex (see below), but either lengthening or shortening the duration on a later test trial can reinstitute the reflex, indicating that the subjects were selecting for duration of the stimulus. More direct demonstrations of duration discrimination have been reported (Creelman, 1962). The phenomenon of temporal conditioning may be considered a demonstration of selection for duration, although this would involve selection for the duration of intertrial intervals without the presence of a specific exteroceptive stimulus. The paradigm simply involves periodic and regular presentation of an unconditional stimulus (e.g., shock) without a prior CS. Temporal conditioning is in evidence when a conditional response (CR) occurs regularly just prior to US onset. Salivation (Pavlov, 1927) and galvanic skin response (Lockhart, 1966) have shown temporal conditioning in modified classical conditioning paradigms. Shock avoidance behavior maintained by the well-known Sidman avoidance schedule is a clear demonstration that animals can attend to or select "time," or the duration between otherwise unsignalled shocks in an instrumental conditioning situation also. We might, then, enlarge our consideration of the category of duration of a stimulus to include duration of either the presence or absence of a stimulus.

### E. Novelty

There remains one last basis for stimulus selection to be discussed in this chapter: "novelty." Without further explaining or justifying the choice of this term, let us simply regard attention to novelty as selection for stimulation which is different from expected stimulation.* Properly speaking, it is not a property of stimuli as are the other categories. Novelty has been studied most extensively in investigating the effects of: (1) simply presenting a stimulus without subsequent reward or punishment, and (2) repeating this stimulus presentation at intervals several times. Initial presentation produces an orienting reflex (OR) (Pavlov, 1927) which is comprised of a constellation of responses including cere-

---

* See Thompson and Bettinger (1970) for a more detailed discussion of the definition of "novelty."

bral vasodilation and peripheral vasoconstriction, pupillary dilation, an interruption in respiration, slowed heart rate (Graham & Clifton, 1966), EEG desynchronization, and skeletal muscle changes which may include orientation or searching for the stimulus source (e.g., head turning, sniffing, etc.) (Sokolov, 1963a, 1963b). The nature of the OR is not dependent upon the particular stimulus change which elicits its appearance; its constellation of components is essentially the same whenever it is evoked. Repeated stimulus presentation leads to a decrease in the vigor or magnitude of these responses until none are evoked at all ("extinction" or "habituation" of the OR). Habituation has been shown to be neither a function of loss of sensory capacity to process the stimulus (e.g., adaptation) not inability to respond (e.g., muscular fatigue). These and other parametric characteristics of habituation have been extensively investigated and analyzed recently (Thompson and Spencer, 1966) and need not be discussed further here. During the course of habituation, or after it is seemingly complete, substitution of a different stimulus for that which has been repeatedly presented may reinstitute the OR. In this sense, occurrence of an OR is an index of attention to change, particularly a change from the expected to the unexpected.

Selection for novelty cuts across all of the categories and dimensions previously discussed. That is, no matter how complex the stimulus, a change in any single stimulus category, dimension, or component could elicit an OR providing that an organism had experienced that stimulus sufficiently often to consider such a change to be "novel." The amount of prior exposure and the degree of change of the several components of the stimulus necessary to elicit an OR cannot be specified *a priori,* but are empirical questions. Note then, that elicitation of an OR can be used as an index of selection for change, but that the change need not be the type of change discussed previously, that is, change in level of ambient stimulation, but might include change in any component of a stimulus which is not continually present, but present aperiodically. The OR provides a convenient index of selection. Let us now consider other ways to measure attention.

## III. THE MEASUREMENT OF ATTENTION

In discussing the categories of stimulus selection, mention was made of some techniques used to determine which aspects of a stimulus control behavior. In this section, we will consider these more formally, with emphasis upon the nature of the technique and its limitations, if any. The treatment here must be brief. Several recent works can be consulted for details of technique as well as theoretical behavioral issues (Mostovsky, 1965; Honig, 1966; Gilbert & Sutherland, 1969).

## A. Receptor Orientation

If queried, most people would assert that they know whether someone is attentive by his general posture, facial expression, and head and eye orientation. These criteria have found wide use also in the laboratory (e.g., Kaada & Bruland, 1960). They are extensively employed in human neonatal and nonhuman studies. We have previously discussed the orienting reflex and noted that many workers consider receptor orientation to be a somatic component of the OR. Such orientation may be investigated more casually. In a classic study, Hernandez-Peon, Scherrer, and Jouvet (1956) attempted to investigate neural processing of sensory stimuli under two conditions: when a cat was visually attentive and when it was not. Visual attention was produced by placing mice in a jar in front of the cat, and it was assumed that the cat was visually attentive while it was looking at the mice. However, these workers also assumed that the cat was attentive only to the visual modality and was not selecting auditory, olfactory, or other input. Horn (1965) has pointed out that this assumption is questionable because the cat may have also been listening for the mouse and attempting to detect its odor. This seems plausible, particularly because the mice enclosed in the jar presumably provided neither their normal auditory nor olfactory cues. Nevertheless, we would agree that receptor orientation (ordinarily eye orientation in experimental studies) is necessary for effective reception of stimulation. Recording of pupillary reflections (Kagan & Lewis, 1965; Salapatek, 1968) provides additional elegance to this method.

We may question, however, whether receptor orientation guarantees selection for the stimulus that is allegedly attended. Mackworth, Kaplan, and Metlay (1964) reported failures to detect changes in the movement of a revolving pointer during visual fixation of a target. Similar findings were reported by Baker (1963). Additionally, it would be difficult to explain selective listening to one voice in a crowd ("cocktail party phenomenon") on the basis of receptor orientation, for clearly more than one voice is heard, although only one may be attended. It would seem that while receptor orientation may sometimes provide an index that something is being selected, it cannot by itself tell us what is being selected. Wundt (1894) claimed that he could shift his attention to an object in his peripheral visual field without moving his eyes; he was probably correct.

## B. The Observing Response

Simply viewing an animal's posture or facial expression in order to determine whether and to what he is attending has the drawback of requiring inference on the part of the observer, and may be too sensitive to observer bias. An alternative consists of requiring the animal to perform a discrete response in order to be able to view a discriminative stimulus. Thus Wyckoff (1952) trained pigeons to press a treadle in order to produce either a red or green light, which served as cues regarding which of two reward contingencies were in effect. The treadle press constituted an objective index of observing behavior, and it provided a stimulus display which in turn controlled the pigeon's pecking behavior. Butler (1953) demonstrated that monkeys would open a viewing window in order to see various objects or parts of the laboratory. Walker (1969) has shown that rats will emit the same number of observing responses (putting their heads through a hole) when permitted to view stimuli of both a simple and complex nature; however, the duration of each observing response was greater for the complex stimulus. Eye movements themselves rather than an arbitrary skeletal motor response may be used as observing response (Schroeder and Holland, 1968). The duration of somesthetic contact with an object (manipulation) has also been used (Hutt & Hutt, 1964).

In these and other experiments, it can be shown that removal of the discriminative stimulus results in loss of the observing response, which while not surprising does indicate that the discriminative stimulus did control the observing behavior. The number, rate, and duration of observing responses thus can serve as an objective index of attention. This is not to say, however, that all attentive behavior includes an overt observing response. For example, particular aspects of stimuli which are presented tachistoscopically can be selected, but the duration of stimulus exposure is too short to permit overt observing responses, including any effective eye movements. (See also Egeth, 1967).

## C. Autonomic Nervous System Responses

In addition to or instead of measurement of striated muscle behavior, investigators commonly record ANS effector action. Heart rate, respiration, and the galvanic skin response are widely used, particularly in studies of habituation of the orienting reflex (e.g., Scholander, 1960; Kagan & Rosman, 1964; Stechler, Bradford, & Levy, 1966). As components of the OR, these measures may be sensitive to a change in any stimulus parameter as well as to stimulus onset itself. Goodman (1969) studying the salamander *Necturus* found that respiration and heart rate were sensitive to novel stimuli, exhibited habituation (as expected), and additionally served as an index of the state of arousal of the animals; under some circumstances, he was able to predict the amplitude of the responses of the cardiac and respiratory systems to a shadow stimulus by noting their steady-state variability prior to trial onset.

It has been pointed out by Hebb (1958) that stimuli serve both cue and arousal functions. This distinction suggests that ANS measures provide information about the state of the organism directly, and indirectly tell us about what it is selecting by revealing that a stimulus has caused a state change. Thus, if following habituation of the OR to a 5000-Hz tone, presentation of a 4995-Hz tone elicits OR (dishabituation), or only some of its components (e.g., slight changes in respiration), we might conclude that auditory frequency was the category selected.

### D. Transfer Tests

The most commonly used indices of the categories or dimensions to which an animal is attending can be grouped under the rubric of "transfer tests." These are characterized by an initial training period with stimulus A (or stimulus complex A) followed at a later time by presentation and testing with stimulus B to determine the extent to which the behavior originally controlled by A is also controlled by B, that is, the degree of transfer from A to B. Thus, although the experimenter does not know the exact nature of the stimuli selected at the time of initial training, he can find out by using transfer tests at a later date.

One variant of this technique involves training on dimension A to some criterion of correct performance, and then adding a second dimension B which is redundant with A, and therefore always correlated with reward when selection of A is rewarded. Transfer is tested by presenting B in the absence of A. The question asked is "To what extent does an animal learn about cue B when it is attending to cue A?" This is a variant of the old continuity–discontinuity controversy previously discussed and comes down to asking whether or not all receptor excitations (stimuli) which are paired with reward come to be associated with the rewarded behavior. This is not the correct place further to discuss the issues involved, which have been summarized by Riley

(1968). This particular technique was used in the studies cited previously by Bruner *et al.* (1955) and Trabasso and Bower (1968).

A second technique involves presenting a stimulus complex which consists of components that can be separated later. For example, the training situation may involve pairing a white horizontal rectangle (rewarded) with a black vertical rectangle (not rewarded). Following learning to some criterion of correct performance, a second task is given in which brightness and orientation are unconfounded. The white horizontal rectangle, still rewarded, may be paired with a black horizontal rectangle. A high level of performance (i.e., continued responding to the white horizontal rectangle) indicates that brightness was originally selected; poor performance, that stimulus orientation was chosen. Similar information may of course be gained by rewarding selection of a black horizontal rectangle paired with a black vertical rectangle. This type of test is particularly helpful in intramodality selection situations, in which noting receptor orientation would provide no information about the particular stimulus dimension selected.

Intramodality selection has been studied in conditioning studies using a complex CS such as simultaneous light and sound. Following establishment of the conditioned response (CR), test trials on which either the light or sound is presented are used to establish the probability of each eliciting the CR. Pavlov (1927) originated this technique, demonstrating the prepotency of auditory over visual stimuli in dogs. Neff and Diamond (1958) found similar results for cats using the same general design in an instrumental situation.

The final transfer technique mentioned here is that of determining the gradient of stimulus generalization. Briefly, initial training may be given with one value of a stimulus dimension (e.g., frequency). Later, testing is ordinarily performed during extinction to the original stimulus A, but test trials are interspersed which have as the stimulus various values of the dimension being tested. The probability of response to an array of values on either side of stimulus A is calculated. A sharp gradient (with its peak at A) is taken to indicate that A was attended. A flat gradient, that is, one on which the probability of response is essentially the same for all stimuli on the dimension (including A), indicates a failure to attend to A and demonstrates that the dimension containing A was not selected. The purpose of generating the gradient during extinction is to preclude altering the response probabilities to the test stimulus either by rewarding or not rewarding responses to them.

In an interesting variant of the standard method, Heinemann, Chase, and Mandell (1968) were able to obtain two very different generalization gradients for the same stimulus dimension within the same testing session. Pigeons were trained to discriminate between two tones of different frequency in the presence of red light. However tone was irrelevant to the schedule of reward when a green light was present. Later testing revealed a sharp gradient of generalization for frequency during red light trials, demonstrating control or attention to frequency; gradients generated during green light trials were flat, indicating, as expected, that frequency was not attended (did not control behavior) under this condition. Blough (1969) has shown the same type of effect, across the visual and auditory modalities rather than within a single modality.

There is yet another aspect of the problem: cue switching during learning. If two cues are highly correlated with each other and the reward or punishment, an animal may utilize one cue early in learning and switch to the other later. Phillips (1968) has found that rats learning a simultaneous brightness discrimination will respond to the brightness cue initially but often switch to olfactory cues which are deposited in the course of the experiment. (Careful design can eliminate this particular problem.) If such switching occurs between stimulus parameters other than modality, the task of determining what was selected by using post acquisition transfer tests is not only unmanageable but also irrelevant to the early training.


E. Vigilance Tasks


These tasks are not concerned ordinarily with examining the categories or dimensions selected. Rather, the stimulus in question is shown to the subjects, and they are pre-instructed (or trained) simply to detect the presence of the stimulus, which will be presented aperiodically. The stimulus may consist of a change in a continuous series of stimuli (continuous performance task) such as detection of an odd movement of a clock hand (Jerison, Pickett, & Stenson, 1965), an "X" in a series of other letters (Mirsky, Primac, & Bates, 1959), or a stimulus embedded in background noise (Deese, 1951). The "twenty dials test" (Broadbent, 1958) requires continuous scanning of all dials to detect a slight change in the position of one dial hand, so that while the subject knows the nature of the signal he must detect, he does not know where it will appear. These and similar tasks may also demand the fastest possible response time, increasing the difficulty for the subjects and providing an additional measure of attention (Fedio, Mirsky, Smith, & Perry, 1961). Detection of stimuli of unknown displayed position may be varied in difficulty also by tachistoscopic display for varying durations (Kornetsky, Mirsky, Kessler, & Dorff, 1959).

Tracking tests, such as visual following (eye movements) or holding a pointer on an irregularly moving target, require continuous detection of and responding to continuous stimuli (Siddall & Anderson, 1955). Stimulus counting makes similar demands on the subject. However, Spong, Haider, and Lindsley (1965), employing flash or click counting, suggest that this actually causes distraction. The rate of stimulus presentation in these situations may be of great importance. Slow presentation rates may permit the subject to select other aspects of his environment, particularly because these task situations are usually uninteresting.

Selective listening experiments seem to fall into the category of tracking tasks, particularly if "shadowing" is required. In such a situation, different messages are presented (dichotically) to the two ears, the subject being instructed to attend to only one. An index of successful stimulus selection is obtained by requiring repetition of the instructed message (shadowing) (Cherry, 1953). A variant of this task, termed "division of attention," involves both shadowing and detection. The subject is required to shadow a message to one ear while detecting a predetermined word or phrase in a message simultaneously presented to the other unattended ear (Broadbent & Gregory, 1963). Treisman and Geffen (1967) has performed several ingenious experiments which indicate that failure to respond to signal stimuli in the unattended ear is due neither to motor limitations, nor, in all probability, to receptor blockade. Studies of selective listening have been almost exclusively applied to humans; however, Kaas, Axelrod, and Diamond, 1967) recently used a clever design with tone patterns to demonstrate selective listening in the cat. We may expect to see further studies in nonhumans using similar techniques.

## F. Summary

It should be clear from the foregoing discussion that "attention" is measured in many ways. General receptor orientation is less sensitive than other methods, for it does not guarantee that selection is taking place, nor does it indicate which particular aspects of a stimulus are being selected. Transfer tests in discrimination learning do provide such information, although at some time following the attentive behavior in question. Additionally, vigilance, tracking, and selective listening techniques permit continual assessment of stimulus selection.

## IV. THE UTILITY OF THE CONSTRUCT "ATTENTION"

Having considered what may be selected and how such selection can be indexed, we return to the problem of the concept of "attention" itself. Our goal is to understand stimulus selection. To what extent, if any, are we assisted by invoking "attention?" The answer may depend upon our usage of this term.

### A. Descriptive Usage

Up to this point, we have adopted the standard behavioral definition of attention as equivalent to stimulus control of behavior; that is, an animal attends a stimulus (dimension or category) if changing that stimulus also changes the animal's behavior. Used in this way, as merely a convenient description of situations in which a certain stimulus controls a given behavior, "attention" has no surplus meaning or referent. "There is no attention; it is but a name for the fact of selection" (Paschal, 1941). However, we may ask whether this simple and straightforward use of "attention" covers all situations of stimulus selection. What about the negative case, that is, situations in which an animal gives no response at all to the presentation of a stimulus? If animals can selectively respond to some stimuli, can they not also selectively ignore (not respond) to other stimuli?

Instances of specific selection *against* stimuli can be cited easily, but one will suffice for present purposes. In a now classic study, Sharpless and Jasper (1956) aperiodically but repeatedly presented a brief tone (e.g., 1 kHz) to sleeping cats. Initially this stimulus produced an orienting response; the authors quantified one aspect of this OR, the duration of electrocortical (ECoG) desynchronization or "arousal." The duration of ECoG desynchronization progressively decreased with repeated trials (i.e., habituated), until presentation of the tone evoked no response at all. The failure to respond was selective however; it was not due to deepening sleep or inability of respond, for when the cats were probed with novel stimuli (e.g., 5 kHz or touch) they promptly exhibited ECoG desynchronization. Yet when the original stimulus was again presented, there was no response. This is a rather clear example of *selective nonresponding*. In fact, we may consider all examples of *bona fide* habituation of behavior to be demonstrations of stimulus selective nonresponding, that is, of attention.

However, all instances of failure to respond to a stimulus are not necessarily instances of selective nonresponding. For example, contrast the above example with a simple signal detection situation in which the subject is instructed to press a button upon detecting a randomly presented tone. An error of omission is often considered to be an instance of lack of attention. However, few workers would consider these two cases to be identical although, in both cases, stimulus presentation did not evoke a response. In the first situation, the evidence indicates that the cats must have perceived the repeated tone, that is, analyzed that stimulus, and on the basis of accruing experience with that singularly insignificant and uninteresting stimulus, decided to not respond. We ordinarily do not attribute this same chain of internal events to the subject who fails to detect a signal.

A child who fails to answer a call to the dinner table while watching television may have either understood the call and decided not to respond, or could have "missed the signal." Thus, conceptually there are two reasons why the stimulus failed to evoke a response. Operationally, two sets of subsequent events also may differentiate between these reasons. If the parent believes that the child merely missed the call, a reprimand may be in order; if "willful disobedience" is the reason, sterner measures are likely to be instituted. The difference between a reprimand and a spanking is quite real; this author maintains that the difference between selective and nonselective nonresponding is equally real.*

Our behavioral definition of attention does not differentiate between these two cases at the time the stimulus is presented. Failure of the child to appear at the dinner table does not differentiate "willful" from "nonwillful disobedience." Fortunately, the definition of attention as stimulus control is still valid if we can differentiate between these two at a later time. In the case of the sleeping cats, presentation of novel "probe" stimuli revealed selection against the original tone. In the case of the human observer, continued testing would have resulted in correct responses on most trials, and the experimenter would assume that the few instances of missed signals were not "willful," i.e., attention to the signals coupled with a specific decision not to respond.

In summary, the definition of attention as stimulus control of behavior seems to be adequate as a description of all instances of stimulus selection. Our previous consideration of the ways stimulus selection is indexed revealed that in the case of response to a stimulus, it may be necessary

---

* The only problem with this distinction is the cumbersome terminology which it entails.

to unconfound stimulus categories or dimensions at a later time, in order to determine precisely what stimulus aspects were selected. Our present consideration of instances of absence of responding shows that attention to a stimulus need not imply a behavioral response to that stimulus. Furthermore, in the case of absence of a response, the experimenter must at a later time determine: first, whether the subject was attending the stimulus and if attention is established; second (as in the case of responding to a stimulus), what specific stimulus attribute(s) were selected.

A purely behavioral definition of attention precludes the possibility of always determining whether and to what an animal is attending at the moment in time of interest, that is, when the selection is being made. Horn (1965) has offered a definition which avoids this problem. "An organism is said to attend to a stimulus when it makes some behavior or *perceptual response* to that stimulus" (italics this author's). Presumably, the perceptual response is present at the time of selection, and if it could be directly recorded, we could dispense with later transfer tests and other indirect behavioral methods. Our assumption here is that there are central nervous system processes which underly the processes of stimulus selection and which occur during or shortly after original stimulus presentation. These assumptions do not appear objectionable even to workers who are not as physiologically oriented as Horn. Thus Jerison (1968), well known for his behavioral research in the field of vigilance and signal detection, considers observing responses to be both psychophysical (behavioral) and physiological events. We may interpret Jerison's "physiological observing responses" to be similar or identical to Horn's "perceptual responses." Naturally, we would be interested in the relationships between perceptual and behavioral responses, but it would seem that the former are necessary for the latter, not the converse. If behavioral responses are considered to be the end product of an interaction between a stimulus and particular CNS events (e.g., "perceptual responses"), then they are less sensitive indices of stimulus selection than those CNS events. Direct observation or measurement of the CNS processes in question might then provide an accurate description of what is being attended or selected at the time such selection is taking place. We will return to this question later.

## B. Explanatory Usage

We have seen that considering "attention" as stimulus control of behavior may provide a convenient rubric for many diverse behavioral situations, but that as such it does not provide an understanding of why or how a given stimulus comes to exert control. However, the construct of attention has been used also in an explanatory sense.

Attention has been invoked as an alternative to differential reward or punishment. For example, Mackintosh (1965) holds that discrimination learning depends upon attention to the appropriate dimension prior to learning the particular value of the dimension which is correct for a given situation. Thus, in a redundant cue situation (e.g., brightness and orientation confounded), response to a given cue ensures equal reward for both dimensions which comprise that cue. Yet later transfer tests will indicate that the two dimensions exert differential amounts of control over behavior. Mackintosh believes that the "dimension analyzer" is switched in first, so that an animal which switches in the brightness analyzer will learn much about brightness cues, but little about orientation cues. Sutherland (1968) takes an extreme position on this issue, holding that the more an animal learns about one cue, the less it will learn about another cue. We have considered the position of Bruner et al. (1955) who believe this to be an empirical rather than theoretical question. Without delving further into the issue, we may point out that differential reinforcement is hard put to explain differential control of behavior by stimuli which receive equal amounts of reinforcement. As an example, Wagner (1969) has found that the amount of control exerted by a stimulus may be dependent upon the relative "validity" of other stimuli present, when there is no differential reinforcement of the stimulus in question.

This issue demands more consideration than that which can be allocated to it in this chapter. The position taken for the sake of considering the neural bases of attention is that many variables can modulate the degree of control which a stimulus may exert over behavior. We may not yet have a complete list. Those which have been identified include (1) genetic and developmental factors, (2) differential reward and punishment, (3) type and level of motivation, (4) amount of prior experience or training, (5) "validity" of incidental cues, (6) cue salience (Trabasso & Bower, 1968), (7) discriminability of other stimuli present (Miles & Jenkins, 1965), and perhaps (8) perceptual hierarchy (Newman & Benefield, 1968). At present there is no generally accepted unified theory which encompasses all of these factors of stimulus control.


## C. Summary

Definitions are neither right nor wrong, neither true nor false. They may be good or bad, depending upon the goal or problem for which they are formulated or employed. Our problem is to consider the neural bases of stimulus selection. The descriptive definition will be used. There are two reasons for choosing the descriptive rather than explanatory definition for this task. First, identification of the neural bases of stimulus selection will constitute an explanation itself. Second, the descriptive definition is neutral with regard to theories of learning and may therefore be broad enough to include all phenomena of possible interest without prejudgments about their right to be included in the problem. Let us turn, then, to neural approaches to attention.

## V. NEURAL MECHANISMS

If we consider, at least for the sake of the present discussion, that attention is in evidence whenever stimulus selection or specific stimulus control of behavior is in evidence, then it would seem that organisms are almost always attentive with respect to some stimulus(i) or other, particularly if one includes as objects of attention both the sensorial and intellectual realms. Even if we discard James' category of intellectual attention, as previously agreed, we still find that animals and people spend most of their time being attentive to one thing or another. There seems to be a rather continual flow. This aspect of attention has largely escaped notice in experimental psychology, perhaps because effector action does not invariably accompany the continual nuances of attention. Pauses between behavioral sequences are, after all, not uncommon. (Whether or not such pauses are filled with "intellectual attention," we leave to some future consideration.)

Attention, then, cannot be equated with the actual behavior that is under stimulus control. Rather, that behavior is an index of brain processes one of whose products is the behavior in question. These cerebral functions constitute the "attentive processes" which underlie attentive behavior, and it is to a consideration of these that we now turn our attention. The reader should understand that attentive processes do not comprise all of brain or central nervous system action. We are concerned only with those neural processes which control *in a selective manner* the effects of stimuli upon ongoing or future behavior, not with the central motor processes which actually produce the behavior itself. This restriction still leaves as potential candidates for attentive processes perhaps more brain systems than we desire. Still, it simply reflects our present knowledge.

Behavioral approaches to attention have yielded at least two major findings with important implications for considerations of the neural bases of attention. First, a great diversity and variety of tasks and behaviors are all subsumed under the common rubric of attention. This implies that the neural substrates of attention may be similarly diverse, so that perhaps no unitary mechanism or CNS subsystem may exist for attentive behavior. Second, a substantial and highly successful technology has evolved which provides objective behavioristic indices of the objects or stimulus characteristics to which an animal attends. However it is often impossible to determine the object(s) of attention at the time such selection is taking place; the animal may have to be "probed" at a later time to reveal its previous selection strategy or choice. As mentioned earlier, this particular behavioral limitation enhances the attractiveness of finding the central attentive processes (CAP) which comprise the substrate of each initial selective act itself. If the CAP were known, they could be recorded in place of (or in addition to) overt behavior, thus providing an accurate index of that which is being attended at the time such selection is actually taking place.

The identification and verification of CAPs comprises a task whose complexity and enormity is presently unknown. If the difficulty of this task were presently appreciated, we might be less bold in our venture for this "Holy Grail." In point of fact, electrophysiological attacks on the problem have continued to grow in number and complexity during the past decade and a half. Most research and theory has been concentrated on two systems: (1) the reticular formation of the brain stem, and (2) sensory systems (primarily visual and auditory). We will consider these in turn shortly, but let us first outline the general strategy used and requirements for findings and validating CAPs.

## A. The Search for Central Attentive Processes (CAPs)

We have implicitly assumed that the identification of the neural processes which comprise the substrate of a given act of attention are to be sought by electrophysiological means, that is by recording some CNS activity concomitantly with the behavior in question. This bias should now be made explicit. Ablation, lesion, and brain stimulation can certainly provide important clues and perhaps even help narrow the search for the specific neural processes which we seek. Pharmacological approaches can also provide powerful assistance, particularly because they may involve systems or functional circuits which are not localized in one part of the brain. Biochemical sampling and assay of neurohumors and tissue during behavior holds much promise, although this approach may provide less specific and detailed data than our task requires. Electrophysiological recording is left by default but need not be defended on this basis alone. It permits continuous recording of brain activity during behavior and has so far proven to be the most powerful approach to an understanding of brain function. The following discussion, particularly the CAPs requirements, will deal in the main with electrophysiological attempts to understand the neural bases of attention.

There are at least four steps or levels of achievement necessary to accomplish identification of a neural substrate of attention.

## 1. Identification of an Electrophysiological Correlate

It is widely assumed that finding a *bona fide* neural correlate of a process, such as learning or attention, would constitute the identification of a neural substrate of that process. However, this is only a necessary first step. In the case of attention, this step entails recording neural activity during stimulus selection in which an objective determination of the bases upon which selection is made are known to the experimenter. It is obviously essential to ensure that the presumed CAP is not a correlate of a process (e.g., increased arousal) which is confounded (accidentally or otherwise) with the act of attention. If later transfer or probe tests are needed to determine what was being selected, the neural data would be stored and later examined for correlates of the selective act in question. Examples of possible or proposed correlates include the frequency spectrum of the electroencephalogram, the amplitude of sensory evoked potentials, and the firing of single units in the neocortex.

## 2. Prediction of Selection

If a correlate is found, it is necessary to determine whether the neural processes are merely correlates of the behavior taking place or are necessary precedents of the selection in question. Thus, neural activity which is invariably correlated with button pressing in a vigilance task might be a correlate of the motor act itself or neural feedback consequent to the act. To qualify as a candidate for a CAP, the neural activity should be a predicative correlate, that is must occur prior to the behavior which indexes the fact that the animal has selected a given stimulus. In practice, this step needs no data beyond that gathered from the first step; it does require an accurate knowledge of the temporal relationships between the behavior and the neural activity.

### 3. Presence in the Absence of Behavior

The first two criteria do not ensure against recording a neural predictive correlate of the intention to respond (e.g., press the button) such as increasing muscular tension or CNS processes which anticipate slight postural changes consequent to the performance of a behavior. In an appetitive task, such anticipatory processes might even be related to the forthcoming food reward. It is therefore necessary to find the correlate even when no behavior is required. Elimination of behavior by paralysis of an animal is an unsuitable control, because it merely eliminates the actual contraction of striated muscle, not the processes which precede release of acetylcholine at the neuromuscular junction. It would be preferable to find the presumed CAP in a situation which requires no overt response, e.g., habituation. However this runs the risk of recording a correlate of the "intention not to act"! There is as yet no generally acceptable solution to this problem. One might be persuaded to accept very short latency neural events (e.g., occurring less than 75 msec after stimulus onset) as constituting something other than correlates of some aspect of performance. In any event, this is a moot criterion for most researchers who have not yet ascended the first two criteria.

### 4. Control of Attention

Ideally, the experimenter should be able somehow to institute or produce the CAP by direct manipulation of the brain and thereby to produce the (type of) selection of which the candidate CAP is said to be the substrate. This may sound Orwellian, but it is not likely to be accomplished by 1984.

With these criteria in hand, we will now consider proposed substrates of attention.

### B. The Reticular Formation

The relationships between the reticular formation and behavior waking and arousal are too well known and documented to require detailed comment here. Naturally, revisions and refinements of the originally proposed functional role of the reticular formation in behavior have been forthcoming over the last twenty years. For purposes of the present discussion, the term reticular formation (RF) is used to refer to that part of the brain stem tegmentum and adjacent posterior hypothalamic zones which have mainly ascending activating effects on the electrocorti-cogram (ECoG) and produce behavioral arousal. In the present context, the term "sleep" refers to "slow-wave sleep" and does not include the REM state.

If there exists one candidate which is widely considered to comprise a unitary substrate for attention or the "vigilant" state, it is the reticular formation. Much support for this position comes from human studies in which the ECoG is a dependent variable. Variations in the ECoG which are systematically related to attention, as indexed by an inde-pendent behavioral measure, are taken to be reflections, at the cortex, of variations in the functional state of the RF.

Mirsky and his associates have performed extensive studies with hu-mans using a continuous performance test (CPT) (Rosvold, Mirsky, Sarason, Bransome, & Beck 1956) which is sensitive to lapses in stimulus detection.* They found that patients with centrencephalic epilepsy (medial brain stem involvement) perform more poorly than those having frontal or temporal epileptic foci (Mirsky & Rosvold, 1963). In other studies, sleep deprivation, chlorpromazine, and barbiturates all caused poor performance on the CPT, during correlated slowing of the ECoG (Primac, Mirsky, & Rosvold, 1957; Mirsky et al., 1959; Mirsky & Car-don, 1962). Insofar as these treatments are believed to depress the RF, it was concluded that the RF was necessary for attention. It has also been proposed that reaction time (a common test of attention) depends partly upon cortical excitability, more specifically on the alpha-wave cycle which may be regulated by the RF (Lindsley, 1952). There is support for this hypothesis (Lansing, 1957; Callaway & Yeager, 1960; Dustman & Beck, 1965; Donchin & Lindsley, 1966). Also, Goodman (1968) investigated the relationship between the amount of multiple-unit activity in the RF of the monkey and visuo-motor reaction times. Short reaction times (less than 300 msec) occurred only when the ambient level of unit activity was within a restricted range; levels of activity higher or lower than this precluded fast responses, supporting the notion that critical levels of RF "tonus" are necessary for optimal readiness to respond to environmental events.

Actually, there have been few direct tests of the involvement of the reticular formation in attentive behavior which include extensive and objective assessment of the behavior itself. In the most extensive survey of this problem, Sprague, Levitt, Robson, Liu, Stellar, and Chambers

---

* A more detailed exposition of pharmacological approaches to attention will not be given. The reader is referred to Callaway and Stone (1960), Glaser (1962) and especially to Mirsky and Tecce (1966).

(1963) actually found that lateral midbrain lesions seemed to produce a deficit in attention while cats with RF lesions exhibited "hyperattentiveness". In their own words:

> Thus we have two contrasting preparations that learn poorly for different reasons: (1) the animal with lemniscal lesions is highly motivated for food, works rapidly, and is unemotional and virtually indistractable, but has difficulty in attention and orientation and (2) the animal with medial reticular lesions has good attention, but is sluggish, has poor motor performance, is easily distractable, and is hyperemotional (p. 280).

These findings actually indicate that both types of lesion produced alterations in attentive behavior, but for different reasons. These findings notwithstanding, even if it is agreed that the reticular formation plays a role in attention, we may inquire into the nature of that role. For example, to what extent is the RF related specifically to stimulation selection? Stimulus selection may be affected in the same circumstances for different reasons. Thus, failure to respond to a signal in a vigilance situation may be taken as an index of a "lapse" of attention. But if the lapse is due to prior sleep loss, so that the subject drowses, then the interpretation of inattention ought to be different than when failure to respond occurs because the subject is adequately attending to another (possibly incidental) stimulus, such as a pain in the toe or an itch. In the first case, the subject cannot be responsive, while in the second he is responsive or attentive, but not to the designated signal. A distinction must be made, therefore, between general factors which have an incidental, but powerful, effect upon stimulus selection, and those which have a much more specific effect. In short, we must not confuse arousal with attention.

## C. Arousal and Attention

Arousal and attention can be differentiated conceptually, a distinction which is often not made experimentally. The terms "vigilant," "aroused," "alert," "activated," and "attentive" have found wide use, but not in a sufficiently consistent manner. A vigilant animal may be one which is either simply wide awake or perhaps additionally is performing well in a signal detection task. An aroused or activated animal is certainly awake, but may be considered attentive or not, depending upon inferences which the experimenter draws from the animal's posture and movements. An attentive animal may be generally ready to interact with its environment or be engaged in some specific selective act, etc. Operational definitions are clearly needed. In any event, there seem to be two senses of use of these and similar terms: (1) to refer to some aspect of the state of wakefulness; (2) to refer to some very specific behavioral interaction with environmental stimuli. At the conceptual level, "arousal" pertains to the former and "attention" to the latter. These two referents are not unrelated. Common sense tells us that in order to be attentive, to behave quite selectively when presented with the array or barrage of stimuli which the environment offers, we must be awake, or aroused. This general conception, that background organismic state is inextricably tied to stimulus selection, has blurred the distinction between the two. An empirical question arises: "Is it possible to dissect apart the general state of waking from attention?" Briefly, yes.

Demonstrations of stimulus selection in the sleeping state have shown that wakefulness is not necessary for attention. For example, Rowland (1957) examined the effects of presenting conditioned (CS) and non-reinforced differential stimuli (DS) to sleeping cats which had previously shown differential conditioned behavior to the two stimuli during the waking state. He found differential responsiveness to the stimuli: the CS produced significantly more behavioral and electrographic arousal than did the DS. Oswald, Taylor, and Treisman (1960) found discriminative arousal (evidenced by the elicitation of K-complexes in the ECoG) to the subject's name versus other names in some, but not all, stages of sleep. Discriminated avoidance behavior, learned in the waking state, may be maintained during sleep (Granda & Hammack, 1961). In addition to discrimination during sleep, it is also claimed that discriminations can be learned during sleep, and carry over to the waking state (Beh & Barratt, 1965). Discriminated selective nonresponding during sleep to a stimulus following habituation is also known (Sharpless & Jasper, 1956; Apelbaum, Silva, Frick, & Segundo, 1960). Finally, Gluck and Rowland (1959) reported both discriminative arousal to a CS and discriminative dearousal (induced slow waves in the ECoG) to a DS in sleeping cats. In summary, an organism can be asleep and attentive, or asleep and inattentive, awake and attentive, or awake and inattentive to external stimuli (e.g., daydreaming). Although they interact, arousal and attention are neither sufficient nor necessary conditions for each other.

Even within the waking state, arousal and attention can be differentiated empirically. Perhaps two studies can serve here to point up this difference. Weinberger and Lindsley (1965) studied behavioral responses in sleeping cats to changes in auditory stimulation under two conditions: (1) noise or click onset for three seconds on a background of relative quiet, and (2) noise or click offset (3 sec interruption) on a background of 16 hours of stimulation. Behavioral responses were found to consist of two components: head lifting, and head turning toward the loud-speaker. These two components are smoothly integrated to stimulus onset, which is the most common life situation. However in the offset condition, head lifting occurred at stimulus offset, but the orientation toward the speaker did not occur until three seconds later, when stimulation was resumed. Thus the behavior consisted of two components: (1) a general arousal component (head lifting) in response to a *change* in ambient stimulus conditions, and (2) head orientation or localization of the sound source, a *stimulus* and *modality specific* response to the onset of auditory stimulation.

Elul and Marchiafava (1964) investigated lens accommodation in the paralyzed cat in response to sensory stimulation. He found that accommodation responses consisted of two phases: (1) a short latency near accommodation in response to unexpected stimulation in any modality, followed by (2) a longer latency response which was specific only to visual stimuli and was appropriate to the distance of the visual stimulus from the eye. Here again, we have a single response system with different components related to (1) general arousal and (2) stimulus specific characteristics.

In both of the foregoing studies, the short latency, nonspecific responses were accompanied by signs of electrographic arousal; in both studies, the two types of responses exhibited habituation with aperiodic repeated stimulation; in both studies, the stimulus-specific behavior habituated more rapidly than the general nonspecific arousal behavior.

The foregoing suggests that neural substrates of arousal level ought to be differentiated from those underlying stimulus selection *per se*. At the very least, the reticular formation ought not to be considered as an essential substrate of attention or the "attentive state" insofar as its general arousal functions are concerned. It may additionally be concerned with the possible modulation of sensory system analytic functions (see below) and therefore cannot be excluded as a candidate for subserving stimulus selection.

## D. Sensory System Function

Most electrophysiological studies of attention have been concerned with sensory system operation. Two extreme points of view may be contrasted: (1) stimulus information is greatly modifiable (enhanced or reduced) as it proceeds from the receptor rostrally to sensory neocortex, and in fact information may be blocked or attenuated as peripherally as the first relay nucleus or receptor itself (e.g., Hernandez-Peon, 1960,

1966); (2) stimulus information is not altered, reaching sensory neocortex unimpeded and unenhanced (Deutsch & Deutsch, 1963). *Ad hoc* arguments can be advanced to support both views. Rephrased, these positions might read: "(1) Animals possess a limited information processing capacity. Attention is accomplished therefore by reducing potential information by sensory blockade and allocating the processing capacity thus saved to the attended information channel." or, (2) "All information must be completely analyzed (and thus reaches neocortex) prior to the allocation of attention because integrated and appropriate responses may be made to novel or meaningful stimulation which is presented to an unattended modality or channel. There is no justification for identifying the locus of filtering below sensory cortex."

There are alternatives to these two views. Perhaps both are correct but apply to different behavioral circumstances. In contrast, maybe both are incorrect, and while information is not modulated at peripheral sensory levels, it is altered as it enters the forebrain (e.g., medial and lateral geniculate bodies for auditory and visual systems, respectively). At the present time, behavioral approaches have not provided a generally acceptable answer to this problem. Thus, based upon the same evidence, Treisman's model (1964) includes some attenuation prior to the cortex while that of Norman (1969) does not.

Direct electrophysiological recording of information throughout a sensory system would seem to be an ideal approach to solve the problem. However, while it is relatively easy to record electrical events, we cannot yet identify them with information. It may seem reasonable to expect evoked potentials in an attended channel to be larger than those in an unattended channel, but this is merely a current and more expensive form of introspection than that of the 19th century. Evoked potential amplitude probably "codes" stimulus intensity per unit time as reflected in the degree of synchronization of the afferent neural volley. It also appears that amplitude, polarity, and waveform are reflections of nearby cellular events such as synaptic potentials and unit firing. Thus, EP amplitude and configuration may be an adequate index of the excitability of the system or brain region, and systematic changes in the EP can serve as "markers" informing us that some systematic neural changes are in evidence. We must be wary, however, of assumptions regarding information *per se* from EP recording (Worden, 1966). At the present time, the particular relationships between the evoked potential, underlying cellular events, and information are the subjects of intensive investigation (MacKay, 1969).

At the very best, the use of EPs as neural dependent variables restricts experimenters to the use of brief or punctiform stimulation, which is surely a negligible amount of all stimulation which sensory systems have evolved to process. At the worst, reliance on evoked potentials may be misleading. In an important recent study, Fehmi, Adkins, and Lindsley (1969) studied visual system EPs during behavioral perceptual masking in monkeys, attempting to determine the relationship between EPs and information used by the animals. The task was to discriminate between a square and triangle presented simultaneously in a weak tachistoscopic flash. Perceptual masking on some trials was accomplished by following this test flash with an intense flash; performance was poor with interflash intervals (IFI) of less than about 30 msec and was essentially perfect at this or longer intervals. The informative test flash EP was completely abolished under conditions of perceptual masking at short IFIs. At IFIs of 30 msec (and greater), a minimal amplitude short latency component of the informative EP was present, from the optic tract through visual cortex, and was sufficient to sustain near perfect perceptual discrimination. With IFIs greater than 30 msec, the informative EP grew in amplitude, and later components became prominent. These findings suggest that the information required to discriminate between the square and triangle was contained in or represented by the minimal amplitude, short latency optic tract evoked potential. Additional amplitude and later components were not necessary.

As an alternative to the evoked potential, the pattern of firing of single sensory system cells may be examined. A limitation is that data from very large numbers of cells must be gathered in order to provide a coherent picture of functional operation. Also, small cells are likely to be underrepresented. This approach may yield more information to us about information modulation in these systems than the EP, because single units are known to code in discrete ways the stimulus categories (previously discussed) which seem to serve as bases for stimulus selection. For example, retinal ganglion cell may respond preferentially to the *presence* ("on fibers") or *absence* ("off fibers") of illumination (Hartline, 1938). While these are modality specific, cells which respond to stimulus change independent of modality have been found in association cortex (Bettinger, Davis, Meckle, Birch, Kopp, Smith, & Thompson, 1967). With regard to *modality*, any cell in a sensory system which responds only to stimulation of that system may be said to code that modality; first-order neurons (e.g., VIIIth nerve) would be the most peripheral coders of modality. *Modality-specific* parameters are coded by neurons which are "tuned" to restricted wavelengths (DeValois, 1965) or frequencies (Kiang, 1965). Units which provide information about the *locus* of stimuli include those with limited receptive fields in the visual (Kuffler, 1953) and somesthetic (Poggio & Mountcastle, 1963) systems, and those that are particularly sensitive to interaural time differences in the auditory system (Galambos, Schwartzkopff, & Rupert, 1959). Units which code *pattern* have been found in the visual (Hubel & Weisel, 1965) and auditory (Whitfield & Evans, 1965) cortices. Finally, in almost all cases, stimulus *intensity* and *duration* are important variables influencing sensory cell firing. At the present time, single-unit studies during behavioral investigations of attention are still few. We can expect an increasing interest in this approach.

With the above considerations in mind, let us turn to an examination of possible sensory system mechanisms which have either been alleged or found to modulate sensory evoked activity and which might therefore be candidates for altering sensory information flow.

There seem to be four obvious ways in which information might be modulated *vis-a-vis* sensory processing. These may be ordered along a continuum of decreasing proximity to the stimulus itself:

(1) receptor orientation,
(2) prereceptor operation,
(3) intrinsic sensory system action,
(4) extrinsic sensory system action.

This ordering may also comprise a continuum of increasing capacity to select stimuli on the basis of increasingly complex criteria.

## 1. Receptor Orientation

The most obvious mechanism is that of altering the position of receptors *vis-a-vis* stimuli. Stimuli may be selected or rejected by appropriate movement of the body and limbs, more usually by the head and eyes, especially for visual, auditory, and olfactory stimuli. The major effect of these behaviors is to alter the effective intensity at the receptor. Although this is somewhat crude, it can be effective and perhaps even essential for further selection by more central mechanisms, by increasing the signal-to-noise ratio within a modality while generally decreasing some inputs to an unselected modality. As noted above, receptor orientation is not sufficient to guarantee selection for the fixated stimuli, although it has been widely used as an index of attention. However, orienting is commonly regarded as necessary for the selection of stimuli, so that failure to orient has been taken as evidence of "neglect" or inattention. Lesion studies have revealed deficits in orientation following injury to regions which do not alter general arousal level. Sprague and his colleagues have performed extensive experiments which indicate that damage to lateral midbrain and subtectal regions, sparing the more medial reticular formation, result in chronic neglect of inputs to all modalities (Sprague *et al.*, 1963). Adey and Lindsley (1959) produced similar but more transient effects in cats by subthalamic lesions. Severely impaired orienting following medial thalamic lesions has been reported by Chow, Dement, and Mitchell (1959). At the level of the neocortex, ablation of primary auditory cortex impairs head orientation to sound (Thompson & Welker, 1963). Lesions of the temporal cortex in primates attenuates visual exploration (Butler & Harlow, 1954; Symmes, 1963).

The above studies indicate that brain damage can depress or eliminate orienting to stimuli. However, this type of behavior may actually be enhanced following brain lesions. Injury to the frontal cortex results in hyperactivity (French, 1959) as well as retarded habituation of orienting (Butter, 1964; Kornorski & Lawicka, 1964; Glaser, 1962). Limbic lesions may produce similar effects (Kluver & Bucy, 1939; Schwartzbaum, Wilson, & Morrissette, 1961; Leaton, 1965).

Receptor orientation may be affected not only by brain lesions, but also by electrical stimulation. Stimulation of sensory systems typically produces appropriate receptor orienting behavior, as might be expected. Stimulation of certain nonsensory sites produces general orienting and searching. Effective loci include the reticular formation and posterior hypothalamus (Segundo, Arana, & French, 1955), amygdala (Kaada & Ursin, 1957), and restricted cortical regions (i.e., medial frontal, cingulate, temporo occipital, orbito-insular-temporal polar) (Segundo *et al.*, 1955; Fangel & Kaada, 1960). Only the reticular formation appears to be essential for producing this behavior. Amygdala and cortical stimulation effects habituate, whereas the effects of RF stimulation do not (Ursin, Wester, & Ursin, 1967). Furthermore, cortical desynchronization effects elicited from the cortex and other forebrain structures are abolished by RF lesions (Velasco, Weinberger, & Lindsley, 1965).

Our understanding of mechanisms subserving receptor orientation behavior is still far from satisfactory. It does appear that certain generalizations are possible at this time. Rostropontine and mesencephalic portions of the reticular formation are ordinarily necessary for wakefulness and to this extent for orientation to stimuli. More caudal brain stem regions are not necessary, at least for the elicitation and habituation of eye orientation (King & Marchiafava, 1963). Tectal and lateral mesencephalic, subtectal and medial diencephalic structures apparently are involved in orienting behavior. At the level of the cortex, sensory projection regions appear to be needed for normal orientation to stimuli within the specific modality. In contrast, the frontal cortex and parts of the limbic system are not needed for the elicitation of orienting but may assist in habituation of that behavior. We should bear in mind that receptor orientation is ordinarily a response to environmental stimulation and therefore cannot alter the impact of stimulation which preceded its appearance. It can modulate the effects of subsequent stimulation.

## 2. Prereceptor Modulation

Gross alteration of receptor orientation can alter effective stimulus intensity over a very wide range. Prereceptor mechanisms in the ear and eye may serve a similar but more restricted intensity modulating function.

*The Ear.* Contraction of the middle ear muscles (MEM) (stapedius and tensor tympani) is capable of reducing stimulus intensity by up to 20 db, particularly for frequencies of less than 1000 Hz (Simmons, 1959). Intense sounds produce brisk (12 msec latency) contraction of the MEM, suggesting to some workers that these muscles function mainly to protect the Organ of Corti. It is now clear that many nonacoustic factors also produce MEM activation. General head and body movements, especially those of the facial musculature (chewing, swallowing, coughing, etc.) are very effective (Carmel & Starr, 1963). Contraction also occurs preceding each vocalization (Saloman & Starr, 1963). It seems likely that MEMs serve to attenuate sounds produced by the individual and so assist stimulus selection by reducing auditory system "noise." Simmons has found continuous small "spontaneous" fluctuations in MEM tonus, and speculates that the stimulus intensity modulation which this produces is important for perception, in a manner similar to the continuous microsaccades produced by the extra-ocular muscles which prevent fading of the retinal image.

The action of the MEM must be taken into account when studying sensory evoked activity in the auditory system. Habituation of auditory evoked potentials (i.e., progressive amplitude diminution during continued click presentation) may depend upon MEM contraction. Guzman-Flores, Alcanaz, and Harmony (1960) found temporally conditioned MEM contractions to periodic click stimulation. EP habituation in the medial geniculate body (MG) and auditory cortex was abolished by removing MEM function by muscle paralysis or surgery. These findings were replicated by Alcaraz, Pacheco, and Guzman-Flores (1961). However, they also demonstrated that reduction of EP amplitude at these loci was independent of MEM activity during presentation of a novel stimulus ("distraction"). Moushegian, Rupert, Marsh, and Galambos (1961) also found EP amplitudes at the auditory cortex and inferior colliculus (IC) to be independent of the MEM not only during distraction, but also during habituation. The reason for this discrepancy is not immediately obvious. Baust and Berlucchi (1964) found that destruction of primary auditory cortex (AI) abolished MEM contraction to acoustic stimuli, interpreting this as evidence for direct centrifugal control of the MEM. However, the relationship may not be that direct. Head orientation movements to auditory stimuli are greatly depressed by AI lesions (Thompson & Welker, 1963), and MEM action might have been originally caused by such movements.

*The Eye.* Eyelid position, pupillary diameter, and lens accommodation serve to modulate stimulus intensity and pattern at the retina. These mechanisms may be of importance for stimulus selection by providing a good retinal image which can be analyzed by more central mechanisms. Additionally, eyelid and pupil action can be very effective in rejecting all visual stimuli. Lens accommodation and behavior have been studied by Elul and Marchiafava (1964). Using an automatic infra-red system with cats, they found a short latency near-accommodation to nonvisual stimuli. This response habituated and was interpreted as being part of generalized orienting to novel stimuli. These findings suggest that accommodation may serve stimulus selection and adaptive behavior by increasing the probability of rapidly obtaining a well focused image to near objects following unexpected stimulation.

As in the auditory system, evoked potentials in the visual system may be affected by prereceptor action. Chiasmatic EPs are critically related to pupil diameter (Fernandez-Guardiola, Roldan, Fanjul, & Castillo, 1961), and habituation of visual cortex EPs was abolished (Palestini, Gallardo, & Armengol, 1964) or attenuated (Fernandez-Guardiola *et al.*, 1961) by pupillary paralysis. Accommodation also alters the amplitude and configuration of evoked potentials in man (Van Hof, Van Hof, & Rietveld, 1966).

Prereceptor mechanisms in the eye and ear serve some selective function by modulating input to the retina and cochlea. This is probably limited mainly to changes in effective stimulus intensity, which in turn may alter evoked activity in the visual and auditory systems. It has not been established that all sensory system EP changes associated with attention and habituation are due to prereceptor modulation of input. It is clear that the intensity and pattern of receptor excitation cannot be disregarded in considering the intrinsic role of the sensory systems in stimulus selection. It is to a consideration of this that we turn.

## 3. Intrinsic Sensory System Action

In the preceding two sections, we have been concerned with mechanisms which might alter the configuration of stimulus energy upon a receptor. But the problem of the neural bases of attention far transcends burying one's head in a pillow and other similarly gross methods of controlling stimulation. These kinds of mechanisms, while often of critical importance in experimental studies of evoked potentials, cannot subserve stimulus selection based upon the fine and subtle distinctions which are so characteristic of attention. Certainly, dropping the jaw to relax one's middle ear muscles is effective in increasing auditory sensitivity, but surely the essence of the problem concerns the fate of sensory input after it has properly and adequately reached our receptors.*

Sensory systems are comprised of descending or centrifugal components in addition to the better known and more widely studied ascending fiber systems. The centrifugal components originate in sensory neocortex for the modalities which are mapped at this level of the neuraxis, somesthetic, visual, and auditory. They may descend, after a variable number of synapses, as far peripherally as the receptor itself, as in the case of the olivocochlear bundle in the auditory system.† Such sensory centrifugal systems (SCF) form possible or established feedback loops (e.g., Fex, 1962) and are obvious candidates for modulators of sensory information processing. There is, in fact, ample physiological evidence that centrifugal fibers do alter sensory activity as measured by modulation of evoked potential amplitude and single-unit firing (Livingston, 1959). However, we cannot assume that these comprise the only mechanisms intrinsic to a sensory system which may alter the action of the system. Changes in neural patterning may be a consequence of the intrinsic organization and activity of the ascending centripetal components as well. Lateral or recurrent inhibition consequent to neuronal activity or changes in the general excitability of sensory neurons could occur without the intercession of a centrifugal mechanism.

Although centrifugal systems are commonly invoked to account for changes in sensory EPs, in fact, we know little about their function in behaving animals. To date, there have been no reports of recordings from such fibers during stimulus selection. Some lesion studies have implicated the olivocochlear bundle (OCB) in perception and attention, but there is insufficient data to provide a general relationship at this time. Buno, Velluti, Handler, and Garcia-Austt (1965) reported that habituation of VIIIth nerve action potentials and the cochlear microphonic in the guinea pig was not found in animals having prior section of the crossed OCB. Dewson (1968), in a very clever experiment, found

---

* Peripheral control, such as the rapid adaptation of some cutaneous receptors, is recognized but not considered in this discussion.

† The olivocochlear system includes two components which project centrifugally: to the receptor (cochlea), and to the cochlear nuclei. There exist both crossed and uncrossed components (Rasmussen, 1964).

that section of the crossed OCB in the monkey produces a decrement in the discrimination of vowel sounds when they are masked by white noise. In the absence of noise, no effect was seen. Capps and Ades (1968) reported an increase in the difference limen for frequency in monkeys with similar section of the OCB. Whitfield (1967) has pointed out that lesions or ablations of the auditory sytsem invariably involve the centrifugal as well as the intended centripetal components, thus rendering interpretations of resultant sensory or discriminatory deficits unclear.

There is no question that an understanding of sensory-centrifugal systems comprise a sizeable portion of needed research in the area of attention, unless unequivocal evidence demonstrates that information flow through a sensory system is unaltered to the neocortex, except perhaps for general changes in the effective intensity or level of the stimuli. There are indications, however, of a much finer organization and action. Thus, Giolli and Guthrie (1967) found that centrifugal projections from the visual cortex of the rabbit to the superior colliculus and pretectal nucleus were organized in a highly specific manner. Projections from the retinotopic cortical quadrants were directed to the corresponding quadrants in the tectum and pretectum. Also, it is erroneous to assume that centrifugal action always has an inhibitory effect (indexed by reduced EP amplitude). While this seems to be the case for that portion of the OCB which projects to the cochlea itself, both excitatory and inhibitory effects have been found for the other part of the OCB system which projects to the cochlear nucleus (Comis & Whitfield, 1967). In the somatosensory system, corticofugal influences upon dorsal column neurons in the gracile nucleus may be either excitatory or inhibitory. Additionally, inhibitory corticofugal effects are restricted to cells which are also subject to afferent inhibition, and excitatory corticofugal effects are limited to cells which may receive afferent facilitation (Gordon & Jukes, 1962).

It is possible that SCFs are part and parcel of normal sensory system functioning, in that they serve to ensure fidelity of information transmission, much as lateral inhibition at the periphery serves to sharpen contrasts and edges. If such is the case, then the modulation of sensory evoked potentials and single-unit activity recorded in the laboratory might signify, not decrements in information, but rather the normal action of the system which ensures an unmodulated flow to the cortex. In this case, SCFs might be said to comprise perceptual but not attentive substrates (Worden, 1966).

Without being able to specify whether centrifugal fibers or another intrinsic sensory system mechanism causes systematic changes in evoked sensory activity, we can review evidence that such changes do occur and,

furthermore, that they are intimately related to attentive processes.*
*Habituation: Selection Against.* Contemporary studies date from
Hernandez-Peon *et al.* (1956). Clicks were continuously presented to
a resting but wakeful cat. Evoked potentials, recorded from the first
auditory relay (cochlear nucleus) were attenuated when the cat excitedly
viewed a mouse. EP amplitude returned to control levels when the cat
ceased orienting. These findings were interpreted to indicate a blockade
of input to an unattended modality (auditory), although there was no
reason to believe that the cat was not also listening for the mouse.
It was subsequently shown that cochlear nucleus EPs are greatly affected
by slight changes in head and ear position *vis-a-vis* the loudspeaker
(Marsh, Worden, & Hicks 1962). Middle-ear muscle contraction during
movement and heightened arousal could also account for these results.
The experiment was finally repeated by Dunlop, Webster, and Simons
(1965). They replicated the original results when the cat was moving
while viewing the mouse, but no EP changes occurred in the absence
of movement Thompson, Bettinger, Birch, Groves, and Mayers (1969)
found no attenuation when stimulus intensity was controlled by use
of a small earphone. Hernandez-Peon and his associates also reported
attenuation of EPs in the visual, olfactory, and somesthetic systems
following repetitive stimulus presentation and termed this phenomenon
"afferent neuronal habituation" (ANH) (Hernandez-Peon, 1960) in contrast to ECoG habituation (Sharpless & Jasper, 1956) and behavioral
habituation.

The mechanism underlying afferent neuronal habituation was believed
to be centrifugal action of the reticular formation upon the sensory
systems (Hernandez-Peon, 1961) (see below). In fact, investigation of
the role of centrifugal auditory fibers in EP habituation in the cochlear
nucleus was attempted (Bach-Y-Rita, Brust-Carmona, Penaloza-Rojas,
& Hernandez-Peon, 1961). Lesions of the lateral mesencephalon, which
presumably interrupted fibers descending to the cochlear nucleus, did
not prevent acoustic habituation.† In any event, the phenomenon of
ANH itself was challenged. In an exemplary study which included stimulus control and the objective measurement, as opposed to arbitrary selection, of evoked potentials, Worden and Marsh (1965) found no EP

---

* Evoked potentials recorded from the scalp of human subjects are treated
separately, because they may comprise association rather than sensory cortex
events. In addition, these EPs are customarily of very long latency (100–500 msec)
and could not therefore represent the primary afferent volley.

† This negative result is not particularly surprising, because there are no known
auditory centrifugal fibers which reach the cochlear nuclei directly from the level
of these lesions (Whitfield, 1967).

habituation in the cochlear nucleus. Their work, in turn, has been criticized by Webster, Dunlop, Simons, and Aitkin (1965), who claimed that habituation takes place within the first 30 sec of click stimulation, not after minutes or hours. Worden and Marsh's design would not have revealed such rapid habituation. Actually, Webster *et al.* confused refractory period or recovery cycle phenomena with habituation. They found "rapid habituation" only for 1/sec and 10/sec stimulation, and their tests for "dishabituation" consisted of slowing the ongoing rate, which led to recovered EPs. This same laboratory later failed to find habituation at the cochlear nucleus (Simons, Dunlop, Webster, & Aitkin, 1966). The issue is far from resolved, however. If habituation of EPs in the cochlear nucleus is in doubt, studies of evoked multiple unit activity (MUA) in this nucleus using paralyzed cats have reported slight (Holstein, Buchwald, & Schwafel, 1969) or pronounced (Kitzes & Buchwald, 1969) habituation. A possibly important difference between these and most EP studies is the use of nonpunctiform stimuli of 1 sec in duration.

There is increasing evidence that habituation of EPs does occur at higher levels of the neuraxis, primarily in the forebrain. Jane, Smirnov, and Jasper (1962) found this to be the case for EPs in the geniculate bodies and cortices of the auditory and visual systems during simultaneous stimulation with clicks and flashes. However Steinberg (1965) found no habituation in the visual cortex. Variables other than stimulus repetition may alter EP amplitude, particularly in the forebrain, and these must be considered or controlled in experiments. For example, EP amplitude in the lateral geniculate nucleus and visual cortex varies directly with arousal level (Khachaturian & Gluck, 1969). Saunders and Chabora (1969) found a reduction in click EPs at the auditory cortex as a function of food deprivation during a 32-hour period; no effects were seen at the cochlear nucleus. Wickelgren (1968a) found great stability in the cochlear nucleus, superior olive, and inferior colliculus across a wide range of arousal in sleeping and waking cats. EPs in the medial geniculate and auditory cortex (and also cerebellar vermis) were quite labile; the late wave of the cortical EP in particular was increased during slow-wave sleep. The use of preparations with middle-ear muscles cut, and the stability of responses in lower levels of the auditory system, strongly suggest that the forebrain effects are due to some intrinsic mechanism rather than stimulus variations at the receptors. Hall (1968) attempted to control the level of arousal by demanding that rats be engaged in an appetitive bar-pressing task at a constant rate of responding. Receptor orientation was controlled, and clicks and flashes, irrelevant to the task, were presented. Habituation was found in the visual cortex, auditory cortex, and medial geniculate bodies. Only the late waves, not the primary volley, were affected. (The optic tract and lateral geniculate were not investigated.) Lower levels of the auditory system were stable. Essentially identical results were found in the auditory system of the cat (Wickelgren, 1968b). Simons *et al.* (1966) reported habituation in both the medial geniculate and inferior colliculus. There seems to be no question that forebrain sensory regions are more labile than lower stations, and it appears that under conditions of control of arousal level, the late components of evoked potentials do habituate. This suggests that the initial sensory volley travels undisturbed from the receptor to the sensory cortex under conditions in which the stimulus is of little interest.

Once again, however, multiple-unit studies have found significant habituation below the forebrain, in the inferior colliculus, as well as in the medial geniculate body (Holstein, Buchwald, & Schwafel, 1969; Kitzes & Buchwald, 1969). It should be noted that, for a considerable number of habituation runs, there was either no habituation or a significant increase in evoked MUA at these sites (Kitzes & Buchwald, 1969).

The studies cited above have not been concerned with the possible relationship between EP habituation and behavioral habituation, which is invariably assumed to develop as the experimenter continues to present stimuli of no consequence to the subjects. Weinberger, Goodman, and Kitzes (1969) measured conjugate eye deviation toward the ear stimulated in waking, locally-anesthetized encephale isole cats. This behavior habituates in 5–30 trials. Aperiodic discrete trials, rather than continuous stimulation, were used. No consistent correlation was found between the amplitude of EPs recorded at the level of the superior olivary complex prior to eye movement and the amplitude of eye movement on each trial. Multiple-unit activity in the mesencephalic RF immediately preceding trial onset was a significant predictor of conjugate deviation amplitude during habituation Weinberger and Imig (in preparation) investigated both EPs and multiple-unit activity in the lateral lemniscus and inferior colliculus of unrestrained rats during habituation of the orienting reflex. Neither EP amplitude nor MUA evoked activity preceding orienting movements (which had a latency of at least 200 msec) were significantly correlated with the magnitude of the behavior during habituation. These studies suggest that behavioral habituation in these situations is not due to changes (presumably a decrement) in evoked auditory system activity in the hindbrain and midbrain. They do not necessarily conflict with EP habituation studies which found changes in the late components at the thalamus and neocortex.

There are several reports of sensory units which exhibit habituation with repeated stimulation. These are sometimes referred to as "novelty detectors." Such cells have been found in the visual (Sokolov, 1966) and auditory cortices (Hubel, Henson, Rupert, & Galambos, 1959; Bogdanski & Galambos, 1960). Some units in the superior colliculus habituate (Horn & Hill, 1966; Horn, 1970), particularly those in the deeper layers (Sprague, Marchiafava, & Rizzolatti, 1968). It is unclear whether or not such cells comprise the afferent limb of the visual system or are part of the efferent tecto-tegmental system which might control ocular behavior. Dubrovinskaya (1966) failed to find habituating neurons in this structure. All of the preceding studies concern vertebrate sensory systems. In a recent series of provocative experiments, Horn and Rowell have demonstrated habituation in visual neurons of locusts (Rowell & Horn, 1968; Horn & Rowell, 1968; Horn, 1970). It is still too early to determine any overall picture from such unit studies; the results are generally scattered, and the percentage of such cells with respect to the total population of the structure involved is still unknown. No careful behavioral analyses have accompanied these single-cell studies.

*Selection for Stimuli.* What is the fate of evoked activity in an "attended" channel? Is it enhanced? We begin again with the work of Hernandez-Peon and his associates. Olfactory bulb rhythmic waves which appear when a mouse is shown to a cat have been interpreted as sensory system facilitation of olfaction (Lavin, Alcocer-Cuaron, & Hernandez-Peon, 1959; Hernandez-Peon, 1966). However, an equally plausible explanation is that they resulted from the cat sniffing. Palestini, Davidovich, and Hernandez-Peon (1959) investigated optic tract EPs to a series of four flash pairs presented at the rate of one per second, when these flashes constituted the CS in classical defensive conditioning. The US (shock) was applied during the fourth pair. After some progress in conditioning, the flashes, in particular the fourth pair, produced EPs of increased magnitude, interpreted as sensory facilitation. The absence of control for pupil size also allows the interpretation that the enhanced amplitude was due to conditioned mydriasis which is a standard response to shock. The authors also claimed a shortened recovery cycle, indexed by increased amplitude of the second flash of each pair. If this proves to be substantiated, it would appear to be a genuine example of enhanced visual system (retinal) excitability.

In point of fact, sensory EP data from all behavioral conditioning studies bears on the present question. No such review will be attempted here.* Suffice it to say that the most general report has been an enhance-

---

* See, for example, Morrell (1961). For recent work which includes specification of the stimulus category controlling behavior and correlated evoked potential changes, see John (1967).

ment of EPs evoked by the CS during conditioning and a reduction consequent to behavioral extinction. These results are not uniform, however. Horn and Blundell (1959) reported a reduction in visual cortex EPs during visual-searching behavior, and Horn (1960) found EP reductions in both the selected and the unselected modality. However, even if it is agreed that enhancement generally takes place, it is not at all established that such an effect is related to the modality of the CS. Rather, such enhancement seems to be a general phenomenon. Khachaturian and Gluck (1969) studied visual EPs in the thalamus and cortex during classical defensive conditioning to an auditory stimulus. The flash stimuli, which were always present in the conditioning chamber and were irrelevant to the conditioning itself, were enhanced during establishment of a conditioned response and declined in amplitude during extinction. Control animals, receiving both CS and US, but unpaired, exhibited the same results. Mark and Hall (1967) found significantly larger late components of evoked potentials in the medial geniculate body and auditory cortex in rats during fear conditioning to an auditory CS. However, the amplitude increases were not specific to CS modality, for when conditioned suppression of bar pressing was brought under control of a visual stimulus, the same changes were seen in the auditory system. In a follow-up study (Hall & Mark, 1967) these workers compared the effects of conditioned suppression training with that of appetitive training and found greater increases in EPs during fear than food conditioning, concluding that fear rather than arousal level was responsible for the effect. Controls for movement and the evocation of EPs by electrical stimulation of the auditory system in part of their study once again support the view that the systematic EP changes are due to some intrinsic mechanisms operating at the level of the forebrain. Feeney (1969) reported similar results during appetitive conditioning in dogs; the effect was present at the cortex also when stimulation of the medial and lateral geniculate bodies was used in place of standard exteroceptive conditioned stimuli.

In addition to conditioning studies, there are several reports of enhanced evoked potentials during "distraction." Jane et al. (1962) presented simultaneous clicks and flashes to cats and at certain times introduced distractors in the form of a rat in a plastic box or a recording of a rat squeaking. Distraction in either modality produced an increase in both the visual and auditory systems at both the thalamic and cortical levels. This is an appealing experimental design, but unfortunately it includes no independent test of what modalities are irrelevant. Perhaps cats listen for rat noises when their enclosure in a plastic box removes such normal cues; cats may look for rats when they hear rat squeaks.

If both modalities were relevant, these findings may constitute genuine facilitation of selected channels. If not, the results support other studies which indicate that the enhancement effects are not related to the objects of attention, but are general.

There is a paucity of data on sensory system activity during vigilance or signal detection tasks in animals. This is surprising in view of the extensive behavioral data in this area. In a very recent study, Kitzes (1970) investigated the excitability of the lower auditory system by recording EPs in the lateral lemniscus during signal detection in the cat. The EPs were produced by white noise pips which signalled the start of a trial and served to mask the signal which was a 1 kHz tone. They were presented alternately, binaurally at the rate of 10/sec. Three seconds after white noise onset, one of two cue lamps was illuminated, indicating whether the signal would be given to the right or left ear on that trial. The signal was presented for 1.5 sec from 3–10 sec following lamp illumination, and correct responses were rewarded with milk. EPs in the lateral lemniscus were recorded preceding lamp illumination and during the foreperiod between lamp illumination and signal presentation, to both contra- and ipsilateral stimulation on both right and left trials. There were no changes in EP amplitude attributable to whether or not the ear stimulated corresponded to the expected signal. However, EPs were significantly enhanced during the foreperiod compared to the pre-lamp period. This effect occurred for both ipsi- and contralateral stimulation and was found for both the ear which was expected to receive the signal and the ear which was not. Insofar as no stimulation or recording was performed with another modality, it cannot be claimed that the facilitation was specific to the auditory system. These results are consistent with the studies cited above, which found a nonspecific facilitation of EPs. In the present case, however, the facilitation was found below the forebrain.

After an extensive review, Sokolov (1963b) concluded that facilitation or increased excitability of sensory systems constitutes part of organismic readiness to interact with the environment under conditions of elicitation of the orienting reflex and during integrated behavior in general. While it remains to be determined whether such facilitation includes receptors, and whether the intrinsic centrifugal systems are implicated, it appears that Sokolov's conclusions are essentially correct to the extent that he postulates a nonspecific facilitation of all modalities. To that extent, the data reviewed here are in agreement. Whether it can be said that increased arousal level, even in animals already in the waking state, is responsible remains a moot question pending the establishment and validation of a generally acceptable direct measure of arousal level.

*Human Cortical Potentials.** This approach to the neurobiology of attention has grown enormously in the past decade, due in part to the introduction of average evoked potential techniques which permit the extraction of very small signals (on the order of 5 $\mu$V) from the human brain. The attraction of using human subjects coupled with many encouraging findings promises to continue the prominence of this approach for the forseeable future. Little more than a cursory sketch can be provided here.† We should recall the caution previously stated that the vast bulk of this work sheds no light on the fate of ascending primary volleys. However, we have already seen from the animal research that forebrain longer latency potentials are the most labile and perhaps most interesting of all sensory system evoked activity.

The vertex is the most frequently used locus for recording human evoked potentials. A complex EP with most components having a latency of 100–500 msec is found. The most labile components, those which seem to be systematically related to task variables, generally occur in the 200–400-msec range, a positive wave having a latency of about 300 msec (P300) is of particular interest.

There are many reports of amplitude enhancement to an attended stimulus and amplitude decrements to an irrelevant or habituated stimulus. A sampling of stimulus modalities and behavioral selection includes the following early reports: visual (Haider, Spong, & Lindsley, 1964; Garcia-Austt, Bogacz, & Vanzulli, 1964), auditory (Davis, 1964; Satterfield, 1965), somatosensory (Debecker & Desmedt, 1966). Interpretation of these effects as reflecting the action of central stimulus selection mechanisms must be tempered with the realization that arousal level (Eason, Aiken, White, & Lichtenstein, 1964), myogenic artifacts (Bickford, Jacobson, & Cody, 1964), and peripheral factors (receptor orientation and prereceptor action) may account for some positive results. A critical factor for the visual system is lens accommodation, minute changes of which produce large changes in human EP amplitude and configuration (Van Hof *et al.*, 1966). Horn (1965) additionally has pointed out that, during habituation or inattention to a visual stimulus, binocular convergence is lessened, resulting in reduced simultaneous

---

* The "contingent negative variation" (CNV) is not discussed here. See Donchin and Smith (1969) for a consideration of the relationships between the CNV and the long latency evoked potential. Karlin (1970) has presented a rigorous analysis of the CNV, human evoked potentials, and attention, and finds reason to believe that neither the CNV nor scalp EPs reflect attention processes. He believes they are correlates of phasic changes in arousal level.

† For a recent overview of this approach, see Donchin and Lindsley, 1969.

foveal excitation from the stimulus possibly causing a reduction in EP amplitude to the unattended stimulus.

More recently, great improvements have been made in this type of study, including control of stimulus reception and more sophisticated task designs and data analysis. Even so, some results have been interpreted as due to changes in arousal level only, rather than attention (Näätänen, 1967). Eason, Harter, and White (1969) found that an arousal component can account for some results, but that genuine enhancement of attended stimuli was also a function of selection *per se,* not merely of arousal. Some particularly interesting studies include Donchin and Cohen (1967) which demonstrated intramodality selective effects for the visual system. Attention (assessed behaviorally) was switched between two visual stimuli; the stimulus attended produced an enhanced P300 wave. Sutton, Braren, and Zubin (1965) and Ritter, Vaughn, and Costa (1968) reported that P300 was enhanced when the nature of the stimulus which evoked it was uncertain. This relationship was found when the stimulus modality was not predictable (click vs. flash), and also within a modality, when the pitch of a tone was unpredictable. Smith, Donchin, Cohen, and Starr (1970) studied the effect of attending to clicks while the subject was engaged in a dichotic listening task. When clicks were attended, P300 was enhanced for clicks presented to both the attended (shadowed) ear and the unattended ear. No selective ear effects were found. These authors interpret the enhancement of P300 in all of these studies as due the fact that a decision regarding the stimulus is being made. Sheatz and Chapman (1969) have reported similar findings and advanced this type of interpretation also.

Gardiner and Walter (1968) performed a clever experiment in which two levels of pitch and intensity were confounded and required attention to each parameter on different trials. This technique ensures constancy of the stimulus under all conditions. They reported complex but systematic changes in the vertex EP as a function of whether or not the subjects had to judge the relative pitch or intensity of a given tone pip.

There is now overwhelming evidence that long latency EPs, which are probably not modality-specific, are sensitive indices of some cerebral process(es) that are related to stimulus selection. The details of this relationship remain to be elucidated. One limitation of research with human subjects is that underlying neuronal processes are inaccessible to the investigator. However Thompson *et al.* (1969) have reported evidence that EPs in the association cortex of the cat, which are also not modality specific, are implicated in attention. The neuronal substrates of this EP are being pursued.

## 4. Extrinsic Sensory System Action

In this section, we briefly consider some brain structures which reside outside of sensory systems but nevertheless are able to alter sensory evoked activity (Livingston, 1959). There is an important need for a current review paper on this topic; such a review will certainly not be attempted here. Perusal of the literature begins to suggest that all of the nervous system extrinsic to the sensory systems can, under some circumstances, modulate some aspect of their activity. Here are two related examples of particular interest.

(1) In paralyzed cats, hippocampal stimulation enhances all components of the auditory cortex EPs, but medial geniculate EPs are unaffected. This effect is mediated via the nonspecific thalamic system and is not limited to the auditory or other sensory regions, but is an aspect of the general regulation of neocortical excitability by the hippocampus acting through the centrencephalic system (Parmeggiana & Rapisarda, 1969). We may speculate that such facilitation is related to that which seems to occur normally during the orienting reflex (see above), a behavior in which the hippocampus has been particularly implicated. (2) In paralyzed cats, caudate stimulation reduces auditory cortex EP amplitude. The medial geniculate EPs are much less affected, and the effect seems to be mediated at the cortical level (La Grutta, Giammanco, & Amato, 1969). Again we may speculate about the relevance of this to attention. The present effect may be related to the behavioral inhibition (and inattention?) which can be induced by caudate stimulation (Buchwald, Hull, & Trachtenberg, 1967).

No discussion of this topic could fail to mention the reticular formation. Previous mention has been made of the importance which Hernandez-Peon attached to the RF. Virtually all sensory system modulation reported by this worker and his colleagues, both facilitatory and inhibitory, was considered to be a function of RF activity. Demonstrations of its effects upon sensory activity in the visual, auditory, somesthetic, and olfactory systems are summarized by Hernandez-Peon (1961). The role of the RF in EP habituation has been questioned on indirect grounds. For example, EP habituation at the cortex may be accompanied by increasing drowsiness and sleep, which is inconsistent with the well-known cortical activating role of the RF; while inhibiting the cochlear nucleus, it should also have been desynchronizing the cortex (Cavaggioni, Giannelli, & Santibanez, 1959). Cortical EP habituation is also enhanced by midbrain section (Mancia, Meulders, & Santibanez-H., 1959a) and retarded by sections caudal to the mesencephalic RF (Mancia, Meulders, & Santibanez-H., 1959b), suggesting that the mesencephalic portion of the RF retards rather than promotes such habituation. These criticisms can be circumvented by appealing to functional diversity within different regions of the reticular formation. A more direct criticism is the finding that reduction of cochlear nucleus EPs by RF stimulation is simply a function of middle-ear muscle contraction, probably accompanying movement produced by arousal (Hugelin, Dumont, & Paillas, 1960).

It would be simple to cast out the baby with the bath water and look with jaundiced eye upon the claims of RF control of sensory processing. However there is substantial evidence supporting neurally-mediated RF modulation of sensory activity (e.g., Hagbarth & Kerr, 1954). Each of the claims of Hernandez-Peon and his coworkers must be examined objectively and on their own merits. Very few attempted replications or control experiments have been performed to date.

A very different approach to and conception of extrasensory modulation during attention has been advanced by Pribram (1967a, 1967b). Space limitations preclude doing complete justice to his elegant formulation; the reader is referred to the original sources. Basically, it is proposed that four different forebrain mechanisms serve to modulate sensory information and thereby control attention: frontotemporal cortex (including the amygdala), hippocampus, sensory-specific intrinsic cortex (i.e., regions of the inferior temporal lobe which have specific effects upon the auditory or visual systems), and polysensory-motor ("association") cortex. The known effects of infero-temporal cortex in modulating sensory system activity are an essential component of Pribram's formulation. Chronic stimulation of this region prolongs the recovery cycle of visual cortex EPs (Spinelli & Pribram, 1966); ablation of insular-temporal cortex in cats (alleged to be the auditory-specific intrinsic cortex in this animal) reduces the recovery cycle in the auditory system (Dewson, Nobel, & Pribram, 1966). (But Schwartzkroin et al. (1969) failed to find any change of recovery cycle in the visual cortex of monkeys following inferotemporal ablation.) Pribram believes that sensory-specific intrinsic cortex reduces redundancy in sensory systems by increasing the recovery cycle, thereby reducing the number of cells which carry information about a particular stimulus at a given time. The reduction in redundancy would increase the number of alternative stimuli which could be processed, thereby increasing the information processing capacity of the system. An important consequence of this model is that the stimulus itself is unchanged as it proceeds to the sensory cortex; what is changed is the number of redundant information channels which it occupies. This formulation is far more sophisticated than early conceptions of general blocking or facilitation of stimulus information.

It has been firmly established that sensory systems are subject to modulating influences from without, and as seen in the previous section, from within. It seems inconceivable that information which is utilized in stimulus analysis and selection is not also altered. We have tantalizing anatomical and physiological facts to support such a claim. These must surely serve as the pillars upon which a bridge to attention will be built. The span must consist of solid neuro-behavioral facts. These are just now beginning to be produced.

### E. Central Integrative Mechanisms

This is the final category of possible neural mechanisms underlying attention. It may, in fact, comprise the most important aspect of the problem, but it is here that our present ignorance is greatest. Into this category are placed all neural mechanisms of attention which do not act upon sensory transmission of information, but rather upon the results of sensory analysis. Into this category also belong presumably all mechanisms which are concerned with the "intellectual attention" of William James. But less esoteric problems may find a home here also. For example, selection based upon the relationships between stimuli (e.g., "larger than") would seem to require a poststimulus analysis mechanism. It should also be clear from the extensive preceding discussion that we do not yet know whether information is altered within sensory systems. The possibility still remains open that even the most simple act of stimulus selection requires central integrative mechanisms, that is, those beyond the sensory analyzers.

Central integrative structures or regions which have been implicated in attention by fact or fancy could comprise a very long list indeed. No attempt will be made here to provide a compendium of these. Those which have been mentioned in other contexts in previous sections include frontal, association, and sensory-specific intrinsic cortices, hippocampus, amygdala, nonspecific thalamic projection system, and subthalamus. The major purpose of this section is simply to remind the reader that the mechanisms of attention may not be restricted to sensory systems. With that reminder, let us pass quickly to a relatively recent and very exciting development in central integrative mechanisms.

The bases of habituation have been attacked in model neural systems which are characterized by having many fewer components than the nervous system as a whole, and in which stimulus control, response magnitude, and single-unit recording are all essential ingredients.

In a series of elegant experiments, Thompson, Spencer, and associates have studied the bases of habituation of the flexion reflex in the spinal cat (Spencer, Thompson, & Neilson, 1966a, 1966b, 1966c). These studies established that the flexion reflex obeys the descriptive laws of behavioral habituation (Thompson & Spencer, 1966), that habituation of this reflex is not a function of alterations in the ability of the motor neurons to respond, and it is not due to changes in effective sensory input. In a later study, it was demonstrated that tonic presynaptic inhibition of afferent terminals did not occur during habituation, nor did tonic presynaptic facilitation occur during dishabituation or sensitization (Groves, Glanzman, Patterson, & Thompson, 1970). Single-unit recordings of interneurons in the cord have identified two types of cells: (1) type H which exhibits a continuous decrement in output in response to iterated stimulation; (2) type S–H which exhibits an initial sensitization (increased firing) followed by habituation (Groves, De Marco, & Thompson, 1969). The two types are located in different layers of the cord. These findings support the authors' contention that habituation and dishabituation (sensitization) are two distinct neural processes which interact to produce the actual behavioral output to a repeated stimulus in a given situation.

Kandel and associates have used the gill-withdrawal reflex in *Aplysia* as a model system for studying habituation. The anatomical substrates are simpler than the spinal cord. These researchers found that the reflex in question follows most of the descriptive laws of behavioral habituation in vertebrates (Pinkser, Kupfermann, Castellucci, & Kandel, 1969). As with the flexion reflex, habituation and dishabituation of the gill reflex were not due to peripheral changes in either the sensory or motor components. Intracellular recordings from motor neurons revealed that habituation and dishabituation were accompanied by changes in the EPSPs (Kupfermann, Castellucci, Pinsker, & Kandel, 1969). In a third study, the reflex arc was simplified to its monosynaptic components. Habituation was found to result from low-frequency depression in the monosynaptic motor neuron EPSPs, while dishabituation produced by application of a stimulus to another pathway produced EPSP facilitation (Castellucci, Pinsker, Kupfermann, & Kandel, 1969). Behavioral habituation and dishabituation in this system, therefore, are not a function of imposed inhibition, but are due to changes in the efficiency of the sensory-motor synapse, the exact nature of which remains to be determined.

## VI. CONCLUDING REMARKS

The stated purpose of this chapter was to present a viewpoint or framework from which our present knowledge of the neural bases of

attention would be evaluated. The perspective which has been emphasized here is that of behavior. From this point of view, approaches to
the cerebral substrates of stimulus selection must concern themselves
with the objects of attention. The bases for or categories selected by
an organism must either be known to or discovered by the experimenter.
They may not be inferred from anthropomorphic similes nor from mere
observation of an animal's posture or expression. In order to determine
the neural mechanisms which are the foundations of attention, the starting point must be behavior and must include a knowledge of what the
organism is selecting for or against. This point has been made before,
recently by Worden (1966), but it is echoed and dealt with in a more
intensive manner in this paper because it seems to lie at the crux of
the whole problem area.

One of the most glaring discrepancies in attention research is that
animal studies are characterized by a failure to determine the bases
of stimulus selection in contrast to the human studies which characteristically do apply accepted behavioral analysis techniques. The animal
studies have been concerned mainly with the question of sensory modulation, as evidenced by the many studies of evoked potential habituation,
or enhancement. The modulation of sensory system processing is certainly of potential significance to questions of attention mechanisms,
but this approach does not constitute a correlative approach to attention
unless it includes objective determination of what the animal is selecting
for or against while these fluctuations in sensory system activity are
taking place.

On the other hand, the studies using human subjects continue to increase in behavioral sophistication. This discrepancy is not due solely
to the fact that humans may be trained quickly by verbal commands,
for we have seen that extensive developments in experimental psychology
have produced techniques for assessing attention in non-humans. The
different emphasis between the human and animal studies may be due
to the fact that psychologists tend to perform the former while neurophysiologists undertake the latter experiments. Insofar as we cannot
presently use humans to investigate the intricacies of sensory system
functioning at subcortical levels, an amelioration of the present situation
may be accomplished by enticing more psychologists to undertake animal
work and by providing neurophysiologists with additional behavioral
training. Perhaps it is not too much to hope that in the coming years
training programs will produce scientists well versed in both.

Another recurrent theme pervading much of the literature in question
is the confounding of general arousal with attention. Previous consideration of this point was sufficiently extensive to preclude detailed com-

ment at this juncture. In summary, I have argued that arousal and attention must be differentiated conceptually and empirically, in order that we may one day find the brain mechanisms subserving stimulus selection. If we fail in this task, we may instead find correlates of the state of arousal which happens to characterize our subjects during an investigation. This is an interesting and worthy problem in itself, but the danger is that we will be deluded into believing that we know something about attention when, in fact, we do not.

What is the fate of sensory information that is selected for or against? We do not know. It must be stressed that we have no certain CNS measures of information. We can record evoked potentials to punctiform stimulation, and seek systematic changes related to behavioral stimulus selection. Such changes, when they are found, indicate that something in a sensory pathway is changing. If additionally we have controlled for peripheral effects, we may conclude that a *bona fide* CNS change has taken place. But the evoked potential is not yet validated as an index of information, only as a convenient marker that something has happened. The Fehmi, Adkins, and Lindsley study discussed previously suggested that only the minimal initial components of the EP are required for information transmission. These components are, in fact, the least labile of all EP components, so perhaps information is not blocked or altered in sensory systems. More data using this approach is needed to arrive at a firm conclusion.

As far as the future is concerned, a more fruitful approach might utilize single sensory unit recording. This strategy might be advantageous, because sensory cells at all levels of the neuraxis have been found to code discrete stimulus properties. Further, stimulation need not be restricted to flashes and clicks. The discrete coding aspects of unit behavior bring us closer to finding central measures of information *per se*. Systematic changes in the way a unit codes a stimulus category, reliably related to acquisition or loss of behavioral control by that stimulus category, would suggest that sensory information is modified during stimulus selection.

What can be said about nonsensory systems, "central integrative mechanisms"? The best data come from model system studies of the cat flexor reflex by R. F. Thompson and his associates, and of the gill-withdrawal reflex of *Aplysia* by E. Kandel and his associates. Both approaches combine careful behavioral measurement with correlated recording of CNS processes. To date, both groups have found that behavioral habituation (in these systems) is due to a change between the sensory and motor systems, and further that it may be caused by a "weak link," that is, a mechanism intrinsic to the reflex arcs, rather than to inhibition imposed from an extrinsic part of the nervous system. Insofar as the reticular core of the vertebrate brainstem may be considered a rostral extension of the central core of the spinal cord, it is not unreasonable to think that the reticular formation may mediate behavioral habituation in the intact animal, (Groves, Lynch, & Thompson, in preparation). At present, firm data are lacking.

It is a truism that the term "attention" refers to many phenomena, but nevertheless the common aspect of stimulus selection binds them together. In any case, there is no justification for assuming that at the neural level the same mechanisms underly all instances of stimulus selection. For example, different neural substrates may mediate selection based upon the various stimulus categories discussed: (1) presence–absence, (2) sensory modality, (3) locus, (4) modality-specific attribute, and (5) pattern. Additionally, the type of mechanism may also be a function of the information demands made upon an organism. Thus, stimulus selection early in training requires more of an organism's information processing capacity than at a later time, when the habit is well practiced. A new driver requires that all of his "attention" be focused on the task at hand; interruptions are not welcome, and only the most relevant or trivial conversation will be attended. Additionally, even with well-practiced tasks, the information-processing load will not necessarily be light. This depends upon the task. For example, during habituation to an occasional stimulus, the load is light; during dichotic listening, heavy. In short, both stimulus category selected and information processing load may determine the type of brain mechanism(s) which form the substrates of stimulus selection. If we have no evidence that the neural mechanisms of attention are multiple, then we have even less evidence that they are unitary.

In farming, the ground must be cleared before it can be tilled, planted, and eventually harvested. So it seems to be in a new field of science. Systematic attempts to find the neural substrates of attention are now midway through their second decade. Much of this time has been spent in clearing the ground. The importance of stimulus control and the action of peripheral mechanisms in sensory systems is now well understood and no longer presents an obstacle to progress. The problem of arousal in studies of attention is now being acknowledged and will come to be controlled. Technological advances in computer processing of neuroelectric data now render objective and quantitative analysis a routine matter. The ground, in fact, appears to have been cleared, with the exception of a rough spot or two. The time is ripe for planting, and the next logical step seems to be careful behavioral analysis coupled with sophisticated neural techniques. The harvest will depend upon this.

In closing, it must be admitted that progress has been slower than we would prefer. With respect to the whole problem of attention, we have advanced relatively little. But from the perspective of the first rather exciting but naive studies of the mid-fifties, we have come a long way. Our modest rate of progress need not be considered as reflecting poorly upon the efforts of the investigators involved. It is more likely a tribute to the immense difficulty of the task which they have undertaken.

# REFERENCES

Adey, W. R., & Lindsley, D. F. On the role of subthalamic areas in the maintenance of brain-stem reticular excitability. *Experimental Neurology*, 1959, **1**, 407–426.

Alcaraz, M., Pacheco, P., & Guzman-Flores, C. Distraccion a estimulos acusticos en gatos con seccion de las musculas del oido medio. *Boletin del Instituto de Estudios Medicos y Biologicos (Universidad Nacional Autonoma de Mexico)*, 1961, **19**, 215–222.

Apelbaum, J., Silva, E. E., Frick, O., & Segundo, J. P. Specificity and biasing of arousal reaction habituation. *Electroencephalography & Clinical Neurophysiology*, 1960, **12**, 829–840.

Bach-Y-Rita, G., Brust-Carmona, H., Penaloza-Rojas, J., & Hernandez-Peon, R. Absence of para-auditory descending influences on the cochlear nucleus during distraction and habituation. *Acta Neurologica Latinoamerica*, 1961, **7**, 73–81.

Baker, C. H. Further towards a theory of vigilance. In D. N. Buckner and J. J. McGrath, (Eds.), *Vigilance: a Symposium*. New York: McGraw-Hill, 1963.

Baust, W., & Berlucchi, G. Reflex response to clicks of cat's tensor tympani during sleep and wakefulness and the influence thereon of the auditory cortex. *Archives Italiennes de Biologie*, 1964, **102**, 686–712.

Beh, H. C., & Barratt, P. E. H. (1965). Discrimination and conditioning during sleep as indicated by the electroencephalogram, *Science*, 1965, **147**, 1470–1471.

Bettinger, L. A., Davis, J. L., Meckle, M. B., Birch, H., Kopp, R., Smith, H. E., & Thompson, R. F. "Novelty" cells in association cortex of cat. *Psychonomic Science*, 1967, **9**, 421–422.

Bickford, R. G., Jacobson, J. L., & Cody, D. T. R. Nature of average evoked potentials to sound and other stimuli in man. *Annals of the New York Academy of Sciences*, 1964, **112**, 204–223.

Blough, D. S. Attention shifts in a maintained discrimination. *Science*, 1969, **166**, 125–126.

Bogdanski, D. F., & Galambos, R. Studies of the auditory system with implanted electrodes: Chronic microelectrode studies. In G. L. Rasmussen and W. F. Windle (Eds.), *Neural mechanisms of the auditory and vestibular systems*. Springfield, Illinois: Thomas, 1960. Pp. 143–148.

Boring, E. G. *A history of experimental psychology*. (2nd ed.) New York: Appleton-Century-Crofts, 1957.

Broadbent, D. E. *Perception and communication*, Oxford: Pergamon Press, 1958.

Broadbent, D. E., & Gregory, M. Division of attention and the decision theory of signal detection. *Proceedings of the Royal Society B,* 1963, **158**, 222–231.

Bruner, J. S., Matter, J., & Papanek, M. L. Breadth of learning as a function of drive level and mechanization. *Psychological Review,* 1955, **62**, 1–10.

Buchwald, N. A., Hull, C. D., & Trachtenberg, M. C. Concomitant behavioral and neural inhibition and disinhibition in response to subcortical stimulation. *Experimental Brain Research,* 1967, **4**, 58–72.

Buckner, D. N., & McGrath, J. J. (Eds.) *Vigilance: a symposium,* New York: McGraw-Hill, 1963.

Buno, W., Velluti, R., Handler, P., & Garcia-Austt, E. Neural control of the cochlear input in the wakeful free guinea-pig. *Physiology and Behavior,* 1965, **1**, 23–35.

Butler, R. A. Discrimination learning by rhesus monkeys to visual-exploration motivation. *Journal of Comparative & Physiological Psychology,* 1953, **46**, 95–98.

Butler, R. A., & Harlow, H. F. Persistence of visual exploration in monkeys. *Journal of Comparative & Physiological Psychology,* 1954, **57**, 258–263.

Butter, C. M. Habituation of responses to novel stimuli in monkeys with selective frontal lesions. *Science,* 1964, **144**, 313–315.

Callaway, E., & Stone, G. Re-evaluating focus of attention. In L. Uhr and J. G. Miller, (Eds.) *Drugs and behavior.* New York: Wiley, 1960. Pp. 393–398.

Callaway, E., & Yeager, C. L. Relationship between reaction time and electroencephalographic alpha phase *Science,* 1960, **132**, 1765–1766.

Capps, M. J., & Ades, H. W. Auditory frequency discrimination after transection of the olivocochlear bundle in squirrel monkeys. *Experimental Neurology,* 1968, **21**, 147–158.

Carmel, P. W., & Starr, A. Acoustical and nonacoustical factors modifying middle ear muscle activity in waking cats. *Journal of Neurophysiology,* 1963, **26**, 598–616.

Castellucci, V., Pinsker, H., Kupfermann, I., & Kandel, E. Neuronal mechanisms of habituation and dishabituation of the gill-withdrawal reflex in Aplysia. *Science,* 1969, **167**, 1745–1748.

Cavaggioni, A., Giannelli, G., & Santibanez-H., G. Effects of repetitive photic stimulation on responses evoked in the lateral geniculate body and the visual cortex. *Archives Italiennes de Biologie,* 1959, **97**, 266–275.

Cherry, E. C. Some experiments on the recognition of speech, with one and with two ears. *Journal of the Acoustical Society America,* 1953, **25**, 975–979.

Chow, K. L., Dement, W. C., and Mitchell, S. A., Jr. Effect of lesions of the rostral thalamus on brain waves and behavior in cats. *Electroencephalography & Clinical Neurophysiology,* 1959, **11**, 107–120.

Comis, S. D., & Whitfield, I. C. Centrifugal excitation and inhibition in the cochlear nucleus. *Journal of Physiology,* 1967, **188**, 34–35P.

Creelman, C. D. Human discrimination of auditory duration. *Journal of the Acoustical Society of America,* 1962, **34**, 582–593.

Dashiell, J. F. *Fundamentals of objective psychology.* Boston, Massachusetts: Houghton-Mifflin, 1928.

Davis, H. Enhancement of evoked cortical potentials in humans related to a task requiring a decision. *Science,* 1964, **25**, 182–183.

Debecker, J., & Desmedt, J. E. Rate of intermodality switching disclosed by sensory evoked potentials averaged during signal detection tasks. *Journal of Physiology,* 1966, **185**, 52–53.

Deese, J. The extinction of a discrimination without performance of the choice response. *Journal of Comparative and Physiological Psychology,* 1951, **44**, 362–366.

Deutsch, J. A., & Deutsch, D. Attention: some theoretical considerations. *Psychological Review,* 1963, **70**, 51–61.

DeValois, R. L. Analysis and coding of color vision in the primate visual system. *Sensory receptors,* Cold Spring Harbor, New York: Society of Quant. Biology, 1965. Pp. 566–580.

Dewson, J. H., III, Efferent olivocochlear bundle: some relationships to stimulus discrimination in noise. *Journal of Neurophysiology,* 1968, **31**, 122–130.

Dewson, J. H., III, Nobel, K. W., & Pribram, K. H. Corticofugal influence at cochlear nucleus of the cat. Some effects of ablation of insulartemporal cortex. *Brain Research,* 1966, **2**, 151–159.

Dobrzecka, C., Szwejkowska, G., & Kornorski, J. Qualitative versus directional cues in two forms of differentiation. *Science,* 1966, **153**, 87–89.

Donchin, E., & Cohen, M. D. Averaged evoked potentials and intramodality selective attention. *Electroencephalography & Clinical Neurophysiology,* 1967, **22**, 537–546.

Donchin, E., & Lindsley, D. B. Averaged evoked potentials and reaction times to visual stimuli. *Electroencephalography & Clinical Neurophysiology,* 1966, **20**, 217–223.

Donchin, E., & Lindsley, D. B. (Eds.) *Average Evoked Potentials—Methods, Results and Evaluations.* NASA SP-191, Washington, D.C., 1969.

Donchin, E., & Smith, D. B. The CNV and the "late positive wave"—two sides of the same coin. *Electroencephalography and Clinical Neurophysiology,* 1969, **28**, 91.

Dubrovinskaya, N. V. The behavior of colliculi neurons in the course of repeated stimulus presentation. In *Orienting Reflex, Alertness, and Attention. 18th International Congress of Psychology, Moscow,* 1966. Pp. 82–83.

Dunlop, C. W., Webster, W. R., & Simons, L. A. Effect of attention on evoked responses in the classical auditory pathway. *Nature,* 1965, **206**, 1048–1050.

Dustman, R. E., & Beck, E. C. Phase of alpha brain waves, reaction time, and visually evoked potentials. *Electroencephalography & Clinical Neurophysiology,* 1965, **18**, 433–440.

Eason, R. G., Aiken, L. R., Jr., White, C. T., & Lichtenstein, M. Activation and behavior: II. Visually evoked cortical potentials in man as indicants of activation level. *Perceptual & Motor Skills,* 1964, **19**, 875–895.

Eason, R. G., Harter, M. R., & White, C. T. Effects of attention and arousal on visually evoked cortical potentials and reaction time in man. *Physiology and Behavior,* 1969, **4**, 283–289.

Egeth, H. Selective attention. *Psychological Bulletin,* 1967, **67**, 41–56.

Elul, R., & Marchiafava, P. L. Accommodation of the eyes as related to behavior in the cat. *Archives Italiennes de Biologie,* 1964, **102**, 616–644.

Estes, W. K. The statistical approach to learning theory. In S. Koch, (Ed.), *Psychology: A study of a science.* Vol. 2. *General systematic formulations, learning, and special processes.* New York: McGraw-Hill, 1959. Pp. 380–491.

Fangel, C., & Kaada, B. R. Behavior "attention" and fear induced by cortical stimulation in the cat. *Electroencephalography & Clinical Neurophysiology,* 1960, **12**, 575–588.

Fedio, P., Mirsky, A. F., Smith, W. J., & Perry, D. Reaction time and EEG activation in normal and schizophrenic subjects. *Electroencephalography & Clinical Neurophysiology,* 1961, **13**, 923–926.

Feeney, D. M. Thalamocortical evoked potentials during appetitive conditioning in dogs. *Proceedings 77th Annual Convention of the American Psychological Association,* 1969. P. 385.

Fehmi, L. G., Adkins, J. W., & Lindsley, D. B. Electrophysiological correlates of visual perceptual masking in monkeys. *Experimental Brain Research,* 1969, **7,** 299–316.

Fernandez-Guardiola, A., Roldan, E., Fanjul, L., & Castillo, C. Role of the pupillary mechanism in the process of habituation of the visual pathways. *Electroencephalography & Clinical Neurophysiology,* 1961, **13,** 564–576.

Fex, J. Auditory activity in centrifugal and centripetal cochlear fibers in cat. *Acta Physiologica Scandinavica, Supplement,* 1962, **189,** 1–68.

French, G. M. Locomotor effects of regional ablations of frontal cortex in rhesus monkeys. *Journal of Comparative & Physiological Psychology,* 1959, **52,** 18–24.

Galambos, R., Schwartzkopff, J., & Rupert, A. Microelectrode study of superior olivary nuclei. *American Journal of Physiology,* 1959, **197,** 527–536.

Garcia, J., & Ervin, F. R. (1968). Gustatory-visceral and telereceptor-cutaneous conditioning—adaptation in internal and external mileus. *Communications in Behavior Biology,* 1968, **1,** 389–415.

Garcia-Austt, E., Bogacz, J., & Vanzulli, A. Effects of attention and inattention upon visual evoked response. *Electroencephalography & Clinical Neurophysiology,* 1964, **17,** 136–143.

Gardiner, M. F., & Walter, D. O. Information processing and auditory evoked potentials in man. *Communications in Behavioral Biology,* 1968, **B,** 115.

Gilbert, R. M., & Sutherland, N. S. *Animal discrimination learning,* London: Academic Press, 1969.

Giolli, R. A., & Guthrie, M. D. Organization of projections of visual areas I and II upon the superior colliculus and pre-tectal nuclei in the rabbit. *Brain Research,* 1967, **6,** 388–390.

Glaser, E. M. Assessment of pharmacological action upon the brain, based on experimental studies of habituation. *Proceedings of the First International Pharmacological Meeting,* Oxford: Pergamon Press, 1962. Pp. 315–324.

Gluck, H., & Rowland, V. Defensive conditioning of electrographic arousal with delayed and differentiated stimuli. *Electroencephalography & Clinical Neurophysiology,* 1959, **11,** 485–496.

Goodman, D. A. Some Brain Reflexes of *Necturus Maculosus,* the Mud Puppy. Unpublished doctoral dissertation, University of California, Irvine, 1969.

Goodman, S. J. Visuo-motor reaction times and brain stem multiple-unit activity. *Experimental Neurology,* 1968, **22,** 367–378.

Goodwin, W. R., & Lawrence, D. H. The functional independence of two discrimination habits associated with a constant stimulus situation. *Journal of Comparative & Physiological Psychology,* 1955, **48,** 437–443.

Gordon, G., & Jukes, M. G. M. Correlation of different excitatory and inhibitory influences on cells in the nucleus gracilis of the cat. *Nature,* 1962, **196,** 1183–1185.

Graham, F. K., & Clifton, R. K. Heart-rate change as a component of the orienting response. *Psychological Bulletin,* 1966, **65,** 305–320.

Granda, A., & Hammack, J. Operant behavior during sleep. *Science,* 1961, **133,** 1485–1486.

Green, D. M., & Swets, J. A. *Signal detection theory and psychophysics.* New York: Wiley, 1966.

Groves, P. M., DeMarco, R., & Thompson, R. F. Habituation and sensitization of spinal interneuron activity in acute spinal cat. *Brain Research*, 1969, **14**, 521–525.

Groves, P. M., Glanzman, D. L., Patterson, M. M., & Thompson, R. F. Excitability of cutaneous afferent terminals during habituation and sensitization in acute spinal cat. *Brain Research*, 1970, **18**, 388–392.

Groves, P. M., Lynch, G., & Thompson, R. F. *Brain stem mechanisms for habituation*. (in preparation)

Guzman-Flores, C., Alcaraz, M., & Harmony, T. Role of the intrinsic ear muscles in the process of acoustic habituation. *Boletin del Instituto de Estudios Medicos y Biologicos (Universidad Nacional Autonoma de Mexico)*, 1960, **18**, 135–140.

Hagbarth, K. E., & Kerr, D. I. B. Central influences on spinal afferent conduction. *Journal of Neurophysiology*, 1954, **17**, 295–307.

Haider, M., Spong, P., & Lindsley, D. B. (1964). Attention, vigilance, and cortical evoked potentials in humans. *Science*, 1964, **145**, 180–182.

Hall, R. D. Habituation of evoked potentials in the rat under conditions of behavioral control. *Electroencephalography & Clinical Neurophysiology*, 1968, **24**, 155–165.

Hall, R. D., & Mark, R. G. Fear and the modification of acoustically evoked potentials during conditioning. *Journal of Neurophysiology*, 1967, **30**, 893–910.

Harris, J. D. Habituatory response decrement in the intact organism. *Psychological Bulletin*, 1943, **40**, 385–422.

Hartline, H. K. The response of single optic nerve fibers of the vertebrate eye to illumination of the retina. *American Journal Physiology*, 1938, **121**, 400–415.

Hebb, D. O. *A textbook of psychology*. Philadelphia, Pennsylvania: Saunders, 1958.

Heinemann, E. G., Chase, S., & Mandell, C. Discriminative control of "attention." *Science*, 1968, **160**, 553–554.

Hernandez-Peon, R. Neurophysiological correlates of habituation and other manifestations of plastic inhibition (internal inhibition). In H. H. Jasper and G. D. Smirnov (Eds.), *The Moscow colloquium on EEG of higher nervous activity*. *Electroencephalography & Clinical Neurophysiology, Supplement*, 1960, **13**, 101–114.

Hernandez-Peon, R. Reticular mechanisms of sensory control. In W. A. Rosenblith, (Ed.), *Sensory communication*. New York: MIT Press and Wiley, 1961. Pp. 497–520.

Hernandez-Peon, R. Physiological mechanisms in attention. In R. W. Russell, (Ed.), *Frontiers in physiological psychology*. New York: Academic Press, 1966. Pp. 121–147.

Hernandez-Peon, R., Scherrer, H., & Jouvet, M. Modification of electric activity in cochlear nucleus during "attention" in unanesthetized cats. *Science*, 1956, **123**, 331–332.

Holstein, S. B., Buchwald, J. S., & Schwafel, J. A. Progressive changes in auditory response patterns to repeated tone during normal wakefulness and paralysis. *Brain Research*, 1969, **16**, 133–148.

Honig, W. K. *Operant behavior: areas of research and applications*. New York: Appleton, 1966.

Horn, G. Electrical activity of the cerebral cortex of the unanaesthetized cat during attentive behaviour. *Brain*, 1960, **83**, 57–66.

Horn, G. Physiological and psychological aspects of selective perception. In D. S.

Lehrman, R. A. Hinde, & S. Shaw (Eds.), *Advances in the study of behavior.* New York: Academic Press, 1965. Pp. 155–216.

Horn, G. Behavioral and cellular responses to novel and repeated stimuli. In R. E. Whalen, R. F. Thompson, M. Verzeano, & N. M. Weinberger, (Eds.), *The neural control of behavior.* New York: Academic Press, 1970.

Horn, G., & Blundell, J. Evoked potentials in visual cortex of the unanaesthetized cat. *Nature,* 1959, **184,** 173–174.

Horn, G., & Hill, R. M. Responsiveness to sensory stimulation of units in the superior colliculus and subjacent tectotegmental regions of the rabbit. *Experimental Neurology,* 1966, **14,** 199–223.

Horn, G., & Rowell, C. H. F. Medium and long term changes in the behaviour of visual neurones in the tritocerebrum of locusts. *Journal of Experimental Biology,* 1968, **49,** 143–169.

Hubel, D. H., Henson, C. D., Rupert, A., & Galambos, R. Attention units in the auditory cortex. *Science,* 1959, **129,** 1279–1280.

Hubel, D. H., & Weisel, T. N. Receptive fields and functional architecture in two nonstriate visual areas (18 and 19) of the cat. *Journal of Neurophysiology,* 1965, **28,** 229–289.

Hugelin, A., Dumont, S., & Paillas, N. Tympanic muscles and control of auditory input during arousal. *Science,* 1960, **131,** 1371–1372.

Humphrey, G. *The nature of learning,* Chapter 6. *Habituation.* New York: Harcourt-Brace, 1933.

Hutt, S. J., & Hutt, C. Hyperactivity in a group of epileptic (and some non-epileptic) brain-damaged children. *Epilepsia,* 1964, **5,** 334–351.

James, W. (1890). *The principles of psychology.* Vol. I. New York: Holt, 1890.

Jane, J. A., Smirnov, G. D., & Jasper, H. H. Effects of distraction upon simultaneous auditory and visual evoked potentials. *Electroencephalography & Clinical Neurophysiology,* 1962, **14,** 344–358.

Jane, J. A., Masterson, R. B., & Diamond, I. T. The function of the tectum for attention to auditory stimuli in the cat. *Journal of Comparative Neurology,* 1965, **125,** 165–192.

Jerison, H. Attention. In D. L. Sills, (Ed.), *International encyclopedia of the social sciences.* New York: Macmillan and The Free Press, 1968. Pp. 444–448. 444–448.

Jerison, H., Pickett, R. M., & Stenson, H. H. The elicited observing rate and decision processes in vigilance. *Human Factors,* 1965, **7,** 107–128.

John, E. R. *Mechanisms of memory.* New York: Academic Press, 1967.

Kaada, B. R., & Bruland, H. Blocking of cortically induced behavioral attention (orienting) responses by chlorpromazine. *Psychopharmacologia (Berlin),* 1960, **1,** 372–388.

Kaada, B. R., & Ursin, H. Further localization of behavioral responses elicited from the amygdala in unanesthetized cats. *Acta Physiologica Scandinavica,* 1957, **42,** Supplement 145, 80–81.

Kaas, J., Axelrod, S., & Diamond, I. T. An ablation study of the auditory cortex in the cat using binaural tonal patterns. *Journal of Neurophysiology,* 1967, **30,** 710–724.

Kagan, J., & Lewis, M. Studies of attention in the human infant. *Merrill-Palmer Quarterly,* 1965, **11,** 95–127.

Kagan, J., & Rosman, B. L. Cardiac and respiratory correlates of attention and an analytic attitude. *Journal of Experimental Child Psychology,* 1964, **1,** 50–63.

Karlin, L. Cognition, preparation, and sensory-evoked potentials. *Psychological Bulletin,* 1970, **73,** 122–136.

Khachaturian, Z. S., & Gluck, H. The effects of arousal on the amplitude of evoked potentials. *Brain Research,* 1969, **14,** 589–606.

Kiang, N. Y-S. *Discharge patterns of single fibers in the cat's auditory nerve. Research Monograph #35.* Cambridge, Massachuetts: MIT Press, 1965.

King, F. A., & Marchiafava, P. L. Ocular movements in the mid, pontine pretrigeminal preparation. *Archives Italiennes de Biologie,* 1963, **101,** 149–160.

Kitzes, L. M. Auditory system activity during selective listening in the cat. Unpublished doctoral dissertation, University of California, Irvine, 1970.

Kitzes, M., & Buchwald, J. Progressive alterations in cochlear nucleus, inferior colliculus, and medial geniculate responses during acoustic habituation. *Experimental Neurology,* 1969, **25,** 85–105.

Kluver, H., & Bucy, P. C. Preliminary analysis of functions of the temporal lobes in monkeys. *Archives of Neurology Psychiatry,* 1939, **42,** 979–1000.

Kornetsky, C., Mirsky, A. F., Kessler, E. K., & Dorff, J. E. The effects of dextroamphetamine on behavioral deficits produced by sleep loss in humans. *Journal of Pharmacology & Experimental Therapeutics,* 1959, **127,** 46–50.

Kornorski, J., & Lawicka, W. Analysis of errors by prefrontal animals on the delayed-response test. In J. M. Warren and K. Akert, (Eds.), *The frontal cortex and behavior.* New York: McGraw-Hill, 1964. Pp. 271–294.

Kuffler, S. W. Discharge patterns and functional organization of mammalian retina. *Journal of Neurophysiology,* 1953, **16,** 37–68.

Kupfermann, I., Castellucci, V., Pinsker, H., & Kandel, E. Neuronal correlates of habituation and dishabituation of the gill-withdrawal reflex in Aplysia. *Science,* 1970, **167,** 1743–1745.

La Grutta, V., Giammanco, S., & Amato, G. The control of the auditory system by the caudate nucleus in the cat. *Archives of Science Biology (Bologna),* 1969, **53,** 1–31.

Lansing, R. W. Relations of brain and tremor rhythms to visual reaction time. *Electroencephalography & Clinical Neurophysiology,* 1957, **9,** 497–504.

Lavin, A., Alcocer-Cuaron, C., & Hernandez-Peon, R. Centrifugal arousal in the olfactory bulb. *Science,* 1959, **129,** 332–333.

Lawrence, D. H. The nature of a stimulus: Some relationships between learning and perception. In S. Koch (Ed.), *Psychology: a study of a science,* Vol. 5. New York: McGraw-Hill, 1963. Pp. 179–212.

Leaton, R. N. Exploratory behavior in rats with hippocampal lesions. *Journal of Comparative & Physiology Psychology,* 1965, **59,** 325–330.

Lindsley, D. B. Psychological phenomena and the electroencephalogram. *Electroencephalography & Clinical Neurophysiology,* 1952, **4,** 443–456.

Lindsley, D. B. Attention, consciousness, sleep and wakefulness. In J. Field, H. W. Magoun, & V. E. Hall (Eds.), *Handbook of physiology,* Vol. 3. Baltimore: Williams and Wilkins, 1960.

Livingston, R. B. Central control of receptors and sensory transmission systems. In J. Field *et al.* (Eds.), *Handbook of physiology,* Vol. 1, Sect. I. Washington, D.C.: American Physiological Society, 1959. Pp. 741–760.

Lockhart, R. A. Temporal conditioning of GSR. *Journal of Experimental Psychology,* 1966, **71,** 438–446.

MacKay, D. M. Evoked brain potentials as indicators of sensory information processing. *Neuroscience Research Program Bulletin,* 1969, **7,** No. 3.

Mackintosh, N. J. Selective attention in animal discrimination learning. *Psychological Bulletin*, 1965, **64**, 124–150.

Mackworth, N. H., Kaplan, I. T., & Metlay, W. Eye movements during vigilance. *Perceptual & Motor Skills*, 1964, **18**, 397–402.

Mancia, M., Meulders, M., & Santibanez-H., G. Changes in the photically evoked potentials in the visual pathway of the cerveau isole cat. *Archives Italiennes de Biologie*, 1959, **97**, 378–398. (a)

Mancia, M., Meulders, M., & Santibanez-H., G. Changes of photically evoked potentials in the visual pathway of the midpontine pretrigeminal cat. *Archives Italiennes de Biologie*, 1959, **97**, 399–413. (b)

Mark, R. C., & Hall, R. D. Acoustically evoked potentials in the rat during conditioning. *Journal of Neurophysiology*, 1967, **30**, 875–892.

Marsh, J. T., Worden, F. G., & Hicks, L. Some effects of room acoustics on evoked auditory potentials. *Science*, 1962, **137**, 280–282.

Miles, C. G., & Jenkins, H. M. Overshadowing and blocking in discriminative operant conditioning. Paper delivered at the meeting of the Psychonomic Society, 1965.

Mirsky, A. F., & Cardon, P. V. Jr. A comparison of the behavioral and physiological changes accompanying sleep deprivation and chlorpromazine administration in man. *Electroencephalography and Clinical Neurophysiology*, 1962, **14**, 1–10.

Mirsky, A. F., Primac, D. W., & Bates, R. The effects of chlorpromazine and secobarbital on the C.P.T. *Journal of Nervous & Mental Disease*, 1959, **128**, 12–17.

Mirsky, A. F., & Rosvold, H. E. Behavioral and physiological studies in impaired attention. In *Psychopharmacological methods*, Oxford: Pergamon Press, 1963.

Mirsky, A. F., & Tecce, J. J. The relationship between EEG and impaired attention following administration of centrally acting drugs. *Proceedings of the Fifth Congress of the Collegium Internationale Neuropsychopharmacologicum*, Washington, D.C. 1966.

Moray, N. Attention. *Selective processes in vision and hearing*. London: Hutchinson Educational Ltd., 1969.

Morrell, F. Electrophysiological contributions to the neural basis of learning. *Physiological Review*, 1961, **41**, 443–494.

Mostovsky, D. I. (Eds.) *Stimulus generalization*. Stanford, California: Stanford University Press, 1965.

Moushegian, G., Rupert, A., Marsh, J. T., & Galambos, R. Evoked cortical potentials in absence of middle ear muscles. *Science*, 1961, **133**, 582–583.

Näätänen, R. Selective attention and evoked potentials. *Annales Academiae Scientarum Fennice*, 1967, **151**, 1–226.

Neff, W. D., & Diamond, I. T. The neural basis of auditory discrimination. In H. F. Harlow, and C. N. Woolsey (Eds.), *Biological and biochemical basis of behavior*. Madison: University of Wisconsin Press, 1958. Pp. 101–126.

Newman, F. L., & Benefield, R. L. Stimulus control, cue utilization and attention: Effects of discrimination training. *Journal of Comparative & Physiological Psychology*, 1968, **66**, 101–104.

Norman, D. A. *Memory and attention: an introduction to human information processing*. New York: Wiley, 1969.

Oliverio, A., & Bovet, D. Transfer of avoidance responding between visual and auditive stimuli presented in different temporal patterns. *Communications in Behavioral Biology*, 1969, **3**, 61–68.

Oswald, I., Taylor, A. M., & Treisman, M. Discriminative responses to stimulation during human sleep. *Brain,* 1960, **83,** 440–453.

Palestini, M., Davidovich, A., & Hernandez-Peon, R. Functional significance of centrifugal influences upon the retina. *Acta Neurologica Latinoamericana.* 1959, **5,** 113–131.

Palestini, M., Gallardo, R., & Armengol, V. Peripheral factors in the study of the habituation of the cortical responses to photic stimulation. *Archives Italiennes de Biologie,* 1964, **102,** 608–615.

Parmeggiani, P. L., & Rapisarda, C. Hippocampal output and sensory mechanisms. *Brain Research,* 1969, **14,** 387–400.

Paschal, F. C. The trend in theories of attention. *Psychological Bulletin,* 1941, **48,** 383–403.

Pavlov, I. P. *Conditioned reflexes,* London: Oxford University Press, 1927.

Phillips, D. S. Olfactory cues in visual discrimination learning. *Physiology and Behavior,* 1968, **3,** 683–685.

Pillsbury, W. B. *Attention,* New York: Macmillan, 1908.

Pinsker, H., Kuppermann, I., Castelluci, V., & Kandel, E. Habituation and dishabituation of the gill-withdrawal reflex in Aplysia. *Science,* 1969, **167,** 1740–1742.

Poggio, G. F., & Mountcastle, V. B. The functional properties of ventrobasal thalamic neurons studied in unanesthetized monkeys. *Journal of Neurophysiology,* 1963, **26,** 775–806.

Pribram, K. H. Memory and the organization of attention. In D. B. Lindsley and A. A. Lumsdaine (Eds.), *Brain function.* Vol. 4. *Brain function and learning* Berkeley: University of California Press, 1967. Pp. 79–112. (a)

Pribram, K. H. The limbic systems, efferent control of neural inhibition and behavior. In W. R. Adey and T. Tokizane (Eds.), *Progress in brain research.* Vol. 27. *Structure and function of the limbic system.* Amsterdam: Elsevier, 1967. Pp. 318–336. (b)

Primac, D. W., Mirsky, A. F., & Rosvold, H. E. Effects of centrally acting drugs on two tests of brain damage. *American Medical Association Archives of Neurological Psychiatry,* 1957, **77,** 328–332.

Rasmussen, G. L. Anatomic relationships of the ascending and descending auditory systems. In W. S. Fields & B. R. Alford (Eds.), *Neurological aspects of auditory vestibular disorders.* Springfield, Massachusetts: Thomas, 1964. Pp. 5–23.

Razran, G. The observable unconscious and the inferable conscious in current soviet psychophysiology: Interoceptive conditioning, semantic conditioning, and the orienting reflex. *Psychological Review,* 1961, **68,** 81–147.

Riley, D. A. *Discrimination learning,* Boston: Allyn and Bacon, 1968.

Ritter, W., Vaughn, H. G., Jr., & Costa, L. D. Orienting and habituation to auditory stimuli: A study of short term changes in average evoked responses. *Electroencephalography & Clinical Neurophysiology,* 1968, **25,** 550–556.

Rosvold, H. E., Mirsky, A. F., Sarason, I., Bransome, E. D., Jr., & Beck, L. H. A continuous performance test of brain damage. *Journal of Consulting Psychology,* 1956, **20,** 343–350.

Rowell, C. H. F., & Horn, G. Dishabituation and arousal in the response of single nerve cells in an insect brain. *Journal of Experimental Biology,* 1968, **49,** 171–183.

Rowland, V. Differential electroencephalographic response to conditioned auditory stimuli in arousal from sleep. *Electroencephalography & Clinical Neurophysiology,* 1957, **9,** 585–594.

Salapatek, P. Visual scanning of geometric figures by the human newborn. *Journal of Comparative & Physiological Psychology,* 1968, **66,** 247–258.

Saloman, G., & Starr, A. Electromyography of middle ear muscles in man during motor activities. *Acta Neurologica Scandinavica,* 1963, **39,** 161–168.

Sanders, A. F. (Ed.). *Attention and performance.* Amsterdam: North-Holland Publ., 1967.

Satterfield, J. H. Evoked cortical response enhancement and attention in man: A study of responses to auditory and shock stimuli. *Electroencephalography & Clinical Neurophysiology,* 1965, **19,** 470–475.

Saunders, J. C., & Chabora, J. T. Effects of appetitive drive on evoked potentials in cochlear nucleus and auditory cortex in cats. *Journal of Comparative & Physiological Psychology,* 1969, **69,** 355–361.

Scholander, T. Intra-individual variability in habituation of autonomic response elements. *Acta Societatis Medicorum Upaliensis,* 1960, **65,** 259–289.

Schroeder, S. R., & Holland, J. G. Operant control of eye movements. *Journal of Applied Behavioral Analysis,* 1968, **1,** 161–166.

Schwartzbaum, J. S., Wilson, W. A. Jr., & Morrissette, J. R. The effects of amygdalectomy on locomotor activity in monkeys. *Journal of Comparative and Physiological Psychology,* 1961, **54,** 334–336.

Schwartzkroin, P. A., Cowey, A., & Gross, C. G. A test of an "efferent model" of the function of inferotemporal cortex in visual discrimination. *Electroencephalography and Clinical Neurophysiology,* 1969, **27,** 594–599.

Segundo, J. P., Arana, R., & French, J. D. Behavioral arousal by stimulation of the brain in the monkey. *Journal of Neurosurgery,* 1955, **12,** 601.

Sharpless, S. K., & Jasper, H. H. Habituation of the arousal reaction. *Brain,* 1956, **79,** 655–669.

Sheatz, G. C., & Chapman, R. M. Task relevance and auditory evoked responses. *Electroencephalography & Clinical Neurophysiology,* 1969, **26,** 468–475.

Siddall, G. J., & Anderson, D. M. Fatigue during prolonged performance on a simple compensatory tracking task. *Quarterly Journal of Experimental Psychology,* 1955, **12,** 601–613.

Simmons, F. B. Middle ear muscle activity at moderate sound levels. *Annals of Otology, Rhinology, & Laryngology,* 1959, **68,** 1126–1143.

Simons, L. A., Dunlop, C. W., Webster, W. R., & Aitkin, L. M. Acoustic habituation in cats as a function of stimulus rate and the role of temporal conditioning of the middle ear muscles. *Electroencephalography & Clinical Neurophysiology,* 1966, **20,** 485–493.

Skinner, B. F. *Science and human behavior.* New York: Macmillan, 1953.

Smith, D. B., Donchin, E., Cohen, L., & Starr, A. Auditory averaged evoked potentials in man during selective binaural listening. *Electroencephalography & Clinical Neurophysiology,* 1970, **28,** 146–152.

Sokolov, E. N. Neuronal models and the orienting reflex. In M. A. B. Brazier (Ed.), *The central nervous system and behavior.* New York: Josiah Macy, 1960. Pp. 187–276.

Sokolov, E. N. Higher nervous functions. The orienting reflex. *Annual Review of Physiology,* 1963, **26,** 545–580. (a)

Sokolov, E. N. *Perception and the conditioned reflex.* Oxford: Pergamon Press, 1963. (b)

Sokolov, E. N. Neuronal mechanisms of the orienting reflex. In *Orienting reflex, alertness and attention, 18th International Congress of Psychology, Moscow,* 1966. Pp. 31–36.

Spencer, W. A., Thompson, R. F., & Neilson, D. R., Jr. Response decrement of the flexion reflex in the acute spinal cat and transient restoration by strong stimuli. *Journal of Neurophysiology*, 1966, 29, 221–239. (a)

Spencer, W. A., Thompson, R. F., & Neilson, D. R., Jr. Alterations in responsiveness of ascending and reflex pathways activated by iterated cutaneous afferent volleys. *Journal of Neurophysiology*, 1966, 29, 240–252. (b)

Spencer, W. A., Thompson, R. F., & Neilson, D. R., Jr. Decrement of ventral root electrotonus and intracellulary recorded PSPs produced by iterated cutaneous afferent volleys. *Journal of Neurophysiology*, 1966, 29, 253–274. (c)

Spinelli, D. N., & Pribram, K. H. Changes in visual recovery function produced by temporal lobe stimulation in monkeys. *Electroencephalography & Clinical Neurophysiology*, 1966, 20, 44–49.

Spong, P., Haider, M., & Lindsley, D. B. Selective attentiveness and cortical evoked responses to visual and auditory stimuli. *Science*, 1965, 148, 395–397.

Sprague, J. M., Levitt, M., Robson, K., Liu, C. N., Stellar, E., & Chambers, W. W. A neuroanatomical and behavioral analysis of the syndromes resulting from midbrain lemniscal and reticular lesions in the cat. *Archives Italiennes de Biologie*, 1963, 101, 225–295.

Sprague, J. M., Marchiafava, P. L., & Rizzolatti, G. Unit responses to visual stimuli in the superior colliculus of the unanesthetized, med-pontine cat. *Archives Italiennes de Biologie*, 1968, 106, 169–193.

Stechler, C., Bradford, S., & Levy, H. Attention in the newborn: Effect on motivity and skin potential. *Science*, 1966, 151, 1246–1248.

Steinberg, R. H. Alterations of averaged photic evoked potentials in cat visual cortex during repetitive stimulation. *Electroencephalography & Clinical Neurophysiology*, 1965, 18, 378–391.

Sutherland, N. S. Outlines of a theory of visual pattern recognition in animals and man. *Proceedings Royal Society Series B*, 1968, 171, 297–317.

Sutton, S., Braren, M., & Zubin, J. Evoked potential correlates of stimulus uncertainty. *Science*, 1965, 150, 1187–1188.

Symmes, D. Effect of cortical ablations on visual exploration by monkeys. *Journal of Comparative & Physiological Psychology*, 1963, 56, 657–763.

Thompson, R. F. The effect of acquisition level upon the magnitude of stimulus generalization across sensory modality. *Journal of Comparative & Physiological Psychology*, 1959, 52, 183–185. (a)

Thompson, R. F. The effect of training procedure upon auditory frequency discrimination in the cat. *Journal of Comparative & Physiological Psychology*, 1959, 52, 186–190. (b)

Thompson, R. F., & Bettinger, L. A. Neural substrates of attention. In D. Mostovsky (Ed.), *Attention: a behavioral analysis*. New York: Appleton, 1970. Pp. 367–402.

Thompson, R. F., Bettinger, L. A., Birch, H., Groves, P. M., & Mayers, K. S. The role of synaptic inhibitory mechanisms in neuropsychological systems. *Neuropsychologia*, 1969, 7, 217–233.

Thompson, R. F., & Spencer, W. A. Habituation: A model phenomenon for the study of neuronal substrates of behavior. *Psychological Review*, 1966, 173, 16–43.

Thompson, R. F., & Welker, W. I. Role of auditory cortex in reflex head orientation by cats to auditory stimuli. *Journal of Comparative & Physiological Psychology*, 1963, 56, 996–1002.

Titchener, E. B. *Lectures on the elementary psychology of feeling and attention*. New York: Macmillan, 1908.

Trabasso, T., & Bower, G. H. *Attention in learning: Theory and research.* New York: Wiley, 1968.

Treisman, A. M. Selective attention in man. *British Medical Bulletin,* **20,** 12–16, 1964.

Treisman, A. M., & Geffen, G. Selective attention: Perception or response? *Journal of Experimental Psychology,* 1967, **19,** 1–17.

Ursin, H., Wester, K., & Ursin, R. Habituation to electrical stimulation of the brain in unanesthetized cats. *Electroencephalography & Clinical Neurophysiology,* 1967, **23,** 41–49.

Van Hof, M. W., Van Hof, D. J., & Rietveld, W. J. Enhancement of occipito-cortical responses to light flashes in man during attention. *Vision Research,* 1966, **6,** 109–111.

Velasco, M., Weinberger, N. M., & Lindsley, D. B. A unitary arousal system revealed by blocking of recruiting responses. *Electroencephalography & Clinical Neurophysiology,* 1965, **20,** 517.

Wachtel, P. L. Conceptions of broad and narrow attention. *Psychological Bulletin,* 1967, **68,** 417–430.

Wagner, A. R. Incidental stimuli and discrimination learning. In R. M. Gilbert and N. S. Sutherland (Eds.), *Animal discrimination learning.* New York & London: Academic Press, 1969. Pp. 83–112.

Walker, E. L. Stimulus produced arousal patterns and learning. Speech presented to the Department of Psychobiology, University of California, Irvine, November, 1969.

Webster, W. R., Dunlop, C. W., Simons, L. A., & Aitkin, L. M. Auditory habituation: A test of a centrifugal and a peripheral theory. *Science,* 1965, **148,** 654–656.

Weinberger, N. M., Goodman, D. A., & Kitzes, L. M. Is behavioral habituation a function of peripheral auditory system blockade? *Communications in Behavioral Biology,* 1969, **3,** 111–116.

Weinberger, N. M., & Imig, T. J. Evoked auditory system activity during behavioral habituation in the rat, (in preparation.)

Weinberger, N. M., & Lindsley, D. B. Behavioral and electroencephalographic arousal to contrasting novel stimulation. *Science,* 1965, **144,** 1355–1357.

White, A. R. *Attention.* Oxford: Blackwell, 1964.

Whitfield, I. C. *The auditory pathway.* London: Arnold, 1967.

Whitfield, I. C., & Evans, F. Response of auditory cortical neurons to stimuli of changing frequency. *Journal of Neurophysiology,* 1965, **28,** 655–662.

Wickelgren, W. O. Effect of state of arousal on click-evoked responses in cats. *Journal of Neurophysiology,* 1968, **31,** 757–769. (a)

Wickelgren, W. O. Effect of acoustic habituation on click-evoked responses in cats. *Journal of Neurophysiology,* 1968, **31,** 777–785. (b)

Worden, F. G. Attention and auditory electrophysiology. In E. Stellar and J. M. Sprague (Eds.), *Progress in physiological psychology,* Vol. 1. New York: Academic Press, 1966. Pp. 45–116.

Worden, F. G., & Marsh, J. T. Amplitude changes of auditory potentials evoked at cochlear nucleus during acoustic habituation. *Electroencephalography & Clinical Neurophysiology,* 1965, **15,** 866–881.

Wundt, W. *Logik: eine untersuchung der prinzipien der erkenntnis.* Stuttgart: Ferdinand Enke, 1894.

Wyckoff, L. B. Jr. The role of observing responses in discrimination learning. *Psychological Review,* 1952, **59,** 431–442.

CHAPTER 6    # Brain Mechanisms
of Memory

E. ROY JOHN

Brain Research Laboratories
Department of Psychiatry
New York Medical College
New York, New York

The work described in this paper was supported by Research Grant MH-08579
from the National Institute of Mental Health. Dr. John is a Career Scientist of
the Health Research Council of the City of New York under Grant #I-375.

199

## I. THE DEVELOPMENT OF OUR IDEAS ABOUT LOCALIZATION OF BRAIN FUNCTIONS

Our perception and interpretation of the content of consciousness, the very meaning of thought, depends on memory. Plato quotes Socrates as saying:

> There exists in the mind of man a block of wax, of different sizes and qualities in different men. This tablet is a gift of memory, the mother of the Muses, and when we wish to remember anything which we have seen or heard or thought, we hold the wax to it and in that material receive its impression as from the seal of a ring. We remember and know what is imprinted as long as the image lasts, but when it is effaced or cannot be taken, then we forget and do not know. (Jowett, 1931).

Neuropsychology sends its roots deep into the past. We draw much knowledge from those who worked before us. We are deeply influenced by the facts which they passed on to us and by traditional ways of looking at certain problems. Some of the problems about the mechanisms of memory which are still unresolved have been of concern to workers in this field for a long time. It is important for us to be familiar with the earlier approaches to these problems, not only to benefit from the discoveries and errors of our predecessors, but to understand the origins of our present beliefs. Because memory is established by a brief experience and lasts so much longer, even for a lifetime, men have long assumed that something is made in the brain when an event registers in memory. In this chapter, we will marshal logic and facts bearing upon this so-called "engram" and relevant to four major problems: (1) Where is the engram? (2) How is a memory made? (3) What is the physical basis of memory? (4) How does remembering occur?

## II. THE LOCALIZATION OF FUNCTION

The problem of localization of memory is a special case of the more general problem of localization of function in the brain. Historically, two diametrically opposite viewpoints on this question have long existed. One, which we shall call the "localizationist position," holds that circumscribed regions mediate specific mental processes, with the brain consisting of an aggregate of separate organs. The other, the "antilocalizationist position," holds that mental activity is the product of the whole brain.

## III. THE LOCALIZATIONIST POSITION

In the second century B.C., Galen suggested that mental processes were localized in the cerebral ventricles. About six hundred years later, Nemesius proposed the posterior ventricle as the seat of the memory, the middle ventricle as the seat of the intellect, and the anterior ventricle as the seat of perception. This idea of three ventricles as the substrate of the major mental abilities was still generally accepted in the Middle Ages. As descriptive anatomical studies of the brain began, attempts continued to identify the parts of the brain which were responsible for mental processes. Various workers suggested the pineal gland, the corpus striatum, the cerebral white matter, the corpus callosum, and other structures as the cerebral centers responsible for mental processes. These suggestions were the first attempts toward detailed functional localization.

In the eighteenth century, a school of psychology emerged which believed that mental processes could be subdivided into separate faculties. As these beliefs became established, a search began for the material substrate of these traits. It was believed that the brain could be subdivided into many organs or centers, each responsible for a separate ability. Anatomical works began to appear which proposed differential mediation of the different mental faculties by various brain regions. Such works suggested, for example, that memory was localized in the cerebral cortex, imagination and reason in the white matter, apperception and will in the basal regions, and integrative processes in the corpus callosum.

Gall (1825) was one of the leading anatomists of the brain of his time. Early in the nineteenth century, accepting the psychology of faculties, he proposed that each mental faculty was based on a definite group of brain cells and suggested that the whole cerebral cortex was an aggregate of organs each responsible for a particular faculty. The faculties which he relegated to particular areas of the brain were those identified by the psychological teachings of his time. Gall constructed very detailed phrenological maps in which domestic instincts, destructive instincts, attraction to food, aptitude for education, instinct for continuation of the race, love of parents, self esteem, and numerous other traits were localized.

Gradually, scientific evidence supporting the ideas of localization began to come from clinical observations on the effects of local brain lesions, on the one hand, and from neurophysiological and neuroanatomical studies, on the other hand. Clinicians argued that, if the brain did not consist of separate centers, one could not understand how localized defects could appear after damage to particular parts of the brain. In 1861, Broca showed the brains of two patients with disturbances in expressive speech who had lesions in the inferior frontal convolution of the left hemisphere. He concluded from this that expressive speech functions were localized in a center for the motor forms of speech in which cells of a particular area comprised a depot of images of the speech movements. A few years later, Wernicke (1874) found a case with a lesion of the superior temporal gyrus of the left hemisphere and a disturbance in speech comprehension, and concluded that the sensory images of speech were localized in this cortical zone.

Encouraged by these discoveries, clinicians in the following years reported the identification of additional centers in the brain. These included areas responsible for visual memory, for mind blindness, word blindness, word deafness, writing skills, formulation of logical propositions, conceptual centers, naming centers, and centers of ideas, in addition to the centers responsible for visual, auditory, tactile, and motor function. In 1884, on the basis of many such observations, Meynert proposed that cortical cells were carriers of particular mental processes and suggested that each new impression was stored in a new and still vacant cell. This was perhaps the earliest hypothesis that single cells mediated the storage of particular memories.

In parallel with the clinical observations supporting ideas of the localization of function, similar evidence was produced from animal studies. In 1870, Fritsch and Hitzig showed that stimulation of certain cortical areas caused contraction of certain muscles. At about the same time, Betz (1874) found giant pyramidal cells in the anterior central gyrus and associated these cells with motor functions. In one of the earliest experimental studies of lesion effects on memory, Munk (1881) showed that extirpation of the occipital lobes caused the loss of visual recognition. In a series of studies by Hitzig (1874), Ferrier (1876), and Bianchi (1895), it was reported that anterior lesions caused disturbances of attention and intellectual activity. These findings, which were suggestive of centers for various sensory and motor functions, stimulated further search for centers of more complex mental functions. Eventually these ideas led some to the belief that complex mental processes could be localized in circumscribed brain areas. These propositions were formally presented in psychiatric texts such as that of Kleist, published in 1934, which contains a well-known chart on cerebral localization. These ideas received support from the teachings of Vogt (1951), a pioneer in cytoarchitectonics, who postulated that the brain was composed of numerous small organs each the seat of a particular faculty.

# IV. THEORIES OF MEMORY LOCALIZATION

Thus, evidence gradually accumulated which supported the belief that sensory and motor functions could be localized in specific regions of the brain. Many of the functions which were being mapped during this period were functions which were only acquired through experience and whose storage represented a form of memory. Further, with the advent of conditioning techniques, learning came to be viewed as a process by which connections were established between input regions responsive to sensory stimuli and output regions responsible for control of muscle movements. It was assumed that, as a consequence of repeated experiences and reinforcement, a neural pathway was gradually elaborated which mediated the influence of the sensory input upon the motor output. The location of this new neural pathway was therefore the locus of the memory for the newly acquired behavior. These ideas about the localization of memory follow easily and naturally from concepts of functional localization in the brain. Numerous connectionistic theories of memory have been formulated to express this intuitively reasonable viewpoint, including those of Tanzi (1893), Pavlov (1903), Ramon y Cajal (1911), Kappers (1917), Child (1924), Holt (1931), Konorski (1948, 1967), Hebb (1949), Toennies (1949), Young (1951), Eccles and McIntyre (1951), Eccles (1951), McIntyre (1953), Thorpe (1956), Milner (1957), Gastaut (1958), Russell (1959), Fessard (1961), Fessard and Szabo (1961), Asratyan (1961), and other more recent workers.

Some of these theories were so-called dual-trace theories, in which short-term memory was postulated to be mediated by a dynamic process, while permanent memory depended upon structural changes. Among such theories, probably the best known are those of Hebb and Konorski.

In his well-known book *The Organization of Behavior* (1949), Hebb proposed that short-term memory was mediated by reverberatory circuits, but that long-term memories were stored by structural changes at synapses. Writing at about the same time, Konorski (1948) proposed similarly that recent memory was mediated by reverberatory processes located in the association cortex, while the subsequent development of stable memory was due to synaptic growth. These ideas of localization of function were incorporated into basic texts of neurology such as that of Nielsen, published in 1947. Writing as recently as 1958, Nielsen states very positively that engrams are located in the hippocampus and the temporal cortex. Visually-minded people have memories which are based on hippocampal–occipital associations. One pathway providing access to the stored patterns for recognition comes from the primary cortical area, and another pathway used for recall comes from the association areas. Thus Nielsen explains the observation that lesions sometimes produce recognition without recall, and recall with blocked recognition. Attributes other than visual properties are stored similarly in the corresponding regions of the brain. All engrams related to an experience are associated by association fibers, and each memory pattern has associations with the diencephalon. According to Nielsen, the engram is asserted to be plastic changes at synapses. Activation of synaptic knobs during stimulation leads to increases in efficiency.

Although they seldom state it with quite as much assurance as Nielsen, many workers feel that memories are localized in the brain. Russell, for example, writing in 1959, says that memory depends on the establishment of pathways in many levels of the central nervous system. The parieto–occipital region is the visual memory center, while the temporal lobe–hippocampal system is responsible for feelings of familiarity. Writing in 1961, Russell and Espir state that the hippocampal–fornix system facilitates storage in the relevant brain areas, and repeat their belief that the posterior parietal lobes store visual memories.

Asratyan (1965a) has reviewed the recovery of functions disturbed by ablations in various parts of the central nervous system. He describes two views about such phenomena: (1) The readjustment of behavior which takes place is due to the plasticity of an equipotential system; (2) The recovery of functions which is observed is due to the stepwise relearning and compensation carried out by various parts of the nervous system, and is not due to the substitution of function. Asratyan believes that conditioned connections for the site of closure (memory) is a chain of cortical internuncial neurons between the centers of the conditioned stimulus and that of the unconditioned stimulus.

These ideas about the locations of temporary connections between the different parts of the brain involved in a conditioned response have been spelled out in great detail by Beritoff (1965). According to this writer, temporary connections between contiguously activated cells in different cortical areas (analyzers) are mediated by association neurons with fibers going through white matter. Temporary connections within an area are mediated by internuncial neurons. Experience establishes an integrated system of stellate cells. Neocortical elements form temporary connections in regard to perceptual experiences, while paleocortical elements mediate emotional experience. Conditioned reflexes are based on connections located exclusively in neo- and paleocortex. The nonspecific structures of the thalamus and the mesencephalon do not contain such connections, nor do the basal ganglia. Images of the outside world are stored in neocortical stellate cells. Connections are formed between simultaneously active stellate cells via internuncial and associative neurons. Each behavioral act implies participation of the entire nervous system, with excitation in some circuits and inhibition in the remainder.

Beritoff proposes that temporary connections are formed between receptive stellate cells when they are simultaneously or consecutively stimulated. This stimulation results in an image of the stimulus. Similar connections are formed between receptive and motor cells by repeated coincidence of activity during the formation of conditioned reflexes. Temporary connection formation implies a morphological change in the cells. This change is postulated to result from a decrease in synaptic space and the facilitation of transmission of impulses in chains of neurons. These changes are faster in cortical cells and persist longer. With respect to this assertion, it is interesting that Olds and Olds (1961), who studied the conditionability of single cells in various regions of the brain, concluded that subcortical and paleocortical neurons could be readily conditioned, while neocortical units rarely if ever changed their mode of response.

A large proportion of the contemporary writers who attribute the mediation of memory to increased synaptic efficiency cite the work of Eccles (1951). Writing very authoritatively, this worker asserted that the memory of all events was dependent on the development and persistence of increased excitatory efficacy across certain synaptic junctions. This assertion was based upon the demonstration that activation of *monosynaptic pathways in the spinal cord* led to prolonged increase in excitatory efficacy of particular synapses. Subsequent work by Eccles and his collaborators showed that the observed changes in these and analogous experiments could not be attributed to increased or decreased synaptic use but were due to unspecific factors. Eccles receives and merits great prestige because of his fundamental contributions to neurophysiology, particularly the neurophysiology of the spinal cord. It is regrettable, however, that his early statements are cited so often in support of the belief that memory is based on increased synaptic efficiency, when the evidence on which those statements were based was completely inadequate. Writing more recently Eccles (1961) has stated that it is the pattern of neuronal activity which is important for memory, not the neurons themselves.

## V. THE ANTILOCALIZATIONIST VIEWPOINT

Throughout the period in which the localizationists were developing their beliefs and the evidence on which those beliefs were based, a diametrically opposed school of thought was marshalling its own arguments. An early representative of this was Haller who, writing in 1769, acknowledged that different parts of the brain might well be involved in different functions, but postulated that the brain acted as a single organ composed of parts of equal importance. Damage to a single region can cause disturbance of various functions, and many of these disabilities can be compensated by the remaining tissue. In what is probably the earliest piece of experimental work supporting the antilocalizationist position, Flourens (1824) showed about the same degree of recovery of function in birds regardless of which part of the brain was damaged. He concluded that the cortex acted as a homogeneous entity. Some years later (1842), he showed that reversing flexor and extensor innervation of the wing in a cock could be compensated, and argued that this was evidence for equipotentiality of function of different regions of the brain. Further experimental studies of a similar sort were done by Goltz between 1876 and 1881. After extirpation of various parts of the cerebral hemispheres, Goltz (1884) reported that dogs showed a variety of marked disturbances of behavior, using general responses as a measure. These disturbances gradually disappeared. The functions were restored, leaving only slight awkwardness. These observations led to the idea that any part of the brain could be associated with ideas and thought, and the defect observed after brain damage was solely related to the size of the lesion.

In 1884, Brown-Sequard provided evidence showing that any region of the cortex could acquire motor properties merely by being associated in its activity over a period of time with the part of the brain which when stimulated caused movement. In 1905, Baer provided a detailed confirmation of Brown-Sequard's observation, voicing again the conclusion that any region of the brain could be made motoric by association over a period of time with the activity of a region causing movement. In 1897, Wedensky published the first of a long series of experiments on the so-called "stability of the motor point" in which the usual interpretation of the observation of Fritsch and Hitzig was challenged. Wedensky showed that the movement which was produced by electrical stimulation of a point on the motor cortex depended on the previous history of stimulation of the animal. If in a dog under light narcosis, shortly after electrical stimulation of the motor point for the extensors of the forepaw (Center $A$), stimulation is applied to the motor cortex regions of the flexors of the forepaw (Center $B$), it is possible to observe a paradoxical effect. The result of stimulation of Center $B$ is as if Center $A$ had been stimulated, and extension rather than flexion of the forepaws occurs.

Similar conclusions came from the work of Lashley (1923), who mapped the precentral gyrus of a rhesus monkey, using electrical stimulation in a series of tests extending over a period of weeks. In each test motor reactions to stimulation of a particular cortical point were essentially constant, and in different tests the general cortical fields from which movements of face, arm, or leg were elicited tended to remain constant, although the borders of the fields varied somewhat. However, within the arm area stimulation of the same point in different tests produced widely different movements, and at different times the same movement was obtained from widely separated and shifting areas. Such results suggested that within the segmental areas the various parts of the cortex might be equipotential for the production of all the movements of that limb, and that the particular movements elicited in any test depended upon the momentary physiological organization of the area rather than upon any point-for-point correspondence between pyramidal and spinal cells. After lengthy studies of the results of different kinds of ablations and lesions on the performance of conditioned responses, Lashley (1929) concluded that a particular type of disturbance cannot be ascribed to a particular brain lesion. Impairment of function is related to the extent of brain damage (the Law of Mass Action), while complex functions can be mediated by different brain areas (the Law of Equipotentiality).

In addition to experimental results, clinical observations provided support for antilocalization ideas. The distinguished neurologist Hughlings Jackson formulated a series of principles in sharp opposition to the ideas of narrow localization (1869). Jackson stated that lesions of circumscribed brain areas seldom lead to complete loss of function. While voluntary movements or speech are often blocked, involuntary movements and utterances frequently remain. Jackson argued against the concept of function as mediated by narrowly circumscribed groups of cells in favor of a complex vertical organization with multiple representation at low brain stem levels, middle motor and sensory cortical levels, and high frontal cortex levels. Thus the localization of the cause of a symptom that is the reason for impairment of some function accompanying local lesion could not in any way be interpreted as evidence for localization of that particular function.

At about the same time, other neurologists suggested that speech should be considered as a symbolic function disturbed by any complex damage to the brain. The so-called Noetic School of neurology held that the principal form of mental process was symbolic, and all brain damage caused depression of symbolic function (e.g., Goldstein, 1948). While accepting the cerebral localization of neurological symptoms, sensations, and elementary processes, Monakow and Mourgue (1928) argued against the localization of symbolic activity in any particular brain region. Head (1926) ascribed speech disturbances to lesions of large areas of cortex and attributed these disturbances to the loss of "vigilance." Goldstein (1948) distinguished between the "periphery" of cortex, in which localized lesions disturb the means of mental activity (elementary functions), and the "central part," treated as equipotential, in which lesions cause change in abstract behavior (higher functions) in accordance with the Law of Mass Action. The ideas of this worker combine the principles of narrow localization with those of equipotentiality.*

# VI. THE LOCALIZATION OF MEMORY

The controversy between the localizationists and the antilocalizationists dealt with the attempt to identify complex mental processes or psychological concepts with the material structure of the brain. The problem of localization of memory was a particular aspect of the more general question of functional localization. Much of the evidence on which theories of memory localization were based came from studies of conditioned responses in which a sensory stimulus came to elicit a new motor movement after a conditioning procedure. It was assumed that the sensory stimulus affected a particular sensory region of the brain, that the conditioned movement was controlled by the motoric regions of the brain, and that conditioning established a new pathway between the sensory region and the motor region so that the sensory stimulus could influence the activity of the motor region. Generations of physiological psychologists have attempted to localize this pathway mediating the new influence of the sensory stimulus on the motor system by destroying various regions of the brain. The failure of such ablation studies has been thoroughly catalogued by Lashley in his paper entitled "In Search of the Engram" (1950a).

Strict correlation of structure with function is difficult even with respect to such relatively species-constant characteristics as sensory input and motor output regions. The variability of the responses elicited by stimulation of the motor system has already been mentioned. Evidence

---

* I wish to acknowledge my indebtedness to A. R. Luria for his excellent review in "Higher Cortical Functions in Man" (1966) from which I have borrowed heavily in summarizing the historical development of the localizationist and antilocalizationist positions.

increasingly accumulates from studies of the unanesthetized, unrestrained animal that many conclusions about functional localization must be seriously questioned. Data which contradict expectations based on "classical" cytoarchitectonic or neurophysiological evidence as well as dramatic evidence of functional compensation abound in the literature. To cite a few recent examples:

(1) Evoked potentials (Doty, 1958) or responses of single neurons (Burns, Heron, & Grafstein, 1960) to visual stimuli can be recorded from a widespread extent of cortex far exceeding the area striata as defined cytoarchitectonically;

(2) Visual discriminations can be established after extensive ablations of cortical and collicular regions of the visual system (Winans & Meikle, 1966; Urbaitis & Hinsey, 1966). Ablations which produce severe sensory deficits in adult cats cause literally no permanent discrimination deficits when performed on kittens (Tucker & Kling, 1966). Further, the severe visual impairment after unilateral removal of the visual cortex can be reversed by subsequent destruction of the superior colliculus on the other side (Sprague, 1966);

(3) Cats can perform visual pattern discriminations after destruction of as much as 98% of the optic tract (Norton, Frommer, & Galambos, 1966);

(4) Cats can relearn an auditory frequency discrimination after bilateral ablation of all cortical auditory areas resulting in complete retrograde degeneration of the medial geniculate body (Goldberg & Neff, 1964);

(5) Extensive bilateral lesions of the thalamic and mesencephalic reticular formation do not produce unconsciousness, loss of arousal, inability to acquire new conditioned responses, or loss of previously acquired conditioned responses if such damage is inflicted in multiple stages (Adametz, 1959; Chow, 1961; Chow & Randall, 1964);

(6) The challenge to strict localization of function even extends to the so-called vegetative centers. A series of specialized receptors located near the midline ventricles of the brain stem play an important role in the regulation of respiration, food intake, and other vegetative functions. These receptors correspond to the classical centers for metabolic regulation. Recent data (Coury, 1967) suggest that these centers constitute portions of regulatory systems which are anatomically quite extensive and diffuse, deployed through the brain at all levels including neocortex.

In spite of the failure of ablation attempts as catalogued by Lashley, there has been a continuing suggestion that certain regions of the brain are importantly involved in memory, particularly the hippocampus and the frontal cortex. A number of experiments, particularly the dramatic observations of Milner and Penfield (1955), have directed attention to the possible role of the hippocampus in the "stamping in" of experience. This proposition seems to receive support from such studies as those of Bureš (Bureš, Burešová, & Weiss, 1960), which show that hippocampal spreading depression can block retention of avoidance learning, and Hunt and Diamond (1957), who reported that bilateral hippocampectomy interferes differentially with performance of avoidance responses to visual and auditory cues and that the effects disappear with overtraining. Yet Grastyán and Karmos (1962) have shown that bilateral removal of the hippocampus in cats does not interfere with the ability to acquire either alimentary or defensive conditioned reflexes. Flynn and Wasman (1960) demonstrated that a defensive reflex could be established during bilateral afterdischarge of the hippocampus following electrical stimulation. A number of investigators have concluded that various behavioral deficits observed after hippocampal disturbance are not due to recent memory loss but can be attributed to discrimination failure (Cordeau & Mahut, 1964), motivational changes (Grossman & Mountford, 1964), complexity of task (Drachman & Ommaya, 1964), or inability to alter previously established behaviors (Webster & Voneida, 1964). These inconsistencies indicate the necessity of using a variety of response measures and methods of intervention in attempts to assess the anatomical localization of memory processes.

Since the work of Jacobsen (1936), there is a long history of belief that the frontal lobe is important for recent memory. Recent evidence seems to indicate that the impairment in delayed response observed after frontal resection is not due to a memory defect. Pribram and Tubbs (1967) have shown that the deficiency vanishes if a longer interval is imposed after each pair of trials. Since performance is restored in spite of the lengthened post-trial period, the defect after frontal lobe injury seems related to the ability to divide a stream of information into its proper segments. After studying the defects observed in man with frontal lesions, Teuber (1959, 1964) concluded that there were no deficits in recent memory.

A great deal of interest has been elicited recently by the studies of interhemispheric transfer of information in the so-called "split-brain" preparation. This preparation has been extensively studied by Sperry and his pupils. Initial results suggested that learning acquired by one-half of the brain was somehow localized to the structures on that side and not accessible to structures on the other side of the brain. Sperry has summarized the more recent results obtained with the split-brain preparation (1962). Cats trained with one eye masked were unable to remember with the second eye what they had learned with the first following section of both the corpus callosum and the optic chiasm. The second eye could be trained to do the opposite task with no interference. In numerous studies by various workers, it was found that section of the cerebral commissures prevented the spread of learning and memory from one to the other hemisphere.

Upon extending these studies to somasthetic and motor learning, transfer between the sides was sometimes found. It has been established that either forelimb can be governed from a single hemisphere in both learned and unlearned tasks. In sensory–sensory conditioning, cross-integration between hemispheres has been demonstrated. It has been found that visual information on one side can be cross-integrated with tactile information on the other side even with section of the midbrain as well as the forebrain commissures. Easy brightness and color discriminations have been shown to transfer from side to side. Brightness transfer occurs even with the split of the quadrigeminal plate. Some signs of the transfer of visual pattern discrimination from side to side have been obtained. Brightness discrimination has been performed by split-brain cats and monkeys when one brightness has been projected in one eye and the other brightness through the second eye. Such discrimination clearly demands integration of the information in the two sides with the memory of the learned responses. Size discriminations have also been established with simultaneous presentation of stimuli of two different sizes to the two eyes. Thus, cross-comparisons of sensory and stored information can be made between the divided hemispheres. Similar results are being obtained for the transfer of conditioned tactile and visual stimuli between the two sides of the split-brain preparation. This transfer has even been observed in animals whose brains have been split as far as the tegmentum of the brain stem. Results of this sort indicate that however memory is stored, access to this stored information can be achieved from different sensory systems under circumstances where the mediating anatomical regions must be such nonsensory-specific structures as the tegmentum of the brain stem, when the sensory commissures connecting the two sides have been completely separated.

On the basis of the kind of considerations which have been here presented, many workers have concluded that memory is not localized to particular brain regions, while at the same time asserting that the functions of speech must be considered an exception and are probably localized. For example, Gerard, writing in 1961, stated that it was highly doubtful that each remembered item was "located at a particular neuron or synapse. Yet some localization is present as shown by aphasic defects, but even these are hardly cell by cell." Ojemann (1966) after reviewing the deficits in function observed in man after damage to various localized brain regions, concluded that there was little evidence for the localization of memory in the brain except for the fact that speech defects were observed with local lesions. McCleary and Moore (1965) state that in the absence of sensory and motor loss, behavioral deficits in animals following various cortical lesions are partial, sensitive to the amount of cortex removed, generalized in nature, and frequently reversible with time. Except for deficits in speech after brain damage, they believe that the same conclusions hold in man. A basically similar position is voiced by Reitan (1964), who concluded that unknown factors wash out the differences in the effects of lesions in man which vary in type and location.

## VII. THE LOCALIZATION OF SPEECH FUNCTIONS

Speech functions obviously depend on a variety of kinds of memory. In view of the widespread belief that deficits in speech function after brain damage are evidence for the localization of memory, it is worthwhile to take a more careful look at the data bearing on this point. The work of Broca and Wernicke, cited earlier, provided the original basis for the belief that speech functions were localized in particular regions of the temporal lobe of the left hemisphere. The recent studies which are most frequently cited as providing support for this viewpoint are those by Penfield and Roberts (1959). Penfield has extensively studied the effects of stimulation of various regions of the exposed cortex in man in the course of operations for neurological disorders. Stimulation of primary motor areas causes movement of various peripheral muscles. Excision of these areas does not block voluntary movement subsequently. Stimulation of primary sensory areas produces contralateral sensation. Excision of these areas produces a defect in sensation. Yet the work of Sprague, cited earlier, suggests that these defects may be due to the release of subcortical inhibition. Stimulation of secondary sensory areas causes ipsilateral sensation. Excision of such areas produces little defect. Harvey Cushing, in 1909, showed that stimulation of the postcentral gyrus in man produced sensation in the opposite limbs. Since then, it has been shown by many neurosurgeons that electrical stimulation of other primary sensory areas and secondary areas causes patients to see, hear, smell, feel, or taste in an elementary way. Patients react to such sensations as imposed by external action and consider the sensation as an artifact.

In 10 cases out of 190 in which Penfield and his colleagues carried out cortical stimulation over a nine-year period, psychical responses to stimulation consisting of experimental illusions, interpreted illusions, or dreamy states were obtained. Each of these ten cases involved stimulation of the temporal lobe. The resulting experiences were recognized as authentic events from the patient's past. Penfield denoted the temporal cortex involved in such experience as the interpretive cortex to distinguish this region from sensory and motor areas and those areas which give no response to stimulation, such as the anterior frontal and posterior parietal regions. The stimulation of interpretive cortex causes an experience described as "a flashback." Similar phenomena appear during epileptic seizures caused by spontaneous discharge in the corresponding temporal regions. Penfield did not conclude that the recording mechanism was actually in the stimulated tissue. Rather, he assumed that the neuronal activity left the area where the electrode was applied and activated the record in some more distant area. He distinguished between experiential responses consisting of specific flashbacks, and interpretive responses consisting of more generalized feelings such as familiarity, novelty, distance, intensity, loneliness, or fear. The flashbacks can be vivid sight and sound in personal interpretations. The person always feels that this is the evocation of a memory rather than a real experience. Experiences evoked in this fashion go forward moment by moment. No still pictures occur, and there is no backward sequence of events reported. Experiences are of a commonplace type, for the most part. There is no crossing between different periods in an individual's past. Experience stops when the electrode is withdrawn, and sometimes it is possible to reactivate the same experience repeatedly beginning at the same point when stimulation begins.

Cortical areas where stimulation caused ideation or speech project to the pulvinar and nucleus lateralis posterior of the thalamus and via centre medianum to Broca's area. Recovery of speech function following cortical lesion and aphasia suggests that the thalamic areas can be used for the ideational mechanisms of speech with the assistance of previously unemployed cortical zones, coordinated with the centrencephalic system. Penfield assumes a central integrating "centrencephalic system" within the diencephalon and mesencephalon, which has bilateral functional connections with the cerebral hemispheres, responsible for integration of the function of the hemispheres and integration of functions between different parts of the same hemisphere. Consciousness accompanies this integrative function and disappears with interruption of function in the centrencephalic system. Penfield considers the mesencephalic reticular formation as part of this system and cites the loss of consciousness after mesencephalic reticular lesion as support for his thesis. In this regard, it must again be pointed out that Adametz (1959) has shown that the mesencephalic reticular formation can be completely coagulated in multiple stages with no subsequent loss of consciousness. Any area of cortex can be removed without the loss of consciousness.

The lateral temporal cortex is the only brain region from which actual earlier remembered experience can be reinvoked by direct stimulation, *and this only in patients with seizures and probable alteration of function of this part of the brain.* Thus, it appears that a memory can be released by an electrical stimulation to a particular place on the temporal cortex of man. Yet animal studies show that a conditioned response can be established to local electrical stimulation of the brain, and stimulation of the region where the conditioned stimulus has been applied gives access to the memory, the criterion being that the conditioned response is produced (Leiman, 1962). Yet, it has been shown that transfer to other regions occurs readily, and if the primary stimulated region is removed, conditioned response can nonetheless occur to the stimulation of other regions (Segundo, Roig, & Sommer-Smith, 1959). Such evidence would indicate that the site of stimulation eliciting a response is not necessarily the site of the memory.

Some insight on contemporary thinking about the localization of the speech function is afforded by studying the transcript of a recent conference on aphasia (Osgood & Miron, 1963). Most participants in this conference agreed that lesions in specific localities produced definite clinical types of aphasia. Yet evidence was presented of the recovery from aphasia after brain surgery. It was proposed that to show the *essential* function of a brain region one would have to demonstrate first that there was no performance after injury, secondly that no spontaneous recovery took place, and thirdly that no relearning was possible. Evidence was presented that after temporal lobe damage resulting in aphasia, retraining was often possible. In bilinguals, one language frequently returns before the other. The general feeling was expressed that words or concepts are not stored in local regions in the sense of occupying specific locations in the cortex. No electrical stimulation carried out by any of the participants had produced organized speech. Stimulation of the cortex caused vowel-like cries or arrest of speech or other distortions. Such effects were obtained from Broca's area and primary and secondary motor areas on the left hemisphere. Stimulation on the right side was usually ineffective. The vocalization could be produced on either side. The general conclusion reached by the participants in the symposium was that language defects were more probable after damage to the left hemisphere than to the right. The more posterior the lesion, the more likely was the development of receptive language difficulties.

The more anterior the lesion, the more likely was the development of expressive aphasia. The participants seemed reluctant to go beyond this in allocating localization of speech functions and memories involved in such functions to particular regions of the brain.

Evidence has been provided by Penfield that Broca's area can be destroyed with essentially complete recovery from the resulting aphasia, and other workers have provided supporting evidence. There is a case of bilateral destruction of Broca's convolution with retained ability to speak. Roberts (Penfield & Roberts, 1959, p. 78) has stated that any acute lesion to any gross part of the left hemisphere may produce some disturbance in speech. This implies a widespread involvement of the cortical surface in the mediation of speech. Similar conclusions are provided by the results of Luria (1962), who has mapped the incidence of speech disorders after wounds to different parts of the brain. Luria's findings indicate clearly that damage to any convolution of the left hemisphere, from the anterior to the posterior boundaries of the brain, can result in speech defects. Analyzing evidence of this sort, Luria has pointed out that, in order to develop an adequate theory of localization, it is necessary first to revise our concepts of function, and second to reject the idea of centers as cell groups which are responsible for mental processes. Luria suggests that function is the product of a reflex system uniting excited and inhibited areas of the central nervous system into a working mosaic, analyzing and integrating afferent input, and establishing a system of temporary connections which achieves equilibrium of the organism in its environment.

Function conceived this way is localized in a network of complex dynamic structures composed of combinations of mosaics of distant points which are united in a common task. Function, particularly higher function, refers to the complex adaptive activity of an organism which is directed toward the accomplishment of some task. Such complex functions are multistage and are mediated by functional systems rather than centers. These functions consist of a set of interconnected steps and are mediated by a complex dynamic constellation of relationships involving different levels of the nervous system. Such a system of functionally united components has a systematic not a concrete structure in which the initial and final links of the system (task and effect) remain stable, and the intermediate system (means of performance of the task) may vary within wide limits. These systems are complex in composition, plastic in their elements, and dynamically self-regulating. Localization of such functions in any circumscribed area is out of the question. Function is accomplished by a plastic system which achieves an adaptive task with a highly differentiated group of interchangeable elements.

Elaborating such ideas, Luria refers to the concept of functional pluripotentialism enunciated by Filimonov (1951, 1957). This concept suggests that no formation of the central nervous system is responsible for only one function. A given region may participate in multiple functional systems which mediate the performance of numerous tasks. Filimonov proposed the concept of graded localization by which he meant that functions are mediated by complex systems at multiple levels. Loss or damage at any level leads to reorganization because of feedback and to the restoration of the disturbed act. These notions are related to ideas of dynamic localization expressed by Ukhtomski (1945), who proposed that functions are localized in dynamic systems whose elements are strictly differentiated. Coordination in timing and speed of action creates a momentary functionally unified center from spatially differentiated groups. Luria has used such concepts to explain the variability of the motor point, the achievement of sensory responses from anterior stimulation, and the fact that extirpation does not cause the loss of functions which are elicited by stimulation.

Response elicited by stimulation at a point depends on what has happened before, that is, on the state of the system. Particular areas of the brain are not fixed centers but points in dynamic systems. It is often observed that the total lesion of a cortical center leads to the initial loss of a function which is gradually recovered. If a local cerebral lesion is subsequently inflicted, it is unlikely to cause a secondary loss of the restored function. The recovery of function is not due to the establishment of vicarious performance by new equipotential centers but to the reorganization of a new dynamic system which is dispersed in the cortex and lower regions. Thus, the restoration of function is conceived of as reorganization rather than the transfer to equipotential areas. Local brain lesion is hardly ever accompanied by total loss of function but usually by disorganization and abnormal performance. Particular functions may be disturbed by very different lesions, and a local lesion may lead to the disturbance of a complex of very different functions. The localization of processes such as perception or memory in discrete areas of the brain seems even less likely than the localization of respiration or movement in an isolated brain area. The localization of higher functions seems less plausible than biological functions.

Luria conceives of the wide dynamic representation of experience via synchronously working cells which excite one another mutually. The material basis of higher processes is the activity of the brain as a whole; that is, the brain is a highly differentiated system whose parts are responsible for the different features of the unified whole. In this view, the character of the cortical intercentral relationship does not remain the same at different stages of development of the function, and the effect of a lesion of a particular part of the brain will differ at different stages of functional development. Some of these ideas are similar to the views of physiological organization upon which speech depends as expressed by Lord Brain (1965).

## VIII. OBJECTIONS TO DETERMINISTIC THEORIES

The discussion thus far shows that it is difficult to provide unequivocal evidence for the localization of a particular memory in a specific brain region. Were such evidence available, it might provide a basis for arguing that the region was involved in an essential way in the mediation of the storage or retrieval of a particular memory. Yet even such evidence would not be an adequate basis to argue for the differential localization of specific memories in *particular* cells *within* a region.

The various considerations which have been presented indicate the general bases on which one can question the validity of connectionistic theories according to which memory must be localized in specific cells in a region. It seems clear that the early conception of memory as consisting of a pathway established by experience in which a group of cells connects some sensory region receiving a conditioned stimulus to some motoric region responsible for the mediation of a learned response requires extensive modification. Similar conclusions were reached by Jasper, Ricci, and Doane (1960), evaluating the results of microelectrode analysis of cortical cell discharge during conditioning. They observed that many units in various areas fire spontaneously at irregular intervals. Changes in the firing patterns of single neurons could be observed in all cortical areas when the conditioned stimulus was presented alone *before* conditioning. Habituation led to widespread changes in the response of neurons in different brain regions. Evaluating these findings, Jasper concluded that a much more dynamic conception of brain mechanisms must be considered before a satisfactory theory of conditioning could be formulated. All parts of the brain seem to be in continuous activity in the alert animal. Many responses can be elicited by the conditioned stimulus before conditioning. Extensive activation or inhibition of neurons in parietal, sensory, motor, and frontal cortex occurs in response to a visual stimulus before conditioning, showing that pathways affecting these neurons exist without a learning experience. Multiple sensory-motor response systems seem to exist. One of these complex systems is selected when it proves successful. No rigid connection seems to be established, because different limb movements are interchangeable for performance of a learned response. It may be worthwhile to point out that the original formulation of memory, as mediated by pathways connecting regions responsive to the conditioned stimulus and regions controlling the learned movements, was because the repetition of experience is necessary in conditioning in order to establish the conditioned response. This need for repetition was interpreted by many workers as reflecting the gradual penetration of a pathway as new connections were established or as synaptic resistance was lowered. But conditioning is only one kind of learning, and even conditioning may occur in one trial. Further, response need not be performed for a conditioned response to be established. The phenomenon of latent learning is well known in which an animal, given an opportunity to explore a situation for some period of time, subsequently demonstrates that he has constructed a mental map of the experimental apparatus when motivation is introduced for particular responses to be performed in that surround. In recent work (John, Chesler, Victor, Bartlett, 1967), we have demonstrated that it is possible for the cat to acquire a conditioned response merely by observing the performance of a trained animal. Such cognitive or observational learning involves the appreciation of relationships between stimuli and can be acquired by animals without the explicit performance of the response. Such phenomena indicate clearly that repetition of a stimulus–response relationship is not necessary for learning to be established.

Such observations imply that learning is far more than establishment of pathways between sensory and motor areas. Gerard (1961) has concluded that it is highly doubtful that remembered items are located at particular neurons or synapses, suggesting that it is far more probable that large numbers of neurons in different patterns are involved in each memory. As cited earlier, Eccles has stated that it is the pattern of neuronal activity which must be important in memory, not the activity of the neurons themselves (1961). Pribram (1960) has suggested that some coded representation of an experience must be established in the posterior intrinsic system, by which he denotes the intrinsic thalamic nuclei and their cortical projection areas. The neuronal patterns forming this representation could be analogous to the cell assemblies proposed by Hebb (1949) and Milner (1957). Alternatively, these patterns might be based upon interacting waves of excitation creating interference patterns, as suggested by Lashley (1950) and Beurle (1956). These ideas are related to the cytological studies of Sholl (1956, 1959), who suggested that the physiological basis of pattern perception could only be specified in statistical terms and by probability laws.

Some readers may consider that the objections to the localization of memory in pathways connecting particular neurons can be adequately answered by assuming that the postulated pathways are diffusely distributed and therefore are localized but anatomically extensive. This position is impossible to refute with the failures of lesion studies, for no matter where lesions might be made, the memory circuits might be someplace else. Rather than explore this issue further, it would seem more profitable to address our attention to the basic assumption, namely, that specific memories are stored in specific cellular circuits, whether diffuse or localized, which by firing indicate recognition of present input as previously recorded. Some general shortcomings of this deterministic hypothesis can be pointed out.

Numerous recent neurophysiological studies have indicated that neuronal processes at all levels involve a probabilistic element. Many workers have proposed quantitative neuronal models in attempts to account for the unit activity which is observed experimentally. As a rule, such models have postulated a random factor influencing spike discharge. Some theorists have endeavored to account for the unpredictable aspect observed in cellular firing by "noisy" processes intrinsic to the cell such as random fluctuations in membrane potential or threshold level. Other workers have located the source of randomness outside the responsive cell, suggesting factors like unpredictability in the time of synaptic excitation. Developments in the statistical analysis of neuronal spike data have recently been reviewed by Moore, Perkel, and Segundo (1966).

It is well known that most cells in the brain are in incessant activity. Such cells may indicate the occurrence of some specific stimulus by a change in their "resting" pattern of discharge. Individual cells can only be described as responsive to peripheral stimuli in a statistical sense, with a variability in response rate and latency which is perhaps attributable to their irregular spontaneous activity. Sequential responses to the same stimulus may well be markedly different. Furthermore, the firing pattern of almost any arbitrarily selected cortical cell can be shown to change in response to local electrical stimulation of almost any accessible cortical area, as well as to a variety of peripheral stimuli (Burns & Smith, 1962; Burns & Pritchard, 1964). In view of this demonstration that many if not all neurons can be more or less directly influenced by most other neurons, no essential purpose would seem to be served by the assumption that new synaptic contacts are formed during learning. Burns and Smith have stated:

> . . . During one second a single neuron does not provide the rest of the brain with sufficient information to identify the presence and nature of the stimulus. Our results suggest that sensory inputs to the brain set up a spatial and

temporal pattern of activity which probably involves most of the cells in the cerebral cortex. It would appear that differentiation of the effects of a stimulus from the "noise" of continual or "spontaneous" activity is only made possible by the simultaneous weak response of many neurons.

Thus, it seems that all neurons in the brain fire occasionally in the absence of any specific input, neurons display great variations in response to any specific input, and any arbitrary stimulus will affect the discharge of most (and perhaps all) neurons within an anatomical system. Such observations provide the basis for formulation of a number of questions which seem crucial to an understanding of the mechanisms of information coding, storage, and retrieval in the brain:

(1) How is the discharge of a cell due to the occurrence of a novel stimulus distinguished from discharge due to the recurrence of a familiar stimulus, since most events will influence the discharge of many cells and since the response of a neuron to a given stimulus is variable?

(2) How is discharge of a cell due to ongoing background activity distinguished from discharge due to the arrival of afferent information which is similar to previous inputs stored in that cell?

(3) From the viewpoint of a central nervous system neuron, how is activity arising from the influx of information to be stored differentiated from activity arising from spontaneous or background discharge?

(4) How are the cells selected which are to mediate a particular memory? Since any stimulus may affect the activity pattern of many cells, how are the cells which will store the occurrence of that experience distinguished from the cells which will not?

(5) How are memories selected for storage? Since all experiences do not seem to register in memory, how do discharges related to experiences which achieve registration differ from those elicited by experiences which will not be stored?

(6) Memories have multiple components reflecting various aspects of the stimulus complex. Are all representational cells for an experience repositories of the full experience or only of constituent fragments thereof? If the former is true, how are the fragments reconstituted from the fact of subsequent cell discharge? If the latter is correct, how are the pieces of a memory represented by different cells unified?

(7) Since cells have a refractory period and are involved in discharges due to a variety of influences, how does the brain recognize an event which impinges on a cell or set of cells responsible for its identification while such cells are in the refractory state?

(8) Once a memory has been laid down in a cell, how is it protected against the overlay of subsequent experience which will also cause discharge of the cell?

Let us assume that memories are in fact stored in particlar cells and are evoked or remembered as a result of the discharge of these cells. If the specific cells in which a memory was stored were to discharge due to spontaneous causes, we would expect to be constantly bombarded by unrelated fragments of recollections. Yet, although cells discharge incessantly, most of us do not live in a random kaleidoscope of our past. Were these cells to discharge due to ongoing new experience, we should similarly expect a confusing interlacing of present events with irrelevant past events, which does not occur. Since most central nervous system neurons discharge intermittently, were specific memories localized to particular cells, we should expect such cells to be busy a significant portion of the time. Were memories stored in such cells interrogated during these busy intervals, readout of stored information should fail to occur. We should be plagued by failure to remember at irregular intervals. Yet most of us are not troubled by intermittently inaccessible memories. Although failure to recover stored material is a common experience, such inability usually persists for much longer than the expected refractory period. Perhaps the reader can pose further expected malfunctions which might be observed were memory stored in particular cells. Although such arguments do not conclusively demonstrate that remembering is not achieved by the discharge of specific cells in particular pathways, they indicate some of the objections that can be raised to the deterministic theories.

The central question underlying evaluation of the plausibility of the deterministic theory of memory is the question of what constitutes an item of information for the brain. If neurons in the brain discharge incessantly, are responsive to a wide variety of inputs, and respond to particular inputs in a variety of ways, the single neuron appears to be an unreliable reporter of the antecedent events preceding its discharge. Unique informational significance cannot safely be attributed by the nervous system to the firing of single nerve cells. This uncertainty would be greatly reduced if the information provided to the brain from the activity of a group of cells were represented by the orderly behavior of the ensemble compared with the random or characteristic discharge pattern. Although some of the cells in an ensemble might discharge spontaneously and some might be fortuitously refractory, and although the different cells in the responsive ensemble might display a wide variety of responses to a stimulus, one might expect that on the average the departure of the activity of an ensemble from its baseline conditions should reflect the effect of a stimulus in a reproducible fashion. Thus, the information in the neuronal network might be represented as the time sequence of coherence, that is, the temporal pattern of order in the activity of the ensemble. We will refer to these temporal patterns of coherence in a population as *modes of oscillation*. If the information contained in the activity of an ensemble of neurons were represented by its mode of oscillation, then storage of that information as a memory would require specification of that mode of oscillation so that the ensemble of neurons might subsequently display the same time course of average activity.

## IX. HOW ARE MEMORIES ESTABLISHED?

Whether memory is the construction of a new pathway or the increased probability of a mode of oscillation, some chemical or physical change must mediate the new capability of the nervous system. This change has been postulated by many to take place in several stages. Many experiments on the stabilization of memory suggest that there is a labile period early in the registration of a memory during which the fixation of experience is susceptible to external interference. Various kinds of perturbations have been demonstrated to accomplish erasure during this period although they are ineffective some time later. Estimates of the duration of the vulnerable stage range from a few seconds to as much as days or even weeks depending on the nature of the test situation, the experimental species, and the strength and type of interfering agent. A survey of this phenomenon was published several years ago by Glickman (1961).

Probably the earliest formulation of such a consolidation theory was provided by Müller and Pilzecker (1900) in an attempt to account for the observation that the ability to recall recently acquired verbal material deteriorated as a function of the interpolation of other tasks. They postulated the existence of a neural perseverative process which was susceptible to external interference in order to explain this retroactive inhibition. More direct physiological evidence for the existence of a consolidation phase was forthcoming from observations of retrograde amnesia resulting from cerebral trauma. In a survey of over 1000 cases of head injury published by Russell and Nathan (1946), over 700 of the individuals studied reported amnesia for events occurring up to one-half hour before the injury. In most patients, the duration of the erased period was only a few moments. These authors concluded that the loss of memory of recent experiences was due to interference with a perseverative process.

Since that time, a wide variety of agents in both human and animal studies has been used to show a marked deterioration of performance for some time after an experience, and the magnitude of the effect increases as the interval between the learning experience and the perturbation decreases. Among the manipulations which have been shown to interfere with consolidation are electroconvulsive shock, anesthesia, anoxia, convulsions induced by a variety of chemical agents, hyperthermia, and cerebral ischemia. Interference with consolidation has also been accomplished by electrical stimulation or by the imposition of spreading depression in a variety of brain regions. The wide variety of perturbations which can interfere with consolidation, and the variety of anatomical regions in which interference has been effective, suggest that no single region of the brain is responsible for consolidation.

These various data provide an adequate demonstration that there is a period following the occurrence of an event during which disturbance of the nervous system will interfere with the registration of an experience. The hypothesis most frequently offered as an explanation for this phenomenon of consolidation is that it depends on the ability of specific neuronal circuits to sustain reverberatory activity. This hypothesis originates from the anatomical studies of Lorente de Nó (1938). It was explicitly proposed by Hilgard and Marquis (1940), Hebb (1949), and numerous other workers, who suggested that reverberatory activity sustains the representation of an experience until permanent structural or chemical storage has been accomplished. This "trace" theory has been reviewed by Gomulicki (1953). Some evidence that stimulation results in a transient reverberation of neural activity has been directly provided by Verzeano and Negishi (1960), who recorded from multiple microelectrodes in the thalamus of the cat. They reported the appearance of recurrent patterns of unit discharge following sensory stimulation, which they interpreted as evidence for continued circulation of a representation of the stimulus through a responsive neural network. The pattern of discharge that was observed varied as the stimulus was changed. Additional evidence for the existence of reverberatory activity has been provided by Burns (1954, 1958), who studied the electrical activity of cortical slabs that were isolated neurally from the rest of the brain while retaining an intact blood supply. Such slabs display a marked diminution of spontaneous electrical activity; however, Burns has observed that a single electrical stimulus train can initiate bursts of electrical activity in these slabs which last for thirty minutes or longer. These bursts can be blocked by a subsequent massive electrical interference but become easier to elicit if the stimulus is repeated. This burst activity has been attributed to reverberatory circuits.

Reports of drug-induced impairment and facilitation of learning and

memory storage are numerous and have recently been thoroughly reviewed by McGaugh and Petrinovich (1965). The tentative generalization about the results of these studies, with a number of exceptions,
might be that anticholinergic substances, barbiturates, or compounds
with depressive action tend to impair learning or retention. Conversely,
anticholinesterase drugs, stimulants, or convulsant drugs in subconvulsive
doses tend to facilitate learning or memory storage. Many substances
which have been found facilitatory, such as strychnine, picrotoxin, nico-
tine, pentylenetetrazol, physostigmine, caffeine, or amphetamine, share
an excitatory effect on the activity of the central nervous system but
are believed to possess different mechanisms of action.

In many of these studies, the drug effects might possibly have been
due to facilitating attention or sensory responsiveness during the subsequent behavioral trials. However, Breen and McGaugh (1961) showed
that post-trial injections of picrotoxin enhanced the learning of mazes
by rats. Westbrook and McGaugh (1964) studied the effects of posttrial
injection of a systemic excitant on the latent learning of a maze by
a group of rats permitted free exploration of the maze without reward.
When reinforcement was introduced following the exploration and post-
trial injection, the experimental group displayed fewer errors than the
controls. Thus, it appears that subjects injected with an analeptic drug
learned more about the floor plan of the maze during free exploration
than did controls. Yet no difference in behavior developed until the
introduction of reinforcement. These data suggest that the drug improved
learning by facilitating memory storage. Petrinovich, Bradford, and Mc-
Gaugh (1965) have explored the effect of post-trial injection of analeptic
drugs on the duration of nonrandom delayed alternation performance
in the rat. These injections enable extension of the interval between
alternation responses appreciably beyond the normal maximum. This
indicates that information about a single choice can be retained for
a markedly prolonged period.

The fact that both strychnine and picrotoxin facilitate storage is informative. Strychnine blocks postsynaptic inhibition, while picrotoxin
blocks presynaptic inhibition (Eccles, 1962). The common effects of these
two substances, in spite of their different locus and mode of action,
indicate that the release of inhibition *per se* may be the crucial factor
in facilitating consolidation. However, pentylenetetrazol injection has
been reported to cause more marked facilitation of learning than either
strychnine or picrotoxin (Irwin & Banuazizi, 1966). This substance blocks
neither presynaptic nor postsynaptic inhibition but seems to achieve
excitatory effects by decreasing the time required for neuronal recovery
after discharge. Such an action might accelerate neuronal transmission

or increase the maximum firing rates that a cell could maintain. The above results might be interpreted as evidence that the drugs which were injected prolonged the period of reverberatory activity, thus in a sense giving the memory a longer period in which to achieve storage. In work relevant to this question, Pearlman, Sharpless, and Jarvik (1961) investigated the effects of strychnine injection immediately following a shock trial in a one-trial learning procedure. Ether anesthesia administered ten minutes after the strychnine had little effect upon retention, indicating that consolidation was already complete. In contrast, normal animals anesthetized ten minutes after the learning trial showed severe impairment of retention. Thus, it appeared that the effect of strychnine was to enable the more rapid elaboration of the structural or chemical basis for long-term storage. These results cannot be attributed to mere lengthening of the reverberatory process, which might be offered as a possible explanation for the results previously cited. It seems reasonable in view of these findings to conclude that these procedures either intensified the reverberatory activity or accelerated the rate of the chemical processes mediating permanent storage of information. The implications of such studies have been analyzed in greater detail elsewhere (John, 1967).

## X. SELF-SELECTION OF REPRESENTATIONAL NEURONS

How are memories selected for storage, since all experiences do not seem to register in memory? Perhaps only those experiences are stored in memory which can achieve excitation in a significant number of neurons, under conditions which permit reverberatory activity to persist during the period necessary for consolidation to take place. This implies the existence of a "storage threshold." Although random variables may contribute to the storage threshold, it seems subject to systematic influence since it is possible to direct one's attention effectively to stimuli to be remembered. Certain situations may sharpen attention in a particularly reliable fashion, changing the excitability of a population of neurons so that a more coherent response will ensue, thus achieving the storage threshold more readily.

How are the cells selected that are to mediate the storage of a particular experience, since most stimuli affect the activity of many cells? Consider the consequences of excitation of a number of neurons in an extensively interconnected network due to some afferent input, a "stimulus." Each of the initially responsive cells has access to a number of neural pathways, a proportion of which are re-entrant and form loops around which an impulse might circulate. The path length of the loops might be as short as two neurons, each stimulating the other, or might be extremely long. The circulation time in a given loop depends on the number of synapses in the circuit, the path length, and the transmission times in the fibers which are involved. In any anatomical region, the distribution of possible path lengths and the corresponding circulation times would depend upon fine anatomical structure, regional microchemistry, and blood supply, and might be expected to be characteristic for that region. At the time of arrival of a specific afferent barrage, certain cells in the population are refractory while others are responsive. The selection of the initially responsive neuron set, therefore, must reflect some fortuitous or chance factors. This initially responsive set now propagates the disturbance into the available set of pathways. Certain of these possible routes are blocked due to refractoriness, while others are momentarily facilitated or inhibited by ongoing activity. The cumulative effects of these constraints plus the inhibitory consequences of the input itself act to terminate the propagation of the disturbance along certain of the possible paths, while other paths sustain propagation long enough to succeed in becoming re-entrant. Only cells in pathways which become re-entrant can participate in reverberatory activity. We assume that sustained activity or inhibition is a prerequisite for permanent storage of information to be accomplished, and furthermore that the effect of reverberation must be upon those cells which mediate the circulation of activity; thus, *these cells and those which they inhibit are necessarily selected as the only set of neurons which could serve to store a representation of the original afferent stimulus configuration.*

Multiple re-entrant pathways undoubtedly exist in parallel and may be thrown into activity at different times. All cells that do not belong to some such pathway or receive its influences would seem to be *necessarily* excluded from participation in the process of storage of information about that specific stimulus. However, it does not seem plausible that the achievement of re-entry can be *sufficient* for the neurons in a loop to participate in storage. On logical grounds, an objection can be raised to the proposition that storage of information is achieved by one iteration around a network involving any number of neurons. It is difficult to understand how the alteration in a cell as a result of one participation in such a circuit would differ from the alteration resulting from a single *spontaneous* discharge, which was not due to membership in a representational set. Actually, a continuum of possibilities must exist in any anatomical region between two extremes. Small loops involving only a few neurons might reverberate at high frequencies many thousands of times, and long loops involving a large number of cells might reverberate at lower frequencies only several times.

The various estimates of consolidation time range from as little as half a minute to as much as twenty minutes. Whatever might be the details of the activity during consolidation, appreciable time is apparently required to achieve long-term information storage in neurons. Most chemical reactions proceed quickly. Why, then, does consolidation require such a long time?

## XI. CRITICAL SUBSTANCE AND CRITICAL SHIFT

Perhaps the reaction which produces the stuff which stores memories requires achievement of a minimum change in the concentration of a critical substance inside the nerve cell, and this change is more than is accomplished by a single neural discharge. Furthermore, the change in concentration due to a single discharge might be dissipated by diffusion or by destruction of this necessary substance. Unless this hypothetical product of discharge is to flood the cell, the normal rate of cell activity and metabolism must maintain its concentration at approximately a steady-state level. Nonrandom or sustained alteration in the pattern or rate of activity in the neuron would tend to shift this balance. Let us define the change in the rate of production of this critical substance in a neuron per unit time after a discharge as $\Delta f$, and the required net change to initiate the storage reaction in any cell, $i$, as $K_i$, the *critical shift*. Then, those cells which could participate in the representation of that experience are those cells for which $\Delta f \times T \geq K_i$. $T$ is equal to the consolidation time for the corresponding cell.

Cells in extremely long loops would be unable to shift concentration sufficiently to outstrip homeostatic regulation, since the unitary increment occurs infrequently. Furthermore, the longer the loop, the greater would be the chance that a participating cell might be captured by competing circuits. The briefer the interval between firings due to reverberation, the greater would seem to be the possibility that a cell would be preempted by representational activity and thereby protected during its consolidation period. Although the preceding discussion directs attention to the effects of a sustained increase in the rate of activity of a given neuron, the same consequences can be envisaged for a sustained decrease in activity. Critical shifts in concentration in some cells might result from accumulation during sustained inhibition. Conversely, critical shifts might consist of lowering the concentration of certain substances.

Obviously, the occurrence of inhibition is of possible informational significance. Inhibition of neural activity is probably an essential aspect of learning.

The critical substance might not be a molecule common to all cells. Various substances might serve with a regulatory role, and they may differ from time to time and from cell to cell. Furthermore, the threshold for critical shift may not be the same for all neurons involved, nor need it be the same under all metabolic conditions. Thus, the achievement of consolidation in a group of cells participating in shared activity may proceed at varying rates in different cells.

These assumptions create a picture of a network in which certain cells participate in reverberations after an afferent barrage. Each cellular discharge is considered to contribute a unitary increment toward a concentration change in a critical substance. Since discharge occurs in varying rates in various loops, increments accumulate at varying rates in different neurons. The rate of change of concentration must exceed some minimum in order to outstrip the homeostatic mechanisms of the cell. This adequate rate must be sustained for a sufficient time to achieve a critical shift in concentration necessary to trigger some storage reaction. Since only the net shift is considered crucial, this model depicts consolidation as a process occurring at different rates in circuits reverberating at different frequencies, all of which participate in the representation of the original event. Since these cells are the only neurons in the nervous system which have been altered by the event, the memory of that event must necessarily be somehow stored in this neural subset initially. Learning often takes numerous experiences although it can occur with a single trial. Certain events seem to register with reliable rapidity. If the necessary shift in concentration which is postulated above occurs in some or all the neurons of a particular mediating loop after a specific trial, consolidation for those cells can be considered as accomplished as a consequence of that single experience. In many cells, the effects of that trial will fail to achieve the critical shift before neural activity returns to the usual level. Residual concentration changes would thereafter be expected to dissipate gradually because of metabolism and diffusion. Unless the cell is again set into sustained activity before normal concentration levels are restored, there will be no lasting effect of the experience in that neuron.

After any particular trial, some neurons are postulated to achieve an altered state (consolidation) in the nonincremental manner which has been outlined. On subsequent trials, stimulus conditions and neural excitability will be somewhat different. Presumably additional sets of neurons will achieve consolidation in a similar way each time the event is repeated. The ability of these neural sets to alter behavioral performance, which is the usual operational criterion that learning has occurred, will depend on a variety of factors. These probably include the percentage of neurons in the population which has achieved consolidation by the relevant time, the variability of state of the system, and the complexity of the stimulus input and of the operationally-defined response. The ability of these altered sets of neurons to mediate altered behavioral response in a reliable way might be expected to increase more or less gradually, that is, incrementally, depending upon the response criterion. In this view, information storage can occur without affecting overt behavior. Whether one chooses to call such storage "memory" becomes a matter of definition.


## XII. THE MULTIPLE-TRACE THEORY


The previous discussion was presented from the relatively simplified viewpoint of what might be called "dual-trace" theory, in that it postulates a labile, short-term memory trace which is probably reverberatory in nature and a long-term memory trace which is stable and somehow constructed as a consequence of the reverberatory activity. Several recent experiments suggest that this picture probably has to be modified.

In mice and goldfish, consolidation is severely disrupted by postacquisition injection of puromycin, an inhibitor of protein synthesis (Flexner, Flexner, & Stellar, 1963; Agranoff & Klinger, 1964). Davis and Agranoff (1966) have shown that puromycin blocks long-term retention if injected immediately after the training session but not if injected one hour later. Yet, if the goldfish are left in the training tank for as long as three hours after completion of training, the period of puromycin susceptibility is correspondingly lengthened. This suggests the existence of an intermediate storage process capable of holding a memory for extended periods before permanent fixation. In addition, puromycin injection does not prevent acquisition of a learned response immediately afterward. However, the performance of such puromycin pretreated animals gradually deteriorates during several hours, and no long-term retention is displayed (Barondes & Cohen, 1966). Similar results have been obtained with pretrial injection of acetoxycycloheximide. Performance of learned responses is unimpaired three hours after training, but deteriorates severely by six hours. Similar phenomena were encountered in the work of Albert (1966a, 1966b), who showed that consolidation of a one-trial learning task could be blocked by post-trial application of cortical

spreading depression or cathodal polarization. Under certain circumstances, recall could be demonstrated for a few hours after this interference, but performance gradually deteriorated and no long-term retention was established. Yet, an intermediate holding process apparently
existed, because subsequent application of surface anodal polarization
reversed these effects, allowing consolidation to proceed and long-term
storage was achieved. Geller and Jarvik (1967) have made a preliminary
report on what seems to be a related phenomenon. Animals tested for
retention of a one-trial learning task immediately after recovery from
ECS show unimpaired performance, which gradually deteriorates. This
observation indicates that performance during this interval was mediated
by a temporary holding mechanism. Additional evidence for the existence
of an intermediate holding process comes from the work of McGaugh
(1967), who has reported that the injection of strychnine up to three
hours *after* ECS almost eliminates the disruption of consolidation of
one-trial learning caused by the electroconvulsive shock.

   These various results suggest that there may be an intermediate holding mechanism among the processes of information storage in the brain.
This intermediate trace is of too long duration to be plausibly attributed
to reverberation, and its ability to survive ECS, spreading depression,
and cathodal polarization further excludes this explanation. Possibly
it consists of a biochemical template which gradually decays. Although
adequate for the mediation of recall for several hours, this mechanism
is not responsible for long-term storage. It is possible that these multiple
traces are organized serially, so that a short-term reverberatory trace

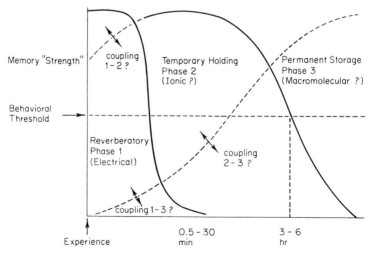

FIG. 1.    Schematic representation of the stages in memory.

induces the intermediate holding mechanism which in turn brings about the processes responsible for long-term storage. Alternatively, these multiple traces might be organized in parallel, so that the intermediate memory process mediates temporary retrieval while consolidation is occurring independently. Obviously, several possibilities can be envisaged. Although further research will be necessary to clarify these questions, we should bear in mind that there are different kinds of memory and that each process may be based upon a different biochemical mechanism. A model of a multiple trace mechanism is shown in Fig. 1.

## XIII. DOES CRITICAL SHIFT IN SOME CELLS IMPLY DETERMINISTIC FUNCTION?

It may seem at this point that the foregoing argument, outlining the processes by which changes in specific cells would occur after an experience, actually provides support for the deterministic formulation which is being challenged. If changes occur in specific cells due to reverberation so that a consolidation process can take place only in those cells, they therefore participate discretely in the storage of information. Clearly, no theory could hope to explain memory without invoking permanent alterations in a definite set of brain cells. Information cannot be stored in a vacuum. Certainly changes must take place in particular cells, and such changes might even consist of synaptic alterations. The critical question is how such changes represent the storage of information and whether activation of a memory or readout of the stored information requires the discharge of unique cells whose activity represents the past experience in a deterministic way.

The essential feature of this model is that information about an experience is stored as changes in specific brain cells but does not influence behavior deterministically. In the preceding discussion, a process has been described by which a large number of cells located in multiple brain regions is affected by the occurrence of an experience in such a way as to bring about some long-lasting consequence, the details of which remain to be discussed. These cells are presumed to have been selected fortuitously and to be distributed in parallel diffusely throughout the brain. The modification of future behavior of the organism as the result of this stored information, involving readout of the stored memory, need not require the participation of any specific cells so that activation of a particular pathway mediates the learned response. The essential features of the proposed mechanisms are that readout may be accom-

plished probabilistically, that different cells may control the same behavior on different occasions, and any given cell may contribute to the
storage of multiple experiences and to the performance of a variety
of learned responses. The effect of an experience is postulated to consist
of alteration in the properties of many cells in various anatomical regions. The consequence of this alteration is suggested to be a change
in the probability of coherent activity in neural populations when the
specified stimulus is subsequently presented. The replacement of baseline
or random activity by coherent activity in an ensemble of cells is proposed as the informationally relevant event.

In this view, the activity of any single cell is important from an
informational viewpoint only insofar as it contributes to the time course
of coherence in a neuronal ensemble, that is, to a mode of oscillation.
It is suggested that the level of coherence or signal-to-noise ratio represents the significance or reliability of the information being processed,
while the specific information content is reflected by the average activity
of the ensemble through time, that is, by the mode of oscillation. These
hypotheses remove the representation of experience from any particular
cell and free the identification of familiarity from dependence on any
pathway. At the same time, the proposed mechanism demands that definite changes occur in a discrete group of cells.

## XIV. MECHANISMS OF STABLE INFORMATION STORAGE

What mechanism might mediate the storage of information in the
stable phase? Since memories are extremely resistant to erasure, persist-
ing through sleep, unconsciousness, and excitement for a good part of
a lifetime once consolidation has been completed, it seems reasonable
to argue that during the consolidation phase something must be made.
Although reverberatory neural activity may be the basis for short-term
representation during the labile phase, long-term memory cannot be attributed to enduring reverberation. Whether information is stored by
the actual growth of new connections between nerve cells or the synthesis
of substances inside neurons or glial cells, whether the responsible mechanisms operate in a deterministic or a statistical manner, these processes
must require changes to occur in the matter of which the brain is constructed—changes in structure or composition. What might be the chemical nature of the change which makes for stable storage? Since information stored in the nervous system can often be retrieved through an
individual's lifetime, can one detect or demonstrate a stability in the

matter of which brain is made which provides a counterpart for the stability of memory? Although the gross morphology of brain seems to be fairly characteristic and stable, radioisotope turnover measurements and other methods provide insight about whether or not any of the molecular species composing the structure are in fact static and persist throughout a lifetime once they are laid down. Such isotope turnover data are available for most of the compounds of brain. There seems to be no significant compound of brain which does not display a remarkably high rate of turnover (Lajtha, 1961; Palladin, 1964.)

The permanence of memory, therefore, probably cannot be attributed to the establishment of new intra- or extracellular structures laid down by permanent chemical molecules. It seems necessary, then, to explain the stable representation of experience as due to some change in configuration or substance mediated by a chemical system which, although itself not stable, is characterized by the fact that the molecules which break down are resynthesized in a specified way as to maintain the essential features of the change. Such template functions are known to be served by the nucleic acids. Furthermore, instinctive behaviors arise because of the influence of DNA and RNA on the cells of the nervous system. Since learning can produce longlasting patterns of behavior as stable as instincts, it seems plausible that analogous mechanisms might be involved. Deoxyribonucleic acid, or DNA, is almost completely localized to the nucleus. Ribonucleic acid, or RNA, is found not only in the nucleus but is distributed on the microsomes and throughout the cytoplasm of the cell in various forms. Since stimuli impinge on the cell at its outer surface, the chemical systems which permanently alter the cellular response to presentation of such stimuli probably modify substances which are found in proximity to cellular surfaces or in the subjacent cytoplasm. Considerations of this sort have led various workers, both in theoretical formulations and experimental explorations, to turn to the possible role of RNA or proteins in the mediation of long-term information storage. Substances located in the cell nucleus may well mediate such changes. In spite of the nuclear localization and greater resistance of DNA to alteration, there is no reason to assume that modification of DNA *action* may not also play a role. A central question which must be considered in this general context is whether the hypothetical mechanism is more likely to be *instructional,* so that the structure of the representational molecule is somehow specified by the information to be stored, or *selectional,* so that one of a preexisting set of possible structures is allocated for a given representational function.

Extensive data which have been reviewed elsewhere (John, 1967) show that the rate of synthesis of RNA in nerve cells is proportional to the total stimulation received by the cell, and that a chemical concomitant of neural activity is stimulation of ribonucleic acid and of protein synthesis. A number of studies have attempted to demonstrate more directly that there is an increase in RNA synthesis in a learning situation. It has been reported that after establishment of conditioned response, presentation of the conditioned stimulus causes an increased turnover of RNA in regions of the brain related to the modality of the conditioned stimulus but not in adjacent regions. Using the so-called "mirror focus" as a prototype of learning, RNA changes in the apical dendrites have been reported after the mirror focus becomes independent. Using labeled uridine, increased RNA synthesis has been demonstrated in the brains of goldfish learning a conditioned avoidance response, but not in the brains of control fish receiving the same total stimulation at random. Similar results have been obtained in mice. Further analysis suggested that the rate of synthesis of a messenger-like RNA in brain increased during learning. Significant changes in base ratios have been found in nuclear RNA in rats in a variety of experimental situations. A reciprocity has been demonstrated between glial and neuronal RNA synthesis. Conditions which cause an increase of certain compounds in neurons seem to cause a decrease of such compounds in glia, and vice versa. This has led some workers to suggest that certain substances might move from glial cells to neurons, since the loss of glial RNA during neural activity exactly balances the increase in neuronal RNA with the same base ratio. The glial cells might thus specify part of the neuronal protein synthesis.

A number of studies have explored the effects of interference with RNA synthesis or destruction of RNA on the storage and retrieval of information. Conditioned planaria display retention of the conditioned response following transection and regeneration, whether the tested animals regenerated from head or tail segments. However, conditioned animals who are transected and permitted to regenerate in a solution containing a low concentration of ribonuclease behave in a different fashion. Only animals regenerated from head segments can perform the conditioned response following such treatment, while animals regenerated from tail segments perform at the random level. It has been shown that intracerebral injection of ribonuclease, but not deoxyribonuclease, trypsin, or serum albumin, blocks retention of a conditioned defensive reflex in mice. Inhibition of RNA synthesis with 8-azaguanine has been shown to increase the number of errors during maze learning without interfering with retention for previously learned maze habits. Inhibition of RNA synthesis using 8-azaguanine has also been demonstrated to increase the consolidation time for a new pattern of activity in the spinal cord of a rat. Conversely, facilitation of RNA synthesis decreased the consolidation time of this same spinal cord activity pattern appreciably. Using mice, it has been shown that facilitation of RNA synthesis decreases the time following an experience during which erasure of the learning can be accomplished by administration of electroconvulsive shock. These data suggest that chemical stimulation of RNA synthesis accelerates the rate at which consolidation is achieved.

Other experiments exist suggesting that increase in RNA facilitates the storage of information and its retrieval. It has been reported that massive injections of yeast RNA to aged individuals result in marked improvement in memory. Animals injected intraperitoneally with yeast RNA before learning sessions acquired conditioned avoidance responses significantly more rapidly than controls who received saline injections and demonstrated greater resistance to extinction. Similar results have been obtained for maze learning in rats. It has been suggested that the injected RNA preempts much of the RNAase available and allows more of the endogenous RNA to survive and accumulate. These effects need not imply direct utilization of yeast RNA for the storage of information in human or animal neural tissue.

Planaria which were fed fragments of conditioned worms acquired the conditioned response more rapidly than planaria which ingested fragments of naive worms. The observation of more rapid learning in cannibalistic worms fed conditioned tissue encouraged a number of workers to attempt to extract "trained" RNA from the brains of conditioned animals and to investigate the possible facilitation of learning in animals receiving injections of such extracts. The initial report of positive results in such experiments led a large number of laboratories to undertake similar investigations. This has developed into one of the most controversial areas of research on memory, with large numbers of workers participating, many of whom report positive results and many of whom report complete failure to obtain any indication of transfer of learning by injection of extracts from trained animals.

Other work suggests that perhaps RNA is not the primary responsible agent for information storage, but represents an agent for the transfer of information to protein, which may be the substance actually responsible for permanent storage. Such findings derive from observation of the effects of inhibitors of protein synthesis, with a resultant impairment of recently learned conditioned responses. A large number of studies indicate that such impairment is reliably achieved utilizing injection of substances such as cycloheximide, acetoxycycloheximide, and puromycin. Further investigations have indicated a marked difference between cycloheximide and puromycin in their effects on hippocampal electrical activity. Puromycin produces marked electrical abnormalities. Thus, it may be that the effects of puromycin on consolidation should not be attributed to interference with protein synthesis but may be related to its effects on the hippocampus, a structure which has been implicated in the short-term storage of information.

These findings not only cast some doubt on whether protein synthesis was crucial for consolidation in these situations, but highlight the hazardousness of interpretation of findings in this research area. Although numerous facts suggest that macromolecular synthesis may well play a' role in consolidation, this is a research area in which there are abundant quantities of data which are extremely difficult if not impossible to reconcile with each other, an area of research in which laboratories have repeatedly reported the inability to replicate results obtained elsewhere, an area of research in which effects which have been clearly demonstrated on one species on one kind of behavior simply cannot be reproduced using other species or other measures of behavior. In the writer's opinion, none of the experimental results which have been obtained is sufficient by itself to warrant the unequivocal conclusion that stable information storage in the brain is mediated by the synthesis of ribonucleic acid or protein. Yet, it must be conceded that a wide variety of experimental procedures has yielded an impressive quantity of positive findings strongly pointing toward ribonucleic acid and protein synthesis as deeply implicated in the function of information storage in the brain.

In the previous discussion, we argued that the information content in the activity of a neuronal ensemble might consist of the time course of coherence. The memory of such information must be stored as an increase in the probability of the particular temporal pattern of coherence which occurred. We have proposed what we call the Derepressor hypothesis to accomplish such storage:

(A) In any cell much of the potential for synthesis of specific substances inherent in the DNA structure is repressed.

(B) Sustained participation of a neuron in representational activity causes a critical shift in the concentration of cytoplasmic materials resulting in the derepression of an inhibited synthesis.

(C) The resulting alteration in cytoplasmic constituents has two consequences: (1) Derepression of that synthesis is thereafter sustained; (2) The reactivity of the neuron to patterns of stimulation is altered.

The Derepressor hypothesis has been discussed in greater detail elsewhere (John, 1967). There are several essential features of this hypothesis. It is assumed that the postulated changes do not occur as a consequence of mere neural activity, but that the activity must be sustained for a sufficient time and at a sufficient rate to achieve a critical shift in the concentration of a critical substance. Since the sustained activity underlying the critical shift arose from participation in a reverberating loop, the neuronal input presumably involved only a portion of the many synaptic contacts of the cell and was characterized by a particular pattern. Thus, the input possessed particular spatio–temporal characteristics. The resulting neuronal discharge reconciled the various spatial influences at different synapses of the same cell, integrating these into a temporal pattern of neuronal response. There seems to be no compelling reason to require that the change in neural reactivity resulting from the derepressed synthesis necessarily restricts the altered probability of neural response to the arrival of impulses with specified distributions at specific synapses. The integrative nature of neuronal response to multiple synaptic inputs might well result in a "smearing" of the contribution of individual synapses.

A great deal of specification would seem to have been accomplished if the cell becomes effectively "tuned" to some temporal pattern integrated over all of its synaptic inputs, which influence cytoplasmic chemical concentrations during the relevant time period. This tuning might be effective at the level of the axon hillock rather than at the synapse. Such tuning would not require faithful reproduction of the events at each synapse, and would also alter response tendencies to partial reproduction of the initial set of input events. Furthermore, it permits alternative inputs to be accepted if temporal constraints are satisfied over the full set of stimuli which occur. Such a formulation would seem to provide advantages of flexibility and overall accuracy while conforming to the probabilistic nature of many of the propositions set forth earlier. The most important consequence of the process envisaged in the Derepressor hypothesis is that cells which have been active over a period of time with a particular pattern of activity become *more capable* of sustaining such a temporal pattern of activity in the future, and thereby *the probability is enhanced that a given mode of oscillation will subsequently be displayed by a particular neuronal ensemble.*

## XV. ELECTROPHYSIOLOGICAL STUDIES OF LEARNING AND MEMORY

For the reasons which have been stated earlier, we feel that it is necessary to reject what we will call the "strong localization hypothesis";

that is, the notion that the memory of experience is stored in a set of cells which construct a pathway from some region of the nervous system responsive to the afferent input to some region of the nervous system which controlled a motor response to the stimulus, and that this set of cells can be localized in a particular anatomical region or regions of the brain. At this stage in our understanding, two possibilities for the mechanism of memory must be evaluated:

(1) *Memory is stored in a diffusely or multiply localized anatomical system involving cells in many brain regions. Connections have been established between these cells during learning, and structure these cells into a memory system. Activation of a specific memory requires the discharge of particular cells in this system. The system cannot easily be disrupted by a lesion, because it is diffusely distributed and organized in parallel. However, memory is still localized in a particular group of cells and the specific connections between them.*

Is it plausible that the mere discharge of certain cells somewhere in the nervous system might be sufficient to represent a particular item of information either about a past or present event? For some, the credibility of this proposition has been markedly enhanced by the observations obtained in the elegant experiments by Hubel and Wiesel (Hubel, 1959; Hubel & Wiesel, 1962, 1963), who have studied the receptive fields of neurons at various levels of the visual system. Their results show that specific neurons in particular structures respond preferentially to discrete components of the stimulus complex. As one moves to successively higher levels of the central nervous system, the complexity of the stimuli which achieve maximal unit response becomes greater. Eventually, levels are reached wherein cells can be found which respond to extremely complex constellations of stimulus features and might be considered as "feature extractors." Similar results have been obtained by Lettvin, Maturana, and McCulloch (1959). Such data may seem to provide support for formulations in which the deterministic response of specific cells "stands for" the occurrence of a particular complex peripheral event. Stabilization or facilitation of pathways achieving that deterministic response might reasonably comprise the memory of that event. Unquestionably, these data do indicate appreciable processing of information in way stations of the visual system between the retina and the primary cortical projection area and progressively more complex specification of the stimuli adequate to elicit maximum unit response at successive levels. This evidence indicates that particular cortical cells respond preferentially to organized features of the afferent input.

Although such response is undoubtedly advantageous for registration

of the information, it does not necessarily follow that the discrete discharge of such a selective cell or set of cells is sufficient for representation
of the peripheral event. First of all, numerous cells are responsive to
a particular stimulus feature, and these cells have considerable anatomical distribution. The ease with which they can be found indicates that
they exist in relative profusion, and are diffusely distributed throughout
cortical areas. These cells may also discharge spontaneously in the absence of the preferred peripheral stimulus, although less intensely than
when optimally excited. Conversely, these cells may not respond identically to each occurrence of the appropriate stimulus. Furthermore, some
of these cells may also show marked changes in discharge when other
events occur. The suggestion that the same cells may represent a multi-
plicity of events receives strong support from such evidence as the continued performance of pattern discrimination by animals retaining only
two percent of the fibers in the optic tract (Norton, Frommer, &
Galambos, 1966). Such observations strongly suggest that information
about a wide variety of stimuli can be transmitted by any neuron in
the visual system. These considerations suggest that the occurrence of
firing in a unique and selectively responsive cell constitutes neither a
necessary nor a sufficient basis for the adequate representation of information about the presence of a unique peripheral event. Although selectively responsive cells may provide the basis for considerable abstraction
and interaction of various features of the stimulus field, it seems necessary to assess the behavior of the whole ensemble of cells in order to
estimate the significance of particular neural events. Preferential response of groups of cells to characteristic configurations of the stimulus
complex could constitute preprocessing of information and provide categories or dimensionality to the incoming excitation. The averaged activity of large ensembles composed of subsets of cells primarily responsive
to various features of the stimulus configuration might constitute the
basis for integration of the multitudinous and somewhat fortuitous responses of individual neurons into a reliable and coherent perception.

A number of experimental observations pose further difficulties for
deterministic extrapolations from receptive field studies. Previous events
can change the response of single units to specific stimuli. For example,
Buchwald and Hull (1966) have shown that a conditioning procedure
can result in sustained inhibition of the response of cortical units to
stimulation of the lateral geniculate. Similarly, Morrell (1967) has
demonstrated that the response of single units in the visual cortex to
specified visual stimuli can be altered by conditioning procedures using
a variety of unconditioned stimuli. A particularly interesting feature of
some experiments is the fact that the response of the unit to the condi-

tioned stimulus alone after pairing was essentially the sum of the responses elicited from the unit by presentation of the conditioned stimulus and unconditioned stimulus separately prior to pairing. These experiments were also noteworthy because of the specificity of the new response, indicated by the differential effects elicited by various stimuli. Data of this sort show that the responses of single units to specific stimulation of a receptive field are, in fact, labile and can be changed by conditioning procedures.

In spite of such evidence, the proposition that information about the specific stimulus might, nevertheless, be represented deterministically by the discharge of a particular neuron or neurons might conceivably still be defended by the argument that the new unit response now uniquely stands for the stimulus contingencies which characterize the conditioning experience. *This contention does not appear tenable in view of data showing that the activity induced in cortical units depends not only upon the immediate afferent stimulus but also upon the configuration of ongoing activity elsewhere in the nervous system.* Spinelli *et al.* have shown that direct stimulation of many brain regions, auditory stimuli, or somatic stimulation can change the receptive fields of single units in the optic nerve, lateral geniculate body, and visual cortex. Changes in the shape of the receptive field as well as in the firing pattern of the unit were observed (Spinelli, Pribram, & Weingarten, 1966; Spinelli & Weingarten, 1966; Weingarten & Spinelli, 1966). Perhaps the strongest evidence against the deterministic model of information coding by specific discharge patterns of particular neurons is provided by the work of Lindsley, Chow, and Gollender (1967) and Chow, Lindsley, and Gollender (1968). These workers have shown that the response patterns of single neurons in the lateral geniculate body to illumination of a spot on the retina of one eye can be altered by subsequent light stimulation of the other eye. This effect could be obtained even though the light stimulation of the second eye alone did not elicit any response from the recorded neuron. Furthermore, by means of a conditioned training procedure, they could obtain one mode of response from some units to illumination of the test spot in the presence of one conditional context and a different mode of response from these units to the same test spot in the presence of the second conditional context. No differential activity was elicited in these neurons by the conditional contexts alone. *The same specific stimulus could, therefore, elicit two alternative response patterns from the same neuron.*

Thus, although single units can display reproducible response patterns to specific stimuli under certain conditions, it seems probable that under normal conditions such response patterns are seldom if ever invariant.

Alteration of unit response patterns has been shown at several levels of the visual system: optic nerve, lateral geniculate, and visual cortex. Unit responses to a specific stimulus may be changed as a function of the configuration of activity elsewhere in the nervous system, by the sequence of events prior to stimulation, or by the environmental context in which the stimulus occurs. In addition, spontaneous discharge of neurons occurs at an appreciable rate, and, furthermore, units often respond to a variety of stimuli. Finally, a common feature of single-unit conditioning studies is the surprisingly high percentage (8–60%) of the units studied which show changes in response during conditioning. Since no unique properties can be attributed to the neurons fortuitously selected by an exploring microelectrode, it is probable that a very large number of cells is altered by any learning experience, and every such cell must be influenced by many experiences. The observed changes in unit response during conditioning look like changes in the temporal pattern of activity, rather than the gating of a new pathway.

In view of these considerations, it seems highly unlikely that the discharge of a given neuron or set of neurons can constitute either a necessary or a sufficient event for the deterministic representation of any specific item of peripheral information within the central nervous system. It would seem impossible to infer the presence or absence of a specified and unique peripheral event merely from the discharge of a single cell or a set of cells in the nervous system of an unanesthetized and unrestrained animal, since the informational significance of such neuronal discharge is contingent upon the recent history of the animal, the prior and present stimulus configuration, and the other ongoing activity in the ensemble. Assessment of the information contained in the activity of a neuronal ensemble would seem to necessitate some form of integration over the ensemble and over some period of time in order to compensate for the contextual dependency and the relative rather than absolute nature of a neuronal response to a stimulus.

(2) *The second possibility is that memory is stored in a volume of cells as temporal patterns of coherent activity or modes of oscillation in which the set of cells can engage. Different items of information need not be coded as the activity of different cells, but might be represented by the same group of cells as different patterns of combination or sequences of activity.*

Evidence from electrophysiological studies of learning is extremely useful in attempting to choose between these two possibilities. The findings obtained from such studies can be categorized into a number of major classes: changes in levels of synchrony or intrinsic brain rhythms associated with presentation of a conditioned stimulus, with occurrence of the orientation response, or with "choice behavior"; phenomena related to changes in steady potentials; and changes in evoked potentials or unit activity as conditioned responses are established to intermittent or rhythmic conditioned stimuli. The voluminous literature on these topics has been reviewed (John, 1961; Morrell, 1961a) and extensively discussed elsewhere (John, 1967).

## XVI. TRACER TECHNIQUE

A major drawback in electrophysiological studies of learning and memory has been the difficulty in identifying that part of the ongoing electrical activity of the brain which represents the processing of information relevant to the acquisition or performance of learned behaviors. We have found *tracer technique* to be particularly useful in enhancing the "signal-to-noise ratio" in such studies (John & Killam, 1959). The signal or *tracer-conditioned stimulus* (TCS) for the behavior under study is presented intermittently at a characteristic rate of repetition. Whatever might be the electrical manifestations of the brain mechanisms responsible for processing information about the TCS, it seems reasonable to expect those mechanisms to act with fair reliability each time that the repetitive TCS is presented. Electrical rhythms which appear in the brain with the frequency of the TCS, and oscillations which are phase locked to the time of occurrence of the TCS, are considered to be *labeled responses* arising from such neural processes.

The appearance of labeled responses in recordings of electrical activity from a particular brain region is *sufficient* evidence to conclude that information about the TCS is influencing the neural processes in that region. Since brain regions may be influenced by such information without displaying electrical activity at TCS frequencies, the appearance of labeled response is not a *necessary* concomitant of participation by a region in processing information about the stimulus. Thus, tracer technique allows us to say with some assurance that those structures which show labeled responses are processing information about the TCS, but does not permit us to say that structures which show no labeled responses are not also processing such information.

It may be necessary to point out that the labeled response which appears in the electrical activity of a brain region is *not* the actual information about the TCS which is being processed. It is merely an electrical sign that some neural activity in that region is regularly occurring with the same temporal characteristic as the TCS, which indicates a probable relationship between that neural activity and the stimulus. Early use of the tracer strategy was limited to relatively low frequencies which could readily be detected in visual inspection of EEG records. With the advent of average response computation methods, it was possible to extend the technique and to study the amplitude and *waveshape* of evoked potentials. By analyzing the detailed characteristics of these various labeled responses, it may prove possible to construct hypotheses and to draw valid inferences about the nature of the underlying neural information processing mechanisms responsible for these electrical manifestations.

## XVII. APPEARANCE OF ELECTRICAL SIMILARITIES IN DIFFERENT BRAIN REGIONS

Many changes in the labeled responses of the brain take place during learning. Some of these changes are due to general factors such as "pseudoconditioning" or sensitization, and do not reflect specific changes due to learning. However, careful use of controls permits identification of some changes which are most probably related to alteration in information processing, storage, and retrieval of information. The methods which have been most useful for the identification of specific changes due to learning are those which utilize the transfer of training from steady to intermittent conditioned stimuli, the transfer of training between intermittent stimuli in two sensory modalites, the transfer of training between peripheral and central conditioned stimuli, the generalization of a previously learned task to the presentation of novel stimuli, and analysis of the differences between correct and incorrect behavioral responses to the same stimulus. All of these techniques permit comparison of the characteristics of electrophysiological activity displayed by a conditioned animal when a particular stimulus either elicits or fails to elicit performance which requires the retrieval of previously stored information. Such studies have shown that during conditioning widespread changes occur in the *distribution* of responses evoked in the nervous system by the conditioned stimulus, as well as changes in the actual *form* of the potential evoked by a stimulus as it acquires informational significance.

In some of our early studies of electrophysiological changes during conditioning, we were surprised to note that certain brain regions sometimes acquired striking similarities in electrical activity during and after conditioning even though these relationships were not previously displayed (John & Killam, 1959). Other workers have seen and commented upon similar phenomena (Galambos & Sheatz, 1962; Yoshii, Pruvot, & Gastaut, 1957; Glivenko, Korol'kova, & Kuznetsova, 1962; Livanov, 1962, 1965; Dumenko, 1967; Knipst, 1967; Korol'kova & Shvets, 1967).

An illustration of this phenomenon from our recent studies is provided in Fig. 2. These average responses were computed from different regions of the brain during four behavioral trials in which a trained cat correctly performed conditioned avoidance responses to a 2.5-Hz flicker CS. Notice the remarkable similarity of the average response waveshapes recorded from bipolar derivations in the reticular formation, lateral geniculate, and visual cortex, as well as from a monopolar visual cortex derivation versus a frontal reference. The extreme electrical similarity between regions illustrated here appears between some but not all structures of the brain and has been observed this dramatically only in highly overtrained animals.

As such observations accumulated, it gradually became apparent that quantitative methods could be used to determine whether the similarity in electrical activity recorded from various brain regions actually increased during conditioning. For this purpose, we utilized techniques of factor analysis (John, Ruchkin, & Villegas, 1963, 1964). In this work, electrophysiological waveshapes which a stimulus elicited in various regions of the brain were digitized, and correlation coefficients were computed between the responses in different brain regions. The resulting

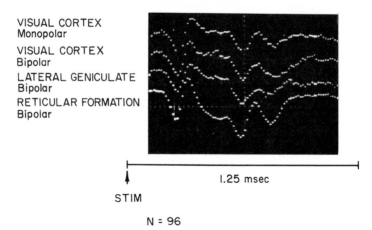

VISUAL CORTEX
Monopolar

VISUAL CORTEX
Bipolar

LATERAL GENICULATE
Bipolar

RETICULAR FORMATION
Bipolar

|— 1.25 msec —|

STIM

N = 96

FIG. 2.   Average response waveshapes recorded from different derivations in a trained cat. Note the marked similarity of the potentials in different brain regions. Cat 222, 2.5 Hz flicker, 4 trials of CAR, 1.25 msec/register. (Data from John, 1967.)

cross-correlation matrix was factor analyzed, and regression equations were constructed which reconstituted the electrical activity in each region of the brain as a weighted linear combination of so-called "generator" waveshapes. We found that it was possible to account quantitatively for the electrical activity observed in a wide variety of brain structures by a linear combination of the generator functions obtained by such analysis. Applying this analysis to the changes in electrical activity of the brain which take place during learning, we observed that the number of terms necessary to reconstruct the electrical activity in the brain of a trained animal decreased. Examination of the regression equations revealed that a variety of structures in the trained brain shared higher loadings on the same factors than was the case before conditioning. *This provided a quantitative demonstration that the coupling or similarity between the electrical signals elicited from different brain regions actually had increased during conditioning.* Similar results have been reported by Livanov (1962), Dumenko (1967), and Knipst (1967). Such results suggest that the waveshape of the electrical response of a brain region to a particular stimulus is not determined merely by the morphology of the region from which the recording is obtained.

## XVIII. RELATIONSHIP BETWEEN WAVESHAPE AND SITE OF STIMULATION

We have studied the relationship between the shape of the evoked potentials recorded in different brain regions and the site at which electrical stimulation is delivered to the brain. Evoked potentials were recorded from a number of different brain regions as conditioned responses were elicited by five different kinds of stimulation. One stimulus was 10-Hz flicker, and the other stimuli were 10-Hz electrical stimulation of the lateral geniculate, reticular formation, nucleus ruber, and pyramidal tract. In this fashion, an array of average evoked potentials was obtained consisting of the responses recorded from ten different anatomical regions to five different kinds of stimuli. These data were divided into two groups, each comprised of the waveshapes displayed by five different structures. In each array, the responses of a given structure to five different stimuli constituted a *row* of averaged evoked potentials, while the effect of a given stimulus on five different anatomical structures constituted a *column*. Each waveshape in a row was then correlated with every other waveshape in that row, yielding a *row matrix*. Similarly, each waveshape in a column was then correlated with every other waveshape in that column, yielding a *column matrix*.

The resulting ten-row and ten-column matrices were then subjected to factor analysis (Ruchkin & John, 1966). The factor analysis of the row matrices provides information about the extent to which the responses evoked in a given brain region by a variety of stimuli display features characteristic to that region. The factor analysis of the column matrices permits evaluation of whether a specified stimulus produces similar and characteristic effects in different anatomical regions. Restated, *the comparison of factor analyses of row and column matrices indicates whether an evoked response is more characteristic of the region from which it is recorded or the stimulus by which it is evoked.*

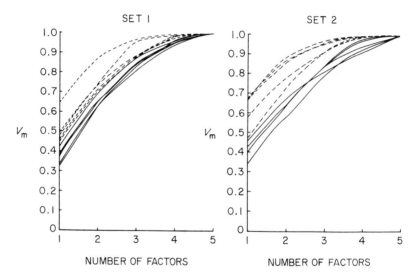

FIG. 3.    $V_m$ curves for factor analyses of correlation coefficients between waveshapes of: (a) averaged responses evoked in five different brain regions by the same stimulus (dotted lines); or (b) averaged responses evoked in the same brain region by five different stimuli (solid lines). Data presented on the left are for five stimuli (10-Hz flicker, 10-Hz electrical stimulation of right lateral geniculate, left pyramidal tract, right nucleus entopeduncularis, or right nucleus ruber) and five structures (right visual cortex, left motor cortex, left medial suprasylvian cortex, right mesencephalic reticular formation, and left nucleus ventralis anterior). Data presented on the right are for the same five stimuli, but the set of five structures included right visual cortex, right putamen, right caudate nucleus, left globus pallidus, and the left caudate nucleus. Note that the dotted curves lie above the solid curves. This means that there is greater similarity between the waveshapes evoked in five different brain regions by the same stimulus than between the waveshapes evoked in the same brain region by five different stimuli. (Data from John, 1967.)

Figure 3 shows the results of the factor analysis of these data carried out on two sets of five different structures. The graphs show the partial communality, $V_m$, that is, the amount the original signal of energy accounted for by the reconstructed signal versus the number of factors used to reconstruct the signal for both row and column matrices. These graphs can be interpreted as reflecting the extent to which different evoked potentials contained common components or had similar waveshapes. The greater the amount of signal energy in common components, the higher will be the $V_m$ curve. These data show at about the 0.01 significance level that *the shape of an evoked potential is determined more by the region from which a propagated disturbance arises than by the region from which the response is recorded*. It must be pointed out that row data were necessarily obtained sequentially, while column data were obtained simultaneously. Although the stability of average response waveshapes in conditioned animals has been found to be quite high on repeated stimulation, these conclusions must be considered tentative until further studies of this sort have been done with control for sequence. However, keeping these reservations in mind, these preliminary findings suggest that information propagating through the brain as a result of nonrandom excitation in some particular structures carries the *local sign* of the originally stimulated structure in its waveshape; that is, the temporal pattern of response to a given stimulus may include the key signature of the region which was initially responsive to that stimulus.

## XIX. RELATIONSHIP BETWEEN WAVESHAPE AND MEANING

Furthermore, the waveshape of the potential evoked by a stimulus may reflect the actual information content of the stimulus as well as its sensory modality. Using visual forms (see Fig. 4), we have demonstrated that the evoked potentials caused by two different geometric forms of equal area have different shape, while the potentials evoked by large and small versions of the same geometric form have similar waveshapes (John, Herrington, & Sutton, 1967). Similar results have been obtained by Clynes, Kohn, and Gradijan (1967) and by Pribram, Spinelli, and Kambock (1967). Additional evidence that evoked potential waveshapes reflect the informational significance of the stimulus has been reviewed recently (John, 1967).

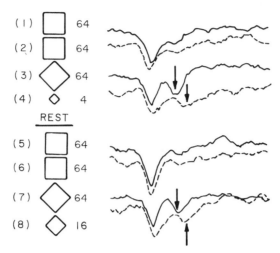

Fig. 4.    Averaged responses from two sessions with the same subject, separated by 30 minutes. All averages based upon 100 repetitions of the stimulus, and a 500-msec analysis epoch. Negative upward. Responses 1, 2, 5, and 6 were to squares with an area of 64 square inches, responses 3 and 7 to diamonds 64 square inches in area, response 4 to a diamond of 4 square inches, and response 8 to a diamond of 16 square inches. Note the new components, marked by the arrows, which appeared in 3 and 7 when the square was rotated 45°. (Data from John, Herrington, & Sutton, 1967.)

## XX. ENDOGENOUS COMPONENTS IN THE RESPONSE OF THE BRAIN TO STIMULI

The results presented thus far indicate that the responses of different brain regions change and become more similar during conditioning, that the response evoked in a particular brain region is not solely determined by the morphology of the neuronal structure but also reflects the site of the primary disturbance in the nervous system, and that the shape of the evoked potential to some extent reflects the informational content of the stimulus which was presented. Not only does the electrical activity of the brain reflect the informational content as well as the physical energy of the stimulus, but evidence exists that the reaction of the organism to the stimulus, *either based on instructional set or previous experience,* is also reflected in the electrical activity of the brain.

### A. Assimilation of Rhythms

The earilest support for this assertion was provided by Livanov and Poliakov (1945), who described what they called "assimilation of the rhythm." If an animal is subjected to a conditioning procedure using an intermittent conditioned stimulus with a particular repetition rate, during the intertrial intervals electrical rhythms at the same frequency as the absent conditioned stimulus appear in the activity of certain brain structures. These rhythms cannot be observed when the animal is in his home cage but appear when he is brought into the training apparatus.

A particularly interesting example of assimilation of the rhythm has recently been provided by Majkowski (1967) and is illustrated in Fig. 5. These data were recorded from both hemispheres of a cat whose brain had been split, including section of the corpus callosum, anterior commissure, posterior commissure, massa intermedia, and the optic tectum. At this stage, the left eye and hemisphere were being trained to a conditioned defensive reflex using a 5-Hz flicker CS. The tracings shown in this figure illustrate spontaneous rhythmic discharge at 5 Hz *during the intertrial interval*. Note that the frequency-specific assimilated rhythms were confined to structures on the side of the brain which was

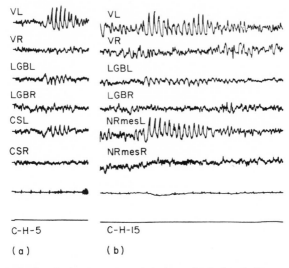

FIG. 5.    Assimilated rhythms recorded from both hemispheres of cat whose brain has been split, including section of corpus callosum, anterior commissure, posterior commissure, massa intermedia, and optic tectum. The tracings shown in parts (a) and (b) of this figure illustrate internal spontaneous rhythmic discharge at 5 Hz. At this stage, the left eye and hemisphere were being trained to a conditioned defensive reflex using a 5-Hz flicker CS. Note that *the frequency specific assimilated rhythm was confined to structures on the side of the brain which was being trained,* but appears at about the same time in different regions. (Data from Majkowski, 1967.)

being trained, but appear at about the same time in different regions. These data show that assimilated rhythms are localized to the "learning hemisphere" of split-brain cats. These differential observations strongly suggest that the spontaneous appearance of frequency specific repetitive responses in various anatomical regions during training with a rhythmic stimulus reflects the establishment of a representational system mediating the storage of information about the stimulus rather than unspecified influences.

### B. Comparison of Correct Responses and Errors

A number of observations permit us to evaluate the functional significance of these endogenous components of the electrical activity of the brain. A particularly interesting insight is afforded by analyzing the electrical activity in the brain of a differentially trained animal when it performs the correct response or an erroneous response to the same conditioned stimulus.

In Fig. 6, we see samples of the electrical activity recorded from the brain of a cat who was conditioned to perform an approach response to a 7.7-Hz stimulus and an avoidance response to a 3.1-Hz stimulus. In both of the trials illustrated in Fig. 6, a 7.7-Hz stimulus was presented to the animal. In the trial shown on the left, the animal correctly performed the approach response for which the 7.7-Hz flicker was the discriminative cue. In the trial shown on the right, the animal erroneously performed an avoidance response, which would have been appro-

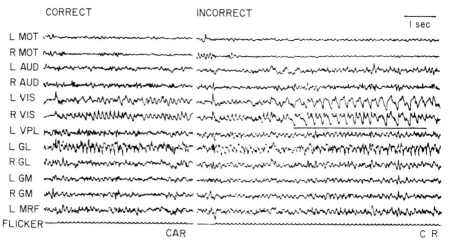

Fig. 6.    Correct vs. erroneous response. (Data from Shimokochi, 1967.)

priate to the 3.1-Hz flicker. Note the marked appearance of 3.1-Hz electrical rhythms in response to the 7.7-Hz stimulus (Shimokochi, 1967). Other examples of this phenomenon have been previously described (John, 1967). Such findings suggest that when a differentially conditioned animal makes a mistake, the electrical activity in certain regions of the brain contains rhythms which are appropriate for the behavior which is displayed but which are inappropriate for the physical stimulus which is actually present. This suggests that the rhythms in question are released from memory rather than caused by the stimulus itself. Such released rhythms have been reported by several authors just before *spontaneous* performance of the corresponding conditioned responses.

## C. Brain Rhythms during Generalization

Figure 7 shows a particularly interesting example of data obtained during generalization from a split-brain cat when a novel stimulus was presented first to the initially trained side and later to the second side following transfer of training (Majkowski, 1967). Using the left eye and hemisphere, this animal was trained to perform a defensive conditioned reflex to a 5-Hz flicker CS. After left-side training, recordings were obtained during generalization of conditioned response upon initial presentation of a novel 12-Hz flicker, to which the cat made the behavioral response previously learned with the 5-Hz stimulus. Examination of the figure shows that *during generalization* to the 12-Hz stimulus, structures on the left side of the brain displayed a marked 5-Hz rhythm. After completion of left brain *differential* training in which the 12-Hz flicker was the negative stimulus, presentation of the 12-Hz flicker to the left eye elicited 12-Hz electrical rhythms on the left side of the brain. After transfer of the conditioned response to the right eye and hemisphere using a 5-Hz cue, generalization was again elicited on presentation of the 12-Hz novel stimulus to the right eye. Notice that the 12-Hz stimulus then occasioned marked 5-Hz activity in right-side structures. After right-eye differentiation, the 12-Hz flicker elicited 12-Hz rhythms on the right side of the brain.

These differential results provide reassurance that the electrical rhythms which are released in the brain during such generalization are not to be attributed to arousal, orientation, or other generalized features of the situation, but are a function of the informational significance of the intermittent stimulus. Repeated observations of this phenomenon, other examples of which have been previously described (John, 1967), suggest that the occurrence of a novel event which resembles a familiar

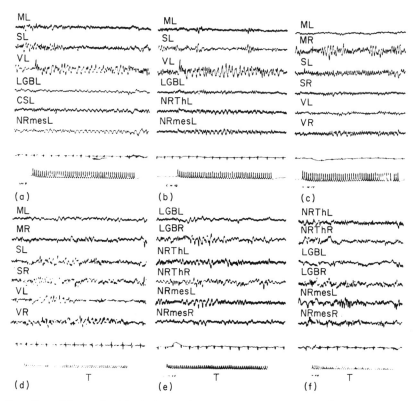

Fig. 7.  Electrophysiological correlates of generalization and differentiation, observed in a "split-brain" cat. Parts (a), (b), and (c) were recorded after the *left eye and hemisphere* had been trained to perform a conditioned defensive reflex to a 5-Hz flicker CS.

*After left-side training:* (a) Recordings obtained during *generalization* of conditioned response upon initial presentation of novel 12-Hz flicker to the left eye, following establishment of CR to the 5-Hz CS. Note marked labeled responses to 5 Hz released in visual cortex (VL), superior colliculus (CSL), and mesencephalic reticular formation (NR mes L) on the left side. Seventh channel shows EKG and EMG and indicates that flexion CR was performed at the end of trial. (b) As differential training was carried out, performance of the CR to the unreinforced 12-Hz signal gradually dropped out. These recordings were obtained during an early nonperformance trial. Note that the 12-Hz signal still elicited marked 5 Hz, clearly visible in the visual cortex, mesencephalic reticular formation, and nucleus reticularis of the thalamus (NR Th L). (c) Records obtained after completion of differentiation. Note that the 12-Hz signal now elicits labeled responses corresponding to the stimulus frequency, particularly marked on the left side.

*After transfer of training to right side:* (d) Recordings obtained during generalization to novel 12-Hz flicker presented to right eye and hemisphere after completion of transfer (T) of the CR to the 5-Hz flicker CS to the right side. Note the 5-Hz labeled responses which appear in some right side structures (R). (e) As differentiation proceeds, generalization is still occasionally displayed. These records stimulus can activate a neural system previously established in a trained animal by repeated presentations of the conditioned stimulus. When activated by the *novel* event, *that neural system seems to enter a particular state,* releasing the mode of oscillation characteristic of response to the *familiar* conditioned stimulus, and *the corresponding behavioral actions are subsequently performed.*

Other studies have provided evidence that not only particular rhythms in the EEG but actual components in evoked potential waveshapes can be released. It has been shown that when a human subject is presented with a sequence of stimuli with a particular patterning in time from which stimuli are occasionally withheld, recordings from particular scalp areas reveal the release of evoked potentials at the time at which the stimulus was *expected* (Rusinov, 1959; Haider, Spong, & Lindsley, 1964; Barlow, Morrell, & Morrell, 1965). Further, it has been shown that the ability of a particular stimulus to elicit an evoked potential depends upon the *set* of the subject (Sutton, Tueting, Zubin, & John, 1967).

## D. Evoked Potentials during Generalization

We have compared the waveshape of average evoked responses elicited when generalization occurs to a novel stimulus with the waveshapes caused by the same stimulus when generalization fails to occur. In Fig. 8, average evoked responses are presented from the lateral geniculate body and nucleus reticularis of the thalamus of a cat, computed under a number of different conditions. The upper waveshape in each column illustrates the evoked potential produced in these structures by presentation of the 10-Hz conditioned stimulus during a number of trials resulting in correct performance of the conditioned response. The middle waveshape illustrates the evoked response elicited by the 7.7-Hz test stimulus during a group of trials resulting in generalization. The lower waveshape shows the average responses evoked by the same test stimulus during trials in which no behavioral performance occurred. The samples used

were taken from a trial in which behavioral response was displayed. Note that the marked 5-Hz labeled activity in some structures is visible on the right as well as on the left side. (f) After completion of differentiation. Notice the clear 12-Hz responses now elicited by the 12-Hz signal. All derivations are bipolar: L, left side; R, right side; M, motor cortex; S, sensorimotor cortex; V, visual cortex; LGB, lateral geniculate body; CS, superior colliculus; NR mes, mesencephalic reticular formation; NR Th, nucleus reticularis of thalamus; seventh channel of all sets indicates EKG and forepaw EMG; eighth channel indicates flicker artifact. (Data from Majkowski, 1967.)

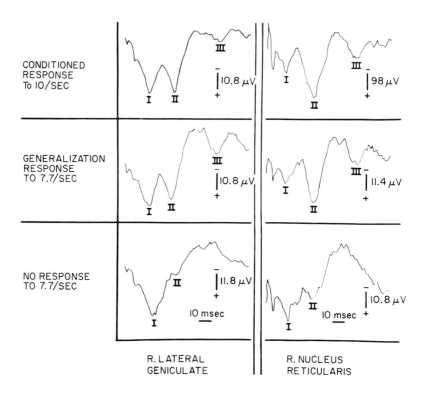

FIG. 8.    Average response computations obtained from the lateral geniculate
nucleus and nucleus reticularis of the cat under various conditions during the
same experimental session. All averages in this illustration are based upon 42
stimulus repetitions from a number of behavioral trials. Analysis epoch was 90
msec.

*Upper records:* Average responses evoked in structures by the 10-Hz conditioned
stimulus (flicker) actually used in training, during repeated correct behavioral
performances.

*Middle records:* Average responses evoked by a novel 7.7-Hz flicker, during
repeated generalization behavior. Test trials with the 7.7-Hz stimulus were interspersed among trials with the actual 10-Hz conditioned stimulus, and were never
reinforced.

*Bottom records:* Average responses evoked by the 7.7-Hz flicker on presentations
when no generalization behavior was elicited. Note the similarity of the waveshape
elicited by the actual conditioned stimulus to the response evoked by the novel
stimulus during generalization. Notice the absence of the second positive component
in the evoked potential when generalization failed to occur. (Data from Ruchkin
& John, 1966.)

in these computations were carefully equated with respect to the time elapsed after stimulus onset. These averages show that the evoked response in these structures contains three positive components (I, II, III) which are clearly seen in the top and middle waveshapes. In trials resulting in generalization, components II and III consistently appeared several seconds before any overt movement of the cat took place. Components II and III are absent when generalization fails to occur. The variance of amplitudes in the sample from which these averages are constructed was computed, and the significance of the differences observed in these components was calculated. The absence of component II during failure of the test stimulus to elicit generalization was significant at the 0.01 level in both structures, and the absence of III was significant in one (John, Ruchkin, Leiman, Sachs, & Ahn, 1965; Ruchkin & John, 1966). However, no significant difference between the various conditions exists for component I.

These results were interpreted to mean that component I was related to the *registration* of the afferent stimulus upon the structure, while component II (and perhaps III) arose from a *reaction* of the neural ensemble to that input, possibly related to the retrieval of stored information. Marked waveshape differences when generalization occurred were seen in other animals treated just like this one, with the definite appearance of a process with the shape and latency of component II in several brain structures during generalization in two of those animals. It is interesting to note the remarkable correspondence shown in Fig. 8 between the waveshape elicited by the actual 10-Hz conditioned stimulus during correct performance of the conditioned response and the waveshape displayed when presentation of the 7.7-Hz test stimulus resulted in the occurrence of generalization. The similarity between the waveshapes under these two conditions is rather extraordinary. Since it is clear that the generalization waveshape cannot be interpreted as a simple evoked response, this demonstrates that the process *released from storage* during readout approximately reproduces the electrical effects of the previously experienced event.

Using approach rather than avoidance situations, similar observations have been obtained, indicating appreciable generality from this phenomenon. Preliminary experiments using computer pattern recognition techniques suggest that the appearance of these late waveshape components may be of utility for the prediction of generalization behavior.

In subsequent studies (John & Ahn, 1966), animals have been trained to perform differential approach and avoidance responses to two stimuli differing in frequency. Generalization tests were then conducted using a novel stimulus of intermediate frequency. *The shapes of the evoked potentials during generalization differed, depending on which behavioral response was performed.*

Evidence has also been obtained that the late waveshape components under discussion here cannot be attributed to unspecific factors of the sort which might merely increase the general excitability of any given brain region such as arousal, focus of attention, the intention to move, or a change in the motivational level (John & Shimokochi, 1966). So-called *conflict* studies have been carried out in which animals have been conditioned to respond to a variety of visual and auditory stimuli with the performance of differentiated approach and avoidance responses. In a conflict trial, two stimuli with contradictory significance are simultaneously presented to the animal, and the evoked potentials elicited by each stimulus are separately computed from the electrical activity recorded from various regions of the brain. Studies of this sort have shown that the late component appears in the evoked potential of the stimulus which effectively controls the decision determining the outcome of the conflict trial, while at the same time the evoked potential caused by the signal which fails to control the behavior does not display the late component. Examination of data from conflict experiments supports the contention that the late components which have been discussed above are related to informational rather than unspecific factors. The probable informational relevance of these late components in evoked potentials is further substantiated by studies which have described the appearance of new late components in the potentials evoked by conditioned stimuli after establishment of conditioned responses (Killam & Hance, 1965; Asratyan, 1965b; Sakhuilina & Merzhanova, 1966).

## XXI. DIFFERENCE WAVESHAPES AND THE READOUT OF STORED INFORMATION

Component II in generalization reflects a process which is markedly evident when a neutral stimulus causes the activation of a memory about previous experience, operationally indicated by the performance of a behavioral response acquired by training to a different stimulus. It seems logically justifiable to invoke readout from memory in order to account for generalization. It is difficult to explain the performance of so unnatural a response as pressing a lever mounted in the wall whenever a novel flicker appears, without assuming mediation by response processes and systems which were established during a previous learning experience. The novel stimulus must trigger the release of neural activity which resembles in some critical ways the past effect of the conditioned stimulus itself.

The most intriguing feature of these data is the suggestion that the retrieval of stored information may actually be symmetrical with the "readin," so that the resulting electrical activity literally reconstructs the process which accompanied registration of the experience. The mechanisms mediating the long-term storage of information in the brain may possess the capacity to reconstruct complex patterns of electrical activity in very large populations of neurons. It appears improbable that such extensive macropotential phenomena would be observed if memories were stored in a restricted specific set of cells whose discharge represented particular past experiences. The relatively crude electrophysiological methods used in these experiments would not be likely to detect such discrete discharge. If it could be conclusively established that retrieval reconstructed average electrical activity in neural ensembles which was statistically comparable to the original influence of the stored information, this would constitute rather striking support for the suggestion that remembering is not accomplished by the deterministic discharge of specific cells but relates to the establishment of a particular mode of oscillation.

One might conceptualize the waveshape during generalization as one which reflects *input plus readout,* while the waveshape when generalization fails to occur reflects *input* alone. Differences in waveshape can be observed in many structures under these two conditions, although at the same time other structures fail to show any difference in the shape of evoked potentials. Reasoning thus, it seemed logical to *subtract* the average response waveshape obtained during nonperformance trials from the waveshapes elicited by the same stimuli when generalization occurred. This operation subtracts the activity during input alone from the activity during input plus readout. (Data used in such computations were always gathered from a period shortly after the onset of the stimulus to just before the first movement was made by the cat being studied. Thus, the possible contribution of movement to the readout component can be excluded.) The resulting "difference waveshape" provides an estimate of the characteristics of the neural process mediating readout of previously stored information. Computation of difference waveshapes across a large number of anatomical structures in the same animal during a common set of stimulus presentations enables several important questions to be answered. If the hypothesis is accepted that the difference waveshape reflects the readout of stored information, then *such readout must occur earliest from the anatomical region where the engram is stored. Measurement of differential latencies for the difference process should identify the region containing the engram, if such localization does in fact exist, as the region with shortest latency.*

The details of the difference waveshape should provide information about the various anatomical regions involved in remembering and the characteristic activity displayed during mediation of the process by different brain structures. In particular, appearance of *similar* difference waveshapes in several brain regions would mean that the same mode of oscillation was displayed by a variety of neuronal ensembles.

Figure 9 shows a set of difference processes computed by subtracting averages obtained during nonperformance to the stimulus from averages obtained during generalization. Examination of these data reveals an unexpected and intriguing fact. Within the limts of time resolution available with the computer parameters used in analysis of these data, the release of the difference waveshape occurs with approximate simultaneity (within less than 1 msec) in the visual cortex, the posterior suprasylvian gyrus, the nucleus ventralis lateralis, and the mesencephalic reticular formation. The distances between these various anatomical regions are so great as to preclude the possibility of propagated conduction between them in so short a period. Furthermore, the shape of the difference process released from some of these structures is highly similar. The system comprising these regions seems subsequently to influence a set of other structures in which the difference process appears successively later, with the most delayed appearance discernible in the anterior part of the lateral geniculate body. Thus, the readout process seems to propagate back to the thalamic nucleus responsible for the afferent input of information about the presence of the stimulus in the environment.

In later studies we have computed difference waveshapes between correct responses and response failures in a differential approach–avoidance situation requiring cats to discriminate between 1-Hz and 2.5-Hz flicker stimuli (John & Shimokochi, 1966). Difference waveshapes have been repeatedly computed from *bipolar* cortical, thalamic, and mesencephalic placements revealing *essentially identical form and latency* of the difference process which was released in these various structures. These findings are illustrated in Fig. 10. Thus, evidence for simultaneous release of activity analogous to that previously presented has been obtained in other cats performing in a different behavioral situation and stimulated in a much lower frequency range. These animals were also overtrained. Additional difference waveshapes computed in these same animals revealed that immediately following acquisition of a new conditioned response after transfer the difference process in the mesencephalic reticular formation has a shorter latency than the difference waveshape observed in other structures. It should be pointed out that in some other structures in the brain of these animals, from which recordings were simultaneously obtained, no comparable readout process could be constructed by the subtraction procedure.

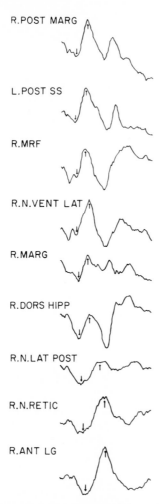

R.POST MARG

L.POST SS

R.MRF

R.N.VENT LAT

R.MARG

R.DORS HIPP

R.N.LAT POST

R.N.RETIC

R.ANT LG

FIG. 9.    "Difference" waveshapes constructed by subtraction of averaged responses evoked by 7.7-Hz test stimulus during trials resulting in no behavioral performance from averaged responses evoked by the same stimulus when generalization occurred. Each of the original averages was based on 200 evoked potentials providing a sample from 5 behavioral trials. Analysis epoch was 62.5 msec. These difference waveshapes begin 10 msec after the stimulus. The onset and maximum of the difference wave has been marked by two arrows on each waveshape. The structures have been arranged from top to bottom in rank order with respect to latency of the difference wave. Note that the latency and shape of the initial component of the difference wave is extremely similar in the first four structures, and then appears progressively later in the remaining regions. (POST MARG, posterior marginal gyrus; POST SS, posterior suprasylvian gyrus; MRF, mesencephalic reticular formation; N VENT LAT, nucleus ventralis lateralis; MARG, marginal gyrus; DORS HIPP, dorsal hippocampus; N LAT POST, nucleus lateralis posterior; N RETIC, nucleus reticularis; ANT LG, anterior lateral geniculate; R, right side; L, left side.) (Data from John, 1967.)

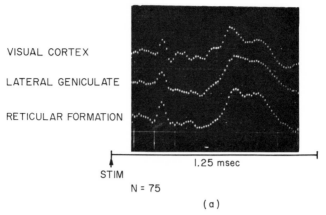

VISUAL CORTEX

LATERAL GENICULATE

RETICULAR FORMATION

STIM
N = 75

1.25 msec

(a)

Fɪɢ. 10.     (a). Difference waveshapes obtained by subtracting average responses computed during three trials resulting in no performance (NR) from average responses computed during five trials resulting in correct performance of the conditioned avoidance response (CAR). All recordings were *bipolar,* and 75 evoked potentials were used in each of the constituent averages. Note the correspondence in latency and waveshape of the difference process in these various regions. (Cat 239, 1-Hz flicker, 5 CAR, 3 NR trials, 1.25 msec/register.)

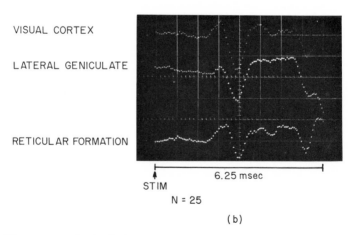

VISUAL CORTEX

LATERAL GENICULATE

RETICULAR FORMATION

STIM
N = 25

6.25 msec

(b)

(b). These were obtained from the same animal as those in (a). However, these results were computed in different trials and illustrate the difference waveshapes from *monopolar* derivations. Twenty-five evoked potentials were used in each constituent average and were taken from three CAR and one NR trials. The onset, first negative peak, and first positive peak in these three structures show remarkable correspondence with respect to latency. Note that the resolution is 0.625 msec/register (spot) in the average response computer. (Cat 239, 1-Hz flicker, 3 CAR, 1 NR trials, 6.25 msec/register.)

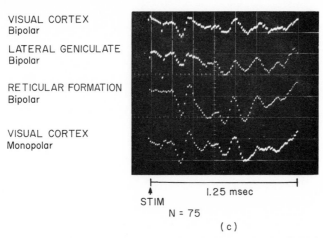

VISUAL CORTEX
Bipolar

LATERAL GENICULATE
Bipolar

RETICULAR FORMATION
Bipolar

VISUAL CORTEX
Monopolar

STIM

1.25 msec

N = 75

( c )

(c). Difference waveshapes from another animal. Seventy-five evoked potentials were used in each constituent average and were taken from three CAR and one NR trials. Note the similarity in the latency and form of the difference waveshape in the three bipolar derivations from reticular formation, lateral geniculate, and visual cortex, as well as the correspondence between the process observed in monopolar and bipolar derivations from the visual cortex. (Cat 222, 2.5-Hz flicker, 3 CAR, 1 NR trials, 1.25 msec/register.)

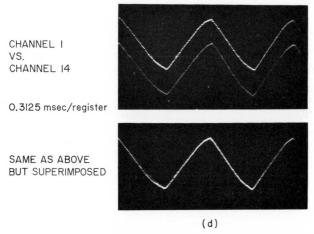

CHANNEL I
VS.
CHANNEL 14

0.3125 msec/register

SAME AS ABOVE
BUT SUPERIMPOSED

( d )

(d). Results of system calibration to check timing accuracy. A sawtooth signal was simultaneously impressed upon the two inputs between which timing errors would be most evident. The amplifier outputs were recorded, retrieved, and averaged using the same equipment as in other parts of this figure. Note that resolution is 0.3125 msec/register. These results indicate that the temporal relationships observed between the difference waveshapes computed in various brain regions reflect the actual timing of physiological processes, with minimal timing error introduced by the measuring apparatus. (Data from John, 1967.)

Reverting to the problem of the localization of the engram, we reach an unexpected conclusion. We argued above that the region in which the difference process appeared earliest would be the site to which engram storage must reasonably be attributed. Either the simultaneous emergence of the readout process in cortical, thalamic, and mesencephalic regions is due to some common influence exerted by an unknown distant structure, or *the representational system comprising the memory of a previous experience involves all of these structures.* In addition, the similarity in the waveshape of the released process suggests that *the readout establishes a common mode of activity in these various ensembles of neurons.* The evidence which has thus far been presented suggests that memory is distributed across a number of structures in the brain. One possibility is that the set of common modes of activity just demonstrated arises independently in each of the structures in which it is observed, and represents the simultaneous activation of portions of a representational system. The second possibility is that the observed synchronous pattern arises in these different brain regions because of the phasing influence of some "pace-maker system," perhaps the intralaminar thalamic nuclei. Further experiments will be necessary to evaluate these alternatives. Perhaps it should be pointed out that the apparent simultaneity of the difference waveshape in different brain regions may be deceptive. These differences were computed by subtracting two averages, and the results hold true *on the average.* It might well be, if one could achieve a sufficient signal-to-noise ratio to look at the single evoked potentials without any necessity for averaging, that some particular region sometimes displays the component which we have identified as reflecting the release of stored information earlier in a trial than do the other regions of the brain. Although the evidence which has been presented seems to provide a strong basis for the conclusion that the function of memory is distributed in a number of structures, it is not sufficient by itself to decide whether the mediation of memory by neurons in those structures is accomplished in a deterministic or a statistical fashion.

## XXII. RELATION BETWEEN SINGLE-UNIT ACTIVITY AND EVOKED POTENTIALS

In order to answer this last question, it will be necessary for us to consider the neuronal activity which accompanies the macropotential phenomena which have been described. It is generally believed that the slow waves recorded from a region are a composite of excitatory and inhibitory postsynaptic potentials plus the after potentials of spike discharges in cell bodies as well as in afferent and efferent fibers coursing through the volume of tissue around the tip of the electrode. Numerous investigations have shown a direct relationship between peripheral stimuli and the firing of single neurons, but until recently, the relationship between unit firings and macropotentials remained obscure, with poor correlations generally reported between extracellular unit recordings and the potentials derived from large electrodes. Gradually data have emerged which help to clarify the picture. Appreciable evidence now exists that surface potentials correlate well with the transmembranal potentials recorded with intracellular electrodes.

Recently, Klee, Offenloch, and Tigges (1965) carried out cross-correlation analysis between EEG potentials and the transmembrane potentials of single cortical neurons, obtaining time series correlation coefficients as high as 0.7. These quantitative results confirm the qualitative conclusions reached by others in cortical, thalamic, and hippocampal neurons (Kandel & Spencer, 1961; Fujita & Sato, 1964; Purpura & Shofer, 1964; Klee & Offenloch, 1964; Creutzfeldt, Watanabe, & Lux, 1966b; Calvet, Calvet, & Scherrer, 1964; Stefanis, 1963). Klee *et al.* interpreted the observed correlations to mean that the electrical rhythms of the electroencephalogram reflect an integration of the fluctuation of membrane potentials in both the cell bodies and dendrites of a large number of neurons. In more recent studies, Creutzfeldt, Watanabe, & Lux (1966a) have demonstrated clear temporal relations between evoked cortical potentials and the transmembranal potential changes of pyramidal cells. In general, surface positivity was correlated with an incoming afferent volley or an excitatory postsynaptic potential (EPSP), while surface negativity tended to be associated with cellular inhibitory post-synaptic potentials (IPSPs). Afferent and efferent volleys and axodendritic and axosomatic inputs all seem to cause characteristic effects on both slow waves and cellular potentials. Pollen and Sie (1964) have also presented evidence that the surface-negative wave is associated with IPSPs generated in deeper layers of the cortex.

The moderate correlation between neuronal transmembranal potentials and regional slow wave activity, together with the fact that neuronal discharge does not always occur at the same level of membrane depolarization (Purpura, Shofer, & Musgrave, 1964), means that unit spike activity and macropotentials cannot be expected to show an immediately noticeable and consistently predictable relationship. Macropotentials seem to reflect the summated effects of slow transmembranal postsynaptic and after potentials over a field encompassing great numbers of neurons and fibers, and thereby may reflect the existence of coherent average processes within the neuronal ensemble. However, the spike activity of any single nerve cell impaled upon a microelectrode might be expected to bear a relationship to such summated waves which was markedly nonlinear and which could only be approximated by statistical evaluation. Systematic relationships between the distribution of unit activity in a population of cells and the macropotentials derived from that region may only become apparent if there is some degree of averaging, either through the simultaneous sampling of more than one unit or by sequentially averaging over time. Using such methods, positive relationships between single-unit activity and slow potentials have been reported by Green, Maxwell, Schindler, and Stumpf (1960), Gerstein (1961), Robertson (1965), Vasilevs (1965), Frost and Gol (1966), and Fromm and Bond (1967). Perhaps the most definite demonstration of the statistical relationship between the discharge of single neurons and evoked potentials in a region comes from the work of Fox and O'Brien (1965). These workers compiled the frequency distribution of spikes from single cells in the visual cortex as a function of time after stimulation with light flashes, summating the responses obtained to several thousand flashes. These frequency distribution curves were then cross-correlated with the averaged evoked potentials recorded from the same region. Correlation coefficients ranged from 0.14–0.88, with 58% of the units studied showing a relationship between spike discharges and local slow waves which was significant at the 0.001 level. Since there is no reason to assume that the arbitrarily monitored units were atypical of the population as a whole, the implication of this study is that a good correlation would be readily obtained between the local evoked potential and the average firing pattern of a large ensemble during the same interval if it were possible to monitor the discharge of thousands of individual neurons simultaneously. This presumed ensemble correlation would arise not because the evoked potential was the envelope of unit discharges, but rather because the evoked potential reflected the average discharge probability of neurons in the region due to modulations of excitability by shifts in transmembranal potentials.

It may be worthwhile to recall here that macropotential changes during conditioning are extremely widespread. In the context of the above discussion, this implies that changes in single-unit activity during conditioning should occur in many regions and should be very marked and easy to detect. That such is indeed the case can be seen from the studies of single unit changes during conditioning which report that a large proportion of the cells observed (from eight to as high as 60 percent) change their response during conditioning (Jasper, Ricci, & Doane, 1960;

Morrell, 1961b; Morrell 1967; Olds & Olds, 1961; Bureš, 1965; Bureš & Burešová, 1965; Kamikawa, McIlwain, & Adey, 1964; Buchwald, Halas, & Schramm, 1965; Hori & Yoshii, 1965; Adam, Adey, & Porter, 1966; Yoshii & Ogura, 1960). Perhaps it is worthwhile to repeat here that examination of data from such studies indicates that units respond to the conditioned stimulus before as well as after establishment of the conditioned response, but the pattern of response to this stimulus changes. This observation, together with the large percentage of cells which seem to be affected by the conditioning procedure, constitutes a powerful argument against the idea of a new pathway as responsible for the storage of information about the stimulus.

## XXIII. CHRONIC MICROELECTRODE STUDIES

In order to study the statistical characteristics of the discharge of neuronal populations over a long period of time and to study the homogeneity of the response characteristics of neuronal ensembles in different anatomical regions, we developed a chronically implantable microdrive capable of carrying multiple microelectrodes (John & Morgades, 1969a; 1969b). This device permits the implantation of two microelectrodes which are held 125 $\mu$ apart. These two electrodes can be moved through the brain at will. Some of the data which have been obtained with this device are relevant to our discussion.

Two microelectrodes were chronically implanted in a cat, and neural activity was studied over a period of more than six months, as the electrodes were moved through a number of brain regions. Appropriate instrumentation permitted separate analysis of simultaneous slow wave activity and unit discharges from the same electrode. Although careful electrode positioning sometimes permitted study of single units (see Fig. 13), the tip diameters of these microelectrodes (2–5 $\mu$) were so selected as to facilitate simultaneous extracellular recording of a local group of several neurons. Different units can be discriminated in such group records by use of pulse-height analysis.

### A. Changes in Unit-Evoked Potential Relations

Early in these studies we observed that the shape of the potentials evoked in the lateral geniculate body by a flash of light varied in different states of the animal. Further, in a given electrode position the rela-

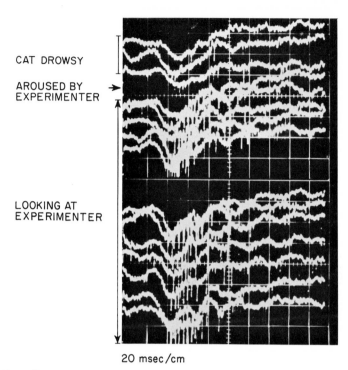

CAT DROWSY

AROUSED BY
EXPERIMENTER →

LOOKING AT
EXPERIMENTER

20 msec/cm

FIG. 11. Responses to successive light flashes. Cat drowsy during first three flashes. Experimenter called cat by name after third flash. Note altered relationship between units and evoked potential. Electrodes in lateral geniculate body. (Unpublished data from John & Morgades, 1967.)

tionship between single unit discharges and the evoked potential *was not constant,* but altered drastically under different conditions. For example, Fig. 11 illustrates the evoked potentials and unit discharges elicited by a series of light flashes. During the first three light flashes, the cat was drowsy. Few unit discharges occurred during this period. After the third flash, the experimenter began to speak the name of the cat, who had become a laboratory pet. While the cat was attentively scrutinizing the person saying her name, not only did the shape of the evoked potential change, but a burst of unit discharges occurred reliably in phase with a particular component of the evoked potential.

## B. Variability of Unit Responses

Although the bursts of unit activity appeared in grossly reproducible relationship to the evoked potential while the cat was alert, detailed

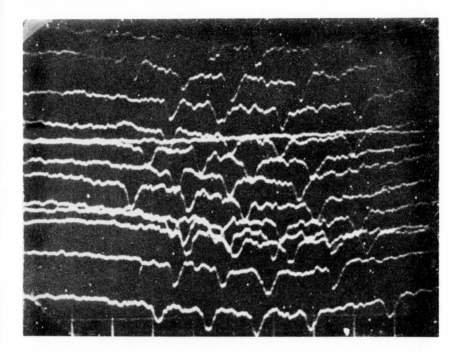

FIG. 12.    Variability in the response to successive light flashes at 1 Hz. (Unpublished data from John & Morgades, 1967.)

examination of the unit responses to single flashes of light revealed marked variability in the number and timing of neuronal discharges. This variability of neuronal response to the stimulus can be seen in Fig. 12.

## C. Similar Unit-Evoked Potential Relationships from Different Groups of Cells

Although examination of simultaneous records from the two microelectrodes (Fig. 13a) showed that they detected cells firing at different times, these different ensembles displayed similar group poststimulus time histograms (PSH) to light flashes. Figure 13b shows PSHs and average evoked responses (AER) to light flashes, recorded from the two microelectrodes in the ventral part of the lateral geniculate body when the cat was drowsy and while it was alert. Small differences in AER waveshape can be seen between evoked potentials recorded from each of the two electrodes monopolar versus a frontal reference. *Major components of the AER were reflected in the features of the group PSH. This*

finding is reminiscent of the correlation between the average evoked
potential waveform and the probability of firing of single cells in the
visual cortex observed by Fox and O'Brien (1965). *The correlation observed at this stage was variable but increased and stabilized after conditioning.* Note the change in shape of both of these measures from both
neuronal ensembles when the state of the animal changed from drowsy
to alert.

Mostly negative-going spike discharges were seen in the first few electrode positions. However, after the electrodes were lowered 3.8 mm, probably into the ventral hippocampus, recordings contained approximately
an equal number of negative and positive–negative spikes. Careful examination of fast oscilloscope tracings showed that these two kinds of spikes
occurred independently in time. This, together with the differential effects
of sodium pentobarbital (30 mg/kg) suggested that these spike types
reflected the firing of two different subgroups of cells in the vicinity
of the electrode tips. The data in Fig. 14 were obtained in Position
5, after the cat had been trained so that it pressed a lever to obtain
food whenever a food dipper on the front panel was lowered. The dipper
was only lowered after presentation of a train of light flashes. Although
careful testing showed that the light flashes had failed to acquire cue
value during this training procedure, the cat trained to the dipper cue
sat motionless and alert in front of the work panel throughout the flicker
presentations. Under these conditions, repeated PSHs were obtained

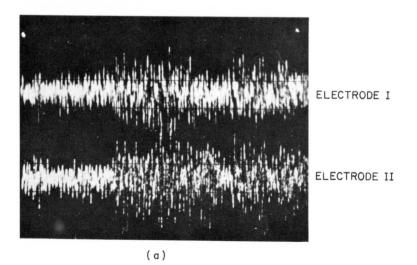

ELECTRODE I

ELECTRODE II

(a)

Fig. 13.    (a). Different cells seen by two electrodes 40 days after implant.
(Unpublished data from John & Morgades, 1967.)

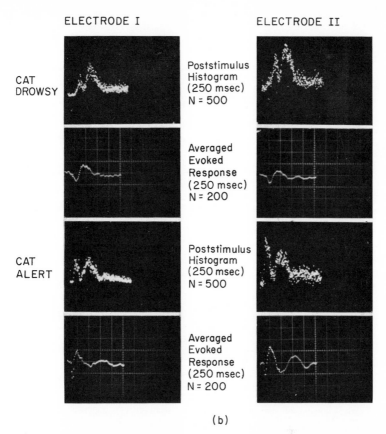

ELECTRODE I                    ELECTRODE II

CAT
DROWSY

Poststimulus
Histogram
(250 msec)
N = 500

Averaged
Evoked
Response
(250 msec)
N = 200

CAT
ALERT

Poststimulus
Histogram
(250 msec)
N = 500

Averaged
Evoked
Response
(250 msec)
N = 200

(b)

(b). Data on the two sides of this figure come from two microelectrodes implanted
125 μ apart in the lateral geniculate body. The upper half of the figure shows
group PSHs and AERs recorded sequentially from the drowsy animal in response
to light flashes. The lower half shows the results of computations performed while
the animal was alert. Note the similarity between the major features of the responses
observed at the two adjacent electrodes, the similarity between the shapes of
the AER and the PSH obtained from the same electrode under the same conditions,
and the change which took place in both of these measures when the state of
the animal was altered. Sample size was 500 for all computations. (Unpublished
data from John & Morgades, 1967.)

which were extremely reproducible and stable over a period of many
weeks. Comparison of the PSHs computed from only negative spikes
with those computed from only positive–negative spikes shows that although the cells responsible for these two kinds of spikes responded
differently to any single flash of light, the two neuronal ensembles displayed extremely similar spike response patterns on the average. Further
examination of Fig. 14 shows but little difference in the pattern of spike

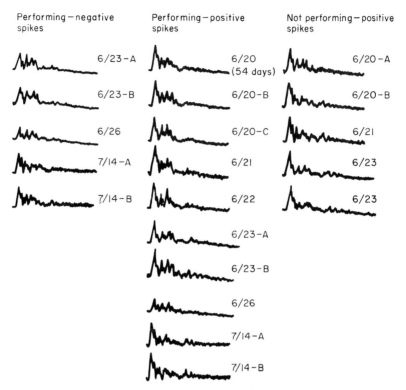

FIG. 14.    Long-term reproducibility of group PSHs from ventral hippocampus neurons in response to 2-Hz flicker. Cat trained to sit at work panel awaiting dipper cue. Note similarity of PSHs of negative spikes (left column) and of positive–negative spikes during flicker preceding correct response (middle column) or failure to respond (right column) to cue. Flicker had no cue value at this stage of training. All computations are based on a sample size of 500 and come from about 10 behavioral trials each. (Unpublished data from John & Morgades, 1967).

discharges between samples of activity obtained when the cat subsequently performed and those taken when the cat failed to perform. This may be due to the absence of cue value for the flicker at this stage of training. When control over the conditioned behavior was subsequently transferred to the flicker, slight changes took place in the responses displayed by the hippocampal neurons. Although differences in certain components were subsequently observed between trials ending in performance and those resulting in no response, additional data are required to decide whether these preliminary observations are consistent.

Figure 15 provides additional data that the neuronal ensembles producing the observed negative and positive–negative spikes display similar statistical patterns, although the two groups of cells seem to fire independently of each other. These data also provide demonstration of the consistent reflection of detailed features of the hippocampal AER in the shape of the PSH of hippocampal neurons. In contrast with the sequential recording used in Fig. 13, corresponding pairs of measures in Fig. 15 were recorded simultaneously.

After the data shown on the left side of Fig. 15 were obtained, the microdrive was advanced 250 $\mu$. Several days later, the right-side records were taken. These results show clearly that the neuronal ensembles at the deeper level have characteristic patterns of response to the condi-

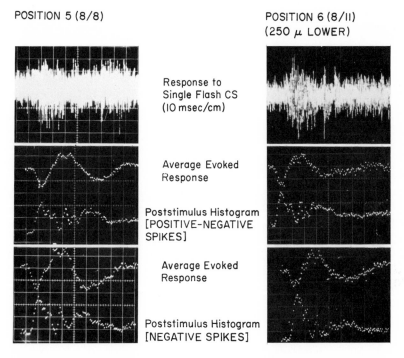

FIG. 15.    Data on left side of this figure come from same region as those in Fig. 14 but were obtained three weeks later. Animal has been trained to press lever for food in response to 2-Hz flicker. Data on right side were obtained three days later, after the electrodes were lowered 250 $\mu$. Note the close similarity between the shape of the average evoked responses and features of the corresponding group poststimulus histogram, the resemblance between PSHs computed from negative and positive–negative spike, and the essential identity of comparable measures obtained from neuronal ensembles at these different levels of the hippocampus. All computations based on a sample size of 500, 1.25 msec/register, and obtained during about 10 behavioral trials each. (Unpublished data from John & Morgades, 1967.)

tioned stimulus which are essentially identical with the patterns displayed by other groups of hippocampal neurons at a higher level. In
further study of this phenomenon, gradients of evoked response and unit
activity were constructed after mapping much larger anatomical domains.
Quantitative study of these gradients indicated that widespread neuronal
populations displayed homogeneous temporal patterns of activity in response to a conditioned stimulus. Thus, the response of extensive neural
ensembles to a conditioned stimulus is statistically uniform.

In another cat, two microdrives were implanted, one in the lateral
geniculate body and one in the hippocampus. Each microdrive carried
two microelectrodes. The cat had previously been trained to perform
differential conditioned responses to two different frequencies of flicker.
Regions were found in the lateral geniculate body and in the hippocampus, where the waveshapes of the potentials evoked by presentation
of a TCS were markedly similar. The waveshapes elicited by the two
discriminanda differed. When novel stimuli were presented to the animal,
the lateral geniculate and hippocampal waveshapes differed from one
another. The gradients of these evoked potentials were mapped by moving the implanted electrodes with the microdrives. These maps showed
clearly that the shape of the evoked potential was related to physiological processes in the vicinity of the electrode tip, and was not the volume-
conducted reflection of a distant dipole or generator process. Poststimulus
time histograms were made in the various electrode positions. These
histograms showed that the times of maximum synchronization in the
two brain regions showing similar evoked potential waveshapes occurred
almost simultaneously. Thus, *the similar waveshapes elicited in different
brain regions by a conditioned stimulus are related to similarities in
the temporal pattern of synchronization in different neuronal ensembles*
(John & Morgades, 1969c).

### D. Summary of Microelectrode Findings

In agreement with what was previously shown for the visual cortex,
we have found, both in the lateral geniculate body and the hippocampus,
that a high correlation exists between the average evoked potential and
the poststimulus histogram. This correlation varies with the state of
the animal, and from region to region of the brain. In general, if neurons
in a region are responsive to a stimulus, the poststimulus histogram
and the evoked potential will be clearly related. When such relationships
are not observed, the neurons in the region do not show marked responsiveness to the stimulus. In such cases, the evoked potential may be due
to slow potentials in fibers coursing through the region. This suggests
that the average evoked response in some regions describes the average

synaptic drive (integrated postsynaptic potentials) impinging on the local neuronal ensemble because of a specific stimulus, which is reflected in the temporal pattern of probability of discharge as measured in a group poststimulus histogram. Further, the characteristics of a large sample of the response patterns of a number of neuronal ensembles to a meaningful stimulus have been analyzed and compared: two ensembles recorded simultaneously from two electrodes 125 $\mu$ apart in the lateral geniculate body, a simultaneously recorded negative spike and a positive–negative spike-producing subgroup in the ventral hippocampus, the same ensemble recorded successfully over a period of many weeks, and two ensembles successively recorded from different levels of the ventral hippocampus 250 $\mu$ apart. The results of these comparisons show that, although the cells of different populations respond in an extremely variable way to any single stimulus, the poststimulus time histograms of adjacent ensembles to a series of repeated stimuli are essentially invariant. Analysis of PSHs in different brain regions which display similar evoked potential waveshapes shows that the neuronal ensembles in regions display similar patterns of synchronization. These findings suggest that in the unanesthetized and unrestrained cat, information about a conditioned visual stimulus is not mediated by the responses of single neurons, which are highly variable. Rather, the informationally relevant activity might be the statistical characteristics of the response patterns of extensive neuronal ensembles. The average evoked response appears to provide an estimate of the responses of such aggregates in many regions of the brain.

## XXIV. CONCLUSIONS

Considering the body of data and argument presented in this chapter, we propose:

(1) The response process to a stimulus in an ensemble of neurons can be viewed as a stochastic process with particular transition probabilities from instant to instant. Although the sequence of transition probabilities is invariant for the response of the ensemble to a particular stimulus, the response of individual neurons is variable.

(2) Change of waveshape observed in learning indicates establishment of a new set of transition probabilities of the ensemble from which the waveshape was recorded.

(3) Memory is the specification of this set of rules, mediated by chemical or structural changes in neuronal ensembles.

(4) The endogenous components of evoked potentials result from

the release of stochastic processes with specified transition probabilities; activation of such stochastic processes constitutes remembering.

(5) The simultaneity and similarity of difference waveshapes observed in different regions of the brain indicate that different neuronal ensembles support stochastic processes with highly similar transition probabilities, and display similar patterns of synchronization.

These various propositions constitute working hypotheses about the nature of memory to be tested in further experimental work.

## REFERENCES

Adam, G., Adey, W. R., & Porter, R. W. Interoceptive conditional response in cortical neurones. *Nature,* 1966, **209,** 920–921.

Adametz, J. H. Rate of recovery of functioning in cats with rostral reticular lesions. *Journal of Neurosurgery,* 1959, **16,** 85–97.

Agranoff, B. W., & Klinger, P. D. Puromycin effect on memory fixation in the goldfish. *Science,* 1964, **146,** 952.

Albert, D. J. The effect of spreading depression on the consolidation of learning. *Neuropsychologia,* 1966, **4,** 49–64. (a)

Albert, D. J. The effects of polarizing currents on the consolidation of learning. *Neuropsychologia,* 1966, **4,** 65–77. (b)

Asratyan, E. A. Some aspects of the elaboration of conditioned connections and formation of their properties. In J. F. Delafresnaye, A. Fessard, R. W. Gerard, & J. Konorski (Eds.), *CIOMS symposium on brain mechanisms and learning.* Oxford: Blackwell, 1961.

Asratyan, E. A. *Compensatory adaptations, reflex activity and the brain* (S. A. Corson, translator). Oxford: Pergamon Press, 1965. (a)

Asratyan, E. A. Changes in the functional state and pattern of electrical activity in cortical areas involved in the establishment of conditioned connection. *Proceedings of the 23rd International Congress of Physiological Science, Tokyo,* 1965, **IV,** 629–636. (b)

Baer, A. Uber Gleichzeitige Electrische Reizung zweier Grosshirnstellen am Ungehemmten Hunde. *Archivfuer die Gesamte Physiologie Pflügers,* 1905, **106.** 523–567.

Barlow, J. S., Morrell, L., & Morrell, F. Some observations on evoked responses in relation to temporal conditioning to paired stimuli in man. *Proceedings of the International Colloquium Mechanisms of Orienting Reaction in Man, Smolenici and Bratislava,* 1965. Published by Slovak Academy of Science, Bratislava, Czechoslovakia, 1967.

Barondes, S. H., & Cohen, H. D. Puromycin effect on successive phases of memory storage. *Science,* 1966, **151,** 594–595.

Beritoff, J. S. *Neural mechanisms of higher vertebrate behavior* (W. T. Liberson, translator). Boston, Massachusetts: Little, Brown, 1965.

Betz, V. A. Two centers in the cortical layer of the human brain. *Mosk. Vrachebn. Vestn.,* 1874, No. 24.

Beurle, R. L. Properties of a mass of cells capable of regenerating pulses. *Philosophy & Transactions of the Royal Society, London, Ser. B,* 1956, **240,** 55–94.

Bianchi, L. The functions of frontal lobes. *Brain,* 1895, **18.**

Brain, Lord. *Speech disorders.* (2nd ed.) London and Washington, D.C.: Butterworths, 1965.

Breen, R. A., & McGaugh, J. L. Facilitation of maze learning with post-trial injections of picrotoxin. *Journal of Comparative & Physiological Psychology,* 1961, **54,** 498–501.

Broca, P. Remarques sur le siège de la faculté du langage articulé. *Bulletin of the Society Anthropology,* 1861, **6.**

Brown-Sequard, C. E. Existence de l'excitabilité motrice et de l'excitabilité inhibitoire dans les regions occipitales et sphenoidales de l'écorce cérébrale. *Comptes Rendus Memoires Societe Biologie,* 1884, 8ᵉ Ser., Pt. 1, **36,** 301–303.

Buchwald, J. S., Halas, E. S., & Schramm, S. Progressive changes in efferent unit responses to repeated cutaneous stimulation in spinal cats. *Journal of Neurophysiology,* 1965, **28,** 200–215.

Buchwald, N. A., & Hull, C. D. Induction of unit inhibition and spindling by stimulation of the lateral geniculate body. *Federation Proceedings Abstracts,* 1966, **25,** 105.

Bureš, J. Discussion. In D. P. Kimble (Ed.), *Anatomy of memory.* Palo Alto: Science Behavior Books, 1965. Pp. 49–50.

Bureš, J., and Burešová, O. Plasticity at the single neuron level. *Proceedings of the 23rd International Congress of Physiological Science, Tokyo,* 1965, **IV,** 359–364.

Bureš, J., Burešová, O., & Weiss, T. Functional consequences of hippocampal spreading depression. *Physiologia Bohemoslovenica,* 1960, **9,** 219–227.

Burns, B. D. The production of afterbursts in isolated unanesthetized cerebral cortex. *Journal of Physiology (London),* 1954, **125,** 427–446.

Burns, B. D. *The mammalian cerebral cortex.* London: Arnold, 1958.

Burns, B. D., Heron, W., & Grafstein, B. Response of cerebral cortex to diffuse monocular and binocular stimulation. *American Journal of Physiology,* 1960, **198,** 200–204.

Burns, B. D., & Pritchard, R. Contrast discrimination by neurones in the cat's visual cerebral cortex. *Journal of Physiology (London),* 1964, **175,** 445–463.

Burns, B. D., & Smith, G. K. Transmission of information in the unanesthetized cat's isolated forebrain. *Journal of Physiology (London),* 1962, **164,** 238–251.

Calvet, J., Calvet, M. C., & Scherrer, J. Étude stratigraphique corticale de l'activité EEG spontanée. *Electroencephalography & Clinical Neurophysiology,* 1964, **17,** 109–125.

Child, C. M. *Physiological foundations of behavior.* New York: Holt, 1924.

Chow, K. L. Brain functions. *Annual Review of Psychology,* 1961, **12,** 281–310.

Chow, K. L., Lindsley, D. F., & Gollender, M. Modification of response patterns of lateral geniculate neurons after paired stimulation of contralateral and ipsilateral eyes. *Journal of Neurophysiology,* 1968, **31,** 729–739.

Chow, K. L., & Randall, W. Learning and retention in cats with lesions in reticular formation. *Psychonomic Science,* 1964, **1,** 259–260.

Clynes, M., Kohn, M., & Gradijan, J. Computer recognition of the brain's visual perception through learning the brain's physiologic language. *IEEE International Convention Record,* 1967, Pt. 9.

Cordeau, J. P., & Mahut, H. Some long-term effects of temporal lobe resections on auditory and visual discrimination in monkeys. *Brain,* 1964, **87,** 177–190.

Coury, J. N. Neural correlates of food and water intake in the rat. *Science,* 1967, **156,** 1763–1765.

Creutzfeldt, O. D., Watanabe, S., & Lux, H. D. Relations between EEG phenomena and potentials of single cortical cells. I. Evoked responses after thalamic and epicortical stimulation. *Electroencephalography & Clinical Neurophysiology,* 1966, **20,** 1–18. (a)

Creutzfeldt, O. D., Watanabe, S., & Lux, H. D. Relations between EEG phenomena and potentials of single cortical cells. II. Spontaneous and convulsoid activity. *Electroencephalography & Clinical Neurophysiology,* 1966, **20,** 19–37. (b)

Cushing, H. A note upon the faradic stimulation of the post-central gyrus in conscious patients. *Brain,* 1909, **32,** 44–53.

Davis, R. E., & Agranoff, B. W. Stages for memory formulation in goldfish: evidence for an environmental trigger. *Proceedings of the National Academy of Science United States,* 1966, **55,** 555–559.

Doty, R. W. Potentials evoked in cat cerebral cortex by diffuse and by punctiform photic stimuli. *Journal of Neurophysiology,* 1958, **21,** 437–464.

Drachman, D. A., & Ommaya, A. K. Memory and the hippocampal complex. *Archives of Neurology,* 1964, **10,** 411–425.

Dumenko, V. N. The electrographic study of relationships between various cortical areas in dogs during the elaboration of a conditioned reflex stereotype. In I. N. Knipst (Ed.), *Contemporary problems of electrophysiology of the central nervous system.* Moscow: Academy of Science, 1967. Pp. 104–112.

Eccles, J. C. Hypotheses relating to the brain-mind problem. *Nature,* 1951, **168,** 53–65.

Eccles, J. C. The effects of use and disuse on synaptic function. In J. F. Delafresnaye, A. Fessard, R. W. Gerard, & J. Konorski (Eds.), *CIOMS symposium on brain mechanisms and learning.* Oxford: Blackwell, 1961.

Eccles, J. C. Spinal neurones: synaptic connections in relation to chemical transmitters and pharmacological responses. In W. D. M. Paton (Ed.), *A symposium on pharmacological analysis of central nervous system action.* New York: Macmillan, 1962.

Eccles, J. C., & McIntyre, A. K. Plasticity of mammalian monosynaptic reflexes. *Nature (London),* 1951, **167,** 466–468.

Ferrier, D. *The functions of the brain.* London: Smith, Elder, 1876.

Fessard, A. The role of neuronal networks in sensory communications within the brain. In W. A. Rosenblith (Ed.), *Sensory communication.* Cambridge, Massachusetts: MIT Press, 1961.

Fessard, A., & Szabo, T. La facilitation de post activation comme facteur de plasticité dans l'establissement des liaisons temporaires. In J. F. Delafresnaye, A. Fessard, R. W. Gerard, & J. Konorski (Eds.), *CIOMS symposium on brain mechanisms and learning.* Oxford: Blackwell, 1961.

Filimonov, I. N. Localization of functions in the cerebral cortex and Pavlov's theory of higher nervous activity. *Klinicheskaya Meditsina,* 1951, **29.**

Filimonov, I. N. Architectonics and localization of functions in the cerebral cortex. In *Textbook of neurology.* Vol. 1. Moscow: Medgiz, 1957.

Flexner, J. B., Flexner, L. B., & Stellar, E. Memory in mice as affected by intracerebral puromycin. *Science,* 1963, **141,** 57–59.

Flourens, M. J. P. *Recherches expérimentales sur les propriétés et les fonctions du système nerveux dans les animaux vertébrés.* Paris: Crevot, 1824.

Flourens, M. J. P. *Examen de phrénologie.* Paris: Hachette, 1842.

Flynn, J. P., & Wasman, M. Learning and cortically evoked movement during propagated hippocampal after discharges. *Science,* 1960, **131,** 1607.

Fox, S. S., & O'Brien, J. H. Duplication of evoked potential waveform by curve of probability of firing of a single cell. *Science,* 1965, **147,** 888–890.

Fritsch, G., & Hitzig, E. Über die elektrische Erregbarkeit des Grosshirns. *Archiv für Anatomie, Physiologie und Wissenschaftliche Medicin,* 1870, **37.**

Fromm, G. H., & Bond, H. W. The relationship between neuron activity and cortical steady potentials. *Electroencephalography & Clinical Neurophysiology,* 1967, **22,** 159–166.

Frost, J. D., & Gol, A. Computer determination of relationships between EEG activity and single unit discharges in isolated cerebral cortex. *Experimental Neurology,* 1966, **14,** 506–519.

Fujita, V., & Sato, T. Intracellular records from hippocampal pyramidal cells in rabbit during theta rhythm activity. *Journal of Neurophysiology,* 1964, **27,** 1011.

Galambos, R., & Sheatz, G. C. An electroencephalograph study of classical conditioning. *American Journal of Physiology,* 1962, **203,** 173–184.

Gall, F. J. *Sur les fonctions du cerveau et sur celles de chacune de ses parties.* Paris: Baillière, 1825. 6 vols.

Gastaut, H. Some aspects of the neurophysiological basis of conditioned reflexes and behavior. In *Ciba Foundation symposium on the neurological basis of behavior.* London: Churchill, 1958.

Geller, A., & Jarvik, M. Unpublished data. Presented by Jarvik at *Neurosciences Research Program work session on Consolidation of Memory Trace,* MIT November, 1967.

Gerard, R. W. The fixation of experience. In J. F. Delafresnaye, A. Fessard, R. W. Gerard, & J. Konorski (Eds.), *CIOMS symposium on brain mechanisms and learning.* Oxford: Blackwell, 1961.

Gerstein, G. L. Neuron firing patterns and the slow potentials. *Electroencephalography & Clinical Neurophysiology, Supplement,* 1961, **20,** 68–71.

Glickman, S. E. Perseverative neural processes and consolidation of memory trace. *Psychological Bulletin,* 1961, **58,** 218–233.

Glivenko, E. V., Korol'kova, T. A., & Kuznetsova, G. D. Investigation of the spatial correlation between the cortical potentials of the rabbit during formation of a conditioned defensive reflex. *Fizicheskii Zhurnal SSSR Sechenova,* 1962, **48** (9), 1026.

Goldberg, J. M., & Neff, W. D. Frequency discrimination after bilateral ablation of cortical auditory areas. *Journal of Neurophysiology,* 1964, **24,** 119–128.

Goldstein, K. *Language and language disorders.* New York: Grune & Stratton, 1948.

Goltz, F. Über die Verrichtungen des Grosshirns. *Pflüger's Archiv Gesamte Physiologie,* 1884, **26.**

Gomulicki, B. R. The development and present status of the trace theory of memory. *British Journal of Psychology, Monograph Supplement,* 1953, **29,** 1–94.

Grastyán, E., & Karmos, G. The influence of hippocampal lesions on simple and delayed instrumental conditioned reflexes. *Physiologie de l'Hippocampe Colloquium International* No. 107, 1962, Paris: C.N.R.S. Pp. 1225–1234.

Green, J. D., Maxwell, D. S., Schindler, W. J., & Stumpf, C. Rabbit EEG "theta" rhythm: its anatomical source and relation to activity in simple neurons. *Journal of Neurophysiology,* 1960, **23,** 403.

Grossman, S. P., & Mountford, H. Learning and extinction during chemically induced disturbance of hippocampal functions. *American Journal of Physiology*, 1964, **207**, 1387–1393.

Haider, M., Spong, P., & Lindsley, D. B. Attention, vigilance, and cortical evoked potentials. *Science*, 1964, **145**, 180–182.

Haller, A. *Elementa physiologiae corporis humani.* Lausanne, 1769.

Head, H. *Aphasia and kindred disorders of speech.* London and New York: Cambridge University Press, 1926. 2 vols.

Hebb, D. O. *The organization of behavior.* New York: Wiley, 1949.

Hilgard, E. R., & Marquis, D. G. *Conditioning and learning.* New York: Appleton, 1940.

Hitzig, E. *Untersuchungen über des Gehirns.* Berlin: Unger, 1874.

Holt, E. B. *Animal drive and the learning process.* New York: Holt, 1931.

Hori, Y., & Yoshii, N. Conditioned change in discharge pattern for single neurons of medial thalamic nuclei of cat. *Psychological Report*, 1965, **16**, 241.

Hubel, D. H. Single unit activity in striate cortex of unrestrained cats. *Journal of Physiology (London)*, 1959, **147**, 226–238.

Hubel, D. H., & Wiesel, T. N. Receptive fields, binocular interaction and functional architecture in the cat's visual cortex. *Journal of Physiology (London)*, 1962, **160**, 106–154.

Hubel, D. H., & Wiesel, T. N. Receptive fields of cells in striate cortex of very young, visually inexperienced kittens. *Journal of Neurophysiology*, 1963, **26**, 994–1002.

Hunt, H. F., & Diamond, I. T. Some effects of hippocampal lesions on conditioned avoidance behavior in the cat. *Proceedings of the 15th International Congress of Psychology, Brussels, 1957.*

Irwin, S., & Banuazizi, A. Pentylenetetrazol enhances memory function. *Science,* 1966, **152**, 100–102.

Jackson, J. H. *Selected writings.* Vol. 2. *On localization.* New York: Basic Books, 1869.

Jacobsen, C. F. Studies of cerebral function in primates: I. The functions of the frontal association areas in monkeys. *Comprehensive Psychological Monographs,* 1936, **13**, 3–60.

Jasper, H. H., Ricci, G., & Doane, B. Microelectrode analysis of cortical cell discharge during avoidance conditioning in the monkey. *Electroencephalography & Clinical Neurophysiology Supplement*, 1960, **13**, 137–155.

John, E. R. Higher nervous functions: brain functions and learning. *Annual Review of Physiology*, 1961, **23**, 451.

John, E. R. *Mechanisms of memory.* New York: Academic Press, 1967.

John, E. R., & Ahn, H. Unpublished observations. 1966.

John, E. R., Chesler, P., Victor, I., & Bartlett, F. Observation learning in cats. *Science*, 1968, **159**, 1489–1491.

John, E. R., Herrington, R. N., & Sutton, S. Effects of visual form on the evoked response. *Science,* 1967, **155**, 1439–1442.

John, E. R., & Killam, K. F. Electrophysiological correlates of avoidance conditioning in the cat. *Journal of Pharmacology & Experimental Therapeutics*, 1959, **125**, 252.

John, E. R., & Morgades, P. P. A technique for the chronic implantation of multiple movable microelectrodes. *Electroencephalography & Clinical Neurophysiology*, 1969a, **27**, 205–208.

John, E. R., & Morgades, P. P. Neural correlates of conditioned responses studied with multiple chronically implanted moving microelectrodes. *Experimental Neurology*, 1969b, **23**, 412–425.

John, E. R., & Morgades, P. P. Patterns and anatomical distribution of evoked potentials and multiple unit activity by conditioned stimuli in trained cats. *Communications in Behavioral Biology*, 1969c, **3**, 181–207.

John, E. R., Ruchkin, D. S., Leiman, A., Sachs, E., & Ahn, H. Electrophysiological studies of generalization using both peripheral and central conditioned stimuli. *Proceedings of the 23rd International Congress of Physiological Science, Tokyo*, 1965, 618–627.

John, E. R., Ruchkin, D. S., & Villegas, J. Signal analysis of evoked potentials recorded from cats during conditioning. *Science*, 1963, **141**, 429–431.

John, E. R., Ruchkin, D. S., & Villegas, J. Signal analysis and behavioral correlates of evoked potential configurations in cats. *Annals of the New York Academy of Science*, 1964, **112**, 362–420.

John, E. R., & Shimokochi, M. Unpublished observations. 1966.

Jowett, B. (Ed.) Theaetetus. In *The dialogues of Plato*, Vol. IV. London and New York: Oxford Univ. Press, 1931. P. 254.

Kamikawa, K., McIlwain, J. T., & Adey, W. R. Response patterns of thalamic neurons during classical conditioning. *Electroencephalography & Clinical Neurophysiology*, 1964, **17**, 485–496.

Kandel, E. R., & Spencer, W. A. Electrophysiological properties of an archicortical neuron. *Annals of the New York Academy of Science*, 1961, **94** (2), 570–603.

Kappers, C. U. A. Further contributions on neurobiotaxis. *Journal of Comparative Neurology*, 1917, **27**, 261–298.

Killam, K. F., & Hance, A. J. Analysis of electrographic correlates of conditional responses to positive reinforcement: I. Correlates of acquisition and performance. *Abstracts of the Proceedings of the 23rd International Congress of Physiological Science, Tokyo*, 1965. P. 1125.

Klee, M. R., & Offenloch, K. Post-synaptic potentials and spike patterns during augmenting responses in cat's motor cortex. *Science*, 1964, **143**, 488–489.

Klee, M. R., Offenloch, K., & Tigges, J. Cross-correlation analysis of electroencephalographic potentials and slow membrane transients. *Science*, 1965, **147**, 519.

Kleist, K. *Gehirnpathologie*. Leipzig: Barth, 1934.

Knipst, I. N. (Ed.) Spatial synchronization of bioelectrical activity in the cortex and some subcortical structures in rabbit's brain during conditioning. In *Contemporary problems of electrophysiology of the central nervous system*. Moscow: Academy of Science, 1967. Pp. 127–137.

Konorski, J. *Conditioned reflexes and neuron organization*. London & New York: Cambridge University Press, 1948.

Konorski, J. *Integrative activity of the brain*. Chicago: University of Chicago Press, 1967.

Korol'kova, T. A., & Shvets, T. B. Interrelation between distant synchronization and steady potential shifts in the cerebral cortex. In I. N. Knipst (Ed.), *Contemporary problems of electrophysiology of the central nervous system*. Moscow: Academy of Science, 1967. Pp. 160–167.

Lajtha, A. Observations on protein catabolism in brain. In S. S. Kety and J. Elkes (Eds.), *Regional neurochemistry*. New York: Macmillan 1961.

Lashley, K. S. Temporal variation in the function of the gyrus precentralis in primates. *American Journal of Physiology*, 1923, **65**, 585–602.

Lashley, K. S. Learning. I. Nervous mechanisms in learning. In C. Murchison (Ed.), *The foundations of experimental psychology.* Worcester, Massachusetts: Clark University Press, 1929. Pp. 524–563.

Lashley, K. S. In search of the engram. *Symposium of the Society Experimental Biology,* 1950, **4**, 454–482. (a)

Lashley, K. S. Functional interpretation of anatomical patterns. *Research Publication Association Nervous Mental Disease,* 1950, **30**, 537–539. (b)

Leiman, A. L. Electrophysiological studies of conditioned responses established to central electrical stimulation. Ph.D. Thesis, University of Rochester, Rochester, New York, 1962.

Lettvin, J. Y., Maturana, H. R., McCulloch, W. S., & Pitts, W. H. What the frog's eye tells the frog's brain. *Proceedings of the Institute of Radio Engineers,* 1959, **47**, 1940–1951.

Lindsley, D. F., Chow, K. L., & Gollender, M. Dichoptic interactions of lateral geniculate neurons of cats to contralateral and ipsilateral eye stimulation. *Journal of Neurophysiology,* 1967, **30**, 628–644.

Livanov, M. N. Spatial analysis of the bioelectric activity of the brain. *Proceedings of the 22nd International Congress of Physiological Science, Leiden,* 1962, 899–907.

Livanov, M. N. The significance of distant brain potential synchronization for realization of temporal connections. *Proceedings of the 23rd International Congress of Physiological Science, Tokyo,* 1965, **IV**, 600–612.

Livanov, M. N., & Poliakov, K. L. The electrical reactions of the cerebral cortex of a rabbit during the formation of a conditioned defense reflex by means of rhythmic stimulation. *Izvestiya Akademiya Nauk. USSR Series Biology,* 1945, **3**, 286.

Lorente de Nó, R. Analysis of the activity of the chains of internuncial neurons. *Journal of Neurophysiology,* 1938, **1**, 207–244.

Luria, A. R. *Higher cortical functions in man.* New York: Basic Books, Consultants Bureau, 1966. Original Russian text published by Moscow University Press, 1962.

Majkowski, J. Electrophysiological studies of learning in split-brain cats. *Electroencephalography & Clinical Neurophysiology,* 1967, **23**, 521–531.

McCleary, R. A., & Moore, R. Y. *Subcortical mechanisms of behavior.* New York: Basic Books, 1965.

McGaugh, J. L. A multi-trace view of memory storage processes. Paper presented at *International Symposium on Recent Advances in Learning and Retention, Rome, Italy,* May 2–6, 1967.

McGaugh, J. L., & Petrinovich, L. Effects of drugs on learning and memory. *International Review of Neurobiology,* 1965, **8**, 139–191.

McIntyre, A. K. Synaptic function and learning. *Proceedings of the 19th International Congress of Physiological Science, Montreal,* 1953, 107–114.

Meynert, T. *Psychiatrie.* Wien, 1884.

Milner, P. M. The cell assembly: Mark II. *Psychological Review,* 1957, **64**, 242–252.

Milner, B., & Penfield, W. The effect of hippocampal lesions on recent memory. *Transactions of the American Neurology Association, 80th Annual Meeting,* 1955, 42–48.

Monakow, C., & Mourgue, R. *Introduction biologique à l'étude du neurologie et de la psychopathologie.* Paris: Alcan, 1928.

Moore, G. P., Perkel, D. H., & Segundo, J. P. Statistical analysis and functional interpretation of neuronal spike data. *American Review of Physiology,* 1966, **28**, 493–522.

Morrell, F. Electrophysiological contributions to the neural basis of learning. *Physiological Review,* 1961, **41**, 443. (a)

Morrell, F. Effect of anodal polarization on the firing pattern of single cortical cells. *Annals of New York Academy of Science,* 1961, **92** (3), 860–876. (b)

Morrell, F. Electrical signs of sensory coding. In G. C. Quarton, T. Melnechuk, & F. O. Schmitt (Eds.), *The neurosciences: a study program.* New York: Rockefeller University Press, 1967. Pp. 452–469.

Müller, G. E., and Pilzecker, A. Experimentalle Beiträge zur Lehre vom Gedachtnis. *Zeitschrift füf Psychologie Supplement,* 1900, **1**, 1–288.

Munk, H. Über die Funktionen der Grosshirnrinde. Berlin: Hirschwald, 1881.

Nielsen, J. M. *Agnosia, apraxia, aphasia.* New York: Hoeber, 1947.

Nielsen, J. M. *Memory and amnesia.* Los Angeles: San Lucas Press, 1958.

Norton, T., Frommer, G., & Galambos, R. Effects of partial lesions of optic tract on visual discriminations in cats. *Federation Proceedings,* 1966, **25**, 2168.

Ojemann, R. G. Correlations between specific human brain lesions and memory changes. *Neurosciences Research Program Bulletin, Supplement,* 1966, **4**, 1–70.

Olds, J., & Olds, M. E. Interference and learning in paleocortical systems. In J. F. Delafresnaye, A. Fessard, R. W. Gerard, & J. Konorski (Eds.), *CIOMS symposium on brain mechanisms and learning.* Oxford: Blackwell, 1961.

Osgood, C. E., & Miron, M. S. (Eds.) *Approaches to the study of aphasia.* Urbana, Illinois: University of Illinois Press, 1963.

Palladin, A. V. (Ed.) *Problems of the biochemistry of the nervous system.* New York: Macmillan, 1964.

Pavlov, I. P. The problem of the study of higher nervous activity and the ways of its experimental solution. *Proceedings of the Military Medical Academy,* 1903, 103–128. Reprinted in *Selected works.* Moscow: Foreign Languages Publishing House, 1955.

Pearlman, C. A., Sharpless, S. K., & Jarvik, M. E. Retrograde amnesia produced by anesthetic and convulsant agents. *Journal of Comparative & Physiological Psychology,* 1961, **54**, 109.

Penfield, W., & Roberts, L. *Speech and brain mechanisms.* Princeton, New Jersey: Princeton University Press, 1959.

Petrinovich, L., Bradford, D., & McGaugh, J. L. Drug facilitation of memory in rats. *Psychonomic Science,* 1965, **2**, 191.

Pollen, D. H., & Sie, P. G. Analysis of thalamic induced wave and spike by modifications in cortical excitability. *Electroencephalography & Clinical Neurophysiology,* 1964, **17**, 154–163.

Pribram, K. H. Theory in physiological psychology. *Annual Review of Psychology,* 1960.

Pribram, K. H., Spinelli, D. N., & Kambock, M. C. Electrocortical correlates of stimulus response and reinforcement. *Science,* 1967, **157**, 94–95.

Pribram, K. H., & Tubbs, W. E. Short-term memory, parsing, and the primate frontal cortex. *Science,* 1967, **156**, 1765–1767.

Purpura, D. P., & Shofer, R. J. Intracellular potentials during augmenting and recruiting responses. I. Effects of injections hyperpolarizing currents on evoked membrane potential changes. *Journal of Neurophysiology,* 1964, **27**, 117–132.

Purpura, D. P., Shofer, R. J., & Musgrave, F. S. Cortical intracellular potentials during augmenting and recruiting responses. II. Patterns of synaptic activities in pyramidal and non-pyramidal tract neurones. *Journal of Neurophysiology,* 1964, **27**, 133–151.

Ramón y Cajal, S. *Histologie du systeme nerveux de l'homme et des vertébres.* Vol. II. Paris: Maloine, 1911.

Reitan, R. M. Psychological deficits resulting from cerebral lesions in man. In J. M. Warren & K. Akert (Eds.), *The frontal granular cortex and behavior.* New York: McGraw-Hill, 1964.

Robertson, A. D. Correlation between unit activity and slow potential changes in unanesthetized cerebral cortex of cat. *Nature,* 1965, **208**, 757–758.

Ruchkin, D. S., & John, E. R. Evoked potential correlates of generalization. *Science,* 1966, **153**, 209–211.

Rusinov, V. S. Electroencephalographic studies in conditioned reflex formation in man. In M. A. B. Brazier (Ed.), *The central nervous system and behavior.* New York: Josiah Macy, Jr. Foundation, 1959.

Russell, W. R. *Brain, memory, learning.* London & New York: Oxford University Press (Clarendon), 1959.

Russell, W. R., & Espir, M. L. E. *Traumatic aphasia.* London & New York: Oxford Univ. Press, 1961.

Russell, W., & Nathan, P. Traumatic amnesia. *Brain,* 1946, **69**, 280–300.

Sakhuilina, G. T., & Merzhanova, G. K. Stable changes in the pattern of the recruiting response associated with a well established conditioned reflex. *Electroencephalography & Clinical Neurophysiology,* 1966, **20**, 50–58.

Segundo, J. P., Roig, J. A., & Sommer-Smith, J. A. Conditioning of reticular formation stimulation effects. *Electroencephalography & Clinical Neurophysiology,* 1959, **11**, 471–484.

Shimokochi, M. Electrophysiological correlates of discrimination learning (I). *Journal of the Physiological Society of Japan,* 1967, **29**, 451.

Sholl, D. A. *The organization of the cerebral cortex.* New York: Wiley, 1956.

Sholl, D. A. A comparative study of the neuronal packing density in the cerebral cortex. *Journal of Anatomy,* 1959, **93**, 143–158.

Sperry, R. W. Some general aspects of interhemispheric integration. In V. B. Mountcastle (Ed.), *Interhemispheric relations and cerebral dominance.* Baltimore, Maryland: Johns Hopkins Press, 1962.

Spinelli, D. N., Pribram, K. H., & Weingarten, M. Visual receptive field modification induced by non-visual stimuli. *Federation Proceedings,* 1966, **25**, 2173.

Spinelli, D. N., & Weingarten, M. Afferent and efferent activity in single units of the cat's optic nerve. *Experimental Neurology,* 1966, **15**, 347–362.

Sprague, J. M. Interaction of cortex and superior colliculus in mediation of visually guided behavior in the cat. *Science,* 1966, **153**, 1544–1547.

Stefanis, C. Relations of the spindle waves and the evoked cortical waves to the intracellular potentials in pyramidal motor neurons. *Electroencephalography & Clinical Neurophysiology,* 1963, **15**, 1054.

Sutton, S., Tueting, P., Zubin, J., & John, E. R. Information delivery and the sensory evoked potential. *Science,* 1967, **155**, 1436–1439.

Tanzi, E. I fattie la induzime ell odierne istologia del sistema nervoso. *Rev. sper. Freniat.,* 1893, **19**, 419–472.

Teuber, H. L. Some alterations in behavior after cerebral lesions in man. In *Evolution of nervous control.* Washington, D.C.: American Association for the Advancement of Science, 1959. Pp. 157–194.

Teuber, H. L. The riddle of frontal lobe function in man. In J. M. Warren and

K. Akert (Eds.), *The frontal granular cortex and behavior*. New York: McGraw Hill, 1964.

Thorpe, W. H. *Learning and instinct in animals*. London: Methuen, 1956.

Toennies, J. F. Die Erregungssteurung im Zentralnervensystem. *Archiv fuer Psychiatrie & Nervenkrankheiten*, 1949, **182**, 478–535.

Tucker, T., & Kling, A. Differential effects of early vs. late brain damage on visual duration discrimination in cats. *Federation Proceedings*, 1966, **25**, 106.

Ukhtomski, A. A. Essays on the physiology of the nervous system. In *Collected works*. Vol. 4. Leningrad, 1945.

Urbaitis, J. C., & Hinsey, J. C. Ablations of cortical and collicular areas in cats: effects on a visual discrimination. *Federation Proceedings*, 1966, **25**, 1167.

Vasilevs, N. N. Relationship between background impulse activity of cortical neurons and electrocorticogram phases. *Bulletin of Experimental Biology and Medicine, USSR*, 1965, **59**, 597.

Verzeano, M., & Negishi, K. Neuronal activity in cortical and thalamic networks. *Journal of General Physiology*, 43 Supplement, 1960, 177.

Vogt, O. Die anatomische Vertiefung der menschlichen Hirnlocalisation. *Klinische Wochenschrift*, 1951. **78**.

Webster, D. B., & Voneida, T. J. Learning deficits following hippocampal lesions in split-brain cats. *Experimental Neurology*, 1964, **10**, 170–182.

Wedensky, N. E. Zeitschrift der rues. Gesellschaft für Volshygiene, 1897. Cited in Wedensky, N. E. Die Erregung, Hemmung, und Narkose. *Archives Gesamte Physiology Pflügers*, 1903, **100**, 1–144.

Weingarten, M., & Spinelli, D. N. Retinal receptive field changes produced by auditory and somatic stimulation. *Experimental Neurology*, 1966, **15**, 363–376.

Wernicke, C. *Der aphasische Symptomenkomplex*. Breslau: Cohn & Weigart, 1874.

Westbrook, W. H., & McGaugh, J. L. Drug facilitation of latent learning. *Psychopharmacologia*, 1964, **5**, 440–446.

Winans, S. S., & Meikle, T. H. Visual pattern discrimination after removal of the striate visual cortex in cats. *Federation Proceedings*, 1966, **25**, 2167.

Yoshii, N., & Ogura, H. Studies on the unit discharge of brain stem reticular formation in the cat. I. Changes of reticular unit discharges following conditioning procedure. *Medical Journal of Osaka University*, 1960, **11**, 1.

Yoshii, N., Pruvot, P., & Gastaut, H. Electroencephalographic activity of the mesencephalic reticular formation during conditioning in the cat. *Electroencephalography & Clinical Neurophysiology*, 1957, **9**, 595.

Young, J. Z. Growth and plasticity in the nervous system. *Proceedings of the Roy. Society, London, series B*, 1951, **139**, 18–37.

CHAPTER 7     **Cognitive Deficit:**
**Experimental Analysis**


MARCEL KINSBOURNE
Division of Pediatric Neurology
Duke University
Durham, North Carolina

## I. AIMS AND METHODS

### A. Introductory Remarks

This discussion of the effects of cerebral lesions on human behavior is motivated by the opportunity these phenomena present of gaining insight into brain mechanisms. The natural historian of disease could consider the consequences of brain damage in relation to the fascinating range and occasional bizarre manner of their expression. The clinician might emphasize the definite diagnostic value of certain well-established brain-behavior relationships. However, we shall consider the exceptional opportunities afforded the investigator of brain function by cases of focal cerebral damage. Human subjects, being responsive to verbal instruction and capable of verbal report, are available to the full range of human experimental psychological methodology, and when they present with focal cerebral deficit, they are of interest to the physiological psychologist, who normally must content himself with more laborious measures when studying behavior in animals. As the action in a moving picture can be clarified by playing it in slow motion, so cognitive processes can become more susceptible to analysis when observed under pathological conditions which slow the rate at which information is processed. The aggregate of behavioral consequences of focal damage to all existing cerebral loci should spotlight the sum total of cerebral contributions to cognition, while each separate contributory process is amenable to separate and selective study. No branch of psychology promises more extensive gains in the understanding of brain mechanisms.

Little of this promise has been fulfilled. The experimental study of psychoneurology is beset by hazards. The complexities involved in the matching of groups for comparison, the inevitable and often elusive sampling biases, the arbitrariness of the single case study, especially when it defies replication—in sum, the multiple interacting variables which are not fully under the experimenter's control, and which could bias the results, have defeated the efforts of many investigators in the field. It will be argued here that these difficulties exist largely because investigators fail to use the everyday concepts and methods of human experimental psychology. Such methods, when used by workers familiar with neurological case material, lead to a more profound analysis of disordered cerebral function than is usually attempted on an experimental basis. Evidence that this is so will first be discussed in principle, then illustrated by instances representative of the author's interests and current preoccupations. These by no means constitute an appraisal or evaluation of the field in its totality.

## B. Relevance of Neuropsychological Findings

Some human experimental psychologists have argued that the effects on behavior of cerebral deficit are irrelevant to the understanding of normal brain mechanisms. They dispute the validity of attributing to a specific brain area the function which is demonstrably disturbed, when that area is inactivated by disease. More generally, they imply that the disease process and adaptation thereto has transformed the organism into some new and qualitatively different state which bears no definable relationship to the normal state, or at least cannot be demonstrated to do so. The line of argument excludes not only neuropsychology but also the whole of physiological psychology from the ambit of fruitful investigation. It is appropriate to examine it with caution.

The brain may be considered as a communication network, incorporating multiple information transmitting channels which lead to and from decision points. A limitation of function, namely the impairment or abolition of the ability to make particular decisions, may result from damage to the decision point and from interruption of input to or output from that point. Those points of the system which are most closely aggregated in cerebral space will be most vulnerable to selective inactivation by focal cerebral injury. The extreme example is the corpus callosum, division of which reliably induces a pure disconnection syndrome (Geschwind & Kaplan, 1962; Myers, 1956) without damage to decision points in either hemisphere. The converse situation, selective degradation of a decision process, can be readily illustrated from the physiology of the brain stem, where decision points often correspond to aggregates (nuclei) of morphologically distinctive neurons. It is less readily demonstrable in the cerebrum, where nuclei seem not to occur. This distinction may be variously interpreted. The neurons that constitute a decision point are widely diffused over the cerebral cortex. But their distinctive function depends on their mode of linkage rather than on physical features of individual neurons, and this is not necessarily reflected in morphological differentiation. Until these alternative possibilities are resolved, we can neither accept nor reject the view that focal lesions may selectively eliminate particular decision processes; in each instance, both possibilities must be kept in mind. If a particular lesion induces a disorder of a mode of processing—such as matching of input to sample from store or serial ordering—irrespective of the nature and modality of input, this is circumstantial evidence that the neural substrate of a decision process or of its output channel is affected. Conversely, the more limited to particular input the deficit, the more likely is a disconnection of the decision point from its proper source of information. If this residual source of uncertainty is freely admitted, there should be no further objection to ascribing localizing significance to functional-anatomical correlates where these are clear cut.

The criticism that inferences about normal brain mechanisms cannot be based on the study of mechanisms in an abnormal organism is so general as to be self defeating. The bounds of normality resist definition. The same argument can be applied to individual differences within a normal population, so that one is driven to admit findings derived from the behavior of any one individual as relevant to none other. No experimental scientist is likely to adopt such an extreme position, although it may be of some philosophic interest.

## C. Biological Factor Analysis

Spontaneously occurring focal cerebral lesions have been described as effecting a "biological factor analysis" (Lashley, 1931) on human higher mental functions. A focal lesion will impair a subset of human performances, leaving the rest intact. What common features unite the performances within a subset, whether defined by conventional or by "biological" factor analysis?

Factors affecting the correlation between different performances may arise at three distinct levels: environmental, physiological, and anatomical. Test performance substantially influenced by previous experiences will depend on the nature and source of that experience: What was the individual taught? What else did he learn incidentally? Clearly, individual differences in experience are liable to be reflected in individual differences in subsequent performance. Secondly, a single cerebral operation may determine the level of achievement in a variety of different tests. Thirdly, if anatomical variation underlies functional disparities, it might well be that, in particular individuals, definite cerebral areas develop to a degree which is substantially independent of the development of other areas, for instance, if these are controlled by separate genes. If that is so, performances controlled by any such area will covary, even if they involve totally distinct cerebral operations, because these operations utilize neural decision mechanisms in the same area. When clusters of abilities are defined, it is necessary to determine whether the cluster coheres for physiological or other reasons. Physiological coherence may be tested by hypothesizing a dimension of mental functioning underlying these abilities. Then further tests may be designed, performance on which should covary with the relevant subset of performances if the hypothesis is correct, but not otherwise. In focal cerebral injury, individual differences arise which are induced by disease rather than by normal variation in cerebral development. Both because these tend to be more striking than those to be found in a normal population and because they can sometimes be attributed to distinctive anatomical loci of injury, they generate a patient population which is particularly useful in defining the physiological significance of the factors that emerge.

## D. The Individual Case Study

The most recent work in neuropsychology has compared groups selected by predetermined criteria. This is in contrast to the older work, which relied mainly on an accumulation of individual case analyses. The group-comparison method is currently fashionable and is supposed to possess scientific values inaccessible to individual case study. This attitude derives from an awareness of individual variation, which in group studies may be randomized out with varying degrees of success by appropriate design and statistical treatment. But there is no inherent advantage in mere large numbers. Much of psychophysics has been established by measures on one or two subjects; physiologists do not, in general, see the need for widespread recruitment of experimental animals if the outcome is, in the individual instance, clear cut. The study in depth of individual cases, if adequately designed and unequivocal in outcome, has definite advantages over mass comparison, in which, due to the staggering heterogeneity of clinical material, it is often necessary to combine data from not entirely comparable cases, thus submerging features of potential importance.

Certain inferences can be based legitimately on single case studies, while others can not. A case study of a characteristic instance of some clinical category can yield important information about the mechanism of a disorder, such that the particular cerebral component process which is at fault is identified. Such a finding can stand without support from large numbers of subjects. If a component process is separable in one case, it is separable in principle, and no model of relevant brain function is acceptable which fails to identify that process as a distinctive event. Furthermore, the individual case study can suggest hypotheses for formal testing of matched groups. Finally, when an individually studied case comes to autopsy and the findings can be related with confidence to the symptomatology during life, a functional and anatomical correlation is established. Within the bounds of individual variation, this correspondence may be regarded as generally valid.

Certain inferences cannot legitimately be made; these include inferences as to relative frequencies of incidence and association of various deficits and their general diagnostic value. In the absence of direct anatomical verification, group studies are more likely to give accurate information as to anatomical–functional correlation than study of the individual case.

The limitations of the individual case study, as detailed above, are substantial. Nevertheless, much of the most fundamental information relevant to neuropsychology may best be derived from experimental studies in depth of individual cases.

## E. The Syndrome

It is everyday medical practice to note constellations of signs and symptoms and to classify such a conjunction as a syndrome, itself indicative of a disease. The associations are probabilistic, not invariant. Partial syndromes abound, and often it is not clear how many ingredients have to be present to justify the diagnosis. This is particularly true because not all ingredients of a syndrome are of equal importance, their relative valuation being unformulated outcome of the interaction of medical instruction and clinical experience, and thus a somewhat individual process. While it may be appropriate for practical medicine, this complex, ill-defined process clearly does not recommend itself for research purposes, and psychologists have seriously objected to medical diagnoses of syndromes supposedly characteristic of cerebral deficit. Critics complain that such syndromes are initially defined on the basis of sparse clinical material anecdotally communicated, and that subsequent confirmation of the conjunction of symptoms could be an artifact of the channeling of attention toward supposedly crucial features and away from others which are actually also present. A clear need exists for appropriately designed correlative studies. One such study was attempted by Benton (1961) in relation to the allegedly characteristic conjunction of finger agnosia, right–left disorientation, agraphia, and acalculia in left-parietal disease (Gerstmann, 1924, 1930). Benton confirmed his own expectations: the four elements occured in conjunction with each other no more frequently than with three other symptoms outside the syndrome as originally defined by Gerstmann, namely, constructional apraxia (drawing disability), reading impairment, and visual retention deficit. Actually, this study demonstrates little more than the difficulty of such an undertaking. The case material was ill defined, and it might well have included enough cases of diffuse brain damage to generate significant correlations between almost any one deficit and any other. Unless only limited focal lesions are studied, it is meaningless to report the absence of a symptom cluster, such as that of the Gerstmann syndrome. The methods for detecting the elements of the syndrome differ widely from those used by Gerstmann and are often complex and nonspecific. Benton's tests for "finger localization" are idiosyncratic and so organized and scored that many different cognitive variables are confounded in the outcome. Of the three putatively "nonGerstmann" elements studied, constructional apraxia is, in fact, a well-known associate of that syndrome (Critchley, 1953); reading difficulty is a complex variable that could arise in a variety of ways; and visual retention is not well understood in relation to its localizing value. Thus, the work does not adequately test Gerstmann's postulate.

Correlative studies of this type, but of valid design, are greatly needed. Cluster analysis is not inappropriate as a validation procedure for the clinical syndrome. However, spuriously high correlations can be generated by the study of diffuse brain disorders, while spuriously low correlations can arise from the use of insufficiently specific test methods. It is, for instance, futile to seek correlations involving factors such as a reading or writing ability, as these complex skills are themselves obviously multifactorial. Studies of this type are best deferred until a sufficient understanding of the clinical situation permits the design and application of test methods which are simple and directly relevant to the issue under investigation.

Observations of the correlations in incidence of the elements of a syndrome is not necessarily the logical means by which a syndrome may be validated. The finding that certain cognitive deficits tend to coincide by no means suggests that the individual deficit may not also occur in other combinations. Indeed, this is a commonplace occurrence in all branches of medicine. If detailed analysis of disordered performance reveals an underlying thread of functional impairment common to the postulated elements, then a *prima-facie* case for an association is made out. This holds for the Gerstmann syndrome (Kinsbourne & Warrington, 1962a) as well as for other constellations of deficits subsequently to be discussed.

Pending validation by appropriate testing, the clinically observed "syndrome" represents an educated guess at a relationship which has interim value in generating hypotheses and experimentation.


## F. Psychometric Methods

Many of the current and most of the early reports on the cognitive effects of brain lesions suffer from the use of test methods which were designed on an opportunistic basis and are incompletely specified and unstandardized. The work is difficult to replicate, and it is hard to assess the significance of a supposed deficit in the absence of reliable information about the subject's general intellectual status. These drawbacks have cast into disrepute many otherwise illuminating reports and have led to a reaction on the part of a group of psychologists who rely entirely on standard tests and discount information otherwise obtained.

Standard psychometric procedures, such as Wechsler's tests, were designed to assess the scatter of abilities in the general population. The wide range of subtests gives an overall measurement which to some extent bears on the ability to form concepts and utilize information based on previous experience. As an overall index of intellectual competence, such a measurement is a valuable adjunct to neuropsychological study, although, strictly speaking, the norms are not applicable to brain damaged populations, since such populations were not represented in the original standardization sample (Wechsler, 1958). Those subtest performances which appear to be unaffected by an injury may give some indication of the premorbid level of intelligence. The intelligence quotient sheds no light at all on selective deficits produced by brain lesions. Indeed, a population of men with substantial cerebral missile wounds may show no overall deficit in tests of this type (Newcombe, 1969). As Hebb (1942) pointed out, focal cerebral deficit does not necessarily affect the availability of stored information or the use of cognitive strategies. The disabilities so caused are often restrictive of the number and nature of operations that the brain can perform rather than of general problem-solving ability or the ability to retrieve stored information. Many such deficits do not involve operations crucial to standard test performance and slip through the psychometric net.

Many attempts have been made to circumvent this difficulty by scrutinizing the profile of the patients' subtest scores to see whether any recurrent pattern of scatter between the individual scores characterizes damage at a given cerebral locus. Thus Smith (1966a), ignoring the now formidable bulk of experimental work on minor hemisphere dominance for certain nonverbal functions (Arrigoni & DeRenzi, 1964; Boller & DeRenzi, 1967; Kimura, 1963; Milner, 1962; Warrington & James, 1967; Warrington, James, & Kinsbourne, 1966), correctly concludes that the psychometric procedures he reviews fail to reveal such dominance. Standard psychometry was not designed for the purpose of analyzing selective deficit. When applied to that end, it proves to be ineffective. Where significant differences do become evident, the results usually cannot be interpreted because the empirically designed test performance in question cannot with confidence be assigned to any particular neural process.

In the hope of achieving relevance while retaining the benefits of standardization, test batteries have been established which attempt to be sensitive to "organicity" of brain disorder and even to have localizing value (Reitan, 1966). Such batteries have the advantage that they are designed for the task in hand. But as they are necessarily constructed prior to research, they embody preconceived notions of the nature of brain mechanisms, which may not be borne out by the subsequent investigation. Very large numbers of observations are needed to make such a battery differentiate between cerebral damage of different pathogenesis and location, and inevitably the test battery becomes a static instrument, most helpful in topographical diagnosis to those extensively familiar with its use. The search from experiment to experiment for converging operations (Garner, Hake, & Eriksen, 1956) is not open to this approach.

The desire to use only those tests which have been documented with normative data in the experimental analysis of cognitive deficit rests on the misconception that when two pathological groups are compared, data from a third, normal group must also be available. Certainly, in order to draw conclusions from a patient's failure in a task, one must be persuaded that a normal person would not have failed. But the type of procedure usually invoked, if well chosen, will be one in which it is obvious that normal subjects would succeed. It is far more hazardous to argue from a patient's failure on a particular procedure to a selective deficit in the area of the failure. Here careful standard background testing is required to exclude the presence of widespread intellectual deterioration, which could lead to an illusion of selectivity of deficit due to neglect of other cognitive processes. For this purpose, standard psychometric tests are essential. It should be possible at reasonably short notice to design experimental procedures with which to pursue hypotheses about the nature of behavioral anomalies. The procedure must be administered in a standard way but need not be standardized on a normal population. Indeed, the use of standardized tests incorporates a further hazard—the assumption that factors which limit normal performance are the same as those which limit pathological performance. For instance, Cohen (1957) found that the factorial content of the Wechsler Digit Symbol Test changes with advancing age of the test population, since performance becomes progressively more vulnerable to perceptual and memory impairments. The test becomes more generalized. Again, Raven's Progressive Matrices are normally a test of "general intelligence" ("g"). When patients with left-hemisphere lesions perform poorly on this test, it may be for reasons of general intellectual deterioration. When patients with right-hemisphere lesions perform badly, it may be for some totally different reason, such as visuo–spatial disability. In normal subjects, the demands on visuo–spatial abilities imposed by the Matrices test are easily met and are not a limiting factor on performance (as witnessed by the low "K" loading). In right-hemisphere cases, the test may be evaluating quite a different process from that which it tests in normal patients; thus, the normative data are irrelevant or even misleading.

### G. Selection of Control Groups

The nature of an investigator's interest is reflected in his choice of control groups—not that controls are invariably required. Certain detailed individual case studies have revealed deficits so widespread and yet so exquisitely selective that to run controls would amount to no more than a ritual incantation. In most investigations, the results are less clear cut, and controls are in order—which controls to choose?

A "brain-damaged" population can be relied upon to perform less efficiently in many respects than normal controls matched with them for age, sex, and socio–economic status. The same is true for an elderly population, as well as for children, mental retardates, and psychotics. The normal adult represents a ceiling level of performance in most experimental contexts, and to show that any other population performs less well is unsurprising, unless it can be shown that a particular pattern of deficit characterizes that group and no other.

It is customary for research studies into the psychology of aging to use young adult controls. The elderly do poorly; would children also have failed? How would the miscellaneously brain damaged have fared? Is there some pattern of deficits in aging that is attributable to the sheer burden of years rather than to a scattered incidence of cumulative brain damage resulting in generally suboptimal cerebral functioning? Again, may the relative failures of the brain damaged on a variety of tasks be manipulated into an index of brain damage? For instance, if children experience similar difficulties, these can in no way be regarded as unique to the damaged brain. There is a practical justification for studying abnormal populations with only normals as reference points, namely, the definition of their handicaps with a view to their rational rehabilitation and reintegration into society. But knowledge of brain mechanisms is further enhanced if it is made clear which constellations of difficulties pertain to which anomalous or pathological cerebral states. Thus, in his study of the amnesic syndrome, Talland (1968) used not only normal subjects but also institutionalized and chronic alcoholic groups as controls. In this way he was able to exclude institutionalization and chronic alcoholism as causative of the amnesia and the underlying lack of drive ("inertia") that he demonstrated. But he has not shown that his inertia is specific to amnesic patients. Were it found, for instance, to be equally marked in patients with frontal lobe disease and no amnesia, it could then be ruled out as a sufficient cause of memory deficit. This is the value of controls chosen from within the brain-damaged population; they help to validate the features specific to a given subset of such subjects and thus provide a test of factors hypothesized to underlie specific behavioral anomalies. The mere fact that such specific factors can be isolated suffices to demonstrate the futility of the search for an index of brain damage; no performance can be imagined which would not be more prejudiced by a lesion in one location than in another. The extent of functional differentiation in the brain is a measure of the extent to which an index of brain damage must fall short of its purpose. The evidence suggests that this differentiation is extreme and that any valid index is correspondingly unattainable.

The number of conceivably relevant variables in neuropsychological group comparisons is so great that control groups could be interminably multiplied. A further possibility remains to be explored, that of double dissociation (Teuber, 1955). If a patient group with damage centered at location $A$ is superior to one damaged at $B$ in respect to task $P$, but inferior in task $Q$, a double dissociation obtains between these groups. This permits the inference of at least one difference between the two groups specific to location of damage, for $P$ may be a nonspecific task, relating, say, to general intelligence or some other variable in which the groups are imperfectly matched. But then it must be admitted that function $Q$ must have been selectively impaired by a lesion at location $A$, since the inferiority in performing $Q$ cannot be accounted for by failure of matching on the other task. The search for double dissociation is a valid means towards progress in neuropsychology.

It is quite another matter when dissociations fail to appear. Thus, Benton and Fogel (1962) regard visual reaction time as a valid measure of cerebral competence, because in their case material it had no specific anatomical correlate. Arrigoni and DeRenzi (1964) accept this argument and add a further task, Raven's Progressive Matrices, again supposedly nonspecific, because its level of performance was not linked to locality of lesion in their case material. This does not necessarily follow. A given task may be performed indifferently for more than one reason, and overall achievement scores will not discriminate between these reasons. An inquiry into the characteristics of failure is required: Are they the same in all groups? As for the variables that do exist, which ones relieve and which aggravate the impairment? Are these variables also identical? Pending such analysis, claims for the reaction-time measure or the Matrices tests are unconvincing.

It is apparent that, if factors specific to particular pathological states are to be isolated, these must be derived from studies in which the experimental population is controlled not only with a normal, but with one or more other pathological populations selected in such a way as to permit the emergence of double dissociations, should they obtain. Should no double dissociations emerge, no conclusions can be drawn.

## H. The Analysis of Group Differences

The basic experimental paradigm in neuropsychological group comparison does not differ from that applicable to other group comparisons, such as those dealing with chronological age (child development and aging studies) and mental age (mental retardation) as independent variables. Experimental and control groups are selected by some objective set of criteria. Significantly lower performance by the experimental group is demonstrated in a particular test situation. That situation is varied along definable dimensions so as to maximize the difference (which identifies the basic nature of the deficit) and so as to abolish it (which demonstrates its selectivity). Overall task difficulty is controlled so as to avoid ceiling effects with the control population.

The point of maximal discrepancy between experimental and control performance identifies the area of disability (nature of limitation on cerebral function). The dimension, variation along which causes equalization of experimental and control performance, indicates the operations which are defective in the experimental group (whether cognitive, motivational, or both). The very possibility of equalization indicates the selective nature of the deficit. The differences between experimental and control groups identify the independent variable with which the deficit is associated.

In most experimental presentations, only fragments of this paradigm are explored, leaving areas of uncertainty in relation to various possible artifacts and contaminating factors. Thus, the independent variable may be incompletely defined, or there may be several independent variables distinguishing the groups (for example, both laterality and size of cerebral lesions). The area of deficit may be incompletely identified because of failure to vary the originally imposed task to make it "simpler" while still discriminating between groups. Thus, test results are equated with hypotheses which purport to define deficits in function, but which merely consist of a statement, often intuitive, about the nature of the test in question. Failure to demonstrate equalization of performance by appropriate variation of test situations calls into question the specificity of the deficit. More frequently, attempts to equalize involve ceiling effects. Control and experimental performance is equal, but this is on simple tests giving near-perfect performance on the part of the control group who might have spare capacity not drawn upon in the task. If complete equalization cannot be achieved, it is not specificity but relative preponderance of the deficit that has been demonstrated. Only if all cognitive task situations which are presented yield approximately the same degree of performance deficit in the experimental group can selectivity of deficit be rejected and a global attribution of deficit justified. Thus impairment may be global or selective; if selective, it may be specific or relative.

Inferiority of an experimental as compared to a control group need not necessarily indicate a straightforward performance deficit. It may indicate inappropriate cognitive strategy. Thus, people accustomed to reading Hebrew will perform less well if required to scan written material from left to right rather than in their customary manner. Under the reverse instructions, however, they will, in turn, do better than the English reading group. Deviant strategy (as opposed to deficit) is revealed if, when the task is modified so as to put a premium on that particular strategy, the experimental group does better than the controls (a situation which cannot occur in the case of a deficit). The deviant strategy may itself be adopted for one of two reasons; because the subject's ability to choose appropriately is impaired, or because the range of strategies available to him is pathologically restricted. In the first case, verbal cueing as to which strategy is appropriate should abolish the faulty performance; in the second case, it would not. An instance of reversible choice of inappropriate strategy is failure on a concept-formation task of patients with the amnesic syndrome, which was readily reversible on additional verbal instruction (Talland, 1968). An instance of restricted range of available strategies is the inability of patients with neglect of the left side of space to reverse the direction of their habitual right to left scan (Kinsbourne, 1966).

## I. Simulation of Cognitive Deficit

Having observed a performance deficit, one usually tries to explain it in terms of some postulated general disorder of function. This postulate may then be tested in terms of "necessity" ("no other mechanism could lead to the observed deficit") and of "sufficiency" ("the mechanism is sufficient to account for the observation"). To determine whether a postulated disorder of cerebral function is both necessary and sufficient to generate particular clinical appearances, one may attempt to simulate the deficit by imposing upon normal subjects the appropriate constraint, analogous to that supposed to have occurred naturally in the patient group. Successful simulation, at the very least, demonstrates consistency of hypothesis with clinical appearances. Failure of simulation decisively demonstrates the inapplicability of the hypothesis under study.

Poppelreuter (1923), doubtful of the proposition that visual-search disorder in his subjects with posterior cerebral injuries could be due solely to restriction of their visual fields, simulated tunnel vision by having normal subjects scan extensive displays through a small but moveable peephole. He found no comparable impairment in visual search and concluded that visual-search defects of cortical origin are not sufficiently explained by visual-field restriction. This finding has since been supported by Luria (1959), who demonstrated the relevance of impaired eye movement in an individual case study, and by Kinsbourne (1966), who, in more than one hundred war veterans with penetrating missile wounds, demonstrated a relationship between slowing of visual search and posterior location of cerebral lesion, even when the presence of field defect was partialled out. With their intact eye movement control, appropriate strategy of spatial exploration, and intact visual memory for relative position, Poppelreuter's normal subjects were able to overcome the effects of visual field restriction.

Conversely, successful simulation of a clinical finding may show that existing concepts suffice, and that new hypotheses are redundant. Siemerling (1890) showed that by cutting down illumination one can induce in normal subjects perceptual difficulties analogous to disorders labeled agnosic when they arise in patients. Again, Dorff, Mirsky, and Mishkin (1965) suggested that the right-temporal lobe is specifically concerned with the visual recognition of letters presented in either visual half-field, because when letters are simultaneously exposed in both half-fields, left-temporal lobectomy cases lose efficiency (as compared to normals) in the right half-field, while right-sided lobectomy cases showed bilateral though less severe effects. For that reason, the right-temporal lobe was held to have bilateral influence in normal functioning. Simulation revealed this hypothesis to be redundant (Kinsbourne, 1966). When similar letter groups are simultaneously briefly exposed to normal subjects, but under two constraints—the letters in one of the half-fields in each trial are either faint or delayed 200 msec—the Dorff findings were closely simulated. Faintness or delay on the right favored identification of letters in the left half-field at the expense of those on the right. Faintness or delay on the left favored the letters in the right half-field so as to reduce or even reverse the advantage of left over right. Compared to efficient normal controls (unmatched for age and general intelligence), any brain-damaged group will show some overall disadvantage. In Dorff's experiment, both right- and left-temporal groups did less well than controls; but while left-to-right scanning habits were preserved in the left lobectomy cases and set up errors to the right of the display, the right-temporal lesions set up a reversed scan tendency and distributed the errors more evenly between the two fields. That right-hemisphere lesions may set up right-to-left scanning habits has elsewhere been demonstrated (Kinsbourne, 1971a). Thus in view of the simulation, the conditions of which would also be expected to modify the direction of visual scan, no further explanatory hypothesis is needed.

At times, an empirical study constitutes attempted simulation of a clinical disorder. Thus it has widely been held that the executive speech difficulty regularly experienced by receptively aphasic subjects is at least partly due to failure to monitor speech output, the feedback of speech output to the auditory system being scrambled by the receptive defect (Alajounanine & Lhermitte, 1963). The notion that speech production normally operates under continual feedback control relies on the inconclusive argument that this is why delayed auditory feedback impairs speech (Yates, 1962). But deafness beginning in adulthood need not disturb speech output, and in essentials, speech output survives the application of masking noise to both ears so as totally to obliterate feedback of all speech signals. Whether speech output is maintained on the basis of kinesthetic feedback is a separate question, as is the role of feedback in the early development of executive speech ability.

Two other studies may be described as cases of simulation in search of a defect. One is "experimental finger dyspraxia" (Jackson & Zangwill, 1952), brought about by introducing a bias into the visual monitoring of finger movements. The other is the "stupid reader" effect (Crovitz, Schiffman, & Rees, 1967), in which oral reading performance is thrown off course by the experimenter who, during a hesitation pause, interjects a word that has just been read out by the subject. The situation is in some ways analogous to delayed auditory feedback, which does disorganize speech. It may well be that further analysis of dyslexia syndromes will reveal a variant in which recently read words perseverate and disrupt reading in just this way.

Constraints on input constitute one form of attempted simulation. The effects of constraints on output, as when random generation of digits is rapidly paced (Badderley, 1962), or when two different motor performances are simultaneously demanded, could with advantage be scrutinized for resemblance to pathologically-impaired performance. Finally, modified central states may have similar effects. In fatigue, a word-finding difficulty ("tip-of-the-tongue effect") may simulate that characteristic form of aphasia; or in perceptual isolation, an abnormal central state is set up which generates visual hyperreactivity (Teuber, 1961) very similar to that induced by certain posterior brain injuries (Kinsbourne & Warrington, 1963b). Pharmacological simulation of the latter situation by mescaline or lysergic acid administration is equally effective.

Finally, computer simulation of disordered behavior presents no greater difficulty in principle than computer simulation of normal behavior; and indeed, insofar as brain lesions simplify the situation by selectively slowing down the target process, it may prove particularly effective and revealing in this setting.

## II. NATURAL HISTORY

### A. Nature of Cerebral Lesion

A traditional premise of neuropsychology is that the location rather than the nature of the cerebral lesion determines the nature of the behavioral change. Within limits, this has been borne out, but it does not necessarily follow that all varieties of lesions produce particular cerebral syndromes with equal frequency, or that they lend themselves equally well to experimental analysis correlated with reliable anatomical localization.

Cerebral tissue may be destroyed by direct impact (head injury, missile wound, surgical excision), neighborhood pressure (tumor, blood clot, abscess) or deprivation of oxygen (vascular obstruction). The damaged cells may become inactivated (causing deficit) or irritable (causing positive phenomena, such as seizures or hallucinations). The damage may have been inflicted suddenly or gradually. When the patient is presented for study, the lesion may be progressing, regressing, or stable, depending on the causative factors, management, and sheer passage of time. It is unduly partisan to attribute particular advantages to one or other of these clinical situations with regard to suitability for psychological study. Different disorders lend themselves to different types of investigation.

For number and range of types of deficit, acute vascular and tumor cases are unrivalled; however, other types of cases are more suitable where precision of anatomical localization is at a premium and a predominance of rather mild deficits no disadvantage.

The most profuse symptomatology is to be found with brain tumor and in the early stages following cerebrovascular occlusion. Such cases lend themselves particularly well to individual study. Selected specifically on the basis of a clinically apparent syndrome, a favorable case may be analyzed in depth with results which, if clear cut, cannot be ignored in any general model of the relevant aspect of brain function. The supply of such cases is usually plentiful, and the bulk of existing neuropsychological knowledge is based on this material.

With tumor and vascular cases, caution is required regarding the basic intellectual equipment of the patient; background psychometry is essential to exclude cases so deteriorated intellectually that they would fail on almost every imaginable test. This is particularly liable to occur in the presence of diffuse blood vessel disease or of tumors large enough to raise intracranial pressure substantially. In such cases, it is up to the investigator to satisfy his audience that sufficient attention has been paid to the patient's intellectual status outside the focal areas of the experiment.

Anatomical verification is most secure at autopsy, but this cannot be arranged to the experimenter's specifications. Failing this, fairly accurate anatomical information is obtained by means of direct surgical intervention—division of commissures (e.g., the corpus callosum), disconnection of cortex from brain stem (e.g., undercutting of frontal cortex), or total excision (e.g., temporal lobectomy). In fact, surgeons can only roughly indicate the area of specific intervention; damage may spread through progressive clotting in blood vessels or spread of infection from the area of incision into previously healthy brain, and the rest of the brain is not immune from coincident disease. Particularly unreliable are surgeons' estimates of the amount of brain excised, since much of this disappears indeterminately down a sucker.

Neurosurgical series have definite advantages for anatomical localization; but they also have the definite drawback that all areas of the brain do not lend themselves equally well to surgical excision. Thus, the student of temporal lobectomy cases will have difficulty in finding an adequate number of parietal lobectomy controls. This disadvantage does not attend the study of patients with penetrating missile injuries of the brain. The distribution of missile wounds of the cortex is more or less random. There is one restriction in that certain areas, such as the superior temporal, overlie vital centers of the brainstem. Consequently, few such cases are available for study.

The study of brain wound cases benefits from the relatively homogeneous population, with respect to age, sex, duration of deficit, availability of premorbid intellectual assessments, and records of the immediate posttraumatic situation. The drawbacks include a substantial residual margin of uncertainty about location and extent of injury, a remarkable scarcity of certain syndromes, such as the agnosias, in the longstanding (Teuber, Battersby, & Bender, 1960) though not acute (Poppelreuter, 1917–18) cases, and an overall tendency to mild deficit necessitating study of large numbers to resolve even a restricted range of problems.

In general, tumor and vascular cases are most suited to detailed individual study, with localizing implications if the case comes to autopsy. Neurosurgical and brain wound cases lend themselves to the evaluation of right–left and front–back differences when available in sufficient numbers. However, the suitability of a particular case for a particular study is best judged on an individual basis, and blanket condemnation of one or other type of case material may safely be ignored.

## B. Duration of Deficit

Loss of an ability in adult life and failure to acquire that ability for developmental reasons are in many ways not strictly comparable. This is because of the different environments that adults and children inhabit and their different life experiences. The adult, comparing his present abilities to their higher previous level which he well remembers, is conscious of grievous, usually irreversible loss and may react emotionally to that knowledge with a passive pessimism which further lowers his performance, or with a bland denial of the disability, which may have bizarre behavioral consequences. The child with developmental deficit knows no other level of functioning. His entire life experience is one of inferiority, specific or general, as compared to his peers. This is liable to set up its own emotional reactions, particularly along the lines suggested by Zigler (1967) for the case of the familial mental retardate—namely, greater dependence on others and on overt and material reward, and correspondingly less inner-directed drive toward success for its own sake. When either brain-damaged adults or developmentally backward children are compared to appropriate control groups, allowances must be made for these biases, which will be reflected in attitudes toward the test situation.

Even in the simpler instance of the adult with acquired disease, the effects on performance of the duration of the deficit is ill understood. These effects are particularly great in nonprogressive disease. When case records of patients with penetrating missile injuries of the cerebrum obtained soon after injury are compared with the findings twenty years later, the extent to which the handicap has receded is remarkable (Newcombe, 1969). How are such changes to be explained? Possible factors are restoration of function or disinhibition of damaged tissue, compensatory activity of undamaged tissue, the adoption of novel strategies suitable to the transformed basic pattern of abilities, and recession of emotional reaction to the situation. Thus physiological, cognitive, and emotional factors may come into play singly or in combination.

Central nervous system neurons do not regenerate. But they do recover function after varying periods of suspended animation, subsequent to damage short of total destruction. For instance, in hemiplegic migraine, transitory vasopasm may lead to transitory neuronal inactivity manifested as neurological deficit, such as hemiplegia, hemianesthesia, or aphasia. This may occur and totally resolve itself dozens of times. A 21-year-old woman was observed in one of many attacks of aphasia and right hemiplegia on a migrainous basis (Kinsbourne, unpublished). Three months passed before the language disorder resolved, but it then did so completely. When episodes of deficit are so frequently repeated, permanent loss of tissue with subsequent compensatory activity of other neuronal systems is hardly to be contemplated in the presence of a finite total brain mass. After some time, temporarily inactivated neurons resume function. This is not to say that compensatory activity is an illusion. An instance is given by Smith (1966b), who describes a case of total left hemispherectomy. An initial global aphasia recovered to an unexpected extent, indicating right hemisphere compensatory activity.

More subtle functional adjustments also happen. In posterior cerebral penetrating missile injury, Poppelreuter (1917–18) found that all but two patients tended to "complete" incomplete forms across hemianopic field defects, a disordered form of behavior related to unawareness of field defect (Warrington, 1962). In a similar series, Kinsbourne (1966) found only one instance of this behavior, in the only patient who remained unaware of his hemianopic field defect. The striking difference between these studies was that, while Poppelreuter worked with acute cases, Kinsbourne studied patients twenty years after the damage was incurred. It would appear that awareness of field defect grows with posttraumatic experience (a form of adult perceptual learning), and the completion tendency recedes. Another instance of adaptation seems to be provided by cases of left-hemisphere infarction with jargon aphasia (Alajouanine, Sabouraud, & DeRiboucourt, 1952). These cases appear at first with a verbal flow of manic proportions but gradually settle down to a semiintelligible verbal output, after which no further improvement occurs (Kinsbourne & Warrington, 1964). Denial of deficit, initially at white heat, settles down over a period of years to a low glow, presumably as a result of nonreinforcement of the more flagrantly abnormal behavior. In cases of longstanding deficit, enhanced motivation may mask disabilities. Thus the somewhat embarrassing finding that, in some tests, subjects with cerebral gunshot wounds were significantly superior to controls comparable in age, sex, and socio–economic background (Newcombe, 1969) is perhaps explained by the tendency of the patient groups to rise to the challenge, rather than by any beneficial effects of lead in the head.

The complex interaction of deficit and sheer passage of time, not to mention the further impact on morale of therapeutic effort, complicate the evaluation of rehabilitation procedures directed at the cognitive consequences of brain injury. No definite evidence exists of any significant success in hastening recovery from the cognitive deficit caused by brain damage, other than that which occurs for nonspecific reasons of the type discussed.

## C. Individual Differences and Cognitive Deficit

Prior to the onset of disease, people are not equal. Genetic and socio–economic differences, reflected in intellectual as well as emotional heterogeneities, influence premorbid performance. What bearing do these have on the results of subsequent testing?

In some cases, previous intelligence test data are available on a patient; he then acts as his own control. At times it is possible to test before and after elective surgery. More usually, however, prior intellectual status has to be inferred from evidence such as length of schooling, school record, and nature of occupation. Since this is only approximate, it is well in individual case studies to attribute significance only to failures in performance far in excess of what would have been predicted on the basis of individual differences. In group comparisons, some attempt to match for such factors is an insurance against artefact. Such matching is relatively simple where homogeneous populations, such as war veterans, are subjects of the experiment, and exceptionally difficult in socially and ethnically mixed populations.

The evaluation of individual emotional differences is far more difficult. Emotional reactions released by disease are often said to represent "exaggerations of premorbid personality." Evaluations of these reactions in a particular patient are usually achieved retrospectively and in deference to preconceived ideas held by the experimenter or witnesses, usually the patient's family. At present, the effect of premorbid personality is imponderable in most cases.

A final possible source of individual variation is that which would arise if there were substantial differences in the cerebral location of particular neural mechanisms in different individuals (Lenneberg, 1967).

Thus, large-scale studies of a variety of test performances have shown that, while particular deficits may emerge typically as the associates of lesions in a particular cerebral area, such deficits are also liable to occur, although with lower frequency, in lesions in other parts of the brain (Hécaen, 1962). However, such findings, might well be generated by inaccuracies in the attribution of anatomical locus to to the disease process and by the multifactorial nature of the performance demanded by the tests in question. It should be kept in mind that, while locus of cerebral representation of function perhaps varies from person to person, there is at present no reason to suppose that it does so to any significant extent.

## III. PERCEPTION

### A. Limitations in Perceptual Capacity

The amount of information that can be processed in a unit of time is limited in the normal adult subject. The capacity is determined by the exact stimulus conditions and response requirements. Thus, normal subjects can identify 3.5 letters or 4 digits displayed for a fraction of a second (Mackworth, 1963). Under "part-reporting" conditions, the equivalent of substantially more items can be dealt with (Sperling, 1960).

The extraction of information from brief visual displays proceeds through an orderly succession of processes. Under any set of conditions, one of these processes will limit the total performance. Under moderately brief exposure conditions, far more is "seen" than can be reported (Sperling, 1960). Therefore, it is some aspect of response formation rather than visual discrimination that limits performance under these conditions.

Span of apprehension is relatively limited in elderly subjects and in children (Wallach, 1963). It is decreased in aphasics (Kinsbourne, 1969) and strikingly decreased in certain patients with left-occipital lesions (Kinsbourne, 1966). In right hemisphere-damaged subjects, the distribution of errors in reponse to supraspan displays is biased to the left (Dorff et al., 1965), and there may exist a tendency to commit false positive errors in relation to the left of the display (Kinsbourne & Warrington, 1962b). Thus span of apprehension may be limited or modified in a variety of biological situations. It should not be assumed that the mechanism of the limitation is the same in each situation, and present knowledge of short-term memory suggests that it involves a number of processes which can be evaluated separately for efficiency in any of the relevant subject groups. The rate of visual information processing depends on the exposure duration and the nature of the stimulus items (Mackworth, 1963), sequential dependencies between items (Miller, Bruner, & Postman, 1956), and the circumstances of the response, whether whole, part (Sperling, 1960), or search for a single target (Sternberg, 1963), immediate or delayed. If we construct a model of the processes involved and identify the component operation that critically limits total performance, we will be able to decide which syndromes of focal brain injury and other pathological states are based on impairment of that, and which on impairment of some other component process. If this procedure succeeds and deficits corresponding to the component processes of the model are identified, this would illuminate the syndrome, validate the model, and, if anatomical correlates are available, assign component processes to these cerebral locations. Such an outcome is not yet in sight, but a discussion of some possibilities will illustrate the direct way in which experimental and neurological psychology bear upon each other.

Simultaneously presented visual stimuli give rise to coded messages which simultaneously arrive at the visual cortex, where they give rise to neural discharges of a duration in excess of stimulation to an extent determined by the neuronal decay characteristic. A rapid sequential process reads this information at a rate of about 10 msec per item (Sperling, 1963) into an intermediate memory store. There the information lingers for about a second (Mackworth, 1963) in visual, that is, not yet recoded, form. During its persistence, information is extracted from this store in "chunks" (Miller, 1956), each chunk being a unitary response encoded in verbal form or as an action pattern. Depending on the situation, the responses become serially overt or are rehearsed silently by recirculation through short-term memory store, to be repeatedly reencoded pending delayed response, written response, or fixation in long-term memory.

The amount which can be incorporated into a whole immediate response depends on the interaction between rate of response formation and duration of persistence of the information in intermediate storage. The more familiar or practiced a response, the faster it is formed (up to a limit of some eight items per second). This corresponds to the maximal rate of vocal and silent counting (Landauer, 1962). The more structured or recodable the stimulus items, the fewer the responses which suffice to empty the store. Therefore, the more practiced and structured the material is, the greater the span will be, and the faster the subject will form responses; the more efficient he is in recoding information into chunks, the greater his span will be as compared to the average. In the delayed response situation, the faster a response is formed, the sooner it will clear the rehearsal loop (permitting other signals to be maintained above noise level) and the more responses can be maintained in the loop.

Disorders will arise:

(1) If there is interruption peripherally or at the first cortical relay of information transmission. This condition manifests itself in the formation of defective sectors in the visual field.

(2) If visual discrimination (serial readout from visual trace to immediate memory store) is impaired. If impairment is severe, misrecognition will result; if it is relative, serial discrimination will be slowed. This will result in a pathological limitation of the span of apprehension at the briefest exposure duration, impairment in visual search performance, and vulnerability of recognition processes to the interfering effects of after-coming masking input, either arising naturally in the environment or introduced experimentally.

(3) If there is premature decay of the contents of immediate memory storage. Span is then limited for all materials, but recognition latencies for items within span will be unaffected.

(4) If response encoding is slowed down. It is this process which, in the normal case, is the major factor limiting capacity. This limitation could become more severe if a particular form of encoding into hand, speech, or other movement is impaired, or if the encoding process is generally prolonged. Where multiple items bear a recognizable relationship to one another, these may be extracted in a single "chunk," expediting clearance of memory store and minimizing the load on the rehearsal loop. If that facility is lost, the patient will prove unable to profit from sequential dependencies between simultaneously exposed items.

An impairment in the rate of response encoding is probably responsible for the phenomenon of disordered simultaneous form recognition (Kinsbourne & Warrington, 1962b). This condition causes certain patients with left-occipital disease (Kinsbourne & Warrington, 1963a) to experience a reading difficulty in which they can only accurately read letter by letter, as well as a difficulty in the identification of pictorial representation of complex events, so-called simultaneous agnosia (Wolpert, 1924). Such patients have a span of apprehension limited to one item (letter, digit, shape, color) and require an increase in exposure duration of up to a second to extend that span to two items. Without such an extension of exposure duration, errors made in identifying the second of two items are of a type suggestive of decay of the visual representation of the second item while it is held in store, pending the slow encoding of the first response. It is significant that, in respect to notions of cerebral localization of function, a unilateral area (left occipital) is in control of encoding for visual stimuli, irrespective of the visual half-field to which they are presented. On the other hand, the right-occipital cortex, when damaged, manifests no evidence of involvement in this process. An instance of a disorder that lends itself to systematic analysis is the decrement in efficiency of "subitizing" (enumeration at a glance) in subjects with right-hemisphere disease (Kimura, 1963; Kinsbourne, 1966; Warrington & James, 1967). When multiple stimuli are briefly exposed, normal subjects can specify their number up to about seven (Hunter & Sigler, 1960). This does not occur by an act of simultaneous apprehension or parallel processing (Kaufman, Lord, Reese, & Volkmann, 1949), but by virtue of an orderly count of the contents of immediate memory store as shown by a steady increment in latency of correct response as the numerosity of the display is increased (Salzman & Garner, 1968). What are the possible mechanisms of limitation of this process in the enumeration disorder of right-hemisphere disease?

(1) The count starts late. If this is the case, response time to a display of one item should not be prolonged, but increments in response time as the display is increased will be normal.

(2) The count is slow. Increments of response time will be proportionally slower than normal.

(3) The count stops prematurely. Response time will be normal up to that level.

(4) Counted items are erroneously recounted. In this case, enumeration errors made by patients will fluctuate around the correct answer. In fact, they do not, but systematically fall short (Kinsbourne, 1966), thus excluding this possibility.

(5) The count proceeds normally, but the trace fades prematurely. Up to the point of the trace fading, response times will be normal.

Clearly, present methods easily suffice to distinguish between these possibilities, and the findings, when available, will specify the disorder with precision. A comparable level of precision may now be sought in any investigation of perceptual disorder.

## B. The Polarization of Attention

At any given time, far more input impinges on the sense organs and is transmitted in recoded form along the sensory projections than is required to trigger appropriate responses of adaptive value. A number of transformations occur in the central nervous system and emphasize those aspects of input likely to be important to the organism, notably by means of simultaneous and successive contrast, the sharpening of discontinuities in space and time. Furthermore, the extraction of invariants from total input aids in the establishment of stable response patterns (Attneave, 1961). Such selection requires the action of a gating mechanism primed to transmit information bearing certain distinctive cues, and to reject the rest. In the normal course of events, such selective attention mechanisms are sensitive to cues relevant to the organism's life experience, its survival, and the satisfaction of its needs (Gibson, 1969). Under certain pathological conditions, it appears that selective attention is cued either by an excess of different inputs, of dubious relevance, or by particular cues not normally crucial or of adaptive value.

The selective attention "filter" has been supposed abnormally permeable in schizophrenia (McGhie, 1965). Such patients are often unusually distractable and responsive to extraneous cues irrelevant to the task set before them in the test situation. This distractability is easy to demonstrate, and it is clear that such patients often do not focus their attention normally. Is this because they are unable to do so?

Subjects fail to focus attention on a task or situation if they lack interest in it, if they have emotional resistance toward participating, if they find that it makes excessive demands on their abilities, or if they are otherwise preoccupied. In the mere demonstration of a failure of selective attention, there is no discrimination between primary physiological causation and distractability secondary to other causes, any or all of which might be applicable to a schizophrenic subject. Thus, the intrusion of pathological thought processes will interrupt concentration on a task and, by changing the expectancies of the subject, might sensitize his selective attention to other ambient stimuli which he incorporates into his abnormal train of thought. Failure to maintain selective attention may be not so much a case of filter incompetence as of a change of set secondary to internal events inaccessible to the examiner, such as disordered thought in schizophrenia. An economical hypothesis would postulate that failure to maintain selective attention is secondary to such a disorder, rather than an independent manifestation of disturbed neuronal activity. Evidence to the contrary would come from the demonstration of some gain to balance the loss in distractibility—for instance, more incidental learning to balance less intentional learning. But no such demonstrations have ever been offered.

Distractibility is also a well-recognized feature of some cases of mental retardation and of so-called hyperkinesis, in which the affected child, usually brain damaged at or before birth, is constantly in motion in proportion to the amount of ambient stimulation. The activity is damped down substantially under conditions of relative sensory impoverishment. Such instances have not been experimentally analyzed in such a way as to permit conclusions about the integrity of the selective attention mechanism.

Breakdowns in selective attention do not appear to characterize patients with focal cerebral damage in any particular location, although perhaps closer analysis of receptive disorders in vision and audition might reveal instances of such a disorder. The selection for attention of dimensions of little adaptive relevance is, however, well exemplified by the not uncommon polarization of attention along the horizontal meridian of the body and of external space (Jackson & Zangwill, 1952). In this disorder, weight is attached to a stimulus in terms of its position relative to the left and right limits of the total stimulus array. Responses are preferentially attached to input from one side of space. In flagrant form, this gives rise to strikingly disordered behavior in men and animals. The situation is conspicuous in many patients with right-parietal disorders. When unoccupied, they tend to lie in bed with head and eyes turned to the right (Bard, 1922). They respond only to conversation addressed to them from their right (Scheller & Seidemann, 1931). Far from compensating for left-sided hemianopia due to peripheral disease, the deficit is aggravated by further withdrawal of the visual field from the central axis of space confronting the person (Luria, 1966). Localization of objects, by pointing, is systematically towards the right. This strikingly maladaptive response is unusual among the consequences of cerebral damage. It is regularly associated with unawareness or even persistent denial of field defect, as well as of left-sided neurological handicap (Babinski, 1914) and characterizes acute as opposed to chronic lesions. In longstanding disease, both unawareness of field defect and withdrawal of attention from that side of space are rare (Kinsbourne, 1966; Teuber et al., 1960).

Right–left polarization of attention is demonstrable both in exteroception [audition (Wortis & Pfeiffer, 1948) as well as vision] and proprioception, although deviation in one of these modalities does not necessarily imply disorder in the rest (Denny-Brown, Meyer, & Horenstein, 1962). Right-hemisphere lesions in right-handed subjects often result in polarization of attention to the right with "neglect" of the left side of the body and of space. Less frequently, or to a less marked extent, left-hemisphere lesions result in the converse change. There is clinical evidence that such changes incriminate the posterior–inferior parietal lobe. While patients with neglect may show more generalized intellectual deterioration as a group than patients with preserved intellect, who show marked neglect of one or another type and of others who are in the converse situation. When patients with or without a given deficit are compared on some general basis, such as an intelligence test battery, it is not surprising to find that affected patients perform less well than controls. There are two reasons for this. First, their specific deficit is likely to interfere with the performance of at least some of the subtests of any intelligence scale with reasonably wide coverage. Secondly, patients who manifest any deficit are likely to have more advanced disease than those who do not, and for that reason they are more likely also to show other signs of disability. For instance, does neglect of space result from a combination of dementia and field defect? To substantiate this claim, that combination would have to be proved both necessary and sufficient to give rise to the clinical syndrome. This demonstration is not feasible, since neglect may occur with both preserved intellect and preserved visual efficiency.

Neglect of space contralateral to a focal hemispheric lesion may be less flagrant and even subclinical but still detectable by appropriate methods. In minor form, it is exceedingly common. Manifestations include the "completion" tendency and reversal of direction of visual scan.

Poppelreuter observed in all but two of his posterior cerebral gunshot wound cases that figures, briefly exposed so as to overlap blind sectors of the field, would usually be reported as complete (as if they were visible even in the area of field defect).

There appears to be polarization of attention toward the side of the lesion. Attention, judged operationally in terms of differential readiness to respond, is diverted to the right side of space and to the rightmost end of any visual display. Information from the left may be ignored when present (neglect) or inferred when absent (completion) ; that source of information is undervalued, while maximum weight is attached to information, irrespective of modality, coming in from the right. This view is further borne out by the results of tachistoscopic presentation of horizontal letter sequences to patients with focal cerebral damage. While the left hemisphere-damaged cases showed an accuracy gradient declining toward the right, such as is also found in normal Western that, because of polarization of attention, patients with right-hemisphere group showed a reversed gradient, such as is manifested by normal readers of Hebrew who scan from right to left (Orbach, 1967). It appears that, because of polarization of attention, patients with right-hemisphere disease begin their scan at the right and proceed leftward.

Although according to Poppelreuter this process is of adaptive value, this is not clear, since the phenomenon amounts to no more than an inference of the unseen on the basis of the seen, which might well be right but, if mistaken, would be maladaptive. Completion is associated with a lack of awareness of field defect (Warrington, 1962) and a failure to explore the affected side of space by eye movement, an obviously maladaptive reaction. Fuchs (1921) postulated that field forces are operative in completion, a notion refuted by Warrington (1962), who demonstrated that the completion tendency is maximal with familiar and namable forms rather than "good" configurations. Kinsbourne and Warrington (1962c) described an analogous completion of incomplete familiar words to the left of the fixation point (backward completion) and have also observed some instances (unpublished) of "forward word completion" in left-parietal disease. Indeed, even in the intact (right) half-field of "backward" completing subjects, a completion tendency to the left of the display was demonstrable.

These observations permit the inference that the normal rather even and roughly symmetrical distribution of attention around the median plane is composed of contributions from the two hemispheres. Each hemisphere acts to bias attention toward the contralateral end of any visual display, whatever its location. When one hemisphere is damaged, its contribution to the overall distribution of attention is diminished, leaving that distribution unbalanced in the manner observed in patients with the unilateral neglect syndrome (Kinsbourne, 1971a). The effect can be simulated in normal people by activating the left (dominant) cerebral hemisphere by imposing a concurrent verbal task (Kinsbourne, 1970).

## C. Illusions and Hallucinations

Illusions consist in the episodic, mistaken identification of one or more aspects of external events or appearances, and hallucinations in the episodic perception of such events or appearances in the absence of corresponding objective external change. In the neuropsychological literature, misidentification of objectively present stimuli has been variously classified in relation to the nature of the pathologically imposed distortion, whether it made the object look larger (macropsia), smaller (micropsia), reduplicated (polyopsia), of a different shape (metamorphopsia), further away (teleopsia), or longer lasting (palinopsia).

The boundaries between mistaken identification due to imperfection in normal perceptual processes and that which is a manifestation of psychopathology cannot be defined, although most relevant episodes can without difficulty be assigned to the appropriate category. Hallucinatory phenomena are profuse in adult schizophrenia and common in a variety of organic cerebral and other neurological diseases, in hypnotic states, following hallucinogen administration, during perceptual isolation, in toxic states and delirium, and (arguably) in normal sleep in the form of dreams. Some distinctions can be formulated, however, between the types of hallucinations which predominate in these various conditions.

Hallucinations may or may not be modality specific. In cases of damage or artificial stimulation of one or another sensory projection pathway or cerebral receiving area, hallucinations will be confined to the relevant modality. The power of "eidetic" subjects to summon up visual images of hallucinatory intensity appears not to be matched by a comparable facility in the auditory sphere. Psychotic hallucinations are predominantly auditory; hallucinogens and perceptual isolation preferentially induce visual phenomena. In hypnosis, toxic delirium, and dream states, both or several modalities are involved, the percepts may be integrated, as in dreams or hynosis, or not, as at times in psychosis. Occasionally taste and smell are involved, and frequently, when brain damage is the cause, the somatic sensations also take part.

Perhaps more fundamental is the amount of credence given to the hallucination and the extent to which it is integrated into ongoing concepts of real events. Psychotic hallucinations are accepted as real; logical inconsistencies do not shake this confidence. In perceptual deprivation and hallucinogen ingestion, the manifestation, although vivid enough, is rejected as nonveridical, not because of lack of verisimilitude in the sensation itself (which may be indistinguishable from that aroused by real external change), but because of knowledge of the other, contravening aspects of the situation. The same applies to the hallucinations of neurological disease, which are rejected as the result of a consciously formulated judgment, reached on the basis of contravening cues from the immediate environment and from expectations founded on past experience. So it is primarily in psychosis that hallucinations form a basis for delusions about the actual state of affairs. This delusional aspect is determined by a pre-existing thought disorder rather than by the hallucinated experience; it is the latter which, in its essential features, often seems to fit into and perhaps be determined by the delusional system. This may simply be an instance of the effect of expectancy on perception. The expectancy is abnormal in this case, but given that abnormal expectancy, the particular type of hallucination that results needs no further explanation.

Misrecognition is a normal everyday experience. It arises from a decision made prematurely on what turn out to be insufficient cues. Familiar (highly probable items, such as words (Howes & Solomon, 1951) and pictures (Oldfield & Wingfield, 1965) are recognized at relatively low-duration thresholds, but consequently are probably more subject to misidentification in the sense of false positive responses. Proofreader's error is an instance. In decision theory terminology, a greater probability (expectancy) causes the adoption of a lower (laxer) recognition criterion. It seems probable that lowered criteria can be the result not only of expectancy changes (whether objectively valid or not) but also of lowered vigilance (sleep-like states, fatigue), confusional states, and intellectual deterioration. This will lead to a more ready acceptance of noisy fluctuation as a "signal" and of an ambiguous signal as the one that was expected. A similar criterion shift may be induced by certain brain lesions. In such cases a shift would be modality specific, leading to decisions made on the basis of signals which are clearly contramanded by the rest of the available information. Therefore, a distinction may be drawn between criterion shifts secondary to general expectancies which, if resulting in false positive recognition, would involve acceptance by the patient of the decisions thus arrived at (i.e., delusions) and shifts which are somehow primarily imposed upon one modality, leading to decisions which may or may not be accepted depending on the state of the subject's thought processes.

It is not always possible to validate a percept by further inspection. Visual misrecognition due to premature closure of the decision mechanism is readily corrected by further inspection (e.g., transient misrecognition of an approaching figure), but auditory stimuli tend to be brief and unavailable for further direct scrutiny. Perhaps for this reason, auditory misinformation is more frequently the substrate for delusion than is visual. However, even in vision in normal adults, "prerecognition" responses have been claimed to retard the ultimately correct identification (Bruner & Potter, 1944); in the interim between responses, a delusion may be said to obtain.

In appropriate circumstances, powerful or biased expectations may lead to misinterpretation of correctly transmitted sensory information or of normally fluctuating "noise" in the sensory system. The other source of hallucinatory experience would be abnormal sensory activity unrepresentative of external change. Such sensory abnormality may be induced by deliberate intervention, such as electrical stimulation of sensory pathways or processing areas. A common instance is the phosphene: a weak current traveling between electrodes applied externally to the temples leads to retinal ganglion cell discharge and a visual percept; simple pressure on the eyeball will have the same effect. Naturally occurring disease processes of the irritative type (glioma of the optic chiasm, posterior fossa tumor) may induce hallucination in sane people (Weinberger & Grant, 1940). Structural changes in the eyeball (corneal or lenticular opacity, retinal detachment) will lead to distorted external appearances, but these anomalies are invariant and, in this respect, unlike hallucinations. Direct stimulation, by whatever agent, of neurons in a sensory projection system may lead to nonveridical signals, that is, to fluctuations of neural noise well in excess of a normally set criterion level (Swets, Tanner, & Birdsall, 1961). Paradoxically, it appears that prolonged absence of stimulation can have a very similar effect. Supersensitivity of denervated structures to circulating neurohumors is well established for peripherally located structures, and comparable changes have been described in central nervous system structures. Anatomical denervation may well be paralleled in this respect by functional denervation, as in the impoverished environment of sensory isolation experiments. Thus accentuation of neural noise may interact with lowered criteria to result in misrecognition of one or several dimensions or attributes of external objects, depending on which analyzing systems are involved. Indeed, insofar as criterion shifts themselves must ultimately reflect neural activity, factors that make for neuronal hyperactivity, if they happen to affect the relevant neurons, would also result in criterion shifts by direct modification of the neuronal activity that underlies criterion shifts. It follows that in any hallucinatory syndrome, the possibility of increased random ("noisy") neuronal activity as well as of criterion relaxation must be considered. In psychosis, selective criterion shifts, resulting from motivational biases, may be a sufficient cause. In eidetic imagery, neuronal activity appears to be heightened, as it may be in organic cerebral pathology. In hypnotic hallucination, criterion shifts may be induced by the experimenter's process of suggestion. In confusion and dementia, the same thing might occur, while in delirium, as in high fever, both spontaneous neuronal firing and criterion shifts could be incriminated, as would also seem likely in the perceptual isolation situation.

This account of the origin of hallucinations remains hypothetical until tested experimentally. Standard decision-theory techniques could be applied to most of the above situations to test the validity of the concept.


## IV. LANGUAGE DISORDER

### A. Language Disorder and Thought

In human society, language is the main vehicle for the communication of specific information, but the influence of language on thought extends beyond its communicative function. The individual's cognitive structure, his mode of thinking, is profoundly influenced by the characteristics of the particular language he speaks. The language influences what he observes, what he remembers, and how he categorizes his observations and memories. It is not necessary to suppose, with Whorf (1950), that what one perceives is directly influenced by what one can name, with the result that the inventory of verbal labels and grammatical forms determines immediate experience. Indeed, there is no experimental evidence to support this extreme view. Rather, in a rich environment where the observer is confronted with far more simultaneously present stimuli than can be encompassed by his span of apprehension, he will selectively attend and choose to respond to those stimulus features which are represented in his linguistic code. Learning the name for an object or an event attracts attention to it, and knowing that name draws attention to it on its subsequent reappearances. Cumulative experience thus selects and preferentially records the incidence and associations of verbally specifiable appearances. The observer's language inventory shapes his life experience; and by means of its communal language, society channels the activity of the recognition process, a system of limited capacity, toward features of the environment which are judged, on the basis of cumulative group experience, as having adaptive value. Different cultures reflect their different ideas about what to expect of life, by virtue of language differing in wealth and type of expression; and, in turn, this verbal bias influences the actual life experience that follows. Thus the structure of the language perpetuates the experience of the group. If it were modified (e.g., curtailed), it is quite believable that the appearances, events, and concepts represented by the censored words would themselves fade from human experience, a phenomenon described by Orwell in relation to the introduction of Newspeak in 1984.

During cognitive development, subsets of experience are aggregated as categories on the basis of observed significant relationships between the items of the subset. By no means does this process of concept formation necessarily rely on verbal mediation. Concept formation has both been observed and induced in animals. This includes the ability to group objects not only in terms of some common selectively altered physical dimension, but also in relation to abstract principles, such as uniqueness ("oddity"), identity ("sameness–difference"), and degree of resemblance ("similarity–dissimilarity"). If even rats are capable of acquiring oddity (Koronakos & Arnold, 1957) or sameness–difference (Kinsbourne, 1967) "learning set," it should not be supposed that language is necessary for abstraction in man or that aphasia necessarily disrupts "categorical behavior" (Goldstein, 1948). Concepts may and will be formed irrespective of language. However, language does trigger the formation of particular concepts, channel concept formation, and expedite it by providing verbal labels with which to group items in categories. Consequently, by developing the words of the language and the concepts they incorporate, adults can cause concepts similar to their own to be formed by their children, thus shaping the developing thought processes.

How might a language or aphasic disorder affect concept formation; how might it affect thinking? Insofar as information flow is restricted for an individual afflicted with such a disorder, he will lack to a greater or lesser extent the raw material for concept formation. For the individual who sustains language impairment in adult years, the effect of this restriction of information flow might be insubstantial, since he will probably already be fully equipped with concepts. But the child who sustains language loss during mental development, particularly the child who is pathologically slow in developing language facility, would be profoundly handicapped in acquiring information upon which concepts may be built, unless energetic remedial efforts utilize whatever other communication channels remain open. Such a child not only lacks specific information, and thus does badly on tests which tap the store of detailed knowledge, but also manifests relative slowness in concept formation due to lack of verbal facility. He has fewer concepts than is normal, and he shows anomalies in the types of concepts formed, these being more dependent than usual on individual observation of a possibly severely restricted environment. These considerations do not suggest that the ability to form concepts will be impaired in the aphasic patient, young or old, but merely that opportunities to form them will be less plentiful than usual.

Intelligence is not unitary, but rather is divisible into verbally mediated processes and those not so mediated. Language disorders prejudice the former but not the latter, and this affects verbal but not nonverbal reasoning processes (Archibald, Wepman, & Jones, 1967; Ettlinger & Moffett, 1970). But this statement is insufficiently explanatory. It is necessary to specify which processes are verbally mediated and which of these could be just as successfully carried out by an alternative nonverbal strategy, should that be necessary. Indeed, it is not at all certain that any intelligent act, other than one which specifically deals with words, could not be based on nonverbal reasoning processes. One depends on the use of words only for those thoughts which are about words. When an aphasic patient fails in verbal reasoning, he fails because he can no longer use words as an adjunct to reasoning, not because he can no longer reason.

These notions can be tested by direct experimentation with aphasic subjects. Besides the use of words, what cognitive faculties are denied them? When test performance of aphasic and nonaphasic brain-damaged subjects are compared on any task not explicitly verbal, a distinction must be made between the implications of the presence and of the absence of a significant deficit in aphasic performance on the task. If the aphasics fail, this might be due to their language disability; or it might be the result of some other deficit associated with it because of vulnerability of the relevant cerebral area to coincident damage and not at all causally connected to the language disorder. Thus the range of cognitive impairment due to aphasia is circumscribed by all those performances in which aphasics succeed, but it may not be accurately estimated by the performances in which they fail.

When is a task demonstrably verbally mediated? Not when verbal processes are shown merely to coincide with performance (Sokolov, 1967), but when they are essential to its appropriate performance, or when an alternative, nonverbal strategy would demonstrably alter the way in which it is accomplished. The verbal processes need not be overt. "Thought is talking to ourselves," claimed Watson (1926). However, while covert verbalization appears to coincide with thinking, there is little evidence that it mediates that process (McGuigan, 1966). When overt, verbal processes, such as verbal responses, do not necessarily indicate a verbally-mediated task. It is the nature of the performance-limiting activity which is crucial, not that of other processes which are also involved but which, unlike those which are rate limiting, are not stretched to capacity.

The latter point is illustrated by an experiment utilizing incomplete representations of familiar objects (Gollin, 1961). These cue-impoverished drawings of graded difficulty were as well recognized, judging from verbal description, by aphasic as by nonaphasic brain-damaged subjects (Kinsbourne, unpublished) and by children delayed in language development as by children not so delayed (Kinsbourne & Peel-Floyd, 1965), the groups in each instance being matched for nonverbal intelligence. It appears that the act of "perceptual closure," which results in correct recognition, is not verbally mediated and therefore is not vulnerable to language disorder; at the same time, the naming responses, relating as they do in this particular test to highly familiar objects, put little strain even on the aphasic subject. Nor can verbalization during task performance necessarily be assumed to contribute an element essential to success in the task. Aphasic patients may make bizarre and inconsequential remarks, purportedly relating to ongoing reasoning processes, which in fact are accurately carried out (Kinsbourne & Warrington, 1964a). The experimental demonstration of performance-limiting verbal mediation, even in normal subjects, is found only seldom in the literature, though impressionistic claims abound. Indeed, the neuropsychological approach might facilitate this study.

Which processes, other than frankly verbal ones, are impaired in aphasia? It may be inferred that such processes involve verbal mediation at some crucial point in the performance. An instance of a test on which aphasic patients perform relatively poorly is the "embedded figure" test, in which the subject is required to pick out an arbitrarily selected configuration which forms part of a larger configuration. In fact, patients with right-hemisphere lesions perform worst of all, but left-hemisphere aphasics still perform less well than left-hemisphere nonaphasics. This is evidence for the contribution of at least two processes to performance on the "embedded figure" test: a right-hemisphere spatial analysis and a left-hemisphere process involving verbal mediation (Teuber & Weinstein, 1956). An alternative view relates the aphasic group's inferiority not to the language disorder itself but to the presence of coincident constructive apraxia. Left-hemisphere patients may have difficulty in copying drawings, difficulty of a type suggestive of an impairment in their ability spatially to analyze the test figure and, on the basis of this, to decide how to organize the manual response (Warrington, James, & Kinsbourne, 1966). Such a constructional apraxia is common in aphasics (Critchley, 1953); and if the aphasic groups in the "embedded figure" studies were more subject to this difficulty in spatial analysis than the nonaphasic left-hemisphere controls, this, rather than the language disorder, might account for the "embedded figure" deficit. This possibility can readily be tested by controlling for constructional efficiency and partialling out intergroup differences in this variable before comparing the "embedded figure" control group. If a significant difference survives such a control, then language mediation will remain a possible factor in "embedded figure" performance.

Finally, if impairment of verbal mediation is a performance-limiting factor on any given task, it should be possible to demonstrate selective deficit in performance of this task on the part of other language-deprived groups, such as the emotionally disturbed and deaf mutes. Such comparisons have not usually held nonverbal intelligence constant between groups and so are difficult to interpret; but, at least in relation to ability to form concepts, it is obviously not the case that the deaf mute or the severely deaf are specifically defective (Rosenstein, 1961).

## B. Language Disorder and Communication

It has become fashionable to distinguish, within the range of cognitive defects, the disorders of communication, and the semiotic disorders. This implies that aphasia is an impairment of the capacity to decode and encode symbols, of which verbal symbols are only one type, albeit a prominent one. If this is so, aphasics should be defective in nonverbal communication in proportion to their verbal defect. This would include such artificial systems as Braille, semaphore, and Morse Code, as well as natural means of communication, such as gesture, mime, and facial expression. In fact, no systematic evidence supports this view. On the contrary, many aphasics become adept at communicating by gesture for the very reason that verbal communication has become difficult. Facial expression is preserved in aphasia. Conversely, facial apraxia, in which facial expression is no longer under volitional control (Nathan, 1947), occurs independently of language disorder.

Even within the sphere of verbal behavior, dissociation occurs between verbal content and intonation. Holding phonemic patterning constant, tone, force, and pitch of speech may vary, and these prosodic variables have semantic implication for the listener. Intonation is one of the means of verbal communication. Does the same neural facility that contributes words, contribute intonation? If so, intonation should be impaired in parallel with other speech functions in aphasia. In Parkinsonism, speech becomes slow, invariant in pitch, and monotonous (hypoprosody), but there is no coincident disorder of verbal formulation. This is a feature of the articulatory output mechanism rather than of its programming by cortical structures. In aphasia, where speech is commonly sparse and halting, intonation is often lost, but so it would be in normal subjects speaking at a comparably slow rate. Those aphasics who speak can generally vary their intonation very effectively, even when the verbal message is totally garbled (Isserlin, 1936); and in jargon aphasia (Alajouanine, Sabouraud, & DeRiboucourt, 1952) the listener may have the impression of someone speaking most expressively in an unknown foreign language. Mechanisms that program prosodic features are evidently not located in the same area as those in which the inherent features of phonemes are programmed.

Rare instances have been reported of patients in whom intonation is specifically disordered; their speech is termed dysprosodic (Monrad-Krohn, 1967). Characteristically, such a patient seems to have developed a "foreign" accent, often described as German or Welsh (Critchley, 1962), usually along with an aphasic disorder. Monrad-Krohn's description of that deficit as an ataxia of intonation is a metaphor rather than an explanation.

Personal studies of dysprosody have provided mechanisms which appear, in retrospect, to be consistent with the findings in the other reported cases. A patient with localized left-posterior frontal damage had a cerebral dysarthria characterized by difficulty in forming certain phonemes and phoneme groups (coincidentally ones with which Germans experience difficulty when learning English). At the same time, speech spectrograms showed that the frequency distribution of her speech remained very level, in contrast with controls who tended especially to lower their pitch at the end of a phrase. The listener gained the impression that the patient actually raised the pitch of her voice at the end of the phrase as might a German, Welshman, or Indian (the latter two accents were attributed to her by some). This illustrates a listener error based on expectancy. Expecting a drop in pitch, the listener interprets failure to drop as an actual rise. If the pitch abnormality had been associated with slow speech, as in Parkinsonism, it would have sounded pathological, and no foreign accent attribution would have occurred. The normal rate of speech and the relatively slight dysarthria permitted the attribution of imperfect rather than pathological English to the speaker.

It follows that intonation is programmed cortically, anterior to the language area of the dominant hemisphere, by mechanisms located adjacent to those that program the phonemic aspect of speech. To a substantial degree, verbal content and intonation can vary independently. When intonation is impaired, its range of variation becomes limited rather than distorted, and the result is monotone. The impression of dysprosody as dialect or accent comes from an interaction between the listener's perception and his expectations.

The dissociation between disorders of prosody and inherent features of verbal output is one of many instances of the multidimensionality of language disorders. Verbal disorder itself occurs in many partial forms; it certainly cannot be regarded as global enough to include disorders of other communication media. Semiotic disorder (Grewel, 1960) is a classificatory concept without physiologic validity.


## C. Language Disorder and Memory

To be constantly useful, the language repertoire must be remembered. Prominent in aphasia is an inability to evoke words or phonemes appropriate to test or real-life situations. In a manner of speaking, the subject has "forgotten" the appropriate words or "signs" of external referents. Usually he can select them accurately in a choice situation, which demonstrates that the failure is one of retrieval from store. For present purposes, this will be regarded as a defect in the use, rather than the remembering, of words. The term "verbal memory" will be restricted to a different process, in which words are remembered as such rather than as labels for things.

Words are useful not only in communication. They may be used for "the registering of the consequences of our thoughts which being apt to slip out of our memory and put us to a new labour, may again be recalled by such words as they are marked by. So that names serve for marks, or notes, of remembrance" (Hobbes, 1950). Thus words are used for the coding of information so that it can be stored more readily and efficiently. For this purpose an appropriate subset of the total vocabulary is specifically associated with the information in question, and that association is retained for subsequent reference. The two components of this process—the allocation of appropriate words to specify the stimulus and the retention and ultimate retrieval of these words—may be considered separately.

When the stimulus is chiefly verbal, the first component is bypassed and the second may be studied in isolation. In this case, verbal memory is measured in terms of the learning of explicitly verbal information, such as word lists or more organized word sequences. In everyday life the defect would manifest itself not only in forgetfulness of what is said but also in impaired memory of such nonverbal input as is habitually encoded for storage in verbal rather than in direct "representational" form.

When the retention of verbal input appears normal, but that of some nonverbal categories of input is impaired, then the first component, the encoding of input into verbal form, may be at fault. Whether it is so will depend on the habitual strategy for memorization of the material in question. If it is customarily stored in direct representational form, the corresponding deficit cannot be referred to an inadequacy in verbal recoding. If, however, correct verbal recoding of input normally enhances retention, a recoding deficit may result in loss of the advantage gained by this tactic and reduce the capacity for retention to that permitted by the less efficient representational process. Covert verbal recoding of ostensibly nonverbal material has been variously demonstrated, for instance with color naming. The relevant process utilizes what has been called the "verbal loop" (Glanzer & Clark, 1963). Glanzer and Clark have shown that misrecognition of previously exposed geometric shapes may be accounted for in terms of confusion among verbal labels. Indeed, memory span and span of apprehension seem to be functions of the verbal recodability of the material rather than of its sheer visual complexity (Warrington, Kinsbourne, & James, 1966). The more readily available an appropriate verbal response (the more pronounceable the input is), the more can be extracted from intermediate memory store before its contents decay into illegibility. In aphasic subjects, the letter span of apprehension is impaired (Kinsbourne, 1966), presumably because they are slow to attach responses to the fading material in temporary storage. Extreme limitation of the span of apprehension in certain cases of left-occipital disease (Kinsbourne & Warrington, 1962b) may represent gross slowing of this process. Some of these patients have shown little or no other evidence of aphasia. This suggests that the neural substrate for visuo–verbal recoding is strategically located between the visual projection area posteriorly and the language production area anteriorly, rather than coextensively with the neural substrate of other language functions.

The demonstration of a limitation in immediate recall of verbal material (apprehension and memory span) on the part of aphasics is important in that it demarcates the deficit from the more general one which characterizes the amnesic syndrome (Talland, 1968), whether acquired following Wernicke's encephalopathy (Wernicke, 1881), bilateral temporal lobectomy (Scoville & Milner, 1957), or encephalitis implicating the hippocampi (Glees & Griffiths, 1952; Rose & Symonds, 1960). In this condition, immediate recall is preserved, but the sometimes overwhelming learning deficit comes into play as soon as even slight interference is inserted between presentation and response (Talland, 1968). This distinction suggests that different mechanisms underlie the aphasic and the amnesic disorder. Aphasia relates to the rate at which familiar material may be sequentially encoded into verbal response from a fading immediate memory trace; amnesia seems to be related more closely to weakness in rehearsal of verbal response prior to utterance or in the course of consolidation into memory storage, that rehearsal being pathologically vulnerable to interference from coincidental activity.

In the aphasic subject, it is perhaps more common to find both encoding of verbal labels and their retention to be impaired rather than only one of these. (Ettlinger & Moffett, 1970). In that case, the memory deficit will affect both verbally presented materials and those nonverbal materials, retention of which is habitually enhanced by verbal loop. Indeed, the finding that aphasic subjects can handle a given material with normal efficiency constitute *prima-facie* evidence that the storage process in question is purely representational. This is an instance of the way in which the study of aphasia can contribute to the understanding of normal cognitive processes.

It follows from these considerations that input varies along a dimension of verbal recodability. An individual will use the strategy of verbal recoding to facilitate memory for material recodable with less than a critical amount of difficulty; a representational form of storage will be applied to material that lends itself only with extreme difficulty to verbal recoding. Efficiency in the retention of nonverbal material will depend, therefore, on the choice of an appropriate storage vehicle, as well as the effectiveness of its use.

Visual arrays used in retention tests may be either frankly verbal or nonverbal ("representational") and may thus vary in the degree to which they lend themselves to recoding in verbal form. Retention scores may be obtained after a single presentation or after repeated display, the two methods giving estimates of memory span and of learning ability respectively; or the two may be combined into a total cumulative score (Kimura, 1963). Retention tests may be by recall or by recognition. The recognition situation gives a direct estimate of efficiency of retention; the recall measure, usually vocal in the case of verbal material or manually mediated when nonverbal drawings are present, is complicated by the possible intervention of output disorders. This test requires rigorous control by means of measurement of the ability to read and to copy while the stimulus material remains on display. The retention of verbal material is particularly prejudiced by left-hemisphere damage (Luria & Karanservat, 1968; Meyer & Yates, 1955; Milner, 1962). Whether this deficit, which has been noted in left-temporal lobectomies even in the absence of clinically apparent aphasia (Kimura, 1963) is due to failure of encoding of material in verbal store or simply of retrieval from store remains to be determined by the use of recognition testing. Furthermore, familiar drawings are better recalled by right- than by left-hemisphere damaged groups (Boller & DeRenzi, 1967). Whether it is because of their familiarity *per se* or because they lend themselves to verbal labeling and thus to more efficient storage is not made clear by the results of these studies. Kimura's finding that nonsense shapes were better retained by left- than by right-temporal lobectomy groups appeared to conflict with the findings of Boller and DeRenzi for paired associate learning of nonsense figures, since in that study left-hemisphere cases were inferior to right to such an extent that they manifested a language deficit. However, it should be recalled that Kimura's series did not include a comparable number of frankly aphasic patients, leaving open the possibility that, had an aphasic group been included in her experiments, this group might have performed even worse than the right-temporal group on her recurring nonsense figure tasks. This illustrates the ambiguity of conclusions about function of cerebral areas on the basis of comparisons which do not include control groups representative of all the major cerebral territories. The sum of data presently available can be reconciled if it is supposed that the right hemisphere (or temporal lobe) is particularly involved in representational memory of material which cannot be verbalized because it is too briefly exposed. When verbalization is made possible by the nature of the material and conditions of exposure, then it is left hemisphere which participates in this function, giving the organism an advantage, in terms of total memory, over and above the capacity of representational memory contributed by the right hemisphere. The evidence for this hypothesis is indirect, largely because experiments to date have not fully dissociated the confounding variables of stimulus familiarity and codability, and because the codability of materials is inferred rather than measured. If the codability of nonsense shapes is expressed in terms of associative value (Vanderplas & Garvin, 1959), then it should follow that in normal subjects the effect of associative value on retention is a function of exposure duration (supposing, as suggested by Boller and DeRenzi (1967), that verbal recoding consumes substantial amounts of time). Moreover, it should prove to be the case that shapes of high associative value are better retained by left-hemisphere patients, the crossover associative value representing the lowest associative point at which verbal recoding confers an advantage in relation to retention. This crossover point should be capable of being shifted in the direction of low associative value by pretraining in the verbal labeling of such figures. Finally, any advantage experienced by right-sided patients who retain coding ability should be maximized by increasing exposure duration of the stimulus material up to the point in time at which the recoding process is normally complete.

Finally, it is still unknown whether, when subjects show an impairment in retention due to failure to utilize verbal recoding, this is because they are incapable of doing so or because they have made an erroneous choice of strategy. This point could be settled by examining the effects of appropriate verbal cueing on the performance of these patients.

Verbal memory deficits are not restricted in their effects to the test situation nor to the retention of verbal information for subsequent reference. A continuous short-term storage process is an ingredient of the comprehension of connected speech, the meaning of which is a function not only of the individual constituent words, but also of their sequential organization. As the meaning of a sentence cumulatively unfolds, with a progressive reduction of uncertainty, information presented early in the sequence has to be retained to modify and illuminate the significance of subsequent items. A severe selective short-term verbal memory deficit could suffice to produce a substantial receptive aphasia for connected speech. Such a patient would not show impairment in the comprehension of isolated words. During the analysis of a case of receptive aphasia, this factor may be isolated by limiting the test vocabulary and presenting it in sequences of graduated length and complexity. If the words are comprehended when presented singly but not when spoken in sequence, a deficit in short-term verbal memory is indicated. The Token Test for receptive aphasia (DeRenzi & Vignolo, 1962) utilizes a vocabulary of two words for specific shape, two for size, and five for color. These are incorporated into increasingly complex instructions. Results on this test were analyzed separately for each of four levels of complexity among adult aphasics (Kinsbourne, 1966) and children with delayed language development (Kinsbourne & Peel-Floyd, 1965). A proportionally greater deficit for the longer sequences suggests that an element of verbal short-term memory deficit contributes to the overall verbal comprehension deficit.

When speech stimuli are successively presented, the required response may be nonverbal (e.g., carrying out a Token Test command) or it may be verbal [e.g., making a matching (sameness–difference) or imitative (repetition) response]. When the response is a single utterance, it is withheld until the input is complete, during which time the early items of input must be maintained in short-term storage by recirculation through a rehearsal loop (Sperling, 1963). The simplest available model would regard the rehearsal as a covert response, utilizing the same neural facility as an overt repetition. This covert response is fed back to the discrimination apparatus. The subject listens to his inner speech. Loss of information during this rehearsal involves "mishearing," so that confusions will be of the acoustic type (Conrad, 1964).

When responses are vocal and multiple, as in the standard memory span situation, overt response to the items presented early in the task may coincide with the rehearsal of subsequent items. This coincidence may be a span-limiting fact, particularly in the aphasic patient. This situation is demonstrated in the case studies of two aphasic patients who had disproportionate difficulty in direct repetition of speech sounds. These patients were able to repeat correctly a single spoken digit. If two were presented so that the second input preceded response to the first stimulus, latency for the first response lengthened and that for the second lengthened disproportionately or even infinitely, insofar as they were unable to respond to that item. There was no comparable difficulty with visual presentation or presentation in mixed modalities, one auditory and, subsequently, one visual stimulus item. There was, however, difficulty if the visual preceded the auditory. When the subjects were asked to hold both speech sounds in memory and then to judge whether they had been the same or different, they succeeded. Indeed, when they were asked to match two or even three successive pairs, they again succeeded with ease. Evidently the deficit was limited to auditory input, where it constituted the second of two rapidly successive stimuli and where a previous stimulus resulted in overt response. The matching situation demonstrates intact rehearsal loop in the absence of concurrent vocalization (Kinsbourne, 1971b).

This combination of findings may be explained as follows: The second of two items presented must be kept in rehearsal during response to the first. When the presentation is auditory, this rehearsal, which is sub-vocal, utilizes the vocal response channel. However, this channel is en-gaged in overt vocal response. The deficit limits the capacity simul-taneously to respond overtly and to recirculate covertly. The rehearsal item is lost or delayed because of competition with the overt response. The site of competition could be in the auditory analyzer, simultaneously confronted with both internal and external feedback, or in the program-ming of several articulatory outputs at the same time. If this interpreta-tion is confirmed by further study, it will provide support for the above-mentioned model of auditory short-term storage. It will also illustrate further the segregation of neural facilities in the brain, without which a relatively selective deficit of this type could not have arisen.

Since Broca's work became known (Riese, 1967), dominant hemisphere representation of speech comprehension has been assumed; and the as-sumption has been supported by numerous instances of receptive aphasia following left-hemisphere damage in dextrals without corresponding sequelae to right-hemisphere disease. Recently, however, a degree of speech comprehension has reportedly been preserved following excision of the left hemisphere (Smith, 1966b). This could be interpreted as re-vealing mechanisms for verbal recoding in the right hemisphere, usually suppressed by the normally functioning left hemisphere (by virtue of inhibition or crosstalk) and still suppressed when the latter is damaged but released from inhibition by total disconnection from left-hemisphere influence. It should follow that, in patients with global aphasia, speech comprehension, as manifested by responses under right-hemisphere con-trol, could be improved by callosal section. This possibility remains to be tested. When some recovery of speaking ability follows upon a severe aphasia, the language deficit may be reinstituted by a subsequent lesion of the other (right) hemisphere, suggesting that dominance for language had shifted to that side (Nielsen, 1946). This has now been confirmed by intracarotid amytal testing (Kinsbourne, 1971b).


## V. SEQUENCING OF INFORMATION

Events occur within a spatio–temporal framework which defines their location as well as their relative spatial position in the succession of circumstances that constitutes the life experience (Lashley, 1951). Does remembering the nature of an event necessarily imply remembering its spatio–temporal location, or are item and order information separately encoded? Everyday experience suggests at least some independence between these two varieties of information, and separate coding of item and order information in memory span was proposed by Crossman (1961). Are they separable experimentally or by intervention of biological change?

The judgment of precedence among rapidly successive auditory events is reportedly impaired in aphasic adults (Efron, 1963) and in children with delayed language development (Lowe & Campbell, 1965), although it is not clear whether the relevant association is with language disorder or with a dominant hemispheric location of lesion, irrespective of aphasia. In the overwhelming memory deficit of the amnesic syndrome, failure of retrieval of information from store in terms of its temporal label has been held responsible for the "confabulatory responses" described in this disorder (Van der Horst, 1932), although this notion remains unproven. These are instances of sequencing of unique and nonrecurrent successions of experimentally or environmentally determined events. An apparently distinct type of sequencing relates to spatio–temporal combinations of events which are recurrent and are associated with conventionally established superordinate categories learned to the point of automatization. There is evidence that the use of this type of sequencing is separable by cerebral disease from the use of temporal labeling of unique and nonrecurrent events.

Gerstmann (1930) reported in certain patients with left-hemisphere lesions the coincidence of a tetrad of deficits discovered by empirical testing. These were a finger-naming and finger-name recognition disorder and difficulty in writing, calculating, and distinguishing left from right. This cluster of symptoms has subsequently been repeatedly identified and referred to a parietal location of lesion which in left-handers can be either in the right or in the left hemisphere (Critchley, 1953). Numerous attempts have been made to rationalize this improbable combination of deficits in terms of a single underlying impairment of cerebral function.

With some risk of tautology, the finger agnosia has been referred to a "localized" lesion of the "body image," of the hypothetical "finger schema." Writing and calculating disorders are derived from or secondary to finger agnosia, because it is necessary to use the fingers in learning to write and "digits" in learning to calculate by counting on the fingers (Critchley, 1953). It remains unclear why a tool used in acquiring a skill should, when impaired, prejudice that skill once acquired and when it no longer need involve that tool (spelling aloud, mental arithmetic). Nor is it differential finger movement but rather wrist movement which controls the written word. The "body-image" notion lacks plausibility and explanatory value.

An alternative view related the syndrome to a supposedly coincident aphasic disorder (Benton, 1959) which, it was claimed, had escaped the notice of previous workers. Subsequently Heimburger, De Myer, and Reitan (1964) reported just such a coincidence. They accounted for previous failures to document this association on the basis of use of insensitive tests. However, since they categorize any spelling disorder as evidence of language dysfunction, they cannot fail to discern aphasia in every complete instance of the Gerstmann syndrome. There are some functions which are specifically related to verbal categorization; these are language functions. Other functions may be involved in the language process as well as in nonverbal performance. The question of whether or not the Gerstmann syndrome transcends the boundaries of verbal skills cannot be resolved by a semantic contest.

Coincidence between the syndrome and aphasia does not amount to evidence of a causal relationship between these disorders and even an infrequent dissociation between the two dismisses the possibility. Their occasional independence (Kinsbourne & Warrington, 1962a) reveals aphasia to be no more than a neighborhood disorder, reflecting contiguous areas of localization. Furthermore, finger agnosia can be elicited by non-verbal tests (Kinsbourne & Warrington, 1962a), which shows that the limitation of function cannot be classified as verbal. These tests identify finger agnosia as an impairment of "finger order sense." The defect affects those fingers which are characterized in terms of relative position on the hand. When this order information becomes unavailable, finger-naming is secondarily impaired. Similarly, the spelling disorder is characterized by a predominance of order errors, in contrast to an aphasic spelling disorder which predominantly introduces letters extraneous to the word to be spelled (Kinsbourne & Warrington, 1964b). The calculation difficulty involves a failure to attach to digits that significance which conventionally attaches to them within a sequence by virtue of their relative position (Stengel, 1944). Right–left disorientation completes this tetrad of deficits of categorization in terms of relative position in a sequence. Spelling and calculation can be regarded in terms of spatial sequence or, equally readily, in terms of temporal sequence.

The sequencing disorder of left-parietal disease does not refer to simple recall of sequential relationships. Patients with this disorder do not lose their way or miss appointments, nor are they unduly forgetful of telephone numbers. They do not forget standard lists, such as days of the

week or months of the year, but specifically experience difficulty with
the categorization of order information for operations such as verbal
labeling and arithmetic. These operations are familiar and overlearned.
Attempts to set up arbitrarily defined sequences and to demonstrate
undue difficulty in learning superordinate categories have so far failed
with such patients (Kinsbourne, unpublished). It may be concluded
provisionally that an operation concerned with the use of spatio–temporal
order information to establish superordinate categories has been isolated
by naturally occurring cerebral disease and appears to constitute a separate component of cognitive functioning. Further work is required to
define this function more precisely.

## VI. SPATIAL PERFORMANCE

Patients with focal cerebral disease sometimes experience difficulty
in manual performance beyond that which would be expected on the
basis of coincident sensory-motor deficit. When this is due neither to
failure to comprehend the task nor to perceptual difficulty, it is referred
to as apraxia, difficulty in the planning and execution of simple single
acts or movement sequences. In motor apraxia, the individual movement
is defective; in ideational apraxia, the component movements may themselves be appropriate, but they are carried out in incorrect sequence.
The acts affected may be familiar and well-practiced ones, such as striking a match to light a cigarette, or arbitrary movement sequences which
are within the scope of normal subjects. A disturbance of one subset
of such acts which deals with the arrangement of items in space in
conformity with a presented or remembered model is called constructional apraxia; and, of the test situations used to study this disorder—
two and three-dimensional block arrangement, matchstick arrangement,
and paper and pencil drawing—the latter has been most fully studied
and will be discussed here in detail.

While a variety of tasks have been used to test for the presence of
constructional apraxia (Critchley, 1953), there is absolutely no evidence
that these are all sensitive to the same defect. Pending the demonstration
of high correlation between various test performances, it is preferable,
when dealing with some such impairment as difficulty in paper and pencil
copying to refer to this by a neutral title such as drawing disability. It
should not be taken for granted that there are correlates of such impairment which are general enough to permit definition of constructional
apraxia in terms as wide as "disturbance in the spatial aspect of forma-
tive activities" (Critchley, 1953).

Failure in the ability to copy simple line drawings by hand has long been regarded as indicative of organic cerebral dysfunction, and this view has been made the basis of tests designed to detect "organicity" in the etiology of abnormal behavior. As always with such tests of "brain damage," the positive findings are more significant than the negative; and it is well known that many cases of substantial cerebral injury fail altogether to manifest such "constructional apraxia" when appropriately tested. It has been proposed (Critchley, 1953) that the disorder occurs only when one or the other parietal lobe is affected by the lesion. While this corresponds well with cumulative clinical experience, it has not so far been experimentally validated, largely because of the difficulty of obtaining large enough series of cases with sufficiently well-defined and localized focal cerebral damage. For this reason, experimentation has confined itself so far to contrasting the drawing disabilities consequent on damage to one or the other hemisphere, leaving intrahemispheric localization for future investigation. The main points at issue have been whether drawing ability is more impaired by right- or by left-sided (minor or major) hemisphere damage, and whether the nature of the impairment is the same irrespective of, or different depending on, the laterality of the lesion.

The isolation of the first and quantitative problem depends crucially on the use of comparison groups of demonstrably equal mean extent and comparable distribution of lesion, as well as on some acceptable metric for assessing the degree of constructional disability. No published study is entirely satisfactory in both respects. When cases are selected as they appear in clinical practice, there is a well-recognized tendency for right-sided disease to appear in more advanced stages than left-sided disease (Wolff, 1962). In major hemisphere damage, the early warning sign of aphasia soon obtrudes on daily life, and this alerts family and friends to the presence of disease. This results in early referral of the patient for treatment. Furthermore, on account of the extreme social importance of language for communication, surgeons tend to be more conservative when excising major hemisphere tissue because of spontaneously occurring cerebral disease. Therefore, inferiority of a right-sided group on drawing tasks, such as that found by Piercy and Smyth (1962), could reflect unbalanced comparison populations rather than the more essential or extensive participation of the minor hemisphere in the drawing performance. Concurrent testing with Raven's Progressive Matrices also revealed inferiority among right-sided cases in Piercy and Smyth's study. In the Matrices procedure, subjects are required at each trial to choose from among a number of pieces, each with a distinctive pattern, the missing piece of a larger design having the same pattern.

Piercy and Smyth regarded both the copying of designs and the Matrices performance as appropriate means of testing for "constructional ability"; therefore, they concluded that the latter ability was more embarrassed in their population by minor than by major hemisphere damage. They then postulated a unitary function with preponderant, but not exclusive, right-sided representation.

Thus the variety of drawing disability following damage to the right (minor) hemisphere is liable to appear the more severe (Heilbrun, 1959; Piercy & Smyth, 1962), although this disparity has not always been found (Warrington et al., 1966) and, when present, has been accounted for on the basis of more severe damage in the right-hemisphere group (Arrigoni & DeRenzi, 1964). This question of relative severity bears upon the view of constructional apraxia as a unitary process, bilaterally represented but localized preponderantly on the right (Piercy & Smyth, 1962), since this would constitute an instance of minor hemisphere dominance. The question of relative severity of damage recedes in importance in the light of evidence that there are at least two components of drawing performance, one contributed chiefly by the major hemisphere and one by the minor hemisphere.

McFie and Zangwill (1960) and Piercy, Hécaen, and Ajuriaguerra (1960) have described the differences they noted in defective copying performances caused by right- and left-sided brain damage. In cases of minor hemisphere disease, the spatial aspect of performance is affected: parts are correctly copied but incorrectly articulated to form the whole design. In major hemisphere cases, errors are described as rudimentary or primitive replications of the model, embodying its general (topological) properties but faulty in detail. Warrington et al. (1966) confirmed these descriptions and specified them in quantifiable form.

In copying simple geometric figures of graded complexity, patients of either type perform correctly up to a critical level of complexity. Beyond this level performance breaks down, even though all segments of the model can be correctly copied in isolation with respect to length, angle, and articulation of lines. Beyond the critical level of complexity, defective performance in left-hemisphere disease is strikingly similar to that which characterizes mentally retarded children and normal children confronted with copying tasks too difficult for their developmental level (Kinsbourne, 1966). "Right-sided" types of errors, on the other hand, do not seem to resemble those made at any stage in the normal development of drawing skill.

"Left-sided" errors are characterized by simplification of the acute and obtuse angle to the right angle, a feature which can be confirmed as characteristic of this group by objective counts of right angles (Warrington *et al.*, 1966). Rectangles are substituted for parallelograms, straight lines for obliques, continuous lines for lines which change in direction at some point along their length. When confronted with his own performance, the patient is aware of its inadequacy and can usually specify the incorrect feature by pointing to it, but he can neither specify it verbally nor describe to the observer how to improve the performance. When setting about the task, he does not systematically construct the drawing in a manner that reveals a prior analysis of the figure into its main components; rather he draws line after line approximately in random sequence. Thus, even when the final replica is adequate, the manner in which it was achieved is typically abnormal. If the figure is similar to one previously practiced and automatized, the automatized performance may be substituted for the correct one, e.g., five-pointed for six-pointed star, Necker cube for opaque box. Instructions to the patient on how to organize his performance are of little avail.

These observations support the generalization that drawing disability of left-sided type stems from an inability to translate a perceptual analysis of the model into the appropriate movement sequences. They do not discriminate between two possible bases for this difficulty: either the perceptual analysis does not occur, or it does occur but cannot be used to program movement patterns. In the former case, it should be possible to show correlated impairment on tests of perceptual analysis, such as the embedded figure test; deficit on this test has been reported in left-hemisphere damaged (aphasic) subjects (Teuber & Weinstein, 1956). In the latter case, only tests requiring manipulation of materials should show the defect.

In its typical form, the right-hemisphere type of drawing disability involves no striking simplification of contours or regression to the right angle. As in the left-sided case, the model is easily recognized, although defective performance is not necessarily recognized in retrospect, as it is in left-sided impairment. Individual elements of the model are appropriately drawn, but in incorrect spatial relationships to each other. Usually the sequence of actions that comprise performance is appropriately organized, at least until overshooting of a line or distortion of an angle unbalances the whole performance. Features that relate to the total form of the model and involve visual memory for their preservation, such as symmetry, are the ones that are commonly lost. Defective or quickly fading visual memory for position could account for this disorder, and such a finding is consistent with the results of other studies that indicate a visual memory deficit in right-hemisphere disease (Benton & Spreen, 1966; Kimura, 1963). It may be supposed that the "spatial" framework within which skilled performance operates consists of the sum of visual impressions of personal position which are retained in short-term store from glance to glance. Even in a direct copying task, a visual retention defect may become performance limiting, if some elements must be remembered while others are reproduced (as will be the case with any but the very simplest figures).

Little is known of the normal mechanism for copying. The type of analysis which follows discovery of defective copying performance in brain-damaged subjects might well trigger a more sophisticated exploration of the factors that limit drawing performance in the normal subject. Drawing disability, which is a common feature in cases of focal brain damage, seems particularly suited to detailed analysis which is based on the fact that certain types of brain damage selectively impair one or another ingredient of total performance.

## VII. THE ANALYSIS OF LEARNING DEFICIT

Learning disorders of developmental as distinct from environmental or emotional origin, have been exhaustively discussed as regards their prevalence, categorization, and neurological and psychometric concomitants (Bakwin, 1968; Kinsbourne & Warrington, 1963c). This debate has had no marked effect on remedial methods which remain empirical or dogmatic. The remote antecedents of his disability are of little relevance to the management of the individual child in need of special education. Until prediction of reading disability (DeHirsch, Jansky, & Lansford, 1965) becomes accurate and its prophylaxis feasible, the situation at ages six to eight, when the cases present, must be the center of attention. Which channels for learning remain open for the child, and which are closed? What manner of presentation of information optimizes upon residual learning ability? To answer these questions and institute rational teaching methods, a systematic analysis of the learning process into its functional components must be undertaken. If each component is separately evaluated for efficiency, a learning profile can be derived for the individual child. This could serve both as diagnostic criterion and as point of departure for innovative remedial methods. Consider the instance of the process of learning to read and write.

Over and above basic language abilities, learning to read involves the retention of visual information and its association with verbal responses. Visual stimuli can vary in many respects—color, contrast, extent, duration, form, orientation, sequential arrangement. Of these, form, orientation, and sequence are relevant to reading, and to each of these are associated verbal responses conventional to the language. This analysis suggests at least nine variants of reading disability, all of which is capable of causing major reading difficulty—failure to discriminate form, sequence, orientation; to retain form, sequence, orientation; to retain the verbal associates of form sequence, orientation. Separate evaluation of each process will generate a "learning profile," which will characterize the individual and serve as a basis for a search for further associates, such as hand preference, soft neurological signs, and the rest. Impairment of each learning process may in turn arise from impaired discrimination of the relevant dimension, inconstant attention to it, or its inadequate retention and association (Kinsbourne & Rosof, 1971). This classification is basic to remedial method. Discrimination deficit may conceivably benefit from intensive perceptual exercise. Attentional disorder might respond to attention-focusing manipulation of the task. Retention may improve with instruction in an appropriate recoding method.

These considerations will be illustrated by reference to one form of remembering: the learning of letter orientation.

Were all letters in English script symmetrical about the vertical axis, reversals could not be made, either by normal or retarded readers. As things stand, however, malorientation of asymmetrical letters in writing, and confusion of mirror-image letters in reading have often been stressed as characteristic or even diagnostic of developmentally retarded readers (Orton, 1936). But reversal errors are also common among younger normal children, on the brink of reading readiness (Ilg & Ames, 1950). Moreover, in the discrimination learning situation differences in orientation present special difficulties for a variety of species, from octopus to adult man. What do orientation errors in these various species have in common, and how does this bear upon the nature of reversals in retarded reading?

When backward readers make reversal errors, they do so, not in a systematic, but in an inconstant manner. This suggests that the reversal tendency is not the result of some bias inbuilt into the perceptual or motor system, but rather reflects uncertainty, with a fifty per cent chance of success. It is likely that as many letters as are reversed in a passage, as many again are oriented correctly on purely chance basis. Why this uncertainty?

The uncertainty could arise at the level of discrimination, of attention, or of retention.

The failure of species such as octopus to learn to discriminate mirror-image forms has been made the basis of theories of shape discrimination (Deutsch, 1960; Dodwell, 1957; Sutherland, 1961), on the assumption that the limitation is perceptual. But while pigeons (Mello, 1965) and cats (Sutherland, 1963) are not so limited, children below the age of seven years also fail (Rudel & Teuber, 1963). Do such children really have a perceptual deficit which later resolves or should we seek another interpretation for the case of the children (not to mention the octopus)?

Simultaneous matching tasks eliminate the memory aspect; merely the instructions need be kept in mind. If the two stimuli differ only in respect of the relevant dimension, and no irrelevant dimensions obtrude, attention is directed to it. Thus the rat is notoriously difficult to train to discriminate mirror-image obliques by traditional methods (Lashley, 1948). Yet this presents no difficulty when the test situation takes the form of a simultaneous sameness–difference matching task, in which memory is eliminated and attention focused on the relevant variable (Kinsbourne, 1967). If the limitation on performance were perceptual, the nature of the experimental situation is immaterial, as long as the physical properties of the stimuli are held constant.

Tests of visual acuity in preschool children utilize the variable of orientation as an indicator of discrimination. The child is asked to indicate the orientation of an E- or a C-form. This, a three year old can do. This observation suggests that with young children, as with rats, the limit on discrimination learning for orientation is not perceptual.

A formal test of this proposition was set up as follows (Kinsbourne & Hartley, 1969). Children were asked to treat "lamb chop" shapes (similar to a "P") oriented in eight different ways as follows:

1. Copy them.
2. Match them by choice from an ensemble.
3. Place them in indicated positions ("setting").

Children as young as three years scored significantly above chance on all three procedures. The "setting" proved easiest, the matching hardest.

The test situation eliminated the memory factor, and the differences between the test situations and between these and the Rudel and Teuber discrimination learning results do not support a perceptual limitation interpretation, at least for children more than three years old. An attentional interpretation is adequate as follows: In matching, the question is "which of these . . . is the same as that?" Regarding form, they are all the same. A child who has not focused attention to the dimension of orientation might well miss the point and fail. In setting, the child is given a form patently identical to the model. He is nevertheless expected to do something. There is no scope to vary anything irrelevant to orientation. This situation attracts attention to that variable.

The attentional hypothesis was further tested by means of discrimination learning procedures (Kinsbourne, unpublished). Three-sided rectangular mirror-image forms were used ($\sqsubset$, $\sqsupset$). Half a group of four-year-old children were first confronted with a simultaneous discrimination task, in which they were shown the shapes one at a time, and each time asked whether the shape was the "correct" one. The other half of the experimental group was started on the successive and transferred to the simultaneous situation. At each trial, the response was confirmed or disconfirmed by the experimenter.

In general, simultaneous discriminations are easier to acquire than successive for three reasons. They dispense with memory load, facilitate discrimination by presenting the discriminanda simultaneously, and by involving highly natural "proximal" (directed to the correct item) rather than arbitrary "distal" response, of the type, "press this button if 'yes,' that one if 'no,'" which are used in successive discrimination. The present variant of successive discrimination learning was designed to dispense with distal response. It follows that superiority of simultaneous over successive discrimination learning in the present situation would indicate involvement of perception and/or memory as performance-limiting factors. In the event, it was the successive discrimination which proved to be substantially easier to learn; and transfer occurred more readily from successive to simultaneous rather than vice versa. Perceptual and memory aspects of the task must have been of little importance. The superiority of successive discrimination learning may be accounted for on an attentional basis.

In simultaneous discrimination, an irrelevant dimension coexists with the orientation variable. This is the relative position of the horizontally adjacent stimuli. "Position habit," according to which the subject persistently turns to one side, is well known from rat experimentation but also occurs with infants (Turkewitz et al., 1968). A subject, human or otherwise, confronted with a discrimination learning problem, formulates a series of hypotheses, testing each in turn until he obtains consistent reinforcement. As many hypotheses are available as there are discriminable physical dimensions distinguishing the stimuli. These dimensions are tested not in random sequence but in a definite order, representing a response hierarchy. Whether this hierarchy is innate or based on early experience is immaterial to the present issue. Position is high up on the hierarchy in many species, and orientation low. The notion that orientation of an object can be an inherent rather than an accidental attribute does not come early to young children. It springs more readily to mind the older the child, and as has been shown can be induced in a given test situation. The crucial point which remains to be clarified is whether the hierarchy is amenable to modification in the young child with generalization of the resultant concept, or whether it is an immutable property of the cerebral apparatus at that stage of maturation.

. While direct evidence is as yet lacking, it seems highly likely that the reversal tendency of older retarded readers represents a persistence of an initially normal phenomenon. The rank order of prevalence of orientation error-reversal in excess of inversions, which in turn predominate over rotations, holds for retarded readers as well as for younger normal children, and indeed also for normal adults when asked to write down the content of brief tachistoscopic presentations of multiple lamb-chop forms (Kinsbourne & Hartley, 1969). Indeed, rats in a jumping stand more readily learn to jump differentially to rotated than inverted, and to inverted than reversed pairs of forms (Kinsbourne, 1971d). For this phylogenetically widely-diffused effect, it would be parsimonious to seek a unitary explanation. An attentional hypothesis invoking a lowly place for orientation on the response hierarchy, satisfies this purpose. Perceptual and memory explanations do not.

Given that it is admissible to apply to retarded readers experience gained from work on younger normal children, methods suggest themselves by which one might attempt to improve the recall and reproduction of letter-orientation. All irrelevant dimensions are removed from the learning situations. Orientation is dealt with specifically, holding form constant and utilizing matching and "setting" techniques which comprise that dimension. Success is judged both by the degree of retention of the learnt ability over time, and the extent to which it generalizes to other forms, in other situations.

Low status on the response hierarchy does not imply that the dimension is ignored. Correct use of the dimension does not imply that the rank order of dimensions in that hierarchy is changed. What varies is rather the rate at which subjects are prepared to discard old and evaluate new hypotheses, and the number of hypotheses they are prepared to test. A normal human adult will be prepared to test the full range of feasible hypotheses. If, however, time is restricted as with tachistoscopic presentation, he may not have had time to register the lowly orientation aspects of forms; hence, the results of the tachistoscopic lamb chop experiments. Dimensions appear to be processed serially, rather than by decisions in parallel. Nor are decisions as to the eight orientations of forms such as the lamb chop made in parallel. Evidence has been obtained that under present experimental conditions decisions are successively made in a binary fashion. For instance, P is registered as follows:

   i. Horizontal or vertical? Answer: *vertical.*
   ii. Semicircles at top or bottom? Answer: *at top.*
   iii. Semicircle facing right or left? Answer: *right.*

Verbalization of this decision process is not implied, it is merely here presented in verbal terms but could readily be formulated as a computer program. If insufficient time is available for all decisions to be made, or if information decay from memory store occurs in inverse sequence to that of acquisition, error at one of two levels may occur: the higher level (two decisions correct) is ꟼ for P; the lower (one decision correct) is b or d for P. This binary decision-making hypothesis accounts for the characteristic and very general relationship for discrimination learning difficulty—reversals > inversions > rotations.

Time restriction is one way to curtail the sequential decision process. Another is the introduction of further dimensions, above orientation on the response hierarchy, which attract the bulk of cognitive effort, leaving orientation the focus of incomplete attention. Thus reversals, and to a lesser extent other orientation errors, have repeatedly been claimed to characterize the copying and visual memory performance of brain-damaged subjects, although this is an inconsistent finding (Warrington *et al.*, 1966). When brain-damaged subjects copy figures, they indeed make more orientation errors than do normal subjects. They also make more errors of other kinds (Benton & Fogel, 1962). When compared to another group that finds copying tasks difficult, the mentally retarded, the incidence of orientation error is no longer excessive in the brain-damaged group (Benton & Spreen, 1966). Task difficulty is the relevant intervening variable. A person engaged in what is for him a difficult copying or visual memory task, concentrates on length, and slope of line and orientation is apt to go by the board. There is a limit on range of cue utilization. He patiently tries again, with the same, or perhaps a little more success. Orientation is again incorrect, but not necessarily in the same way as before. The orientation error is not the result of a specific response bias, but is rather due to the fact that this dimension is left to chance. Then it could not be the case that orientation errors are specific to one kind of diminution in cerebral competence, namely, that due to brain damage. Orientation errors are liable to contaminate copying and drawing performance when, for whatever reason, the task is difficult.

Special education at times involves, not necessarily by design, some of the principles here developed. The kinesthetic method of reading improvement forces the subject, as he runs his fingers over the letter shape to attend to its characteristics undisturbed by other input. So-called perceptual exercises help perhaps not so much by virtue of improving discriminative skills, but rather by focusing attention on relevant dimensions of what is normally perceived. Auditory training of the severely deaf forces the person to concentrate upon auditory cues, for him an exacting task, when he would much rather ignore sound and seek for coincident correlated visual information (for instance, lip reading). So may teaching of children with reading disability be effective by virtue of focusing attention on relevant cues, however hard to perceive and retain. Slow learners are not nonlearners. To acquire a given amount of information, they have to apply themselves more intensively and for longer periods of time. Nor is the appropriate method of teaching one of reiterating what they have already failed to learn. Rather it is necessary to eliminate irrelevant dimensions, such as the excess of extraneous material thrown in by the producers of contemporary reading manuals, for the purpose of making reading instruction "fun," and logically demonstrate, dimension by dimension and distinctive feature by distinctive feature, the material to be learned.

## VIII. ANATOMICAL BASIS OF CEREBRAL FUNCTION

The foregoing discussion has centered upon analysis of behavioral mechanisms and has referred only infrequently to the anatomical location of the cerebral lesions that modify these mechanisms. This is largely because such information is often not available. Relatively few thoroughly studied cases are followed to autopsy, and, of these, fewer still have limited cerebral disease in a well-defined location. Fortunately, substantial advance in neuropsychological study can be made without detailed knowledge of anatomical locations of disease processes, because the logic of such a study is characterized by two questions which must be asked in the right order. What is the nature of the processes which may be selectively impaired by a focal cerebral lesion? What is the location of the neural substrate of each of these processes?

In the attempt to localize cerebral function, contradictory results can arise from inappropriate questioning of either type. Certainly, there is little possibility of arriving at precise functional–anatomical correlations if fully documented and pathologically studied material (which would be preferable) is not available. On the other hand, even if it were, the results would have little consequence for our knowledge of brain mechanisms, if the processes to be localized are not of a kind likely to be subserved by simple, segregated neural facilities. Thus, the failure of the classical search for centers of reading, writing, and calculating in the brain should not be interpreted as evidence against localization of function in that structure; rather, the failure may occur because the researcher is asking the wrong questions. It should not be supposed that activities as complex and multifactorial as reading, writing, and calculating need be represented in a limited and clearly demarcated cerebral area. However, it may well be the case that the various component processes that underlie each of these activities are themselves subserved by clearly-defined neural aggregates. For this reason, the primary emphasis should be placed on functional analysis of the behavioral deficits which result from focal cerebral lesions, so as to reveal the nature and range of the type of process which may be selectively impaired. Most of the foregoing discussion was devoted to this type of functional analysis; and it is apparent that certain functions, such as sequencing of information, matching of sample from input to sample from store, and verbal recoding are susceptible of rather precise anatomical location with respect to their neural substrate or at least in relation to those cerebral areas which when damaged cause selective impairment of these functions. Progress in neurological psychology is not limited by too small a supply of patients with clearly-defined ascertainable anatomical lesions of the cerebral hemisphere, but rather by our inadequate understanding of the way in which behavior disintegrates. Determining the nature of the processes which may be selectively impaired in cerebral hemisphere damage will require study of comparable sophistication and depth to that which, in human experimental psychology, is devoted to the normal adult. It is anticipated that attempts at anatomical localization of function will succeed in the future, to the extent that valid processes are defined for the localization attempt.

It is no longer possible to sustain a "mass-action" or "equipotentiality" (Lashley, 1931) interpretation of cerebral functioning. The roles of certain areas, such as the motor strip, and the auditory and visual receiving areas, are already well defined. The participation in the total behavior of the organism of other parts of the brain, such as the postero–inferior parietal areas and the temporal lobes is becoming clearer. The question may be rephrased, however. Within how large an area of the cerebral cortex are neurons equipotential? For instance, the left-temporal lobe seems to subserve verbal memory. Within that lobe, do all neurons equally or potentially equally subserve that function, or is there a further segregation? We no longer need to debate the principle of whether function is localized in the cerebral cortex. Our concern will rather be to determine where and how minute and anatomically discrete that localization is for each of the processes that together constitute higher mental functioning.

In summary, the behavioral consequences of human brain lesions may be regarded in terms of limitations on the rate and accuracy of information processing and restrictions on the repertoire of cognitive strategies. The methods of human experimental psychology are no less applicable to brain-damaged than to intact subjects. Their application makes it possible to extend the formulation of brain-behavior relationships to the wide variety of processes which are not amenable to study in animals because they are restricted to man. While this stage of development of human neuropsychology is only just beginning, it has, in principle, already become clear that the cerebral hemispheres in man are highly differentiated in relation to the separate though interlocking cognitive processes that contribute to normal behavior. The bulk of the work remains; to identify all these component processes, establish specific measures for the efficiency of each, and relate each to that cerebral area which is crucial to its optimal functioning.

## REFERENCES

Alajouanine, T., & Lhermitte, F. Some problems concerning the agnosias, apraxias and aphasia. In L. Halpern (Ed.), *Problems of dynamic neurology*. Jerusalem: Hadassah, 1963.

Alajouanine, T., Sabouraud, B., & DeRiboucourt, B. Le jargon des aphasiques; desintegration anosognostique des valeurs semantiques du language. *Journal de Psychologie*, 1952, **45**, 158, 293.

Archibald, Y. M., Wepman, J. M., & Jones, L. V. Nonverbal cognitive performance in aphasic and non-aphasic brain damaged patients. *Cortex*, 1967, **3**, 275–294.

Arrigoni, G., & DeRenzi, E. Constructive apraxia and hemispheric locus of lesion. *Cortex*, 1964, **1**, 170–197.

Attneave, F., In defense of homunculi. W. A. Rosenblith (Ed.), In *Sensory communication*. New York: Wiley, 1961. Pp. 777–782.

Babinski, J. Contribution a l'étude des troubles mentaux dans l'hemiplegie organique cerebrale (Anosognosie) *Revue Neurologique*, 1914, **27**, 845–848.

Badderley, A. D. *Some psychological aspects of the coding of information*. Ph.D. dissertation, University of Cambridge, 1962.

Bakwin, H. Developmental disorders of mobility and language. *Pediatric clinics of North America*, Vol. 15. Philadelphia, Pennsylvania: Saunders, 1968.

Bard, L. De l'intervention das la lecture de reflexes de direction des yeus d'origine verbale. *Archives of Ophthalmology Par.*, 1922, **39**, 5–21.

Benton, A. L. *Right-left discrimination and finger localisation development and pathology*. New York: Hoeber and Harper, 1959.

Benton, A. L. The fiction of the "Gerstmann Syndrome," *Journal of Neurology, Neurosurgery & Psychiatry*, 1961, **24**, 176–181.

Benton, A. L., & Fogel, M. L. Three-dimensional constructional praxis. *American Medical Association Archives of Neurology*, 1962, **7**, 347–354.

Benton, A. L., & Spreen, O. Visual memory test performance in mentally deficient and brain-damaged patients. *American Journal of Mental Deficiency*, 1966, **68**, 630–633.

Boller, F., & DeRenzi, E. Relationship between visual memory defects and hemispheric locus of lesion. *Neurology*, 1967, **17**, 1052–1058.

Bruner, J. S., & Potter, M. D. Interference in visual recognition. *Science*, 1944, **164**, 424–425.

Cohen, J. The factorial structure of the WAIS between early adulthood and old age. *Journal of Consulting Psychology*, 1957, **21**, 283–290.

Conrad, R. Acoustic confusions in immediate memory. *British Journal of Psychology*, 1964, **55**, 75–83.

Critchley, M. *The parietal lobes*. London: Arnold, 1953.

Critchley, M. Regional "accent," demotic speech and aphasia. In *Livre jubilaire de Dr. Ludo van Bogaert*. Brussels: Medica Acta Belgica, 1962.

Crossman, E. R. F. W. Information and serial order in human immediate memory. In C. Cherry (Ed.), *Information theory 4th London symposium* London & Washington, D.C.: Butterworth, 1961.

Crovitz, H., Schiffman, H., & Rees, J. N. Simulation of mental deficiency: the stupid reader effect. *Psychological Report*, 1967, **20**, 834.

DeHirsch, K., Jansky, J. J., & Lansford, W. S. *The prediction of reading, spelling and writing disabilities in children: a preliminary study*. New York: Columbia University, 1965.

Denny-Brown, D., Meyer, J. S., & Horenstein, S. The significance of perceptual rivalry from parietal lesions. *Brain*, 1962, **75**, 433–471.

DeRenzi, E., & Vignolo, L. A. The token test: a sensitive test to detect receptive disturbances in aphasics. *Brain*, 1962, **85**, 665–678.

Deutsch, J. A. The plexiform zone and shape recognition in the octopus. *Nature*, 1960, **185**, 443–446.

Dodwell, P. C. Shape recognition in rats. *British Journal of Psychology*, 1957, **48**, 221–229.

Dorff, J. F., Mirsky, A. F., & Mishkin, M. Effects of unilateral temporal lobe removal in man on tachistoscopic recognition in the left and right visual fields. *Neuropsychologia*, 1965, **3**, 39–51.

Efron, R. Temporal perception, aphasia and deja vu. *Brain*, 1963, **86**, 403–424.

Ettlinger, G., & Moffett A. M. Learning in dysphasia. *Neuropsychologia* 1970, **8**, 465–474.

Fuchs, W. Untersuchengen über das Sehen der Hemianopiker and Hemiamblyopiker. II. Die totalisierende Gestaltauffassung. *Zeitschrift für Psychologie* **86**, 1921, 1–14.

Garner, W. R., Hake, H. W., & Eriksen, C. W. Operationism and the concept of perception. *Psychological Review*, 1956, **63**, 149–159.

Gerstmann, J. Finger Agnosie: eine umschriebene Störung der Orientierung am eigenen Körper. *Wiener Klinische Wochenschrift*, 1924, **37**, 1010–1112.

Gerstmann, J. Zur Symptomatologie der Hirn parietal and mittleren occipital-Windung. *Nervenarzt*, 1930, **3**, 691–695.

Geschwind, N., & Kaplan, E. A human cerebral deconnection syndrome. *Neurology*, 1962, **12**, 675–685.

Gibson, E. J. *Principles of perceptual learning and development*. New York: Appleton-Century-Crofts, 1969.

Glanzer, M., & Clark, W. H. The verbal loop hypothesis: binary numbers. *Journal of Verbal Learning and Verbal Behavior,* 1963, **2**, 301–309.

Glees, P., & Griffith, H. B. Bilateral destruction of the hippocampus (cornu Ammonis) in a case of dementia. *Monatsschrift für Psychiatrie und Neurologie,* 1952, **123**, 193–204.

Goldstein, K. *Language and language disturbances.* New York: Grune and Stratton, 1948.

Gollin, E. S. Further studies of visual recognition of incomplete objects. *Perceptual & Motor Skills,* 1961, **13**, 307–314.

Grewel, F. Asemiotic disorders and localization. In H. A. Biemond (Ed.), *Recent neurological research. Research in neuropsychology.* Amsterdam: Elsewier, 1960.

Hebb, D. O. The effect of early and late brain injury upon test scores and the nature of normal adult intelligence. *Proceedings of the American Philosophical Society,* 1942, **85**, 275–292.

Hécaen, H. Clinical symptomatology in right and left hemisphere lesions. In Mountcastle, (Ed.), *Interhemispheric relations and cerebral dominance,* Baltimore: Johns Hopkins Press, 1962. Pp. 215–243.

Heilbrun, A. P. Lateralization of cerebral lesion and performance on spatial—temporal tasks. *AMA Archives of Neurology,* 1959, **1**, 282–287.

Heimburger, R. F., DeMyer, W., & Reitan, R. M. Implications of Gerstmann's Syndrome. *Journal of Neurology, Neurosurgery & Psychiatry,* 1964, **27**, 52–57.

Hobbes, T. *Leviathan,* New York: Dutton, 1950.

Howes, D. H., & Solomon, R. L. Visual duration threshold as a function of word probability. *Journal of Experimental Psychology,* 1951, **41**, 401–410.

Hunter, W. S., & Sigler, M. The span of visual discrimination as a function of time and intensity of stimulation. *Journal of Experimental Psychology,* 1960, **26**, 160–179.

Ilg, F. L., & Ames, L. B. Developmental trends in reading behavior. *Journal of Genetic Psychology,* 1950, **76**, 29–312.

Isserlin, M. Aphasie. In O. Bumke and O. Foerster (Eds.), *Handbuch der Neurologie.* Vol. 6. Berlin: Springer, 1936.

Jackson, C. V., & Zangwill, O. L. Experimental finger dyspraxia. *Quarterly Journal of Experimental Psychology,* 1952, **4**, 1–10.

Jackson, J. H. *Royal London Ophthalmology Hospital Reports,* 1876, **8**, 436.

Kaufman, E. L., Lord, M. W., Reese, T. W., & Volkmann, J. The discrimination of visual number. *American Journal of Psychology,* 1949, **62**, 498–525.

Kimura, D. Right temporal lobe damage. *AMA Archives of Neurology,* 1963, **8**, 264–271.

Kinsbourne, M. Limitations in visual capacity due to cerebral lesions. *Proceedings of the Eighteenth International Congress of Psychology, Moscow,* 1966, 120–127.

Kinsbourne, M. Sameness–difference judgments and the discrimination of obliques in the rat. *Psychonomic Science,* 1967, **7**, 183–184.

Kinsbourne, M. Long term effects of penetrating missile wounds on cerebral function. Unpublished manuscript, 1969.

Kinsbourne, M. The cerebral basis of lateral asymmetries in attention. *Acta Psychologia,* 1970, **33**, 193–201.

Kinsbourne, M. A model for the mechanism of unilateral neglect of space. *Transactions of the American Neurological Association,* 1971a. **95**, 143–145.

Kinsbourne, M. The mechanism of conduction aphasia. *Proceedings of the Academy of Neurology,* 1971b.

Kinsbourne, M. The minor cerebral hemisphere as a source of aphasic speech. *Archives of Neurology;* in press, 1971c.

Kinsbourne, M. Discrimination of orientation by rats. *Psychonomic Science,* 1971d, **22**(1), 50.

Kinsbourne, M., & Warrington, E. K. A study of finger agnosia. *Brain,* 1962a, **85,** 47–66.

Kinsbourne, M., & Warrington, E. K. A disorder of simultaneous form perception. *Brain,* 1962b, **85,** 461–486.

Kinsbourne, M., & Warrington, E. K. A variety of reading disability associated with right hemisphere lesions. *Journal of Neurology, Neurosurgery and Psychiatry,* 1962c, **25,** 339–344.

Kinsbourne, M., & Warrington, E. K. The localizing significance of limited simultaneous form perception. *Brain,* 1963a, **86,** 696–702.

Kinsbourne, M., & Warrington, E. K. A Study of visual perseveration. *Journal of Neurology, Neurosurgery and Psychiatry,* 1963b, **26,** 468–575.

Kinsbourne, M., & Warrington, E. K. Developmental factors in reading and writing backwardness. *British Journal of Psychology,* 1963c, **54,** 145–156.

Kinsbourne, M., & Warrington, E. K. Jargon aphasia. *Neuropsychologia,* 1964a, **1,** 27–37.

Kinsbourne, M., & Warrington, E. K. Disorders of spelling. *Journal of Neurology, Neurosurgery, and Psychiatry,* 1964b, **27,** 224–228.

Kinsbourne, M., & Peel-Floyd, C. Cue deprivation in relation to impaired language development. *Proceedings of the Congress of Phoniatrics and Logopedics, Vienna,* 1965.

Kinsbourne, M., & Hartley, D. Distinctive feature analysis in children's perception of simple shapes. Proceedings of the Society for Research in Child Development, 1 1969.

Kinsbourne, M., & Rosof, D. Systematic analysis of selective reading difficulties. *Proceedings of the Society for Pediatric Research,* 1971.

Koronakos, C., & Arnold, W. J. The formation of learning sets in rats. *Journal of Comparative & Physiological Psychology,* 1957, **40,** 11–14.

Landauer, T. K. Rate of implicit speech. *Perceptual Motor Skills,* 1962, **15,** 646.

Lashley, K. S. Mass action in cerebral function. *Science,* 1931, **73,** 245–254.

Lashley, K. S. The mechanism of vision. XVIII. Effects of destroying the "visual association" areas of the monkey. *Genetic Psychological Monograph,* 1948, **37,** 107–166.

Lashley, K. S. The problem of serial order in behavior. In L. A. Jeffres (Ed.), *Control mechanisms in behavior.* New York: Wiley, 1951.

Lenneberg, E. *Biological basis of language.* New York: Wiley, 1967.

Lowe, A. D., & Campbell, R. A. Temporal discrimination in aphasoid and normal children. *Journal of Speech & Hearing Research,* 1965, **8,** 313–317.

Luria, A. R. Disorders of simultaneous perception in a case of bilateral occipitoparietal brain injury. *Brain,* 1959, **82,** 437–449.

Luria, A. R. *Higher cortical functions in man.* London: Tavistock, 1966.

Luria, A. R., & Karanservat, A. Disturbances of auditory-speech memory in focal lesions of the deep regions of the left temporal lobe. *Neuropsychologia,* 1968, **6,** 97–109.

McFie, J., & Zangwill, O. L. Visual-constructive disabilities associated with lesions of the left cerebral hemisphere. *Brain,* 1960, **83,** 243–260.

McGhie, A. In *Studies on psychosis.* T. Freeman, J. L. Cannon, and A. McGhie, (Eds.), London: Tavistock, 1965.

McGuigan, F. S. Thinking. *Studies of covert language processes.* New York: Appleton, 1966.

Mackworth, J. F. The duration of the visual image. *Canadian Journal of Psychology,* 1963, **17,** 62–81.

Mello, N. Interhemispheric reversal of mirror-image oblique lines after monocular training in pigeons. *Science,* 1965, **148,** 252–254.

Meyer, V., & Yates, A. J. Intellectual changes following temporal lobectomy for psychomotor epilepsy. *Journal of Neurology & Neurosurgery Psychiatry,* 1955, **18,** 44–52.

Miller, G. A. Human memory and the storage of information. *IRE Transactions on Information Theory,* 1956, **2,** 129–137.

Miller, G. A., Bruner, J. S., & Postman, L. Familiarity of letter sequences and tachistoscopic identification. *Journal of General Psychology,* 1956, **40,** 129–139.

Milner, B. Laterality effects in audition. In Mountcastle, (Ed.), *Interhemispheric relations and cerebral dominance.* Baltimore: Johns Hopkins Press. 1962. Pp. 177–195.

Monrad-Krohn, G. H. Dysprosody. *Brain,* 1967, **70,** 405.

Myers, R. E. Function of corpus callosum in interocular transfer. *Brain,* 1956, **79,** 358–363.

Nathan, P. W. Facial apraxia and apraxic dysarthia. *Brain,* 1947, **70,** 449–478.

Newcombe, F. *Missile wounds of the brain.* Oxford: Oxford University Press, 1969.

Nielson, J. *Agnosia, apraxia & aphasia,* 2nd edition. New York: Hafner, 1946.

Oldfield, R. D., & Wingfield, A. Response latencies in naming objects. *Quarterly Journal of Experimental Psychology,* 1965, **17,** 273–281.

Orbach, J. Differential recognition of Hebrew and England words in right and left visual fields as a function of cerebral dominance of reading habits. *Neuropsychologia,* 1967, **5,** 127–134.

Orton, S. T. *Reading, writing and speech problems in children.* New York: Norton, 1936.

Piercy, M., & Smyth, V. Right hemisphere dominance for certain non-verbal intellectual skills. *Brain,* 1962, **85,** 775–790.

Piercy, M., Hécaen, H., & Ajuriaguerra, J. de. Constructional apraxia associated with unilateral cerebral lesions; left and right sided cases compared. *Brain,* 1960, **83,** 225–242.

Poppelreuter. W. *Die psychischen Schädigungen durch Kopfschuss im Kriege 1914–1917* Leipzig: Voss, 1917–18. 2 vols.

Poppelreuter, W. Zur Psychologie und Pathologie der optischen Wahrnehmung, J. ges. Neurol. Psychiat., 1923, **83,** 26–152.

Reitan, R. M. Problems and prospects in studying the psychological correlates of brain lesions. *Cortex,* 1966, **2,** 127–154.

Riese, W. The early history of aphasia. *Bulletin Journal of Medicine,* 1967, **21,** 322–334.

Rose, F. C., & Symonds, C. P. Persistent memory defect following encephalitis. *Brain,* 1960, **83,** 195–212.

Rosenstein, J. Perception, cognition and language in deaf children. *Exceptional Children,* 1961, **27,** 276–284.

Rudel, R. G., & Teuber, H.-L. Discrimination of direction of line in children. *Journal of Comparative & Psychological Psychology,* 1963, **56,** 892–898.

Salzman, Z. J., & Garner, W. R. Reaction time as a measure of span of attention. *Journal of Psychology,* 1968, **25,** 227–241.

Scheller, H., & Seidemann, H. Zur Frage der optisch-räumlichen Agnosie. *Monatschr Psychiatry & Neurology,* 1931, **81,** 97–189.

Scoville, W. B., & Milner, B. Severe memory deficit after bilateral hippocampus lesions. *Journal of Neurology, Neurosurgery & Psychiatry,* 1957, **20**, 11–21.

Siemerling. Ein Fall von sogenannter Seelenblindheit nebst anderseitigen cerebralen Symptomen. *AMA Archives of Psychiatry,* 1890, **21**, 284–299.

Smith, A. Certain hypothesized hemispheric differences in language and visual functions in the human adult. *Cortex,* 1966, **2**, 109–126. (a)

Smith, A. Speech and its function after left (dominant) hemispherectomy. *Journal of Neurology & Neurosurgery Psychiatry,* 1966, **29**, 467–471. (b)

Sokolov, A. N. Speech-motor afferentiation and the problem of brain mechanisms of thought. *Soviet Psychology,* 1967, **6**, 3–15.

Sperling, G. The information available in brief visual presentations. *Psychological Monograph,* 1960, **74**, 11 (whole No. 498).

Sperling, G. A model for visual memory tasks. *Human Factors,* 1963, **5**, 19–31.

Stengel, E. Loss of spatial orientation, constructional apraxia and Gerstmann's syndrome. *Journal of Mental Science,* 1944, **90**, 753–760.

Sternberg, S. High-speed scanning in human memory. *Science,* 1963, **153**, 652–654.

Sutherland, N. S. Shape discrimination by animals. *Experimental Psychological Society Mongraph,* 1961, I.

Sutherland, N. S. Cat's ability to discriminate oblique rectangles. *Science,* 1963, **1939**, 209–210.

Swets, J. A., Tanner, W. P., & Birdsall, T. A. Decision processes in perception. *Psychological Review,* 1961, **68**, 301–340.

Talland, G. A. *Deranged memory.* New York: Academic Press, 1968.

Teuber, H.-L. Physiological psychology. *Annual Review of Psychology,* 1955, **6**, 267–296.

Teuber, H.-L. Sensory deprivation, sensory suppression and agnosia; notes for a neurologic theory. *Journal of Nervous Mental Disease,* 1961, **132**, 32–40.

Teuber, H.-L., Battersby, W. S., & Bender, M. B. *Visual defects after penetrating missile wounds of the brain.* Cambridge: Harvard University Press, 1960.

Teuber, H.-L., & Weinstein, S. Ability to discover hidden figures after cerebral lesions. *AMA Archives of Neurology Psychiatry,* 1956, **76**, 369–379.

Turkewitz, G., Gordon, B. W., & Birch, M. G. Head turning in the human neonate; effect of prandial condition and lateral preference. *Journal of Comparative & Physiological Psychology,* 1968, **59**, 189–192.

Van der Horst, L. Uber die Psychologie des Korsakow Syndroms. *Monatsschrift für Psychologie und Neurologie,* 1932, **83**, 35–67.

Vanderplas, J. M., & Garvin, E. A. The association value of random shapes. *Journal of Experimental Psychology,* 1959, **57**, 147–162.

Wallach, M. A. Perceptual recognition of approximation to English in relation to spelling achievement. *Journal of Educational Psychology,* 1963, **59**, 57–62.

Warrington, E. K. The completion of visual forms across hemianopic field defects. *Journal of Neurology, Neurosurgery & Psychiatry,* 1962, **25**, 208–217.

Warrington, E. K., & James, M. Tachistoscopic number estimation in patients with unilateral cerebral lesions. *Journal of Neurology, Neurosurgery & Psychiatry,* 1967, **39**, 668–676.

Warrington, E. K., James, M., & Kinsbourne, M. Drawing disability in relation to laterality of cerebral lesions. *Brain,* 1966, **89**, 53–82.

Warrington, E. K., Kinsbourne, M., & James, M. Uncertainty and transitional probability in the span of apprehension. *British Journal of Psychology,* 1966, **47**, 7–16.

Watson, J. B. *Behaviorism*. People's Trust Publishing Company, 1926.

Wechsler, D. *The measurement and appraisal of adult intelligence*. Baltimore: Williams and Wilkins, 1958.

Weinberger, L. M., & Grant, F. C. Visual hallucinations and their neuro-optical correlates. *Archives Ophthalmology*, 1940, **23,** 166–199.

Wernicke, C. *Lehrbuch der Gehirnkrankheiten für Arzte und Studierende*. Stuttgart: Thieme, 1881.

Whorf, B. L. *Four articles on metalinguistics*. Foreign Institute, Department of State, Washington, D.C., 1950.

Wolff, M. G. In Mountcastle (Ed.), *Interhemispheric integration and cerebral dominance*. Baltimore: Johns Hopkins Press, 1962.

Wolpert, I. Die Simultanagnosie, *Z. ges. Neurol. Psychiatry*, 1924, **93.**

Wortis, S. B., & Pfeiffer, A. Z. Unilateral auditory spatial agnosia. *Journal of Nervous & Mental Disease*, 1948, **108,** 181–186.

Yates, A. J. Delayed auditory feedback. *Psychological Bulletin*, 1962, **60,** 213–232.

Zigler, E. Familial mental retardation: a continuing dilemma. *Science*, 1967, **155,** 292–298.

# Author Index

Numbers in italics refer to the pages on which the complete references are listed.

349

# Subject Index